CW00536927

([illegible])
Moravia
ZHX

Moravian
ZHX

A

COLLECTION

OF

HYMNS,

FOR THE USE OF THE

PROTESTANT CHURCH,

OF THE

UNITED BRETHREN.

NEW AND REVISED EDITION.

Come before his Presence with Singing. PSALM c. 2.

I will sing of thy Power; yea, I will sing aloud of thy Mercy. Ps. lix. 16.

Let the word of Christ dwell in you richly, in all Wisdom; teaching and admonishing one another in Psalms, and Hymns, and spiritual Songs, singing with grace in your hearts to the Lord. Col. iii. 16.

I will sing with the Spirit, and I will sing with the Understanding also. 1 Cor. xiv. 15.

Manchester,

PRINTED BY R. & W. DEAN;

and Sold by

HENRY HASLOP, NO. 8, NEVIL'S-COURT, FETTER-LANE, LONDON; BINNS, BATH; LAMB, BRISTOL; AND AT THE BRETHREN'S CHAPELS IN GREAT BRITAIN AND IRELAND.

1809.

CONTENTS.

PREFACE.

THE Hymn-Book printed in the year 1801, for the use of the PROTESTANT CHURCH of the UNITED BRETHREN being out of print, a new edition is now published.

As this hymn-book is also intended for the use of our missions in the English dominions abroad, where holy baptism is frequently administered to adults; and as the same is at times administered here, we have added a few hymns, that may be suitably used on such occasions.

The hymns translated from the German are distinguished by an asterisk [*]; those not marked in this manner, are English compositions.

In order to find any single verse, the INDEX does not contain the first line of each HYMN only, but of each VERSE in this collection. The lines which begin a hymn are also marked in the index with an asterisk [*].

The numbers of the tunes, placed over the hymns, have a reference to the second index, which points out the tunes for the hymns that occur in this book.

May all, who use these hymns, delight in and experience at all times the blessed effects of the apostle Paul's advice, (EPHESIANS v. 18, 19.) " Be filled with the

Spirit, speaking to yourselves in psalms and hymns and spiritual songs, singing and making melody in your heart to the Lord," yea anticipate already, whilst in the body, though in an humble and imperfect strain, the song of the innumerable company of angels, and the spirits of just men made perfect, (Heb. xii. 22, 23.) who being redeemed out of every kindred and tongue, and people, and nation, and having washed their robes and made them white in the blood of the Lamb, (Rev. v. 9. and vii. 14.) are singing in perfect harmony, (Rev. v. 12,—14) "Worthy is the Lamb that was slain, to receive power, and riches, and wisdom, and strength, and honor, and glory, and blessing, for ever and ever." Amen!

March 1st. 1809.

LITURGY

OF THE

CHURCH OF THE UNITED BRETHREN.

THE CHURCH LITANY.

LORD,	*Have mercy upon us!*
Christ,	*Have mercy upon us!*
Lord,	*Have mercy upon us!*
Christ,	*Hear us!*

Lord God, our Father, which art in heaven!

Hallowed be thy name; thy kingdom come; thy will be done on earth, as it is in heaven; give us this day our daily bread; and forgive us our trespasses, as we forgive them that trespass against us; and lead us not into temptation; but deliver us from evil. For thine is the kingdom, and the power, and the glory, for ever and ever. Amen!

Lord God, Son, thou Saviour of the world!
Be gracious unto us!
Lord God, Holy Ghost!
Abide with us for ever!

Cong. Most Holy, Blessed Trinity!
We praise Thee to eternity. :||: :||:

Thou Slaughter'd Lamb, our God and Lord!
To needy pray'rs thine ear afford,
And on us all have mercy!

From coldness to thy merits and death,
From error and misunderstanding,
From the loss of our glory in thee,
From the unhappy desire of becoming great,
From self-complacency,
From untimely projects,
From needless perplexity,
From the murdering spirit and devices of Satan,
From the influence of the spirit of this world,
From hypocrisy and fanaticism,
From the deceitfulness of sin,
From all sin,

Preserve us, gracious Lord and God!

By all the merits of thy life,
By thy human birth and circumcision,
By thy obedience, diligence, and faithfulness,
By thy humility, meekness, and patience,
By thy extreme poverty,
By thy watching, fasting, and temptations,
By thy griefs and sorrows,
By thy prayers, and tears,
By thy having been despised and rejected,

Bless and comfort us, gracious Lord and God

By thine agony and bloody sweat,
By thy bonds and scourgings,
By thy crown of thorns,
By thy cross and passion,
By thy sacred wounds and precious blood,
By thy dying words,
By thy atoning death,

By thy rest in the grave,
By thy glorious resurrection and ascension,
By thy sitting at the right hand of God,
By thy prevailing intercession,
By the holy sacraments,
By thy divine presence, (Matth. xxviii. 20.)

Bless and comfort us, gracious Lord and God!

Cong. We humbly pray with one accord;
Remember us, most gracious Lord!
Think on thy suff'rings, wounds, and cross,
And how by death thou savedst us;
For this is all our hope and plea
In time and in eternity.

We poor sinners pray,

Hear us, gracious Lord and God!

Rule and lead thy holy christian church;
Increase the knowledge of the mystery of Christ, and diminish misapprehensions;
Make the word of the cross universal among those who are called by thy name;
Unite all the children of God in one spirit; (John xi. 52.)
Abide their only Shepherd, High-Priest and Saviour;
Send faithful laborers into thy harvest;
Give spirit and power to preach thy word;
Preserve unto us the word of reconciliation till the end of days,
And through the Holy Ghost, daily glorify the merits of thy life, sufferings and death;
Prevent, or destroy, all designs and schemes of Satan, and defend us against his accusation;
For the sake of that peace which we have with thee, may we, as much as lieth in us, live peaceably with all men; (Rom. xii. 18.)

Grant us to bless them that curse us, and to do good to them that hate us;
Have mercy upon our slanderers and persecutors, and lay not this sin to their charge; (Acts vii. 60.)
Hinder all schisms and scandals;
Put far from thy people all deceivers and seducers;
Bring back all that have erred, or have been seduced;
Grant love and unity to all our congregations;
Hear us, gracious Lord and God!
Thou Light and Desire of all nations! (Mat. iv. 16. Hag. ii. 7.)
Watch over thy messengers both by land and sea;
Prosper the endeavors of all thy servants to spread thy gospel among heathen nations;
Accompany the word of their testimony concerning thy atonement, with demonstration of the Spirit and of power; (1 Cor. ii. 4.)
Bless our congregations gathered from the Negros, Greenlanders, Indians, Hottentots and Esquimaux;
Keep them as the apple of thine eye; (Deut. xxxii. 10.)
Deliver the people of Israel from their blindness;
And bring all nations to the saving knowledge of thee; *Hear us, gracious Lord and God!*

MIN. O praise the Lord, all ye heathen!
CONG. Praise him, all ye nations!

Give to thy people open doors to preach thy gospel, and set them to thy praise on earth;
Grant all ministers of the church soundness of doctrine and holiness of life, and preserve them therein;
Sprinkle all thy servants with thy blood;
Keep our episcopacy precious before thee;
Help all elders to rule well, especially those who labor in the word and doctrine; (1 Tim. v. 17.)

That they may feed thy church, which thou hast purchased with thine own blood; (Acts xx. 28.)

Hear us, gracious Lord and God!

Watch graciously over all kings, princes and governments, and hear our intercessions for them all;

Grant and preserve unto them thoughts of peace and concord;

We beseech thee especially to pour down thy blessings in a plentiful manner upon our gracious Sovereign King George, the Queen, the Prince and Princess of Wales, and upon all the Royal Family;

Grant that our King may enjoy a long and happy reign over us; preserve him in thy faith, fear and love, that he may walk before thee as thy servant, and protect thy true religion in these nations; *

Guide and protect the magistrates of the land, wherein we dwell, and all that are put in authority; and grant us to lead under them a quiet and peaceable life in all godliness and honesty;

Hear us, gracious Lord and God!

---

* Bless both Houses of Parliament, at this time assembled, and direct their councils.

To be prayed in times of war, directly after the petitions for the King.

Grant, O Lord, unto our King, in these times of danger, thy gracious counsel, that in all things he may approve himself the father of his people.

Be thou the gracious protector of these nations, and of our fellow subjects in all parts of the world.

Turn the hearts of our enemies; defeat every evil design against us, and continue to show thy tender mercy unto this united kingdom, as thou hast done in the days past.

Cause us to bow down before thee, to confess our sins, and to acknowledge with contrite hearts, that it is of thy mercy that we are not consumed;

Stop, in thy tender mercy, the effusion of human blood, and make discord and wars to cease;

To this end, put into the hearts of the rulers of the nations, thoughts of peace, that we may see it soon established, to the glory of thy name;

 Hear us, gracious Lord and God!

Supply O Lord, all the wants of thy church;

Let all things be conducted among us in such a manner, that we provide things honest, not only before God, but also before men; (2 Cor. viii. 21. Rom. xii. 17.)

Bless the sweat of the brow, and the faithfulness in handicraft business;

Let none entangle himself with the affairs of this life; (2 Tim. ii. 4.)

But may all our labor of body and mind be hallowed unto thee;

Hear us, gracious Lord and God!

O thou Preserver of men!

Send help to all that are in distress or danger;

Strengthen and uphold those who suffer bonds and persecution for the sake of the gospel;

Defend, and provide for the fatherless children, and widows, and all who are desolate and oppressed;

Be the support of the aged;

Make the bed of the sick, and, amidst all their sufferings, let them feel that thou lovest them; (Ps. xli. 3.)

And when thou takest away men's breath, that they die, then remember, that thou hast died, not for our sins only, but also for the sins of the whole world; (1 John ii. 2. Rom. v. 18.)

Hear us, gracious Lord and God!

Now, Lord, thou who art over all, God blessed for ever!

Be the Saviour of all men; (1 Tim. iv. 10.)

Yea, have mercy on thy whole creation; (Rom. viii. 19, 22.)

For thou camest, by thyself to reconcile all things unto God, whether things on earth, or things in heaven; (Col. i. 20. Eph. ii. 16.)

Hear us, gracious Lord and God!

Thou Saviour of thy body! (Eph. v. 23.)

Bless, sanctify, and preserve every member of thy church;

Grant that each, in every age and station, may enjoy the powerful and sanctifying merits of thy holy humanity; and make us chaste before thee in soul and body;

Let our children be brought up in the nurture and admonition of thee; (Eph. vi. 4.)

Pour out thy Holy Spirit on all thy servants and handmaids; (Acts ii. 18.)

Purify our souls, in obeying the truth, through the Spirit, unto unfeigned love of the brethren; (1 Pet. i. 22.)

Hear us, gracious Lord and God!

Keep us in everlasting fellowship with the church triumphant, and let us once rest together in thy presence from all our labor!

Hear us, gracious Lord and God!

O Christ, Almighty God! *Have mercy upon us!*

O thou Lamb of God, which takest away the sin of the world, *Own us to be thine!*

O thou Lamb of God, which takest away the sin of the world, *Be joyful over us!*

O thou Lamb of God, which takest away the sin of the world, *Leave thy peace with us!*

O Christ, *Hear us!*
Lord, *Have mercy upon us!*
Christ, *Have mercy upon us!*
Lord, *Have mercy upon us!*

To be used after the CHURCH-LITANY on solemn occasions.

UNTO the Lamb that was slain, (Rev. v. 12)
And hath redeemed us out of all nations of the earth; (Rev. v. 9.)
Unto the Lord who purchased our souls for himself; (Acts xx. 28.)
Unto that Friend who loved us, and washed us from our sins in his own blood; (Rev. i. 5.)
Who died for us once, (Rom. vi. 10, 11. 2 Cor. v. 15.)
That we might die unto sin; (1 Pet. ii. 24.)
Who rose for us,
That we also might rise; (1 Cor. xv.)
Who ascended for us in heaven,
To prepare a place for us; (John xiv. 2, 3.)
CHOIR. And to whom are subjected the angels, and powers, and dominions; (1 Pet. iii. 22.)
To him be glory at all times,
In the church that waiteth for him, and in that which is around him,
CHOIR. From everlasting to everlasting,
Amen!
Little children, abide in him; that, when he shall appear, we may have confidence, and not be ashamed before him at his coming, (1 John ii. 28.)

CONG. In none but him alone I trust for ever,
In him, my Saviour.

The Lord bless thee, and keep thee!
The Lord make his face shine upon thee, and be gracious unto thee!
The Lord lift up his countenance upon thee, and give thee peace!
CHOIR. In the name of Jesus,
Amen.

The bishop or minister shall say:

I Believe in the One only God, Father, Son, and Holy Ghost, who created all things by Jesus Christ, and was in Christ, reconciling the world unto himself.

I believe in God, the Father of our Lord Jesus Christ, who hath chosen us in him, before the foundation of the world;

Who hath delivered us from the power of darkness, and hath translated us into the kingdom of his dear Son;

Who hath blessed us with all spiritual blessings in heavenly places in Christ; who hath made us meet to be partakers of the inheritance of the saints in light; having predestinated us unto the adoption of children by Jesus Christ to himself, according to the good pleasure of his will, to the praise of the glory of his grace, wherein he hath made us accepted in the Beloved.

CONG. *This I verily believe.*

MIN. I thank thee, O Father, Lord of heaven and earth! because thou hast hid these things from the wise and prudent, and hast revealed them unto babes: even so, Father! for so it seemed good in thy sight.

Father! glorify thy name!

CONG. *Our Father, which art in heaven; Hallowed be thy name; thy kingdom come; thy will be done on earth, as it is in heaven; give us this day our daily bread: and forgive us our trespasses, as we forgive them that trespass against us; and lead us not into temptation, but deliver us from evil; for thine is the kingdom, and the power, and the glory, for ever and ever, Amen.*

MIN. I believe in the name of the only begotten Son of God, by whom are all things, and we through him;

I believe, that he was made flesh, and dwelt among us; and took on him the form of a servant;

By the overshadowing of the Holy Ghost, was conceived of the virgin Mary; as the children are partakers of flesh and blood, he also himself likewise took part of the same; was born of a woman;

And being found in fashion as a man, was tempted in all points like as we are, yet without sin;

For he was the Lord, the Messenger of the covenant, whom we delight in. The Lord and his Spirit hath sent him to proclaim the acceptable year of the Lord:

He spoke that which he did know, and testified that which he had seen: as many as received him, to them gave he power to become the sons of God.

Behold the Lamb of God! which hath taken away the sin of the world,

Suffered under Pontius Pilate, was crucified, dead and buried;

Went by the Spirit and preached unto the spirits in prison;

The third day rose again from the dead, and with him many bodies of the saints which slept;

Ascended into heaven, and sitteth on the throne of the Father; whence he will come, in like manner as he was seen going into heaven.

CONG. The Spirit and the bride of Christ say, come!
Let ev'ry one that heareth, answer, come!
Amen! come, Lord Jesus! come, we implore thee;
With longing hearts we now are waiting for thee;
Come soon, O come!

MIN. The Lord will descend from heaven with a shout, with the voice of the archangel, and with the trump of God, to judge both the quick and the dead.

This is my Lord, who redeemed me, a lost and undone human creature, purchased and gained me from all sin, from death, and from the power of the devil,

Not with gold or silver, but with his holy, precious blood, and with his innocent suffering and dying;

To the end that I should be his own, and in his kingdom live under him and serve him, in eternal righteousness, innocence, and happiness;

So as he, being risen from the dead, liveth and reigneth, world without end.

CONG. *This I most certainly believe.*

MIN. I believe in the Holy Ghost, who proceedeth from the Father, and whom our Lord Jesus Christ sent, after he went away, that he should abide with us for ever;

That he should comfort us, as a mother comforteth her children;

That he should help our infirmities, and make intercession for us with groanings which cannot be uttered;

That he should bear witness with our spirit, that we are the children of God, and teach us to cry, Abba, Father!

That he should shed abroad in our hearts the love of God, and make our bodies his holy temples;

And that he should work all in all, dividing to every man severally as he will.

To him be glory in the church, which is in Christ Jesus, the holy, universal Christian church, in the communion of saints at all times, and from eternity to eternity; CONG. *Amen.*

MIN. I believe, that by my own reason and strength I cannot believe in Jesus Christ my Lord, or come to him;

But that the Holy Ghost calleth me by the gospel, enlighteneth me with his gifts, sanctifieth and preserveth me in the true faith;

Even as he calleth, gathereth, enlighteneth and sanctifieth all Christendom on earth, which he keepeth by Jesus Christ in the only true faith;

In which Christian church he forgiveth me and every believer all sin daily and abundantly.

CONG. *This I assuredly believe.*

MIN. I desire to depart, and to be with Christ, which is far better; I shall never taste death; yea, I shall attain unto the resurrection of the dead: for my body, which I shall put off, this grain of corruptibility, shall put on incorruption: my flesh shall rest in hope:

And God, who brought again from the dead our Lord Jesus, that great Shepherd of the sheep, through the blood of the everlasting covenant, will also once quicken the bodies here interred, beeause the Spirit of God hath dwelt in them. CONG. *Amen.*

We poor sinners pray, *Hear us, gracious Lord and God!*

MIN. And keep us in everlasting fellowship with our brethren N. N. and with our sisters N. N.* who are entered into the joy of their Lord; (and whose bodies are buried here)

---

* Here are mentioned in each congregatoin the names of those, who departed into eternal rest since the preceding Easter.

Also with the servants and handmaids of our church, whom thou hast called home within this year, and with the whole church triumphant; and let us once rest with them in thy presence.

CONG. *Amen.*

They are at rest in lasting bliss,—Beholding Christ our Saviour;
Our humble expectation is—To live with him for ever.

MIN. Glory be to Him who is the resurrection and the Life; He was dead, and behold! He is alive for evermore;

And he that believeth in Him, though he were dead, yet shall he live.

Glory be to Him in the church which waiteth for Him, and in that which is around Him; for ever and ever,

CONG. *Amen.*

Grant us to lean unshaken—Upon thy faithfulness,
Until we hence are taken—To see thee face to face.

MIN. The grace of our Lord Jesus Christ, and the love of God, and the communion of the Holy Ghost, be with us all;

CONG. *Amen.*

LITANIES at BAPTISM.

BAPTISM OF CHILDREN, No. 1.

(After the singing of some suitable verses, and a short discourse:)

Min. CHRIST, thou Lamb of God, which takest away the sin of the world,

Cong. Leave thy peace with us! Amen.

M. By thy holy Sacraments,

C. Bless us, gracious Lord and God!

T. 90. *C.* An infant we present to thee,
As thy redeemed property,
And thee most fervently intreat
This child thyself to consecrate
By Baptism, and its soul to bless
Out of the fulness of thy grace.

M. Baptism is the answer of a good conscience towards God, the washing of regeneration and renewing of the Holy Ghost, which is shed on us abundantly through Jesus Christ our Saviour.

Children may also be made partakers of this grace,

For Christ hath said, "Suffer little children to come unto me, and forbid them not, for of such is the kingdom of heaven."

(Then the child which is to be baptized, is brought in, and the minister offers up a suitable prayer; or sings an appropriate verse; for example:)

T. 14. a. *M.* Be present, Lord! tho' water fails
To cleanse a soul from sin,
Yet while we pour it, let thy blood
Now make this infant clean.

M. Ye, who are baptized into Christ Jesus, how were ye baptized?

C. Into his death.

M. Into the death of Jesus I baptize thee N. N. in the name of the Father, and of the Son, and of the Holy Ghost.

(During the imposition of hands the minister continues:)

Now art thou buried with him, by baptism, into his death;

C. In the name of Jesus, Amen.

T. 79. p. 2. His death and passion ever,—Till soul and body sever,
Shall in thy heart engrav'd remain.

M. Now therefore live, yet not thou, but Christ live in thee! And the life which thou now livest in the flesh, live by the faith of the Son of God, who loved thee, and gave himself for thee.

T. 132. a. p. 2. *C.* This grant according to thy word,
Thro' Jesus Christ, our only Lord,
O Father, Son, and Spirit.

M. The Lord bless thee, and keep thee!
The Lord make his face shine upon thee, and be gracious unto thee!
The Lord lift up his countenance upon thee, and give thee peace! *C.* In the name of Jesus, Amen.

(Questions which may be put to the children, and answered by them.)

What is baptism?
May children also be made partakers of this grace?
What is the ground of this hope?

BAPTISM OF CHILDREN. No. 2.

(After the singing of some suitable verses, and a short discourse:)

Min. O THOU Lamb of God, which takest away the sin of the world,

Cong. Have mercy upon us, and give us thy peace!

M. By all the merits of thy life, sufferings, death and resurrection,

C. Bless us, gracious Lord and God!

M. Baptism was instituted by our Lord Jesus Christ, who said unto his disciples, "Go ye, and teach all nations, baptizing them in the name of the Father, and of the Son, and of the Holy Ghost: teaching them to observe all things, whatsoever I have commanded you."

He annexed this promise to it, "He that believeth and is baptized, shall be saved."

By baptism we are made partakers of the forgiveness of and cleansing from sin, by the blood of Jesus Christ, who loved the church, and gave himself for it, that he might sanctify and cleanse it with the washing of water by the word.

As many of us as have been baptized, have put on Christ.

T. 22 a. *C.* The Saviour's blood and righteousness
Our beauty is, our glorious dress;
Thus well array'd we need not fear,
When in his presence we appear.

T. 83. d. *M.* Are the children heirs of Heav'n?
Have they part in Christ our Saviour?
C. Yea, this grace to them is giv'n,
They are objects of his favor;
For he saith: Bring them to me*,
Heav'n is theirs assuredly.

(Here the child is brought in, and the minister either offers up a suitable prayer, or sings an appropriate verse, for example:)*

T. 1. *M.* Thou Friend of children, in thy arms of love
Receive this child, let it thy mercy prove;
And cleanse it with thy blood, that it may share
In all thy merits: Jesus, hear our pray'r!

(Questions which may be put to children, and answered by them.)

Who instituted baptism?
What promise did he annex thereto?
What are the benefits whereof we are made partakers by baptism?

M. Ye who are baptized into Christ Jesus, how were ye baptized?

C. Into his death.

M. Into the death of Jesus I baptize thee N. N. in the name of the Father, and of the Son, and of the Holy Ghost.

(During the imposition of hands the minister continues:)

Now art thou buried with him, by baptism, into his death;

C. In the name of Jesus, Amen.

T. 184. p. 2. *C.* May his atoning death and passion,
His agony and bitter pain,
Until thy final consummation
Deep in thy heart engrav'd remain!

M. Now therefore live, yet not thou, but Christ live in thee! And the life which thou now livest in the flesh, live by the faith of the Son of God, who loved thee, and gave himself for thee.

T. 58. *C.* That our Lord's views with thee may be attain'd,
We recommend thee now, with faith unfeign'd,
To the Father's blessing, to the Son's favor,
The Holy Spirit's guidance, now and ever,
The angels' guard.

M. The Lord bless thee, and keep thee!
The Lord make his face shine upon thee, and be gracious unto thee!
The Lord lift up his countenance upon thee, and give thee peace!

C. In the name of Jesus, Amen.

BAPTISM OF ADULTS.

T. 22. *Cong.* CHRIST, the almighty Son of God,
Took on him human flesh and blood,
And willingly gave up his breath
To save us from eternal death.

Praise to the Father, and the Son,
And Holy Spirit, Three in One,
That we're from condemnation freed,
Since Christ our ransom fully paid.

(After a short discourse follow these petitions:)

Min. Lord God, our Father, which art in heaven!

C. Hallowed be thy name; thy kingdom come; thy will be done on earth, as it is in heaven; give us this day our daily bread; and forgive us our trespasses, as we forgive them that trespass against us; and lead us not into temptation; but deliver us from evil. For thine is the kingdom, and the power, and the glory, for ever and ever. Amen.

M. Lord God, Son, thou Saviour of the world!
C. Be gracious unto us!

M. Lord God, Holy Ghost!
C. Abide with us for ever!

T. 132. a. p. 2. C. Thou slaughter'd Lamb, our God and Lord;
To needy pray'rs thine ear afford,
And on us all have mercy!

M. By thy divine presence,
By thy holy sacraments,
C. Bless us, gracious Lord and God!

(Questions put to the candidate for baptism)

M. Dost thou believe in Jesus Christ, the only begotten Son of God, by whom are all things and we through him?
Answer. I do.

M. Dost thou believe, that he is thy Lord, who redeemed thee, a lost and undone human creature, purchased and gained thee from all sin, from death, and from the power of the devil, not with gold or silver, but with his holy, precious blood, and with his innocent suffering and dying?
Answer. I verily believe it.

M. Dost thou desire to be cleansed from sin in the blood of Jesus Christ, and to be buried into his death by holy baptism?
Answer. That is my sincere desire.

M. Dost thou desire to be embodied into the congregation of Christ, by holy baptism, which is the laver of regeneration, and renewing of the Holy Ghost, and in his kingdom to live under him, and serve him, in eternal righteousness, innocence, and happiness?
Answer. That is my sincere desire.

v. 155. *C.* Unto *him*, O Lamb of God,
Open thy salvation's treasure—In rich measure;
Graciously *his* sins forgive,—*Him* receive,
Grant *him* peace and consolation;
Join *him* to thy congregation,
As the purchase of thy death.

v. 22. a. The water flowing from thy side,
Which by the spear was open'd wide,
Be now *his* bath; thy precious blood
Cleanse *him*, and bring *him* nigh to God.

(During the last verse the candidate for baptism kneels down, and the following question is put to the Congregation:)

M. Ye who are baptized into Christ Jesus, how were ye baptized?

C. Into his death.

M. Into the death of Jesus I baptize thee N.N. in the name of the Father, and of the Son, and of the Holy Ghost.

(During the imposition of hands the minister continues:)

Now art thou washed, justified and sanctified by the blood of Christ: therefore live, yet not thou, but Christ live in thee! And the life, which thou now livest in the flesh, live by the faith of the Son of God, who loved thee, and gave himself for thee.

C. Amen, Hallelujah! Hallelujah!
Amen, Hallelujah!

(Then, the Congregation kneeling, and the person baptized falling prostrate, the following verses may be sung:)

v. 22. *C.* May Christ thee sanctify and bless,
His Spirit's seal on thee impress;
His body torn with many a wound
Preserve thy soul and body sound!

The blood-sweat trickling down his face,
Thy condemnation doth erase;
His cross, his suff'rings, and his pain,
Thy everlasting strength remain.

The Father, Son, and Holy Ghost,
Will thee protect, we humbly trust.

(During the last, or any other suitable verse, the Congregation rises, and the minister pronounces the blessing:

M. The Lord bless thee, and keep thee!
The Lord make his face shine upon thee, and be gracious unto thee!
The Lord lift up his countenance upon thee, and give thee peace!

C. In the name of Jesus, Amen.

BAPTISM OF ADULTS FROM THE HEATHEN.

Min. OUR Lord Jesus Christ,
Cong. Be gracious unto us!

M. By thy divine presence,

C. Bless us, gracious Lord and God!

M. By all the merits of thy holy humanity, life, sufferings, death, and resurrection,

C. Bless us, gracious Lord and God!

T. 22. *C.* Lord Jesus Christ, all praise to thee!
That thou didst deign a man to be,
And for each soul which thou hast made
Hast an eternal ransom paid.

T. 132. *a.* O Jesus Christ, thou Son belov'd
Of thy celestial Father,
By whom all enmity's remov'd,
And all the lost find succor;
Thou slaughter'd Lamb, our God and Lord,
To needy pray'rs thine ear afford,
And on us all have mercy!

T. 127. O Lamb of God unspotted,—Our crucified Saviour,
Who hast to shame submitted,—With patient meek behavior;
Thy bearing our transgression—Hath sav'd us from damnation;
Have mercy on us, O Jesus! O Jesus!

T. 30. Lift up thy pierc'd hands, O dearest Saviour,
Now pour out on *him* (them) that grace and favor,
Which in thy loving—And kind heart for *him* is ever moving.

(*After these or other verses suited to this transaction have been sung, and a short discourse delivered concerning the aim of baptism, and the grace imparted by it to those who receive it, the minister shall put the following questions to the candidate:*

M. Dost thou believe, that thou art a sinful creature, and dost, on account of thy sins, deserve the wrath of God, and eternal punishment?

Answer. I do believe it.

M. Dost thou believe, that Jesus Christ became a man for us, and by his innocent life, sufferings, blood-shedding, and death, reconciled us poor sinful creatures to God?

Answer. I verily believe it.

M. Dost thou believe, that he hath purchased for thee by his blood and death, remission of sins, life and happiness?

Answer. I verily believe it.

M. Wilt thou in this faith be baptized into the death of Jesus, and be washed from thy sins in his blood?

Answer. That is my sincere desire.

M. Dost thou also desire to be delivered from the power of sin and of Satan, and to be received into the fellowship of Jesus Christ, and of those who believe in him?

Answer. That is my sincere desire, and I renounce the devil and all his works and ways.

T. 22. *C.* Soul, body, spirit, Lord! are thine,
The purchase of thy blood divine,
O take *him*, as thy property,
And keep *him* thine eternally!

(During this verse the candidate for baptism kneels down, and the minister prays that he may be cleansed from all his sins in the blood of Christ; delivered from guilt and punishment, and from the dominion of sin and Satan; buried by baptism into the death of Jesus, and raised together with him unto newness of life, and thus, together with all Believers, received into and made a partaker of the fellowship of the Father, and of the Son, and of the Holy Ghost.)

T. 75. *C.* Thro' thy atoning blood,
That precious healing flood,
Purge off all sin and sadness,
And fill *his* heart with gladness;
Lord, hear thou *his* confession,
And blot out *his* transgression.

OR, T. 22. *C.* The water flowing from thy side,
Which by the spear was open'd wide,
Be now *his* bath, thy precious blood
Cleanse *him*, and bring *him* nigh to God.

(After singing one of these, or any other suitable verses, follows the baptism:)

M. I baptize thee N. N. into the death of Jesus, in the name of the Father, and of the Son, and of the Holy Ghost;

C. Amen.

M. Now art thou buried with Christ, by baptism, into his death; therefore, from henceforth live, yet not thou, but Christ live in thee! And the life which thou now livest in the flesh, live by the faith of the Son of God, who loved thee, and gave himself for thee.

T. 14. a. *C.* With awe and heartfelt thankfulness,
Him in the dust adore;*
He who hath look'd on thee in grace,
Hath bliss for thee in store.

* *During these words the Congregation kneels down, and the person baptized falls prostrate, during which some more verses may be sung, for instance:*

T. 22. a. *C.* May Christ thee sanctify and bless,
His Spirit's seal on thee impress;
His body torn with many a wound
Preserve thy soul and body sound.

OR, T. 22. *C.* The Saviour's blood and righteousness,
Thy beauty is, thy glorious dress;
Thus well array'd thou need'st not fear,
When in his presence all appear.

OR, T. 79. p. 2. *C.* His death and passion ever,
Till soul and body sever,
Shall in thy heart engrav'd remain.

T. 22. *ALL.* All pow'r and glory doth pertain
Unto the Lamb, for he was slain,
And hath redeem'd us by his blood,*
And made us kings and priests to God.

* *At these words the Congregation rises, and the minister pronounces the blessing of the Lord:*

M. The Lord bless thee, and keep thee!
The Lord make his face shine upon thee, and be gracious unto thee!
The Lord lift up his countenance upon thee, and give thee peace!

C. In the name of Jesus, Amen.

T. 11. a. *C.* Praise on earth to thee be giv'n,
Never ceasing praise in heav'n;
Boundless wisdom, pow'r divine,
Love unspeakable are thine!

Of the Holy Communion.

NOTE. IN the church of the United Brethren there is no prescribed form of words used at the administration of the Holy Communion. The service is opened by singing verses expressive of a penitent, contrite heart, after which a prayer for absolution is offered up. The Congregation rising, a verse is sung and the bread is consecrated by pronouncing the words of Institution, thus:

"*Our Lord Jesus Christ, the same night in which he was betrayed, took bread, and when he had given thanks, he brake it, and gave it to his disciples, and said, Take eat: this is my body, which is given for you. This do in remembrance of me.*"

The blessed bread is then distributed by the Minister and his assistants, to each communicant, during the singing of hymns, treating principally of the sufferings and death of our Lord: After all the communicants have received the bread, the Minister repeats the words: *Take eat, this is the Lord's body given for you:* The congregation partake altogether at the same time, kneeling, either in silence, or while a verse is sung, expressive of the solemn act. The congregation rising, verses of thanksgiving are sung, after which the Minister consecrates the wine, by pronouncing the words:

"*After the same manner also, our Lord Jesus Christ took the cup, when he had supped, gave thanks, and gave it to them, saying, Drink ye all of it: this is my blood, the blood of the New Testament, which is shed for you and for many, for the remission of sins. This do ye, as oft as ye drink it, in remembrance of me.*"

The Minister then partaking of the blessed cup, delivers it to his assistants, by whom it is administered to the congregation; during which hymns are sung treating of the remission of sins in the blood of Jesus and its healing and sanctifying power.

The service is closed with such hymns as treat of brotherly love, communion with Christ, and thankfulness for his incarnation and death.

DOXOLOGIES.

To be used at Ordinations.

NOTE. THE service being opened by the singing of the *Veni, Creator Spiritus* (Come Holy Ghost, come Lord our God!) or some other suitable hymn, the Bishop addresses the congregation in an appropriate discourse, ending with a charge to the candidate (or candidates) for ordination, after which he offers up a prayer, imploring the blessing of God upon the solemn transaction and commending the candidate (or candidates) to his grace, that he may be endowed with power and unction and the influences of the Holy Ghost for preaching the word of God, administering the Holy Sacraments, and for doing all those things, which shall be committed unto him, for the promotion of the spiritual edification of the Church: The Bishop then proceeds to ordain the candidate (or candidates) with imposition of hands, pronouncing the following, or similar words:

I ordain *(consecrate)* thee N: N: to be a Deacon (Presbyter) *(Bishop)* of the Church of the United Brethren, in the name of the Father, and of the Son, and of the Holy Ghost: And may *the Lord bless thee, and keep thee! The Lord make his face shine upon thee, and be gracious unto thee! The Lord lift up his countenance upon thee, and give thee peace! In the name of Jesus, Amen.*

[N. B. At the consecration of Bishops, three, or at least two, Bishops are required to assist; and the words used are such as particularly refer to the charge committed to them in the Church.]

The Bishop having returned to his place, kneels down with the whole Congregation, all worshipping in silent devotion, while the following *Doxologies* are sung in a solemn manner by the Choir, the Congregation joining in the *Amen, Hallelujah!*

The service is concluded with a short hymn and the Bishop pronouncing the Blessing.

To be used at the Ordination

(a:) *Of* Deacons.

Glory be to Thy most meritorious Ministry,
O Thou Servant of the true Tabernacle,
Who didst not come to be ministered unto,
But to minister!
Amen, Hallelujah! Hallelujah!
Cong. Amen, Hallelujah!

(b:) *Of* Presbyters.

Glory be to thy most holy Priesthood,
Christ, Thou Lamb of God!
Thou, who wast slain for us;
Who, by one offering, hast perfected for ever them that are sanctified!
Amen, Hallelujah! Hallelujah!
Cong. Amen, Hallelujah!

(c:) *the Consecration of* Bishops.

Glory be to the Shepherd and Bishop of our souls,
The great Shepherd of the sheep, through the blood of the everlasting Covenant;
Glory and obedience be unto God the Holy Ghost, our Guide and Comforter!
Glory and adoration be to the Father of our Lord Jesus Christ,
Who is the true Father of all, who are called children on earth and in heaven!

O might each pulse thanksgiving beat!
And ev'ry breath His praise repeat!

Amen, Hallelujah! Hallelujah!
Cong. Amen, Hallelujah;

LITANY AT BURIALS.

No. 1.

LORD, *Have mercy upon us!*
Christ, *Have mercy upon us!*
Lord, *Have mercy upon us!*
Christ, *Hear us!*

Lord God, our Father, which art in heaven!

Hallowed be thy name; thy kingdom come; thy will be done on earth as it is in heaven; give us this day our daily bread; and forgive us our trespasses as we forgive them that trespass against us; and lead us not into temptation, but deliver us from evil. For thine is the kingdom, and the power, and the glory, for ever, and ever. Amen.

Lord God, Son, thou Saviour of the world!

Be gracious unto us!

By thy human birth,
By thy prayers and tears,
By all the troubles of thy life,
By thine infirmities and pains,
By all the grief and anguish of thy soul,
By thine agony and bloody sweat,
By thy bonds and scourgings,
By thy crown of thorns,
By thine ignominious crucifixion,
By thy sacred wounds and precious blood,
By thy atoning death,
By thy rest in the grave,
By thy glorious resurrection and ascension,
By thy sitting at the right hand of God,
By thy divine presence,
By thy coming again to thy church on earth, or our being called home to thee,

Bless and comfort us, gracious Lord and God!

Lord God, Holy Ghost!

Abide with us for ever!

T. 83. Cong. Christ is risen from the dead,
Thou shalt rise too, saith my Saviour,
Of what should I be afraid?
I with him shall live for ever;
Can the HEAD forsake HIS limb,
And not draw me unto him?

I am the resurrection and the life, saith the Lord; he that believeth in me, though he were dead, yet shall he live. And whosoever liveth and believeth in me, shall never die.

Therefore, blessed are the dead, which die in the Lord from henceforth; yea, saith the Spirit, that they may rest from their labors.

O death, where is thy sting? O grave, where is thy victory? The sting of death is sin, and the strength of sin is the law; but thanks be to God, which giveth us the victory through our Lord Jesus Christ. *Amen.*

T. 580. Cong. This body now to rest convey'd,
Into the earth like Jesus' laid,
Like his shall rise again:
Christ soon in glory will appear,
Then we, and these interred here,
With him o'er death shall ever reign.*

We poor sinners pray, Hear us, gracious Lord and God!

And keep us in everlasting fellowship with our brother (sister) N. N. whose remains we here inter, and with the whole church triumphant, and let us once rest with him (her) in thy presence from all our labor. *Amen.*

Our late brother (sister) desired to depart, and to be with Christ, which is far better; and he (she) shall never taste death, but attain unto the resurrection of the dead; for this body, which he (she) hath put off, this grain of corruptibility, shall put on incorruption. His (her) flesh here rests in hope.

The Father and the Son, who quicken whom they will, and the Spirit of him, who raised up Jesus from the dead, will also quicken this body, because the Spirit of God hath dwelt in it. *Amen.*

T. 22. Cong. The Saviour's blood and righteousness
My beauty is, my glorious dress;
Thus well array'd, I need not fear,
When in his presence I appear.

* During the singing of this verse, the corpse is laid into the grave.

None of us liveth to himself, and no man dieth to himself, for whether we live, we live unto the Lord, and whether we die, we die unto the Lord; whether we live therefore or die, we are the Lord's; for to this end Christ both died, and rose, and revived, that he might be Lord both of the dead and living.

Blessed and holy is he, that hath part in the first resurrection; on such the second death hath no power, but they shall be priests of God and of Christ.

T. 58. CONG. The Spirit and the bride of Christ say; come;
Let ev'ry one that heareth answer: come;
Amen, come, Lord Jesus; come, we implore thee;
With longing hearts we now are waiting for thee,
Come soon, O come!

Glory be to Him who is the Resurrection and the Life, who vivifieth us as long as we are dying: and after we have obtained the true life, doth not suffer us to die any more.

Glory be to Him in the church which waiteth for Him, and in that which is around Him; for ever and ever, *Amen.*

The grace of our Lord Jesus Christ, the love of God, and the communion of the Holy Ghost, be with us all. *Amen.*

LITANY AT BURIALS.

No. 2.

LORD, *Have mercy upon us!*
Christ, *Have mercy upon us!*
Lord, *Have mercy upon us!*
Christ, *Hear us!*

Our Father, which art in heaven; Hallowed be thy name; thy kingdom come; thy will be done on earth, as it is in heaven; give us this day our daily bread; and forgive us our trespasses, as we forgive them that trespass against us; and lead us not into temptation, but deliver us from evil. For thine is the kingdom, and the power, and the glory, for ever and ever, Amen.

O Father, accept us as thy children in thy beloved Son, Jesus Christ, who came forth from thee, and came into the world, was made flesh, and dwelt among us, took on him the form of a servant, and hath redeemed us, lost and undone human creatures, from all sin and from death with his holy and precious blood, and with his innocent suffering and dying; to the end that we should be his own, and in his kingdom live under him and serve him, in eternal righteousness, innocence, and happiness: so as he is risen from the dead, liveth and reigneth world without end.

Therefore, blessed are the dead which die in the Lord from henceforth: yea, saith the Spirit, that they may rest from their labors.

Whosoever liveth and believeth in Christ, shall never die, for he is the Resurrection and the Life, and went to prepare a place for us, and will come again, and receive us unto himself, that where he is, there we may be also.

Meanwhile none of us liveth to himself, and no man dieth to himself, for whether we live, we live unto the Lord, and whether we die, we die unto the Lord; whether we live therefore or die, we are the Lord's; for to this end Christ both died, and rose, and revived, that he might be Lord both of the dead and living.

Blessed and holy is he, that hath part in the first resurrection; on such the second death hath no power, but they shall be priests of God and of Christ.

O death, where is thy sting? O grave where is thy victory? Thanks be to God, which giveth us the victory, through our Lord Jesus Christ.

T. 14. Cong. Now to the earth let these remains*
In hope committed be,
Until the body chang'd obtains
Blest immortality.

We poor sinners pray, Hear us, gracious Lord and God!

And keep us in everlasting fellowship with our brother (sister) (or with this child) N. N. whose remains we here inter, and with the whole church triumphant, and let us once rest with him (her) in thy presence from all our labor.

Amen.

* During the singing of this verse, the corpse is laid into the grave.

(* As touching children, Jesus saith; "Suffer little children to come unto me, and forbid them not, for of such is the kingdom of God. Verily I say unto you, whoever shall not receive the kingdom of God as a little child, he shall not enter therein.")

We desire to depart, and to be with Christ, which is far better: we shall never taste death; and we shall attain unto the resurrection of the dead; for the body, which we shall put off, this grain of corruptibility, shall put on incorruption: our flesh shall rest in hope.

The Father and the Son, who quicken whom they will, and the Spirit of him who raised up Jesus from the dead, will also quicken this body, because the Spirit of God hath dwelt in it.

Glory be to Him who is the Resurrection and the Life! He was dead, and behold He liveth for evermore! And he that believeth in Him, though he were dead, yet shall he live.

Glory be to Him in the church which waiteth for Him, and in that which is around Him; for ever and ever, *Amen.*

T. 79. CONG. While here, the great salvation
Procur'd by Jesus' passion
Our fav'rite theme shall be;
By virtue of his merit,
We shall true life inherit
In heav'n to all eternity.

The grace of our Lord Jesus Christ, the love of God, and the communion of the Holy Ghost, be with us all. *Amen.*

---

* To be used only at the burial of a child.

A

COLLECTION OF HYMNS, &c.

I. Of the WORD of GOD.

1.* T. 119.

HOLY Lord, :||:
Holy and almighty Lord!
Thou who, as the great Creator,
By all creatures art ador'd;
Source of universal nature!
And to man, redeem'd by Jesus' blood,
Gracious God! :||:

2 Thanks and praise, :||:
Lord our God, be ever thine,
That thy word to us is given,
Teaching us, with pow'r divine,
That the Lord of earth and heaven,
Everlasting life for us to gain,
Once was slain. :||:

3 Day nor night :||:
Never let us hold our peace;
In his blood-bought congregation
Never shall his praises cease;
God, as man, made an oblation,
Suffer'd, bled & dy'd, my soul for thee,
Joyful be! :||:

4 Lord our God, :||:
May thy precious, saving word,
Till our race is here completed,
Light unto our path afford!
And, when in thy presence seated,
We to thee will render, for thy grace,
Ceaseless praise. :||:

2.* T. 22.

GOD's holy word, which ne'er shall [cease,
Proclaimeth pardon, grace and peace;
Directs to Jesus and his blood,
And teacheth us the will of God.

2 As fallen creatures could not bear
The awful voice of God to hear,
By men the Spirit of the Lord
Reveal'd God's holy cov'nant word.

3 This sacred word exposeth sin,
Convinceth us that we're unclean;
Points out the wretched, fallen state
Of all mankind, both small and great.

4 It also shews God's boundless grace
Toward the fallen human race,
Eternal life to ev'ry one
Who turns to Jesus Christ his Son.

5 This gospel cheers the poor in heart,
And heav'nly riches doth impart;
Sets forth the myst'ry of the cross,
And that Christ's blood aton'd for us:

6 It gathers God's elected flock,
Grounds them on Jesus Christ the rock,
Serves to instruct us and reprove,
Confirms our hope, inflames our love;

7 Preserves believers in the faith
Of Christ and his atoning death;
Prompts us to do God's holy will,
And leads us safe to Salem's hill.

8 Receive our cordial thanks, O Lord,
For granting us thy holy word;
O may we thereby guided be,
Till we in heav'n shall dwell with thee!

3.* T. 84.

DEAREST Jesus! we are here,
By thy word to gain instruction;
Grant to us an open ear,
And thy Spirit's manuduction;
That we, freed from things terrestrial,
May aspire to joys celestial.

2 Reason gives no saving light
Unto fallen human nature;
But thy Spirit clears our sight,
Makes the sinner a new creature;
And by his divine emotion,
Prompts our hearts to true devotion.

3 Holy Ghost, eternal God,
We now humbly ask the favor:
Shed in all our hearts abroad
The great love of God our Saviour:
Bless our pray'r and meditation,
And accept our supplication.

4. T. 106.

SPIRIT of truth, essential God,
Who didst the saints of old inspire,
Shed in their hearts thy love abroad,
And touch their lips with sacred fire:
Thou Guide divine, who dost impart
The truth to man, instruct each heart!

2 Most holy and almighty Lord,
Whose presence fills both earth and heav'n,
May we believe thy written word,
Which was by inspiration giv'n:
Thou only canst thyself explain,
As truth divine, to fallen man.

3 Come, thou divine Interpreter,
Our sloth and ignorance thou know'st:
Ah, teach us humbly to revere
The Father, Son, and Holy Ghost,
For all the mercy, truth and grace,
We in the holy scriptures trace.

5. T. 22.

'TWAS by an order from the Lord,
The ancient prophets spoke his word;
His Spirit did their tongues inspire,
And warm'd their hearts with heav'nly fire.

2 O God! mine eyes with pleasure look
On the dear volume of thy book;
There my Redeemer's face I see,
And read his name, who dy'd for me.

3 Let the false raptures of the mind
Be lost and vanish in the wind;
Here I can fix my hope secure;
This is thy word, and must endure.

6.* T. 22.

LORD Jesus, with thy children stay
Till dawn of thy eternal day;
And let thy glorious gospel light,
Till then, dispel the gloom of night.

2 In these degen'rate evil days
We pray for constancy and grace,
That we keep pure, most gracious Lord,
Thy holy sacraments and word.

3 Thy sacred word is all our boast;
In this thy church can boldly trust:
This doth alone to bliss direct;
All other doctrines we reject.

4 Lord, from such teachers us preserve
Who from the holy scriptures swerve,
And by false doctrines would deceive
Those who thee love and thee believe.

5 The cause and glory, Lord, are thine;
Thy word is pure, and truth divine:
Assist us to rely on thee,
And keep us thine eternally.

7.* T. 16.

FROM the doctrines I'll ne'er waver,
In the holy scriptures stor'd;
O what sweetness do I savor
In each sacred cov'nant-word!

2 And if I myself examine
While the book I 'fore me hold,
To each truth my heart saith Amen,
One the other doth unfold.

3 Speak, O Lord, thy servant heareth
With deep awe attentively;
What thy holy word declareth
Shall my rule and practice be.

8. T. 22.

FAIN would I, dear Redeemer, learn,
Fain what is excellent discern;
Thy will would search, my duty know;
O let thy word the secret show!

2 Sigh after sigh to thee I send,
That I thy word may comprehend,
That word, which learnt & understood,
Affords the soul a lasting food.

3 Let human arts make others wise,
My learning from the cross shall rise;
Thy wounds, thy passion, death and grave,
Is all the knowledge that I crave.

4 With pity view me at thy feet,
To be instructed, Lord, I wait;
Here will I lie, nor wish to rise
Till by thy cross I am made wise.

9. T. 22.

O HOW I love thy holy word,
Thy gracious covenant, O Lord!
It guides me in the peaceful way;
I'll think upon it all the day.

2 What are the mines of shining wealth,
The strength of youth, the bloom of health!
What are all joys compar'd with those
Thine everlasting word bestows!

10. T. 14.

JESUS, thy word is my delight;
There grace and truth are seen:
Ah, could I study day and night,
And meditate therein!

2 The gospel, as a polish'd glass,
Thy glory lets us see;
And by beholding there thy face
We're render'd like to thee.

3 O Lamb of God, the book unseal,
And to our hearts explain;
Let all its life and spirit feel,
And heav'nly wisdom gain.

4 That thou for us didst live and die,
Make known to us, dear Lord;
To us the promises apply,
Contained in thy word.

11. T. 97.

HERE in thy presence we appear,
Lord Jesus Christ, thy word to hear;
Our wand'ring thoughts and hearts incline
With thirst t'imbibe thy word divine;
That all our minds drawn from this earth to thee,
May love thee more, and serve thee faithfully.

2 God Holy Spirit, now impart
Thy unction to each longing heart;
Us with thy heav'nly light and fire,
To sing, to pray, and preach inspire;
Thus blest, in spirit and in truth shall we
Give praise unto the Father, Son, and Thee.

12.* T. 58.

MOST gracious God; to thee we render praise,
Since thy blest word, replete with truth and grace,
Teacheth us to know thee and seek thy favor;
To us it proveth a life-giving savor,
Through Jesus Christ.

13.* T. 97.

GIVE us thy Spirit, Lord, that we,
With gladness and humility,
The holy scriptures may believe,
And with a grateful heart receive,
As thy own word, to make us truly wise,
And not as man's invention or device.

14.* T. 83.

O WHAT peace divinely sweet
Fills my soul, when I've the favor
To sit down at Jesus' feet,
And his gracious words to savor!
Then I open heart and ear;
What he saith finds entrance there.

15.* T. 11.

LET the splendor of thy word
Light unto our path afford;
That we in thy truth and grace
May proceed throughout our race.

II. Of the Fall and Corruption of Man, and his Redemption by Christ.

16.* T. 212.

WHEN Adam fell, the frame entire
Of nature was infected; [dire,
The source, whence came the poison
Was not to be corrected,
But by God's grace, which saves our race
From mis'ry and destruction;
The fatal lust, indulg'd at first,
Brought death as its production.

2 By one man's guilt we were enslav'd
To sin, death, and the devil;
But by another's grace are sav'd,
Through faith, from all this evil:
And as we all, by Adam's fall,
Were sentenc'd to perdition;
So for us hath Christ by his death
Regained life's fruition.

3 Since God bestow'd his only Son
On his rebellious creature,
To save our souls, which were undone,
And free our sinful nature
From shame and guilt, by his blood spilt,
His death and resurrection;
Do not delay! make sure, this day,
Thy calling and election.

4 I send my cries unto the Lord,
My heart implores this favor,
To grant me of his living word
A never-failing savor; [claim
That sin and shame may lose their
To hinder my salvation;
In Christ the scope of all my hope,
I fear no condemnation.

5 His word's a lamp unto my feet;
My soul's best information;
My surest guide and path to meet
Eternal consolation;
This light where-e'er it doth appear,
Revealeth Christ our Saviour
Unto the lost, who firmly trust
In him alone for ever.

17.* T. 132.

OUR whole salvation doth depend
On God's free grace and spirit;
All our best works can ne'er defend
A boast in our own merit:
Derived is our righteousness
From Christ and his atoning grace;
He is our Mediator.

2 Who can maintain the bold conceit,
That fallen man is able
T' observe, by means of nat'ral light,
The first and second table!
The Lord a feigned work abhors;
Mere flesh increaseth but the curse
Of our entail'd corruption.

3 The law cry'd, "justice must be done,
Or man doom'd to damnation;"
But Mercy sent th' eternal Son,
Who purchas'd our salvation,
Fulfill'd the law in its extent,
And gave its wrath a thorough vent,
To spare the sons of Adam.

4 Christ, having all the law fulfill'd,
Through his blest cross and passion,
Is now the Rock whereon we build
Our faith and whole salvation:
We call him Lord our Righteousness,
Whose death hath purchas'd life and
And ransom'd us for ever. [grace,

5 The law reveal'd sin's sinfulness,
Enhanc'd the accusation;
The gospel tenders saving grace,
To sinners consolation,
Bids all lay hold on Jesus' cross;
The law could ne'er retrieve our loss,
Ev'n with our best performance.

6 True faith by Jesus in us wrought,
By works is manifested;
That faith is empty, which is not
By works of love attested:
Yet faith alone us justifies;
Love to our neighbor but implies,
We are sincere believers.

18.* T. 166.

WHEN the due time had taken place,
God look'd upon the sons of men,
Saw them a sinful, cursed race,
Perverse, polluted and unclean:
Then Jesus came to set us free,
And for our guilt to shed his blood;
His death procur'd our liberty,
And reconcil'd us unto God.

2 Our Lord now calleth constantly:
"Come, sinners, come to me and live;
Surrender ye yourselves to me,
Repenting sinners I receive:
My life I freely gave for you;
Now all your wants I will supply,
Yea, pardon, rest, and life bestow;
O turn to me, why will ye die?"

3 Sinners, attend to Jesus' voice;
He is the Lord our Righteousness:
Mourn not, but in his name rejoice,
Accept of his redeeming grace:
He fills the hungry soul with good,
The thirsty heart may take its fill;
He guides us in the narrow road
That leads to Salem's blessed hill.

4 Ah! come Lord Jesus, hear our pray'r
Thou worthy Son of God most high!
We humbly ask: our souls prepare,
That we may to thy mercy fly;
That we may all believe on thee,
And on thy flesh and blood may feed,
True members of thy body be,
For ever join'd to thee our Head.

19.* T. 89.

IN thine image, Lord, thou mad'st me,
Gav'st me being out of love;
Though I fell, yet thou hast sent me
Full redemption from above:
Sacred Love, I long to be
Thine to all eternity.

2 Love! before I life obtained
I was chose to bliss by thee:
Thou, O God, hast not disdained
To become a man like me;
Love almighty and divine!
I would be for ever thine.

3 Love! who hast for me endured
Keenest pains of death and hell,
Love! whose suff'rings have procured
More for me than tongue can tell,
Sacred Love, &c.

4 Love! my Life, and my Salvation,
Light and Truth, eternal Word!
Thou alone dost consolation
To my sinking soul afford.
Love almighty, &c.

5 Love! thy yoke I gladly carry,
It is easy, gentle, light;
Grant that I may ne'er be weary
Thee to serve with all my might.
Sacred Love, &c.

6 Love! who interced'st in heaven
For my soul when I'm opprest,
Bear'st my worthless name engraven
Upon thy high-priestly breast.
Love almighty, &c.

7 Love! thou me wilt raise to glory
From the grave, the bed of dust,
And as conqu'ror place before thee
Crown'd with bliss among the just.
Sacred Love! I long to be
Thine to all eternity.

20.* T. 590.

THE true good Shepherd, God's own Son
From all eternity,
Urg'd by his love, exchang'd his throne
For human misery;
His wand'ring sheep gone far astray
He sought with pungent pain,
And did for all a ransom pay
To bring them home again.

2 One of those sheep, in deserts lost,
Art thou, my sin-sick soul;
His life it hath the Shepherd cost
To save and make thee whole;
Now hear his voice with gratitude,
Call on his saving name;
For thee he shed his precious blood,
And now his own doth claim.

21. T. 79.

THOU holy, spotless Lamb of God!
Didst leave thy glorious, blest abode,

In love to sinners vile,
To bleed for fallen Adam's race,
Who were accurs'd, unclean and base,
Entangled fast by Satan's guile.

2 Thou, for their sake who hated thee,
Didst shed thy blood upon the tree,
Thy life for ours didst give; [paid,
Thou bar'st our curse; our debt was
Thy soul for sin an off'ring made,
Thou dy'dst, that we with thee might live.

[blood,
3 Thus hast thou bought us with thy
That price accepted was by God
With him we are at peace;
No wrath remains on any one,
Who will but come unto the Son,
Take and put on his righteousness.

4 Never may I depart from thee;
Thou hast procur'd my liberty,
Thanks to thy boundless grace!
Thy wounds, whereon I trust by faith,
My refuge are from sin and death,
My feeble soul's abiding-place.

22. T. 22.

[bled
GIVE thanks that Jesus Christ hath
Upon the cross in Adam's stead,
And freed us from th' unhappy fall;
Thank him for this, ye sinners all!

2 Thanks, that he by his death & cross,
Hath sav'd us and restor'd our loss;
Thanks, that by his most precious blood,
All that was spoil'd is now made good.

3 Permit me therefore thee to praise,
O Lamb of God, with grateful lays,
For all the pain thou didst endure,
For me salvation to procure.

4 O let me by the Spirit's light
Thy cross's myst'ry know aright,
That I on thee my faith may place,
Till I shall see thee face to face.

23.* T. 221.

[love,
YE bottomless depths of God's infinite
In Jesus Christ to us reveal'd!
'Its motions how burning, how flaming they prove!
Though from man's wisdom quite conceal'd.
Whom dost thou love? Sinners, the vilest race;
Whom dost thou bless? Children, who scorn'd thy grace;
O Being most gracious! whom angels adore,
Thou takest delight in the worthless and poor.

[God,
2 Our thirsting can never, O merciful
Extend as far as doth thy grace;
On us thou more blessings and love hast bestow'd,
Than stripes deserv'd our trespasses;
O teach us to trust thy fidelity,
And closely united with Christ to be,
The Spirit's kind teachings in all things to prove,
Yea live to thy honor, thee serve, praise and love.

3 We pray thee, O Being most gracious and mild,
Instruct our minds and teach us now,
So that in Immanuel, thine image and child,
How great thy name is, we may know.
Ah! shew us how easy it is to bear
Thy yoke, and to trust thy paternal care,
That till the short period of this life shall end,
Our faith and our love may the Author commend.

24. T. 14.

HOW sad our state by nature is!
Our sin how deep it stains!
How Satan binds our captive souls
Fast in his slavish chains!

2 But there's a voice of sov'reign grace
Sounds from the sacred word:
"Ho! ye despairing sinners, come,
Believe in Christ the Lord."

3 My soul, obey the gracious call,
And haste to gain relief;
I would believe thy promise, Lord;
O help my unbelief!

4 To the dear fountain of thy blood,
Incarnate God! I fly:
Here let me wash my spotted soul
From crimes of deepest dye.

5 A guilty, weak and helpless worm,
Into thy arms I fall:
Be thou my strength and righteousness,
My Jesus, and my All.

25. T. 582.

NOT one of Adam's race,
If in the balance try'd,
Can, by his works of righteousness,
'Fore God be justify'd.
The works which we have done
Are all, alas! unclean;
But we are sav'd by faith alone,
And cleans'd thereby from sin.

2 Ye sinners, who with grief
Your condemnation feel,
Look up to Jesus for relief,
And to his blood appeal:
God gave his only Son
That sinners who believe,
Might not be lost, but be his own,
And in his kingdom live.

26. T. 14.

I, WITH the fallen human race,
Lay welt'ring in my blood;
Cover'd with shame and deep disgrace,
And banish'd far from God.

2 The loving Jesus passing by,
His bowels yearn'd to see
Me wretched sinner helpless lie
In deepest misery.

3 Inclin'd to me in tenderness,
My soul he would relieve
From all its mis'ry and distress,
He said, "Arise, and live."

4 He wash'd away my ev'ry stain,
And cleans'd me in his blood;
Deck'd me with righteousness divine,
And brought me nigh to God.

5 My heart no condemnation fears,
Nor hell, nor Satan dreads,
Christ as the mercy-seat appears,
His blood my pardon pleads.

6 Against the fiercest pow'rs of hell,
He is my strength and shield;
Within his wounds I safely dwell;
He fights, I win the field.

7 Since he became my sacrifice,
My bonds and chains he broke;
Now to my willing neck he ties
His soft and easy yoke.

8 A pardon'd sinner I remain,
But sin its pow'r hath lost,
Sin still I have, but grace doth reign,
Mercy is all my boast.

9 Arise, O happy soul, rejoice,
In endless happiness;
Open to thee is paradise,
Go in, and take thy place.

27. T. 22.

LORD, I am vile, conceiv'd in sin,
And born unholy and unclean;
Sprung from the man whose guilty fall
Corrupts his race, and taints us all.

2 Soon as we draw our infant breath
The seeds of sin engender death;
The law demands a perfect heart,
But we're defil'd in ev'ry part.

3 O God! create my heart anew,
And form my spirit pure and true;
O make me wise betimes to see
My danger and my remedy.

4 Behold, I fall before thy face;
My only refuge is thy grace:
No outward forms can make me clean,
The leprosy lies deep within.

5 My sin I feel, my guilt I know,
Thy blood can make me white as snow;
Lord, let me hear thy pard'ning voice,
And make my broken heart rejoice.

28. T. 22.

WHEN justice did demand its due,
And sins increas'd the dreadful strife,
My Saviour to my succor flew,
And by obedience bought my life.

2 My ransom from the pow'r of sin
Could not be paid on other terms:

Run, hide thyself, my soul, within
Thy bleeding Saviour's out-stretch'd arms.

3 When law condemns, and justice cries
For dreadful vengeance without end,
To Jesus then I turn my eyes;
He tells me, he will stand my friend.

4 God on these terms is reconcil'd,
And I his gracious heart have won:
Now I am deem'd his favor'd child,
In Jesus his beloved Son.

5 What can be laid unto my charge?
When God saith, "Freely I forgive!"
Tho' Satan on my crimes enlarge,
Christ saith, I shall not die, but live.

6 The curses which the law of God
Pronounc'd o'er me, he freely bore;
I'm now, by faith in Jesus' blood,
Acquitted of sin's dreadful score.

7 Away then doubts and anxious fears!
Be silent all my needless sighs;
My Saviour wipes away my tears,
O'er sin and death I conqu'ror rise.

8 Jesus! be endless praise to thee,
Let sinners loud thy lauds proclaim;
Of old their sins could pardon'd be,
And Jesus always is the same.

29. T. 580.

ARISE, ye who are captive led,
Complain no more, for Christ our Head
From sin can set you free:
Redemption Jesus freely gives,
Repenting sinners he receives,
He came to save both thee and me.

2 He meekly all our sorrows bore,
Us fallen sinners to restore
To life and liberty:
For us he suffer'd deep distress,
Was without form or comeliness;
O depth of love! O mystery!

3 Th'almighty Judge condemned was,
That he by death might gain our cause;
The Prince of life was slain:
And since he suffer'd in our stead,
We need no condemnation dread,
Eternal life in him we gain.

4 The Holy One, made sin for us,
Was nail'd to the accursed cross,
And shed his precious blood;
Thus he obtain'd a righteousness
For all who mourn for pard'ning grace,
Thro' Jesus we have peace with God!

5 Rejoice, O heav'ns, and earth reply!
With praise, ye sinners, fill the sky,
All grace his death procures;
Your woes to blessings he will change,
You in his children's order range,
Thro' him eternal life is yours.

III. Of the Incarnation and Birth of Jesus Christ.

30.* T. 97.

JESUS, th' almighty Son of God,
Takes up with mortals his abode;
He who was sworn to Abraham,
Who ever was and is the same,
Came in due time and mysteries reveal'd,
Which from the world's foundation were conceal'd.

2 We, dead in sins and trespasses,
The narrow way to life and peace
Had neither will nor pow'r to find;
Nor were our stubborn hearts inclin'd
To wish, or ask, that happiness to know,
Which love alone on sinners could bestow.

3 Then Love brake forth, "Behold me still
"Prepar'd, O God, to do thy will!
"I freely come, I freely die,
"For guilty man to satisfy;
"I in his stead will hang upon the tree,
"From sin, and death, and hell to set him free."

4 And thus, to save our souls from guilt,
Our Surety's precious blood was spilt;

The sins of all on him were laid,
And he for all hath fully paid: [ceive
Now God, as children, freely will re-
Repenting sinners who in Christ be-
lieve.

5 Out of mere grace unmerited,
Salvation showers on our head;
Because the Lamb was crucify'd,
Because the Lord of glory dy'd,
Are we invited to receive a crown,
Before the world was made ordain'd
our own.

31.* T. 22.

TO God we render thanks and praise,
Who pity'd mankind's fallen race,
And gave his dear and only Son,
That us, as children, he might own.

2 What grace, what great benevolence!
What love, surpassing human sense!
For this great work, no angel can
Him duly praise, much less a man.

3 The Word eternal did assume
Our flesh and blood, and man become;
The First and Last with wonder see
Partake of human misery.

4 He came to seek and save the lost;
We sinn'd, and he would bear the cost,
That we might share eternal bliss;
O what unbounded love was this!

5 For what is all the human race,
That God should show such matchless
grace,
To give his Son, that we might claim
Life everlasting in his name.

6 How wretched they who still despise
Jesus, the Pearl of greatest price!
Such as neglect to hear his voice,
Must perish by their own free choice.

7 Unhappy those who turn away,
Or such as carelessly delay
To meet their Saviour, tho' he came
Their souls from mis'ry to reclaim.

8 Come, sinners, Jesus will receive
The worst of sinners; come and live!

"I'll dwell with you," our Saviour
saith;
Receive him in your hearts by faith.

2 Your crimes and self-made holiness,
Your carnal reason and distress
Give up, and trust to Christ alone,
Who did for all your sins atone.

10 Thus sav'd by God's unbounded
grace,
You'll humbly render thanks and praise,
With all the num'rous ransom'd host,
To Father, Son, and Holy Ghost!

32. T. 590.

BEHOLD, to us a Child is born,
To us a Son is giv'n;
Unto the wretched and forlorn
Descends the Lord from heav'n:
The promis'd seed, Immanuel,
The everlasting God, [hell
Comes down to save from death and
Poor sinners by his blood.

2 Great is the hidden mystery
That God became a man!
He had from all eternity,
In mercy form'd a plan
To save from mis'ry and distress
The fallen human race;
And now the Sun of Righteousness
His healing beams displays.

3 The Father lov'd us as his own,
Tho' we from him had stray'd,
And freely gave his only Son
To suffer in our stead.
The Son in love to us, declar'd:
"I come to do God's will;"
And in this fallen world appear'd,
His counsel to fulfil.

4 The Holy Ghost had long foretold
That Jesus should appear;
And thus the patriarchs of old
Did his salvation share:
Of him blest Mary did conceive,
The holy child she bore:
And he instructs us to believe
In Christ, and him adore.

5 Thus Father, Son, and Holy Ghost,
In this decree are one,
To save us sinners, vile and lost,
By Jesus Christ the Son:
The Father's love we plainly trace
In Christ th' incarnate God;
What we possess of life and grace
The Spirit hath bestow'd.

6 Come sinners, view th' incarnate Word,
Who us and all things made;
This helpless Babe is Christ the Lord,
Though in a manger laid.
For us to die is Jesus born,
Adore his saving name,
Rejoice, rejoice! for all that mourn
May his salvation claim.

33.* T. 151.

HOW shall I meet my Saviour?
How shall I welcome thee?
What manner of behaviour
Is now requir'd of me?
I wait for thy salvation,
Grant me thy Spirit's light,
Thus will my preparation
Be pleasing in thy sight.

2 While with her fragrant flowers
Thy Zion strews thy way,
I'll raise with all my powers
To thee a grateful lay:
I'll thee, the King of glory,
For thy great goodness praise,
And thankfully adore thee
Throughout my future days.

3 What hast thou not performed
From death to rescue me!
While I was so deformed
By sin and misery;
Fair gifts of my creation
Quite lost, made me despair;
But thy blest incarnation
Brought my redemption near.

4 I lay in fetters groaning,
Thou cam'st to set me free;
My shame I was bemoaning,
With grace thou clothedst me;
Thou raisedst me to glory,
Endowedst me with bliss,
Which is not transitory,
As worldly grandeur is.

5 Love caus'd thy incarnation,
Love brought thee down to me!
Thy thirst for my salvation
Procur'd my liberty:
O Love beyond all measure!
Wherewith thou dost embrace
Mankind, 'midst all that pressure
Which since the fall takes place.

6 No sinful man's endeavor,
Nor any mortal's care,
Could draw his sov'reign favor
To sinners in despair:
Uncall'd, he comes with gladness
Us from the fall to raise,
And change our grief and sadness
To songs of joy and praise.

7 Be not cast down, nor frighted
At sin, though e'er so great;
No! Jesus is delighted
The greatest to remit:
He comes, repenting sinners
With life and love to crown,
And make them happy winners
Of glory like his own.

34.* T. 50.

JESUS, all praise is due to thee,
That thou wast pleas'd a man to be!
O'ershadow'd by the Spirit's pow'r,
A virgin thee conceiv'd and bore.
Hallelujah!

2 The Son of God, who fram'd the skies,
Now humbly in a manger lies;
He, who the earth's foundations laid,
A helpless infant now is made. Hal.

3 Th' eternal and almighty God
Assumes our feeble flesh and blood;
He deigns with sinful men to dwell,
Is God with us, Immanuel. Hal.

4 He is the Sun of righteousness,
Which riseth with resplendent grace,
And doth dispel sin's gloomy night,
That we may share his saving light. Hal.

5 To grant us pardon, peace and rest,
He in this world became a guest,

And open'd, thro' himself, the way
To life and everlasting day. Hal.

6 For therefore poor on earth he came,
That we might all his riches claim,
To make us heirs of glory bright,
With all the ransom'd saints in light.
Hal.

7 For us these wonders hath he wrought
To show his love, surpassing thought:
Then let us all unite to sing
Praise to our Saviour, God and King.
Hallelujah!

35.* T. 157.

RISE my soul, shake off all sadness,
Christ is near—thee to cheer;
Angels sing with gladness:
Unto you is born a Saviour
On this day;—don't delay
To accept God's favor.

2 Our eternal, kind Creator
Leaves his own—glorious throne,
And assumes our nature:
From perdition full exemption
To procure,—and endure
Death for our redemption.

3 O th' amazing demonstration
Of his love,—which we prove
By his incarnation!
If mankind by him were loathed,
How could he—deign to be
With our nature clothed?

4 See your Saviour in a manger;
'Midst his own,—yet unknown,
Treated like a stranger;
Tended by an earthly mother:
Him believe,—and receive,
He is Christ your Brother?

5 Lo! he in the manger lieth;
Full of grace,—truth and peace,
Sweetly thus he crieth:
"Cease my brethren, now from grieving,
Anxiousness—and distress;
Your loss I'm retrieving."

6 Ye that feel quite poor and needy,
Come, who will,—take your fill,
All things now are ready:
He is come to be your Saviour,
Full of love,—to remove
Guilt and curse for ever.

7 Jesus, hear my supplication,
Grant me grace—to embrace
Thee as my salvation:
Then like Simeon, (O what favor!)
I desire—to retire
Hence in peace for ever.

36. T. 166.

INFINITE Source, whence all did [spring,
Thou of all things the Head and Lord,
Thou mighty and eternal King,
Who art in heav'n and earth ador'd,
Thou whom the heav'ns cannot contain,
Didst deign to leave thy throne above,
To be an infant poor and mean:
O myst'ry deep! O boundless love!

2 The cause of this, I know it well,
Was thy great love and my great woe;
I was an heir of death and hell,
This prompted thee to stoop so low;
My mis'ry mov'd the God of grace,
Who in the Father's bosom lay,
When the due time had taken place
His deep compassion to display.

3 What off'ring shall I bring to thee,
Immanuel, my King and God!
Thou who vouchsaf'st a man to be,
To save me by thy precious blood;
Thou to whom angels praises sing,
"Peace upon earth, good will to men;"
To whom the sages humbly bring
Their gifts, tho' thou appear so mean.

4 This will I do, thou Child divine!
I'll give thee that for which thou cam'st;
My soul and body, Lord, are thine,
And them in love to me thou claim'st.
My humble sacrifice receive,
Dear Jesus! born to bleed for me,
That I by faith in thee might live,
And with thee live eternally.

37. T. 58.

O come and view the greatest mystery!
He who made all the world, the seas
and sky,

Now is born an infant: the virgin Mary,
Upon her arms, the Lord of hosts doth
carry, A feeble child.

2 He who prepar'd for ev'ry bird a nest
And gave the foxes holes wherein to rest,
Poverty endured, became a stranger
In his own world; then rested in a
manger The Lord of all!

3 But why was Jesus born in poverty?
Why did our Maker in a manger lie?
'Twas that he might purchase life and
salvation,
And gain for us a glorious habitation
In realms of bliss.

4 O Jesus Christ, thou only holy child,
How canst thou show such love to sinners spoil'd?
But since thou thus lovest, we now
adore thee,
We humbly praise thy name and bow
before thee, Hallelujah!

5 Thy sacred meritorious infancy
Our crown and everlasting glory be!
From world, sin and Satan, keep us
estranged,
Till we shall once around thy throne
be ranged For evermore.

38. T. 590.

COME ye redeemed of the Lord,
Your grateful tribute bring,
And celebrate, with one accord,
The birth of Christ our King:
Let us with humble hearts repair
(Faith will point out the road)
To little Bethlehem, and there
Adore th' incarnate God.

2 All glory to Immanuel's name
The choirs of angels sing;
Gladly these heralds peace proclaim,
Peace from our God and King:
Well might the shepherds haste away
This wond'rous Babe to see;
Well might the sages homage pay,
Before him bow the knee.

3 We too have reason to rejoice,
When we this myst'ry view,
That God assum'd our flesh and blood.
O wonder ever new!
We humbly in the dust adore;
Lord, who is like to thee!
That thou, vile sinners to restore,
Hast deign'd a man to be.

39. T. 126.

SINNERS, with adoration
Receive this wond'rous Child,
Who came and brought salvation,
Th' eternal Father styl'd:
Behold him with our nature drest,
Divested of his glory,
In his own world a guest.

2 With his blest incarnation
His glorious work began,
A needful preparation
For his whole future plan;
Had not his body been prepar'd,
He never could have suffer'd,
Nor we his nature shar'd.

3 Behold! laid in a manger,
The Ancient of all days;
Upon this heav'nly Stranger
With awe and rev'rence gaze;
He, who the world's foundation laid
Must now be fed and nourish'd
By creatures whom he made.

4 Though to his boundless mercy
No limits can be set,
Yet without controversy
The mystery is great;
Angels into its depths can't pry,
'Tis great, immense, stupendous;
Jehovah, born to die!

40.* T. 169.

ARISE my spirit, bless the day
Whereon the ages' Sire
A Child became; thy homage pay,
Receive him with desire.
This is the night in which he came,
Was born, and put on human frame,
Us sinners to deliver
From sin and death for ever.

2 Welcome, thou Source of ev'ry good,
O Jesus, King of glory!

Welcome, thrice welcome, Lamb of
To this world transitory! [God,
In grateful hymns thy name I'll praise,
With heart and voice throughout my
For thy blest incarnation [days;
Procured my salvation.

3 Ah Jesus! thy unworthy bride
Deserved to be loathed,
And yet thou hast her to thyself
Upon the cross betrothed:
Her portion had been infamy,
Eternal shame and misery,
Hadst thou not left thy glory:
Who can enough adore thee!

4 O lovely Infant! thou art full
Of grace above all measure;
Thou art more precious to my soul
Than ev'ry other treasure:
Come, Jesus, come, abide with me,
O let my heart thy dwelling be;
Then I, without cessation,
Shall joy in thy salvation.

41. T. 580.

ALL glory be to God on high!
Ye sons of Adam, fill the sky
With praise and thankfulness;
God, mov'd by everlasting love,
Decreed with his dear Son above,
A sinful world to save and bless.

2 Stand still, and see what God hath
His only and beloved Son [done;
For us he freely gave;
For us, and for the num'rous race
Of cursed sinners vile and base!
Yea, ev'n the worst he came to save.

3 He as a poor mean Child was born,
His birth no palace did adorn,
A manger was his bed;
Look, look upon this rising Sun,
Till tears of love your eyes o'er-run:
This lovely babe is Christ our Head.

42. T. 11.

WHAT good news the angels bring!
What glad tidings of our King!
Christ the Lord is born to-day,
Christ, who takes our sins away.

2 He who rules both heav'n and earth,
Hath in Bethlehem his birth;
Him shall all the faithful see,
And rejoice eternally.

3 Lift your hearts and voices high,
With hosannas fill the sky:
Glory be to God above,
Who is infinite in love!

4 Peace on earth, good will to men!
Now with us our God is seen:
Angels join his name to praise,
Help to sing redeeming grace.

5 Jesus is the loveliest name;
This the angel doth proclaim;
Sinners poor he came to save,
They in him redemption have.

6 They who see themselves undone,
And take refuge to the Son,
They shall all be born again,
And with him in glory reign.

43.* T. 11.

ALL the world give praises due!
God is faithful, God is true:
He to man doth comfort send
In his Son, the sinners' Friend.

2 What the fathers wish'd of old,
What the promises foretold,
What the seers did prophesy,
Is fulfill'd most gloriously.

3 My Salvation, welcome be;
Thou, my Portion, praise to thee!
Come, and make thy blest abode
In my heart, O Son of God.

4 Grant thy comforts to my mind,
Since I'm helpless, poor and blind;
O may I in faith abide
Thine, and never turn aside.

5 Jesus, when in majesty
Thou shalt come my judge to be,
Grant in grace that I may stand
Justify'd at thy right hand.

44.* T. 22.

IMMANUEL, to thee we sing,
Thou Prince of life, almighty King,

That thou, expected ages past,
Didst come to visit us at last.

2 Thou Lord, tho' heaven belongs to
On earth a stranger deign'st to be[thee,
Thou clothest all, yet wear'st a dress
Which doth the poorest state express.

3 Thou dost a mother's nursing need,
Who dost the whole creation feed;
Thou who control'st the sea and wind,
In swadling-clothes art now confin'd.

4 On wither'd grass reclines thy head,
A wretched manger is thy bed:
Tho' thou appear'st among thine own,
No kindness unto thee is shown.

5 I thank thee, gracious Lord, that thou
On my account didst stoop so low:
O that my words, my works and ways
May all proclaim thy matchless praise!

45.* T. 22.

CHRIST, whom the virgin Mary bore,
We all with humble hearts adore;
O might all nations, tribes and tongues,
To our Immanuel raise their songs.

2 God who to all things being gave,
The fallen human race to save,
Assum'd our feeble flesh and blood,
And for our debt as Surety stood.

3 He who the wants of all supplies,
Now in a manger helpless lies,
He who the whole creation feeds,
An earthly mother's nursing needs.

4 The angels at his birth rejoice,
And sing his praise with cheerful voice;
The shepherds, hearing Christ is born,
To Jesus, our chief Shepherd, turn.

5 Thanks to the Father now be giv'n,
Who sent his Son to us from heav'n:
Thanks to the Son who saves the lost,
Thanks to our Guide the Holy Ghost.

46.* T. 22.

TO-day we celebrate the birth
Of Jesus Christ, who came on earth,
Man as his property to claim,
And from perdition to redeem.

2 Awake, my heart; my soul, rejoice;
Look, who in yonder manger lies!
Who is that Child, so poor and mean?
'Tis he, who all things doth sustain.

3 Welcome, O welcome, noble Guest!
Who sinners not despised hast,
But cam'st into our misery;
How shall we pay due thanks to thee?

4 Immanuel, incarnate God,
Prepare my heart for thy abode:
O may I, through thy aiding grace,
In all I do, shew forth thy praise.

47. T. 16.

CHRIST the Lord, the Lord most [glorious,
Now is born; O shout aloud!
Man by him is made victorious;
Praise your Saviour, hail your God!

2 Praise the Lord, for on us shineth
Christ the Sun of righteousness;
He to us in love inclineth,
Cheers our souls with pard'ning [grace.

3 Praise the Lord, whose saving splendor
Shines into the darkest night;
O what praises shall we render
For this never-ceasing light!

4 Praise the Lord, God our Salvation,
Praise him who retriev'd our loss;
Sing with awe and love's sensation;
HALLELUJAH, GOD WITH US!

48. T. 585.

HAIL, thou wond'rous infant stranger,
Born, lost Eden to regain;
Welcome in thy humble manger,
Welcome to thy creature man!
Hail Immanuel :||: thou who wast ere time began.

2 Say, ye blest seraphic legions,
What thus brought your Maker down?
Say, why did he leave your regions,
Why forsake his heav'nly throne?
Notes melodious :||: tell the cause:
"Good will to man."

3 We this offer'd favor needed,
Hence we join your theme with joy;

We by none will be exceeded,
While we laud this mystery;
And with wonder :||: God incarnate glorify.

49. T. 22.

MAKER of all things, Lord our God,
Now veil'd in feeble flesh and blood,
To reconcile and set us free
From endless woe and misery;

2 What heights, what depths of love
In thy blest incarnation shine! [divine
Let heav'n and earth unite their lays
To magnify thy boundless grace.

50. T. 14.

HOSANNA to the royal Son
Of David's ancient line!
His natures two, his person one,
Mysterious and divine.

2 The root of David here we find,
And offspring is the same;
Eternity and time are join'd
In our Immanuel's name.

3 Blest He that comes to wretched men
With peaceful news from heav'n!
Hosannas in the highest strain
To Christ the Lord be giv'n!

51. T. 155.

CHRIST, the sov'reign Lord of all,
Was a Babe laid in a manger,
A poor Stranger;
'Midst the people styl'd his own
Quite unknown;
In the world, which he created,
Disavow'd, despis'd and hated;
Him our Lord and God we own.

2 O thou Day-spring from on high!
When we, lost in deepest wonder,
Duly ponder,
On thy love in coming down
From thy throne,
To save sinners from damnation!
For thy love and great compassion,
Thee we praise, thank and adore.

52.* T. 14.

A Wond'rous change Christ with us
The praise is his alone; [makes;
His own t'impart, our nature takes,
To raise us to his throne.

2 In servant's form, lo! he appears,
Our freedom to obtain;
To show his love, our shame he bears,
And glory thus we gain.

53. T. 14.

BOTH to the Seraph and the worm
God's goodness doth abound,
He calms the sea, calls forth the storm,
And fructifies the ground.

2 But yet his mercy to man's race
More richly was display'd;
He pity'd us in our distress,
And therefore flesh was made.

3 That he as man might sympathise
With every grief we feel,
And being made a sacrifice
With blood our pardon seal.

54. T. 240.

ALL hail, Immanuel,
Eternal Word, all hail!
O Jesus, sinners' friend,
Whose mercy knows no end,
Love made thee condescend,
With men to make abode,
And, veil'd in flesh and blood,
To bring us nigh to God;
Thy sacred name we bless,
Jesus, Jesus,
Full of truth and power;
Blessed, blessed,
Blessed evermore!

55. T. 586.

I will rejoice in God my Saviour,
And magnify this act of love;
I'm lost in wonder at his favor, [move,
Which him to leave his throne could
To take upon him human nature,
To suffer for his wretched creature,
Dire anguish, keenest pain,
And death-pangs to sustain,
My soul to gain.

56.* T. 58.

O Sing, all ye redeem'd from Adam's fall,
Your Hallelujahs join, both great and small;
Praise ye God rejoicing, for our salvation
This Child was born; this blest, divine donation Is God with us.

57.* T. 39.

TO God our Immanuel made flesh as we are,
Our Friend, our Redeemer, and Brother most dear,
Be honor and glory! Let with one accord
All people say, Amen! Give praise to the Lord.

IV. Of the Name of Jesus, and his Walk on Earth.

58.* T. 146.

LORD Jesus, when I trace
Thee as the great Creator,
With fear I hide my face;
But when in human nature
I see thy deep distress,
And lowliness of heart,
I freely must confess
That thou my Brother art.

2 Therefore I'll thee adore
With deep humiliation,
And own thee evermore
Lord of the whole creation;
But thy humanity,
Thy birth, thy life, and death,
Unite my soul to thee,
While here on earth I breathe.

59. T. 14.

HOW sweet the name of Jesus sounds
To a believer's ear!
It sooths his sorrows, heals his wounds
And drives away his fear.

2 It makes the wounded spirit whole,
And calms the troubled breast;
'Tis manna to the hungry soul,
And to the weary rest.

3 Jesus! the Rock on which I build,
My Shie da n d hiding-place,
My never-failing treas'ry fill'd
With boundless stores of grace.

4 Jesus my Shepherd, Saviour, Friend,
My Prophet, Priest, and King;
My Lord, my life, my way, my end,
Accept the praise I bring.

5 Weak are the efforts of my heart,
And cold my warmest thought;
But when I see thee as thou art,
I'll praise thee as I ought.

6 Till then I would thy love proclaim
With ev'ry fleeting breath;
And may thy saving Jesus' name
Refresh my soul in death.

60. T. 14.

JESUS, I love thy charming name,
'Tis music to my ear;
I gladly would thy praises sound,
That earth and heav'n might hear.

2 Yes, thou art precious to my soul,
In thee is all my trust;
Jewels to me are gaudy toys,
And gold is sordid dust.

3 O may thy name still cheer my heart,
And shed its fragrance there!
The noblest balm for all its wounds,
The cordial of its care.

4 I'll speak the honors of thy name,
With my last lab'ring breath;
When speechless, thou shalt be my [hope,
My joy in life and death.

61.* T. 58.

SACRED name of Jesus,
So great and holy,
That all our tongues can never praise thee truly As thou deserv'st.

2 Holy name of Jesus,
Though men blaspheme thee,
I will adore, whene'er I hear or name thee, With gratitude.

3 Precious name of Jesus,
How sweet and blessed
Art thou to souls, who mourning and distressed Upon thee call!

4 Cheering name of Jesus,
Whence comfort floweth;
No angel like a contrite sinner knoweth Thy pow'r divine.

5 Lovely name of Jesus,
Whoe'er confideth
In thee obtains a treasure which abideth, And never fails.

6 Saving name of Jesus,
In which salvation
Is preach'd to ev'ry kindred, tongue and nation, Might all thee praise!

7 Faithful name of Jesus,
In thee I've trusted,
And of thy faithfulness on earth have boasted, And shall in heav'n.

8 Blessed name of Jesus,
How efficacious
To save to sanctify and to preserve us! Thee we adore.

9 Jesus, blessed Jesus,
Name so revered
By all believers; they can ne'er be wearied In praising thee.

10 Name for ever sacred,
For ever precious;
Let all within us echo Jesus, Jesus! For evermore.

62. T. 119.

JESUS' name, :||:
Source of life and happiness;
In this name true consolation
Mourning sinners may possess;
Here is found complete salvation:
Blessed Jesus, we thy name will praise
All our days. :||:

2 God with us, :||:
God appears in human frame;
In his name rejoice with gladness,
Since to save lost man he came;
None need sink in hopeless sadness,
For Immanuel is now with us,
God with us. :||:

63. T. 11.

JESUS is our highest good,
He hath sav'd us by his blood;
May we love him evermore,
And his saving name adore.

2 Jesus, when stern justice said,
"Man his life hath forfeited,
"Vengeance follows by decree,"
Cry'd, "Inflict it all on me."

3 Jesus gives us life and peace,
Faith, and love, and holiness;
Ev'ry blessing, great or small,
Jesus for us purchas'd all.

4 Jesus therefore let us own,
Jesus we'll exalt alone,
Jesus hath our sins forgiv'n,
Jesus' blood procur'd us heav'n.

64. T. 14.

MY God a man! a man indeed,
An infant truly poor;
Born, for a sinful race to bleed,
Salvation to procure.

2 Who can describe the loveliness
Which was, blest Child, in thee?
Thy whole deportment heav'nly grace,
And true humility.

3 According to th' appointed plan
My infant Saviour grew,
In favor both with God and man,
In years and stature too.

4 My Saviour learned Joseph's trade,
Was call'd a carpenter, (*Mark* 6. 3.)
And therefore, that he earn'd his bread,
We justly may infer.

5 Often oppress'd with human care,
He to his Father sighs,

Or spends the night in fervent pray'r,
And offers tears and cries.

6 Again, as Teacher of Mankind
I see my humble Lord:
How cheerfully was he inclin'd
To preach the saving word!

7 To comfort men was his delight,
To help them in distress;
He ready was, by day and night,
To pardon, heal and bless.

8 Oft he was hungry, spent and sad,
In his own world a guest,
And of his own no place he had,
His weary head to rest.

9 Ah, might my heart a mirror be,
Reflecting Jesus' grace,
That all, who my behaviour see,
May some resemblance trace.

10 Grant me that meek and lowly mind,
Thou hast on earth display'd,
Which in thy holy life I find,
My Pattern, Lord and Head.

65. T. 11.

SEE, my soul, God ever blest
In the flesh made manifest!
Human nature he assumes,
He, to ransom sinners, comes.

2 He fulfill'd all righteousness,
Standing in the sinner's place;
From the manger to the cross,
All he did, he did for us:

3 All our woes he did retrieve,
He expir'd that we might live;
By his stripes our wounds are heal'd,
By his blood our pardon's seal'd.

4 Lord, conform us to thy death,
Raise us to new life by faith,
Through thy resurrection's pow'r,
May we praise thee evermore.

5 Circumcise our sinful hearts;
Purify our inward parts;
Lord, destroy the carnal mind,
That in thee we peace may find.

6 In thy righteousness array'd
Let us triumph and be glad;
Let us walk with thee in white,
Let us see thy face in light.

66.* T. 14.

IMMANUEL's meritorious tears
Assuage our ev'ry pain,
His bitter suff'rings, cries and pray'rs,
Our fav'rite theme remain.

2 When Jesus' suff'ring life we trace,
In ev'ry scene we find,
That he a man of sorrows was,
Though of unspotted mind.

3 All they who weeping now go forth,
And bear the precious seed,
May in our Saviour's walk on earth
Pattern and comfort read.

4 Among the evils of the fall
Which soul and body grieve,
This the most dreadful is of all,
That sin to us doth cleave.

5 Whene'er the Holy Ghost displays
To our benighted hearts,
That we are wretched, vile and base,
And light to us imparts,

6 How do we blush with conscious shame,
While tears of anguish flow!
And did we not the suff'ring Lamb,
The Friend of sinners know;

7 A contrite heart would never cease
To weep most bitter tears;
But faith in Jesus' saving grace
The mourning sinner cheers.

8 When we have that great bliss attain'd
To find, that in all need,
Christ is our Counsellor and Friend,
Then are we help'd indeed.

9 O 'tis the greatest happiness,
When of his peace divine
We have a feeling, and he says,
" Fear not, for thou art mine."

10 Our thankful tears then testify
That Jesus wept for us,
And we, possessing heav'nly joy,
For him count all things loss.

11 Yet tears of grief at times bedew
Our cheeks, while here we stay;
When we in heav'n his face shall view,
He'll wipe all tears away.

67. T. 14.

O my dear Saviour, when thy cares,
Thy toils for me I read,
My eyes run o'er with grateful tears,
And I bow down my head.

2 Thy suff'ring life I cannot trace,
Or read thy sacred word,
But I'm o'ercome with thankfulness
To thee, my gracious Lord.

3 What am I, Lord, that thou so much
Should'st love and value me?
Vile dust I am, yet thou for such
Didst bear thy misery.

68. T. 22.

MY dear Redeemer, God and Lord,
I read my duty in thy word;
But in thy life the law appears
Set forth in living characters.

2 Such was thy truth, and such thy zeal,
Such def'rence to thy Father's will,
Such love and meekness so divine,
I would transcribe and make them mine.

3 Cold mountains and the midnight air
Witness'd the fervor of thy pray'r;
The desert thy temptations knew,
Thy conflict and thy vict'ry too.

4 Be thou my pattern; let me bear
More likeness of thine image here;
And at thy right hand me confess,
Arrayed in thy righteousness.

69. T. 58.

LAMB of God, my Saviour,
O set before me
Thy matchless love, and by thy grace procure me A mind like thine.

2 Thy humiliation
How meritorious!
Thy birth in poverty, and life laborious, Teach me to stoop.

3 Thy flight into Egypt,
Amidst great danger,
Teach me to be a pilgrim here and stranger, Where'er I am.

4 Thy unspotted childhood,
And meek behaviour,
Teach me to be a little child for ever
Before thy face.

5 Thy unfeign'd obedience
And true subjection
Unto thy parents, form to like affection
My stubborn heart.

6 Thy forty days fasting,
Thy self-denial,
Thy being sorely try'd, in ev'ry trial
Deliver me.

70. T. 580.

THE wise men from the East ador'd
The infant Jesus as their Lord,
Brought gifts to him their King:
Jesus, grant us thy light, that we
The way may find, and unto thee
Our hearts, our all, a tribute bring.

2 May Jesus Christ, the spotless Lamb.
Who to the temple humbly came
The legal rights to pay,
Subdue our proud and stubborn will,
That we his precepts may fulfil,
Whate'er rebellious nature say.

71. T. 14.

O SON of God and man, receive
This humble work of mine;
Worth to my meanest labor give,
By blessing it with thine.

2 Servant of all, to toil for man
Thou wouldst not, Lord, refuse:
Thy Majesty did not disdain
To be employ'd for us.

3 In all I think, or speak, or do,
Let me show forth thy praise;
Thy bright example still pursue
Through all my future days.

4 By faith thro' outward cares I go,
From all distraction free;

My hands alone engag'd below,
My spirit still with thee.

5 When thou, my Saviour, shalt appear,
Then gladly may I cry,
"The work thou gavest me while here
"Is done—to thee I fly."

72.* T. 22.

MAY all those blessings on us flow,
And in our lives their virtue show,
Which from the manger to the cross,
Thou, Lord, hast merited for us.

V. Of the Sufferings and Death of Jesus Christ, and his Resting in the Grave.

73. T. 114.

WHAT human mind can trace the condescension
Of our almighty Maker's love to man?
No angel can the hidden myst'ry scan;
Redeeming love, thou art past comprehension;
Yet by the Spirit's teaching we can prove,
From Jesus' agony, that God is love.

2 Pursue, my soul, the sacred meditation,
And view the agonizing Lamb of God;
See him oppressed with the pond'rous load
Of all thy sins, to purchase thy salvation:
He riseth with a heart-affecting look,
And with his foll'wers passeth Cedron's brook.

3 My spirit now with solemn, deep devotion,
Doth follow Jesus to Gethsemane;
There he, on my account, doth weep and pray,
O'ercome with horror at the bitter potion:
Yet to his Father's will he is resign'd.
Grant me, dear Jesus, thy obedient mind.

4 I see my Saviour kneeling, groaning, weeping,
He prostrates on the ground and prays for me,
Yea trembling wrestleth in an agony;
And while his sad disciples all are sleeping,
His soul in grief, his eyes in tears are drown'd,
His sweat as drops of blood falls to the ground.

5 By all thy grief, thy tears and supplication,
Thy bloody sweat, thy bitter agony;
O grant that I may love thee ardently:
Be thou, dear Lord, my life and consolation!
Whene'er temptation would my soul beset,
I'll pray to thee, and think of Olivet.

74. T. 580.

BEHOLD! how in Gethsemane
Th' incarnate God doth sweat for thee
Till drops of blood fall down;
For thee the Lord lies prostrate there,
Hear his thrice-utter'd, mournful pray'r,
Mark ev'ry dol'rous sigh and groan.

2 I'm lost in wonder and amaze;
Here I'll abide and melt and gaze,
'Tis God's beloved Son!
How heavy is the weight he bears!
His soul is fill'd with grief and fears,
Lo! now the bitter cup comes on.

3 Lord, dost thou suffer thus for me?
Dost thou endure such misery,
To give me life and peace?
Then will I bear this on my heart,
"My all is purchas'd with thy smart,
Thy sweat & blood sign my release."

75. T. 96.

OFTEN I call to mind the place
Gethsemane, to which the Lamb,
Who lov'd to be in loneliness,
With his disciples often came,
Where, out of boundless love to me,
He wrestled in an agony.

2 There, overwhelm'd with grief, he said:
"My soul is sorrowful to death;"
And suff'ring freely in my stead,
He drank the bitter cup of wrath;
Now on his knees, then on his face,
He weeps, and sweats, and bleeds, and prays.

3 So lov'd me the eternal God,
That he became the Son of man,
And took my sin's prodigious load.
My soul, admire his gracious plan!
Thy stripes, thy guilt and curse he bore;
Believe and thankfully adore.

76.* T. 99.

MOST awful sight! my heart doth break,
Oh! it can ne'er my mind forsake
How thou for me hast wept & prayed:
Might I for thy soul's agony,
When wrestling with death bitterly,
Lord, as thy trophy be displayed!

77.* T. 36.

GOD, in a garden, suffers in our nature!
He faints, who cheers and comforts every creature;
An angel strengthens his Creator yonder: Adore and wonder.

78.* T. 54.

COME, congregation, come and see
Thy Saviour in Gethsemane;
Here is a scene which with amaze
Must strike thee; here astonish'd gaze:
Thy Maker prays.

79.* T. 185.

MY Redeemer, overwhelm'd with anguish,
Went to Olivet for me;
There he kneels, his heart doth heave and languish
In a bitter agony;
Fear and horror seize his soul and senses,
For the hour of darkness now commences:
Ah, how doth he weep and groan,
For rebellious man t' atone!

2 How is Jesus' sacred soul oppressed
With our sins' prodigious load!
Tho' an angel comforts the distressed,
Weak and fainting Lamb of God!
Yet what trembling seizeth him all over
Tears and sweat and blood his visage cover,
And in drops fall on the ground,
While his heart in grief is drown'd.

3 Jeers and stripes and mock'ries he endured,
Meek and patient, in our stead;
How are Jesus' gracious eyes obscured:
View his wounded back and head;
He, whom whips and thorns have lacerated,
Is the Lord, who all things hath created:
Ah, his pungent grief and smart,
Melt and break my stubborn heart.

4 See him bear his cross, in deep affliction,
On his sore and wounded back,
Led to Calvary for crucifixion,
Where his limbs they stretch and rack;
As a Lamb he's led unto the slaughter,
And his soul is poured out like water:
Vinegar and gall he tastes,
While his suff'ring body wastes.

5 Now behold him weeping, bleeding, crying,
'Midst two thieves, upon the cross;
Lo, he bows his sacred head; and dying,
Life eternal gains for us.
Lord, afford us all thy Spirit's unction,
To consider this with heart's compunction:
Might our words and actions prove
That we know thy dying love.

6 Our enraptur'd hearts shall ne'er be weary
On our dying Lord to gaze;
At his cross, in faith, we wish to tarry,
There shall be our hiding-place.
May his dying look remain engraven
On our hearts: for pardon, life & heaven
Our Redeemer then procur'd,
When he death for us endur'd.

7 Therefore all his agony and passion,
And his sin-atoning death,

Shall remain, through grace, our faith's foundation,
While we draw our vital breath:
Thus shall neither honor, wealth nor pleasures,
Rob our souls of everlasting treasures;
Jesus, both by day and night,
Shall remain our sole delight.

8 Could we tune our hearts and voices higher
Than man's most exalted lays,
Yet, till join'd to the celestial choir,
Cold would prove our warmest praise:
Jesus' love exceeds all comprehension,
But our love to him we scarce dare mention;
We may weep beneath his cross,
But he wept and bled for us.

9 O delightful theme past all expression:
"Thy Redeemer dy'd for thee!"
Ah, this prompts my deepest adoration,
When I hear, "He dy'd for me."
Might my thoughts, my words and whole behaviour,
Prove that I believe in Christ my Saviour;
Yea, my love to Jesus show
His to me, in all I do.

10 Lamb of God! thou shalt remain for ever
Of our songs the only theme;
For thy boundless love, thy grace and favor,
We will praise thy saving name:
That for our transgressions thou wast wounded,
Shall by us in nobler strains be sounded,
When we, perfected in love,
Once shall join the church above.

80.* T. 151.

THOU Source of my salvation,
Thou Conqu'ror of my death,
Who didst, as my oblation,
In torrents yield thy breath;
Who bar'st the dreadful sentence
Due to our cursed race,
To screen my soul from vengeance;
Accept my thanks and praise.

2 I'll go with thee, my Saviour,
Up to mount Calvary;
And view with spirit's fervor
All thou hast done for me.
Thus, with intense devotion,
I follow thee each step,
While tender love's emotion
Makes heart and eyes to weep.

3 I see my Saviour languish
In sad Gethsemane,
Till through his pores, in anguish,
The blood ev'n forc'd its way;
The load which him oppresses,
I, I, deserv'd to feel;
The bloody sweat of Jesus
Doth soul and body heal.

4 My Saviour, was betrayed,
Reproach and suff'rings met;
My sins the Lord conveyed
'Fore Pilate's judgment seat;
These, these did him deliver
Into the foe's dire hand;
I should have felt for ever
The pangs my God sustain'd.

5 Behold the man! he's bearing
Our curse, meek as a Lamb!
And now, behold them rearing
Him on the cross's stem!
There to complete his passion,
His sorrows, pain and woe,
His blood for our salvation
In copious streams doth flow.

6 Thou for thy foes intreatest;
Lord Jesus, who was I?
Thy friends thou not forgettest;
Turn, Lord, to me thine eye!
Thy mouth now grace declareth
To the repenting thief;
My guilty soul this cheereth,
Of sinners I am chief.

7 Thou anxiously complainest,
"My God forsaketh me!"
"I thirst," thou then exclaimest,
Yet none refresheth thee.
Thy passion being ended,
Thou cry'st, "Tis finished!
"My spirit be commended
"To God!"—'Twas finished.

8 My heart with love is glowing,
I see my Saviour die;
His head I see him bowing,
This brought me endless joy!
He gave his soul an off'ring
For sin, that I might live;
He sav'd me by his suff'ring,
To him myself I give.

9 Thou God of my salvation,
In whom I trust by faith,
Who hast for my transgression,
Lain in the dust of death;
I place upon thy merit,
While here, my confidence;
And will commend my spirit
To thee, when I go hence.

10 Lord, grant me thy salvation
And peace divine, I pray,
While here 'midst tribulation
On earth below I stay;
Till I shall stand before thee,
And for redeeming grace,
With all the saints in glory,
My Hallelujah raise.

81.* T. 594.

WITH painful penance thoughts distressed,
In spirit I my Saviour view;
I see him mourning and oppressed,
While floods of tears his cheeks bedew:
To change my sorrow into gladness,
His sweat was mix'd with blood; and he,
Fill'd with unutterable sadness,
Trembled and agoniz'd for me.

2 O'erwhelm'd with grief and rack'd with torment,
He's pain'd in ev'ry weary limb;
They who should watch with him lie dormant,
An angel comes to comfort him:
O how heart-piercingly he prayed,
When he his Father did accost,
To have the bitter cup delayed:
Here is my soul in wonder lost!

3 I see his countenance defiled,
His forehead spit on I behold;
I see him laugh'd at and reviled,
Sharp-pointed thorns his head infold:
Thus to the multitude displayed,
His back with scourges raw & torn,
A reed he beareth, is arrayed
In purple, and then hail'd in scorn.

4 Breathless and almost suffocated,
He bears the cross's pond'rous weight,
Already feels what him awaited,
The dismal scenes of torment great.
I see him now in sore affliction
Ascend the brow of Calvary;
'Tis here I view his crucifixion,
Thereby it was he saved me.

5 I see his hands and feet extended
Upon the cross in keenest smart;
I see him as his life he ended,
I see the spear transfix his heart:
Thus closed he his bitter passion,
Expiring on th' accursed tree,
Then horror seiz'd the whole creation,
But streams of grace came over me.

6 The thought of blood & water bursting
From God, my rock, o'ercomes my heart;
I for that living flood am thirsting,
O may it stream through ev'ry part!
Lord, for thy love, with adoration,
I'll thank and laud thee all my days;
Long as I live, shall each pulsation,
And ev'ry breath declare thy praise.

7 This awful, blessed meditation
Oft fills my soul with conscious shame;
Since Jesus dy'd for my salvation,
Who to his mercy had no claim:
How poor I am, how void of glory,
Thou, Lord, know'st best; but yet when I,
With all my ailments come before thee,
My suit is granted presently.

8 Thou, Jesus, art my God and Saviour,
Thee will I serve with all my pow'r,
On thee I'll meditate for ever,
And for thy goodness thee adore:
Thy dying love hath captivated
My heart, and now my chief delight,
Until to heav'n I am translated,
Is to enjoy thee day and night.

82. T. 167.

[stooping,
GREAT High-priest, we view thee
With our names upon thy breast,
In the garden, groaning, drooping,
To the ground with horrors prest.
Angels saw, struck with amazement,
Their Creator suffer thus;
We are fill'd with deep abasement,
Since we know 'twas done for us.

2 On the cross thy body broken
Cancels ev'ry legal charge;
Pleading this authentic token,
Guilty souls are set at large;
All is finish'd, truth hath said it,
Doubt no more, believe your Lord;
To frail reason give no credit,
You have his unerring word.

3 Lord, we fain would trust thee solely,
'Twas for us thy blood was spilt;
Suff'ring Saviour, take us wholly,
Take and form us as thou wilt;
Thou hast borne the dreadful sentence
Pass'd on man's devoted race:
Grant us faith, and true repentance,
They're thy gifts, thou God of grace.

83. T. 243.

GO, follow the Saviour,
Consider his travail,
Adore him for ever,
Ye sinners, and marvel;
It is for you—he suffers so.

2 With tears interceding
Your load he sustaineth,
And sweating and bleeding
Your pardon he gaineth;
All who believe—he'll freely save.

3 He's mock'd and defamed,
'Midst scourging and torture;
By sinners is blamed,
And led to the slaughter;
While thorns disgrace—his royal face.

4 Behold the Lord Jesus,
For you he is wounded,
He bleeds to release us;
His love is unbounded!
For evermore—his name adore.

5 When to the cross nailed
He hung on the mountain,
That we might be healed;
Blood, as from a fountain,
Flow'd from his wounds.—There
health abounds.

6 Our meek suff'ring Saviour
Pray'd for his oppressors,
And gained God's favor,
For us vile transgressors;
He thus displays—his boundless grace.

7 When he had prevailed,
And all was accomplish'd,
By prophets revealed;
He cried: "It is finish'd!" [dead.
Then bow'd his head—and join'd the

8 Accept for thy passion,
Most merciful Saviour,
Our deep adoration:
Remain thou for ever
Our highest good,—O Lamb of God!

84.* T. 243.

BLOOD worthy of praises!
Come streaming from Jesus
O'er us, and all classes
Of sinners, and bless us;
We humbly flee,—and call on thee.

2 In Olivet's garden
Before the Jews bound him,
Most heavily laden
I kneeling have found him, [ground.
Blood-sweat around——bedews the

3 Thy blood-sweat, dear Saviour,
Rain on me like water;
For all the world over
Nought can bless me better:
O precious flood!—O holy blood!

4 So sore was he smitten,
So cruelly used,
With scourges so beaten,
All over so bruised:
That in amaze—on him I gaze.

5 Thy blood-streams and bruises,
Thy agonies, Saviour!
Thy wounds' healing juices
Have sav'd us for ever [sighs.
From tears and cries—from grief and

6 His cross see your Saviour
Compelled to carry,
With patient behaviour,
Submitting, till weary,
And sore oppreest—He sinks at last.

7 Just ready for slaughter,
The nail-holes they bored,
While exquisite torture
He lamb-like endured;
Dumb did he bear—the pain severe.

8 The Lamb yonder nailed
Gain'd for us salvation,
Our pardon is sealed
By his bitter passion:
A healing stream—flows down from him.

9 O dear bleeding Saviour!
I long to embrace thee,
While thousand drops cover,
Hang on thee and grace thee;
And catch the juice-thy wounds diffuse.

10 For all thy wounds painful,
Which glad I remember,
I hourly am thankful,
And praise their whole number;
Me, dearest Lamb!-thou sav'st by them.

85.* T. 151.

O Head so full of bruises,
So full of pain and scorn,
'Midst other sore abuses
Mock'd with a crown of thorn!
O head ere now surrounded
With brightest majesty,
In death now bow'd and wounded!
Saluted be by me.

2 Thou countenance transcendent,
Thou life-creating Sun
To worlds on thee dependent;
Now bruis'd and spit upon!
How art thou grown so sallow!
How are those gracious eyes,
Whose radiance knew no fellow,
Clouded in cruel wise!

3 Thy cheeks, through heavy dolor,
Are marred, fall'n, and wan;

Thy lips, depriv'd of color,
Spoke heav'nly truth to man;
Thy body, ah! how wasted,
Death's horror did reduce
Thy strength, and quite exhausted
Each drop of vital juice.

5 O Lord, what thee tormented,
Was my sin's heavy load!
I had the debt augmented
Which thou didst pay in blood:
Here am I, blushing sinner,
On whom wrath ought to light;
O thou my health's beginner!
Let thy grace cheer my sight.

5 Own me, Lord, my Preserver,
My Shepherd, me receive;
I know thy love's strong fervor
By all thy pain and grief.
Thou richly hast supplied
My soul with heav'nly food,
For which I've often sighed,
Thy holy flesh and blood.

6 I'll here with thee continue,
(Though poor, despise me not)
I'm one of thy retinue:
As were I on the spot,
When, earning my election,
Thy heart-strings broke in death;
With shame and love's affection
I'll watch thy latest breath.

7 O what a consolation
Doth in my heart take place,
When I thy toil and passion
Can in some measure trace;
Ah! should I, while thus musing
On my Redeemer's cross,
Ev'n life itself be losing,
Great gain would be that loss.

8 I give thee thanks unfeigned,
O Jesus! Friend in need!
For what thy soul sustained
When thou for me didst bleed:
Grant me to lean unshaken
Upon thy faithfulness,
Until from hence I'm taken
To see thee face to face.

9 Lord, at my dissolution
Do not from me depart,
Support, at the conclusion
Of life, my fainting heart;
And when I pine and languish,
Seiz'd with death's agony,
O by thy pain and anguish
Set me at liberty.

10 Lord, grant me thy protection,
Remind me of thy death
And glorious resurrection,
When I resign my breath:
Ah then, though I be dying,
'Midst sickness, grief and pain,
I shall (on thee relying)
Eternal life obtain.

86.* T. 36.

DEAR Jesus! wherein art thou to be blamed,
Why is death's sentence against thee proclaimed?
What is thy crime? of what art thou accused, While thus abused?

2 I see thee scourg'd, plung'd in a sea of sorrows,
Beat in the face, thy back plough'd with deep furrows,
Thy temples crown'd with thorns, in mock'ry hailed, To the cross nailed.

3 Why was thy soul with hellish pain surrounded?
Alas, my sins have thee, my Saviour, wounded!
I should have waded thro' this sea of anguish, Which made thee languish.

4 There is no good at all in my whole nature;
Sin hath diffus'd its shame through ev'ry feature;
I had deserv'd eternal consternation,
And condemnation.

5 How highly wonderful is this proceeding!
The Shepherd for his wand'ring sheep is bleeding;
The Master pays for servants' misbehavior, That loving Saviour!

6 O boundless love! O love beyond expression,
Constraining thee to choose such bitter passion!
I lived in the world's and sins enjoyment, Thou barest torment.

7 O greatest King! whose power is unbounded,
How can thy mercy be aright expounded?
Mysterious depth! th' incarnate God is sighing, For sinners dying.

8 Thy dying love all other love doth swallow,
My mind to trace its limits is too shallow;
For such compassion, and for love so tender, What shall I render?

9 One thing I'll gladly do to give thee pleasure,
No more to sin I'll yield in any measure:
Lest it again seduce my mind and senses To old offences.

10 But as my strength is far too weak and feeble
To crucify my flesh and innate evil:
Lord, let thy Spirit graciously direct me, From sin protect me.

11 Unto thy praise my all I'll gladly venture,
Upon thy shame and cross I'll freely enter;
Nor pain, nor death, shall change my resolution, Nor persecution.

12 Do not despise, I pray, my weak endeavor
To praise and love and serve thee, dearest Saviour:
Take soul and body, Lord, as an oblation For all thy passion.

13 When thou shalt give to me a crown of glory,
When all is swallow'd up that's transitory,
Then shall my voice be suited to the matter, And praise thee better.

87.* T. 152. or 9.

CHRIST, who saves us by his cross,
Who in nought offended,
He was in the night for us
Betray'd, apprehended,
Led before a wicked race,
Falsely was accused,
Laugh'd at, mock'd, spit in the face,
Shamefully abused.

2 In the morn, at the sixth hour,
He was led with fury,
As a foe of civil pow'r,
'Fore a heathen jury,
Who him try'd, but found him free
Of th' imputed treason;
Herod mocked him, yet he
Found for death no reason.

3 At nine was the Son of God
By the scourges furrow'd,
And the thorny crown forc'd blood
From his sacred forehead.
With a purple garment mock'd,
On all sides assailed,
He must bear the cross to which
He was to be nailed.

4 He at noon was on the cross
Rear'd for our transgression,
Where he pray'd and bled for us,
To procure salvation:
The spectators shook their heads,
Had him in derision,
Till the sun his beams withdrew
From so sad a vision.

5 At three Jesus cry'd, "My God,
Why am I forsaken?"
Having vinegar and gall,
Which was offer'd, taken,
He then yielded up the ghost!
Pause, my soul, and wonder;—
Then the temple's vail was rent,
Rocks were cleft asunder.

6 When the Lord of glory dy'd,
Not a bone was broken,
But a soldier pierc'd his side
For a lasting token:
From thence stream'd a double flood
Of a cleansing nature;
Both the water and the blood
Wash the guilty creature.

7 Joseph, having leave obtain'd,
And got spices ready,
From the cross (by love constrain'd)
Took our Saviour's body:
Had it, with all decent grace,
To his own tomb carry'd;
Where the keepers for three days
To secure it tarry'd.

8 Grant, O Christ, thou Son of God,
Through thy bitter passion,
That we, as thy smart's reward,
Joy in thy salvation:
That we ever weigh the cause
Of thy death and suff'ring,
Yea for this, though poor we are,
Bring thee our thank-off'ring!

88.* T. 79.

O World, see thy Creator
Extended, like a traitor,
Upon the cross's tree!
Behold him, while expiring,
And for mankind acquiring
Thereby life, grace and liberty.

2 Draw near: thou wilt discover,
How blood and sweat all over
His sacred body dyes;
Out of his heart most noble,
For inexhausted trouble,
Sighs are successive foll'wing sighs.

3 Who hath thee thus abused,
Dear Lord, and so much bruised
Thy most majestic face?
Thou art no sin's transactor,
Thou art no malefactor,
Like others of the human race.

4 I, I, and my transgressions,
Which by my own confessions
Exceed the sea-shore sands;
These, these have been the reason
Of thy whole bitter season,
Of all thy bruises, stripes and bands.

5 I ought to have been pained,
And fast for ever chained
Both hand and foot in hell;

The bonds and scourges tearing,
Which thou, my God, wast bearing,
My soul, my soul deserv'd to feel.

6 I'll be with the beholders,
And see thee on thy shoulders
Bear my prodigious load:
Thou tak'st the curse-infliction,
Giv'st for it benediction;
Thy death procures my peace with God.

7 As Surety thou presentest
Thyself, to die consentest
For me in debt all o'er;
A crown of thorns thou wearest,
All scorn and pain thou bearest,
With patience never known before.

8 Into death's jaws thou leaping
Provid'st for my escaping,
Lest I its sting should prove;
My curse and condemnation
Thou bear'st, for my salvation:
O most unheard-of fire of love!

9 The highest obligations
Bind me through all life's stations,
T' express my thanks to thee;
Weak as I am and feeble,
As far as I am able,
I'll yield thee service willingly.

10 While here on earth I'm living,
I nothing have worth giving
To thee for all thy pain;
Yet shall thy passion ever,
Till soul and body sever
Deep in my heart engrav'd remain.

11 Its fresh representation
Shall raise my admiration,
Where'er I turn or move;
I'll take it for a mirror
Of innocence, for terror
To guilt, but seal of truth and love.

12 How greatly man incenses
The Lord by his offences;
God's holiness how stern;
How rig'rous he chastiseth,
When he with wrath baptizeth;
This from thy suff'rings will I learn.

13 From thence I'll be taught truly,
How to be pure and holy,
Resign'd, compos'd and still;
How patiently to suffer,
When any to me offer
Rude acts of malice and ill-will.

14 I'll be my flesh denying,
And gladly crucyfying,
With Christ, each sinful lust:
What in thy sight is odious
I'll leave, howe'er commodious,
By help and strength which thou bestow'st.

15 Thy sighs and groans unnumber'd,
And, from thy heart encumber'd,
The countless tears forth prest;
These shall at my dismission,
To final rest's fruition
Convoy me to thy arms and breast.

89.* T. 165.

THOUSAND times by me be greeted,
Jesus, who hast loved me,
And thyself to death submitted
For my treasons against thee:
Ah! how happy do I feel,
When 'fore thee I humbly kneel
At the cross where thou expiredst,
And true life for me acquiredst.

2 Jesus, thee I view in spirit,
Cover'd o'er with blood and wounds;
Now salvation, through thy merit,
For my sin-sick soul abounds.
O who can, thou Prince of Peace,
Who didst thirst for our release,
Fully fathom all that's treasur'd
In thy love's design unmeasur'd!

3 Heal me, O my soul's Physician,
Wheresoe'er I'm sick or sad;
All the woes of my condition
By thy balm be now allay'd:
Heal the hurts which Adam wrought,
Or which on myself I've brought;
If thy blood me only cover,
My distress will soon be over.

4 On my heart thy wounds for ever
Be inscrib'd indelibly,
That I ne'er forget, dear Saviour,
What thou hast endur'd for me:
Thou'rt indeed my highest good,
End of all solicitude;
Let me, at thy feet abased,
Be to taste thy friendship raised.

5 With the deepest adoration
Humbly at thy feet I lie;
And, with ardent supplication,
Unto thee for succor cry;
My petition kindly hear;
Say, in answer to my pray'r:
"I will change thy grief and sadness
Into comfort, joy and gladness."

6 Jesus, at my dissolution
Take my longing soul to thee;
Let thy wounds at the conclusion
Of this life, my refuge be!
When in death I close mine eyes,
Let me wake in paradise,
And in endless bliss and glory
With the saints in heav'n adore thee.

90.* T. 168.

JESUS, Source of my salvation,
Conqu'ror both of death and hell!
Thou who didst, as my oblation,
Feel what I deserv'd to feel:
Thro' thy suff'rings, death and merit,
I eternal life inherit;
Thousand, thousand thanks to thee,
Dearest Lord, for ever be!

2 O how basely wast thou used,
Buffeted and spit upon!
Scourg'd and torn, and sorely bruised,
Thou the heav'nly Father's Son:
Me, poor sinner, to deliver
From the devil's pow'r for ever!
Thousand, &c.

3 Lord, thy deep humiliation
Paid for my presumptuous pride;
I need fear no condemnation,
Since for sinners thou hast dy'd:
Thou becam'st a curse, dear Saviour,
To restore me to God's favor.
Thousand, &c.

4 Lord, I'll praise thee now and ever
For thy bitter pain and smart,
For thy agonizing shiver,
For thy wounds and pierced heart;
For thy stooping under sentence
Of God's wrath and fiery vengeance:
For thy death and love divine,
Lord, I'll be for ever thine.

91.* T. 165.

CHRIST, thy wounds & bitter passion,
Bloody sweat, cross, death, and tomb,
Be my daily meditation,
Till I to thy presence come.
When a sinful thought would start,
Ready to seduce my heart,
Thy sore pain effectually
Me forbid with sin to dally.

2 Should my bosom with lewd passion
Be inflam'd, and burn with sin,
Let the thoughts of thine oblation
Quench that spreading fire within.
Would the tempter make his way
To my heart, Lord, grant I may
By thy wounds, thy pain and anguish,
All his vile intrusions vanquish.

3 Would the world with gay temptation
Draw me to its own broad way;
Let me think upon thy passion,
And the load which on thee lay:
Sure the sweat and precious blood
Of the dying Lamb of God
Can arm me, on each occasion,
To oppose th' infatuation.

4 Lord, in ev'ry sore oppression,
Let thy wounds be my relief;
When I seek thine intercession,
Add new strength to my belief.
Ah, the feeling of thy peace
Sets my troubled heart at ease,
And affords a demonstration
Of thy love and my salvation.

5 All my hope and consolation,
Christ, is in thy bitter death;
At the hour of expiration,
Lord, receive my dying breath.
Most of all, when I go hence,
Let this be my confidence,
That thy deep humiliation
Hath procured my salvation.

92.* T. 126.

O Lord, when condemnation
And guilt afflict my soul,
Then let thy bitter passion
The rising storm control:
Remind me, that thy sacred blood
Hath cancell'd my transgressions
By paying what I ow'd.

2 O wonder far exceeding
All human thought and sense!
Heav'n's Sov'reign was seen bleeding
To wipe off my offence:
The Prince of life gave up his breath
For me, whose vile rebellion
Deserv'd an endless death.

3 Though sins exceed a mountain,
Or sands on ocean's shore,
The everlasting fountain
Of Jesus' blood hath pow'r
To wash all sin and guilt away,
And save me from that terror
Which held me in dismay.

4 My heart, while here 'tis moving,
Shall beat with fervent praise
To thee, who art so loving
To the lost human race:
Thy dying words and agony
Shall be my meditation,
Till I am call'd to thee.

5 Lord, let thy bitter passion
Dwell always in my mind,
To raise an indignation
'Gainst sin of ev'ry kind;
That henceforth I may ne'er forget
The greatness of that ransom,
Which paid my endless debt.

6 All pains and tribulations,
Contempt and worldly spite,
Help me to bear with patience;
And always fix my sight
On that unerring rule of faith,
Thy blessed steps to follow,
Until my latest breath.

7 O may my life and labor
Express what thou hast done,
By love towards my neighbor,
By serving ev'ry one
Without self-int'rest or disguise;
And may thy pure example
Be my best exercise!

8 When I give up my spirit
To thee my Judge and God,
O then apply the merit
Of thy atoning blood;
And let my faith its pow'r display,
And rest upon thy promise
To save me in that day.

93.* T. 167.

O The love wherewith I'm loved,
O the undeserved grace;
Thou, O Love, by mercy moved,
Tak'st upon thee my distress!
As a Lamb led to the slaughter
Goest to the cross's tree,
Seal'st thy love with blood and water,
Bear'st the world's iniquity.

2 Love, so strikingly displayed
In thy tears and bloody sweat:
Love, by sinful men betrayed,
Dragg'd before the judgment-seat:
Love, who for my soul's salvation,
Willingly didst shed thy blood,
Through thy death and bitter passion
I am reconcil'd to God.

3 Love, who as my bleeding Saviour
Didst my heart in righteousness
Unto thee betroth for ever,
Ah, I thank thee for thy grace:
Love, who thus himself engaged,
Let my mis'ry and my smart
Now entirely be assuaged
In thy wounded bleeding heart.

4 Love, who hast for me endured
Death upon the accursed tree,
And eternal bliss procured,
Fill my soul with love to thee.
Lord, how hast thou captivated
My else cold and lifeless heart!
Let me till to heav'n translated
Never more from thee depart.

94.* T. 216.

A Lamb went forth, and bare the guilt
Of all the world together,
Most patiently his blood he spilt
To pay for ev'ry debtor;
He freely took sin's heavy load,
To reconcile us unto God;
All comfort he refused:
He underwent reproach and blame,
Death on the cross, with stripes and [shame,
And said, "I freely choose it."

2 This Lamb is God omnipotent,
The sovereign Creator,
The Son, who by the Father sent,
Assum'd our feeble nature;

O love no human tongue can tell,
O love divine, unsearchable!
God gave his well-beloved
To suff'rings, death, and to the grave,
That he lost man thereby might save;
His mercy thus he proved!

3 Jesus, I never can forget
The pangs thou hast sustained;
I'll thee, long as my pulse doth beat,
Adore with thanks unfeigned;
Yea, thou shalt be my heart's delight;
Thou, when I sink in death's dark night,
Shalt be my consolation;
In life and death I will be thine,
And on thy faithfulness recline
With humble resignation.

4 My song in thy great loveliness,
Both day and night shall center;
Amidst all wants and feebleness,
I'll on thy service venture:
My life's whole stream for thee shall flow
O may, by all I speak or do,
Thy holy name be praised!
And all that thou hast done for me,
Upon my heart indelibly
For ever be impressed!

5 Thou canst true comfort to me yield
In my life's ev'ry station;
In combat thou dost prove my shield,
In grief my exultation;
In happy hours, the source of joy;
And when all other meat doth cloy,
This manna shall support me;
In thirst thou shalt my well-spring be,
In solitude my company,
At home and on a journey.

6 What harm can I from death sustain,
Since thou art my salvation?
From scorching heat thou art my screen,
In pain my consolation; [breast,
When gloomy thoughts surround my
Thou, Lord, alone canst give me rest,
'Tis by thy pow'r I conquer:
Thou art, when storms of trials blow,
And toss my vessel to and fro,
My sure and stedfast anchor.

7 When I in heav'n shall rest with thee,
Thou God of my salvation,
Thy blood and righteousness shall be
My glorious decoration:
Thou on my head wilt place a crown,
Thus shall I stand before the throne
Of thy dear heav'nly Father,
Dress'd in salvation's robe, with thee
To live to all eternity,
In bliss no tongue can utter.

95.* T. 152. or 9.

JESUS I am richly bless'd
By thy bitter passion;
O how is my soul refresh'd
In the meditation
On the pain and deep distress,
Which thou hast endured!
By thy death for me a place
Is in heav'n procured.

2 Jesus, who hast once been dead,
Now for ever livest;
Thou in ev'ry time of need
Kindly me relievest,
And dost help to me afford:
Faithful Lord and Saviour,
Give me what thy death procur'd,
And I'm rich for ever.

96.* T. 51.

WHEN Jesus hung upon the cross,
Expiring to retrieve our loss,
Bereft of consolation,
Sev'n dying words he spoke which claim
Our serious meditation.

2 First for his foes he intercedes,
And with his Father for them pleads,
(His matchless goodness showing);
He saith, "Forgive them; they know not
What they to me are doing."

3 Weigh next the pardon and relief
Bestow'd on the repenting thief,
The object of his favor:
"To day thou shalt in paradise
"Be with me, and for ever."

4 Observe the sympathy and care
Which he for John and Mary bare:
"Behold thy son, O mother;
O John, thy mother there behold."
Thus, Christians, love each other.

5 Hark! how the meek & suff'ring Lamb
Doth on the cross, "I thirst" exclaim;
Such thirst the Lord sustained
For our salvation: but now he
Joy for his grief hath gained.

6 Next take to heart his anguish great,
When, press'd beneath sin's pond'rous weight,
All comfort from him taken,
He cries aloud, "My God, my God,
Why hast thou me forsaken?"

7 "'Tis finish'd," was the solemn word,
When for mankind our dying Lord
Had gain'd complete salvation;
Ye mourning sinners, all rejoice
To hear this declaration.

8 The last, attention due demands:
"O Father, now into thy hands
I recommend my spirit!"
He bow'd his head, gave up the ghost,
That we might life inherit.

9 All those who here enjoy, by faith,
The blessed fruits of Jesus' death,
True bliss in him possessing,
Find in his seven dying words
A treasure of rich blessing.

97. T. 168.

O BEHOLD your Saviour wounded,
Hanging on th' accursed cross;
None hath e'er the love expounded,
Our Redeemer show'd to us:
Hear him at his crucifixion
Pray for foes 'midst keen affliction,
"O forgive them; they don't know,
Heav'nly Father, what they do."

2 At his cross's foot now tarry,
View his languid, marred face,
Mark his care for John and Mary;
To the thief he offers grace.
Ah, he thirsts with love unshaken;
"God! why hast thou me forsaken?"
And "'Tis finish'd!" Jesus cries,
Yields his spirit, droops and dies.

98.* T. 168.

SINCE with awe in strains melodious,
Sing with awe: Behold the Man!
Yea repeat in tones harmonious,
Ah, Behold, behold the man!
On thy dying look, dear Saviour,
I will fix my eyes for ever;
I am never tir'd to gaze
At thy lovely bleeding face.

2 Oh! this makes me think with sighing
I'm the cause: Behold the Man!
Then his love which I'm enjoying,
Comforts me: Behold the Man!
Ah! that terribly abused
Countenance so marr'd and bruised,
Makes my eyes with tears o'erflow,
Till to him I've leave to go.

3 Wounded head, back plough'd with furrows,
Visage marr'd: Behold the Man!
Eyes how dim, how full of sorrows,
Sunk with grief: Behold the Man!
Lamb of God, led to the slaughter,
Melted, poured out like water;
Should not love my heart inflame,
Viewing thee, thou slaughter'd Lamb.

99.* T. 217.

When thou in death didst bow thy head
All nature, Lord, was struck with wonder;
The op'ning graves gave up their dead
Earth trembled, rocks were rent in sunder:
Then felt the pow'rs of hell below
Their last irrevocable blow;
Thy aim was then by right obtained,
To free the souls by Satan chained;
Now, thro' thy anguish and distress,
The captives find a full release.

2 Thou, who the nail-prints dost retain,
Tho' to thy glorious throne ascended,
Whose side's incision doth remain,
And thorn-marks which thy head once rended:
This is thy most transcendent form
Which doth our hearts transport and warm,
As thou upon the cross didst languish,
Extended there in keenest anguish;
Or, as thy body, pale and dead,
In the cold sepulchre was laid.

3 'Tis the most lovely attitude
Wherein we can behold our Saviour,
When by the eye of faith he's view'd,
With blood and bruises stain'd all over.

For, more than all that can be said
Of Jesus Christ, our Lord and Head,
Doth sparkle in our heart's recesses:
The blessed fruits of his distresses
We richly can enjoy by faith,
While meditating on his death.

4 Christ's agony, his death and blood
Shall be our joy and consolation,
The grace unmerited bestow'd
On us our constant meditation;
Fresh proofs of his fidelity,
And Shepherd-care we daily see;
He will continue still to feed us,
Till he at last will thither lead us,
Where all his glories shall be seen
Without a vail to intervene.

100.* T. 594.

ONE view, Lord Jesus, of thy passion
Will make the fainting spirit glad;
This yields us solid consolation,
When thy dear blood, so freely shed,
Pervades and heals both soul and body,
When thou dost give to us thy peace;
Ah, then our arms of faith are ready,
Thy cross, O Jesus, to embrace!

2 No drop of blood thou deemd'st too precious,
To shed for worthless worms like me;
O that thy fire of love, dear Jesus,
Inflam'd my heart with love to thee!
May thy atoning death and passion,
Thy agony and bitter pain,
Until my final consummation
Deep in my heart engrav'd remain.

3 O might I live in the enjoyment
Of all my Lord for me hath gain'd!
Might this be daily my employment,
To muse upon what he sustain'd!
O may his hands, whereon engraven
My poor&worthless name doth stand,
Support me, till I in the haven
Of endless joy shall safely land.

101.* T. 14.

MY life-supplying element
Is Jesus' blood and death;
My soul is eagerly intent
To live therein by faith.

2 Lord Jesus! who is like to thee!
O might by night and day
My spirit upon Calvary,
That scene of suff'ring, stay.

3 How that blest moment I regard,
When thou didst bow thy head!
O had my list'ning ear but heard
The groan that left thee dead!

4 How highly favor'd had I been,
Had I with John stood by,
And my beloved Saviour seen
In keenest anguish die!

5 Beholding, with deep reverence,
Thy side for me then pierc'd,
With what emotion had I thence
Seen blood and water burst!

6 It is as tho' my eyes now view'd
This heart-affecting sight,
And ev'ry scene depicted stood
'Fore me in clearest light.

7 O might thy dying love divine
Become to me more clear,
And smile in ev'ry smile of mine,
And flow in ev'ry tear.

8 When I depart, my latest breath
To thee, Lord, shall ascend,
As a thank-off'ring for thy death;
Thus, blest my race will end.

102.* T. 14.

SEE, world, upon the shameful tree
Thy Maker sinks in death!
Cover'd with stripes and wounds for thee
Thy Saviour yields his breath.

2 Behold his body stain'd with blood,
Out of his tender heart
Deep sighs and groans he sends to God
In his excessive smart.

3 Thou Prince of glory knew'st no sin;
What caus'd thee then such pain?
Thou harmless, undefil'd and clean,
What caus'd thee to be slain?

4 My sins, as num'rous as the sands
Upon the ocean's shore,
Have been the cruel, murd'rous hands
That wounded thee so sore.

5 What anguish, what tormenting pain
Thy soul did rack and tear!
All this thou freely didst sustain,
But I deserv'd to bear.

6 Thou on thy shoulders took'st the
To ease my burden'd heart: [whole,
Thou bar'st the curse, to bless my soul,
And heal'st me by thy smart

7 Thy wondrous love to evidence
Thou wouldst my Surety be:
Thyself wouldst pay my debt immense,
Thereby to set me free.

8 Thou art destruction to the grave,
Death's enemy severe;
That each in bondage as its slave,
Might now be sav'd from fear.

9 My debt to thee, God, who art love,
Weak words can ne'er express;
I cannot here, if there above,
Return due thankfulness.

10 Grant me the grace, while I am here,
(Since I can nothing give)
Thy suff'rings in my heart to bear,
And by thy death to live.

103. T. 14.

BEHOLD the Saviour of the world
Imbru'd with sweat and gore,
Expiring on th' accursed cross,
Where he our sorrows bore!

2 Compassion for man's fallen race
Brought down God's only Son,
To veil in flesh his radiant face,
And for their sins atone.

3 Who can to love his name forbear,
That of his suff'rings hears,
And finds the ransom of his soul
Was blood as well as tears?

4 When earth and hell's malicious
Encompass'd thee around, [pow'rs
Thy sacred blood, O Son of God,
Stream'd forth from ev'ry wound:

5 Till death's pale ensigns o'er thy cheeks,
And trembling lips were spread;
Till light forsook thy dying eyes,
And life thy drooping head.

6 Joy for thy torments we receive,
Life in thy death have found;
For the reproaches of thy cross
Shall be with glory crown'd.

7 May we a grateful sense retain
Of thy redeeming love;
And live below like those that hope
To live with thee above!

104. T. 14.

ALAS! and did my Saviour bleed,
And did my Sov'reign die?
Would he devote his sacred head
For such a worm as I?

2 Was it for crimes that I had done,
He groan'd upon the tree?
Amazing pity! grace unknown!
And love beyond degree!

3 Well might the sun in darkness hide
And shut his glories in,
When God th' almighty Maker dy'd,
An off'ring for my sin.

4 Thus might I hide my blushing face,
While Jesus' cross appears;
Dissolve, my heart, in thankfulness,
And melt my eyes in tears!

105. T. 22.

WHEN I by faith my Saviour see
Expiring on the cross for me,
Satan and sin no more can move,
For I am fill'd with Jesus' love.

2 His thorns and nails pierce thro' my heart,
In ev'ry groan I bear a part;
I view his wounds with streaming eyes;
But see! he bows his head, and dies!

3 Come, sinners, view the Lamb of God,
Wounded and dead, & bath'd in blood!
Behold his side, and venture near,
The well of endless life is here.

4 Here I forget my cares and pains;
I drink, yet still my thirst remains;
Only the fountain-head above
Can satisfy the thirst of love.

5 O that I thus could always feel!
Lord, more and more thy love reveal!
Then my glad tongue shall loud pro-
The grace and glory of thy name. [claim

6 Thy name dispels my guilt and fear,
Revives my heart and charms mine ear;
Affords a balm for ev'ry wound,
And Satan trembles at the sound.

106. T. 14.

BEHOLD the loving Son of God
Stretch'd out upon the tree;
Behold him shed his precious blood,
And die for you and me.

2 Why is his body rack'd with pains,
And wrung with keenest smart?
Why flows the blood from all his veins,
Why torn with grief his heart?

3 All righteousness did he fulfil,
No sin did ever know;
He never thought nor acted ill;
Why was he wounded so?

4 Alas! I know the reason why:
Our num'rous sins he bore;
This caus'd his bitter agony,
This wounded him so sore.

5 But hence our confidence begins;
For we may boldly say,
That thus, by bearing all our sins,
He took them all away.

6 Our God is fully reconcil'd,
His justice satisfy'd;
Each sinner may become his child,
Since Jesus bled and dy'd.

7 Come then, ye needy sinners, come,
If ye accept, he'll give;
O suffer him to lead you home;
Whoever will, may live.

107. T. 22.

THERE hangs the Saviour of mankind,
His visage marr'd, his head reclin'd:
His bleeding hands, his bleeding feet,
Declare his love divinely great.

2 His flesh is torn with whips and nails;
His strength decays, his spirit fails:
His side is pierc'd, his heart is broke:
Our sins upon himself he took.

3 The thieves expiring on each side
Proclaim the crimes for which they dy'd:
But what, dear Saviour, hast thou done?
Thou dyd'st for sin, but not thine own.

4 Jesus, and didst thou bleed for me?
O great, O boundless mystery!
I bow my head in deep amaze,
And silently adore thy grace.

108. T. 582.

GO forth in spirit, go
To Calv'ry's holy mount;
See there thy Friend between two
Suff'ring on thy account. [thieves,

2 Fall at his cross's foot,
And say, "My God and Lord,
Here let me dwell, and view those wounds,
Which life for me procur'd."

3 Fix on that face thine eye;
Why dost thou backward shrink?
What a base rebel thou hast been
To Christ, thou now dost think.

4 Fear not; for this is he
Who always loves us first,
And with white robes of righteousness
Delights to deck the worst.

5 Or art thou at a loss
What thou to him shalt say?
Be but sincere, and all thy case
Just as it is display.

6 His blood thy cause will plead,
Thy plaintive cry he'll hear,
Look with an eye of pity down,
And grant thee all thy pray'r.

109. T. 14.

BEHOLD the Saviour of mankind
Nail'd to the shameful tree;
How vast the love that him inclin'd
To bleed and die for thee!

2 Hark how he groans! while nature shakes,
And earth's strong pillars bend;
The temple's vail in sunder breaks,
The solid marbles rend.

3 'Tis done! the precious ransom's paid,
"'Tis finish'd!" Jesus cries;
Behold he bows his sacred head,
He bows his head, and dies.

4 Salvation thus did he obtain,
O mystery divine!
O Lamb of God, was ever pain,
Was ever love like thine!

110. T. 22.

THE cross, the cross, O that's my gain,
Because on that the Lamb was slain;
'Twas there my Lord was crucify'd,
'Twas there my Saviour for me dy'd.

2 The stony heart dissolves in tears,
When to our view the cross appears;
Christ's dying love, when truly felt,
The vilest, hardest heart doth melt.

3 Here will I stay, and gaze a while
Upon the Friend of sinners vile;
Abas'd, I view what I have done
To God's eternal, gracious Son.

4 Here I behold, as in a glass,
God's glory, with unveiled face;
And by beholding, I shall be
Made like to Him who loved me.

5 Here is an ensign on a hill,
Come hither, sinners, look your fill;
To look aside, is pain and loss;
I glory only in the cross.

6 Here doth the Lord of life proclaim
To all the world his saving name;
Repenting souls, in him believe;
Ye wounded, look on him and live.

7 No flaming sword doth guard the place,
The cross of Christ proclaims free grace:
All pilgrims who would heaven win,
By Jesus' cross must enter in.

111. T. 96.

O Love divine, what hast thou done!
Th' incarnate God hath dy'd for me!
The Father's co-eternal Son
Bore all my sins upon the tree:
Th' incarnate God for me hath dy'd;
My Lord, my Love is crucify'd!

2 Behold him, all ye that pass by,
The bleeding Prince of life and peace!
Come see, ye worms, your Maker die,
And say, was ever grief like his!
Come feel, with me, his blood apply'd:
My Lord, my Love is crucify'd!

3 Is crucify'd for me and you,
To bring us rebels back to God;
Believe, believe the record true,
Ye all are bought with Jesus' blood:
Pardon for all flows from his side;
My Lord, my Love is crucify'd!

4 Then let us sit beneath his cross,
And gladly catch the healing stream,
All things for him account but loss,
And all give up our hearts to him:
O may we nothing know beside
The Lamb of God as crucify'd.

112. T. 11.

LET me dwell on Golgotha,
Weep and love my life away!
While I see him on the tree
Weep, and bleed, and die, for me!

2 That dear blood, for sinners spilt,
Shows my sin in all its guilt:
Ah! my soul, he bore thy load;
Thou hast slain the Lamb of God.

3 Hark! his dying word: "Forgive,
Father, let the sinner live;
Sinner, wipe thy tears away,
I thy ransom freely pay."

4 While I hear this grace reveal'd,
And obtain my pardon seal'd,
All my soft affections move,
Waken'd by the force of love.

5 Farewell world, thy gold is dross,
Now I see the blood-stain'd cross;
Jesus dy'd to set me free
From the law, and sin, and thee!

6 He hath dearly bought my soul;
Lord, accept, and claim the whole!
To thy will I all resign,
Now, no more my own, but thine.

113. T. 583.

I Kneel in spirit at my Saviour's cross,
Where he in blood expired for his foes:
With deepest rev'rence humbly I adore
My dying Lord who all my sorrows bore.

2 I, sinful worm, with awe before him bow, [view:
While I the deep unfathom'd myst'ry
Poor man must highly valu'd be indeed,
For whom so great a ransom-price was paid. [maintain,
3 This blessed truth I firmly will
That my Creator for my sins was slain:
May this constrain me gladly to obey,
And love the Lord, who took my sins away.

114. T. 232.

BEHOLD, my soul, the Lamb of God
Baptiz'd with tears, and sweat, and blood,
Spent, comfortless, forsaken:
See, how he bows his head and dies,
While to the world the sun denies
His light, and rocks are shaken.
My dear Redeemer, let thy smart
Subdue my cold and lifeless heart;
Teach me thy dying love to know,
And in return with love to glow;
Thy love divine—My heart incline,
Lord, to be thine,
Till I in death my soul resign.

115.* T. 588.

'TIS finish'd now,
Salvation's finish'd now!
Redeemed sinners bow,
Adore and wonder,
That earth and heaven's Founder
Now sinks in death. :||:

2 Look up and see,
By faith look up and see,
His heart was pierc'd for thee;
The Rock of ages,
Whose stream thy thirst assuages,
Was rent for thee. :||:

3 The precious flood
Of water and of blood,
Of sin-atoning blood,
Now freely floweth
On him, who Jesus knoweth
As Lord and God. :||:

4 We are redeem'd,
Redeem'd to endless bliss,
Our souls rejoice at this;
With hearts enlarged,
We see our debt discharged,
Our ransom paid. :||:

5 O sing again,
Sing still in higher strain
Unto the Lamb once slain;
Bring for salvation
Praise, thanks and adoration,
Hallelujah! :||:

116. T. 14.

THERE is a fountain fill'd with blood
Drawn from Immanuel's veins;
And sinners plung'd beneath that flood
Lose all their guilty stains.

2 The dying thief rejoic'd to see
That fountain in his day;
And there have I, as vile as he,
Wash'd all my sins away.

3 E'er since, by faith, I saw the stream,
Thy flowing wounds supply,
Redeeming love hath been my theme,
And shall be till I die.

4 Then in a nobler, sweeter song,
I'll sing thy pow'r to save;
When this poor lisping, stamm'ring
Lies silent in the grave. [tongue

117.* T. 151.

THY blood so dear and precious,
Love made thee shed for me:
O may I now, dear Jesus,
Love thee most fervently:
May the divine impression
Of thy atoning death,
And all thy bitter passion,
Ne'er leave me while I've breath.

118.* T. 583.

WHENE'ER the suff'ring Lamb of [God I see,
It raiseth grief and joy alternately;
Grief, since I caus'd him all his bitter pain,
Joy, since thereby he life for me did gain.

119. T. [illegible]0.

ALL hail! thou Lamb of God,
Bearing sin's pond'rous load:
Thanks for thy agony,
Thy bloody sweat for me,
Thy suff'ring willingly;
All hail, 'midst pain and scorn,
Spit upon, crown'd with thorn,
And by the scourges torn!
All hail, in purple clad.
Sinners, sinners,
Ah! behold the Man!
Sinners, sinners,
Ah! behold the Man!

2 Bearing the cross's weight,
Thou mountest Calv'ry's height,
I weeping follow thee,
For all is done for me,
For me, thine enemy!
All hail! as in my stead,
Thou, a sin-off'ring made,
In torments bow'st thy head;
Thanks for thy pierced side!
Sinners, sinners,
All ye who pass by,
Hearken, hearken,
Mark his dying cry!

3 "'Tis finish'd," Jesus cries,
He bows his head, and dies;
The vail is rent in twain,
Burst is the captive's chain,
Man is restor'd again!
All hail! in death though pale,
Victorious Lamb! all hail!
Then did thine arm prevail;
O glorious sacrifice!
Ever, ever
To thy promis'd word
Faithful, faithful
Saviour, God and Lord!

120.* T. 208.

HAPPY meditation
On my Saviour's passion,
On his death and grave;
It can't be expressed
What a feeling blessed,
At such times I have,
When I Christ in spirit view,
In his suff'ring scenes revising
My Lord agonizing.

2 All the pains and sorrows
He endured for us;
All the tears he shed,
When he in the garden,
Bearing our sin's burden,
In soul's anguish pray'd:
Yea, each part of toil and smart
In my soul excites a motion
To intense devotion.

3 Soul, from toil reposing,
Languid eyes, just closing,
Side, pierc'd with a spear;
Limbs, to pain inured,
Feet, for me thro' bored,
Hands, the nails did tear;
Head, by right divinely bright,
Crown'd with pointed thorns & bruised,
Spit on and abused;

4 Breast, which heaves with sorrows;
Back, plough'd o'er with furrows,
From the scourges sore;
Arms, in pain extended,
Shoulders, raw and wounded,
Hair distain'd with gore;
Sacred Lips, in death how pale!
Jesus Christ, thy bitter passion
Prompts my adoration.

5 Lamb of God, thus dearest
Thou to me appearest;
O might I each breath
Spend, while here I'm living,
In praise and thanksgiving
For thy wounds and death!
A poor sinner still I am,
Ah! behold me with compassion,
Grant me consolation.

121. T. 581.

MET around the sacred tomb,
Friends of Jesus, why those tears?
'Midst this sad sepulchral gloom
Shall your faith give way to fears?
He will soon, ev'n as he said,
Rise triumphant from the dead.

2 Hidden from all ages past
Was the cross's mystery,
Doubts awhile a veil had cast
O'er that first dear family;
Till they saw him, and believ'd,
And as Lord and God receiv'd.

3 Now with tears of love and joy,
We remember all his pain,
Sighs and groans and dying cry;
For the Lamb for us was slain,
And, from death our souls to save,
Once for us lay in the grave.

4 Hither, sinners, all repair,
And with Jesus Christ be dead,
All are safe from Satan's snare,
Who to Jesus' tomb have fled;
Here the weary and opprest
Find a never-ending rest.

5 Wounded Saviour, full of grace,
Hast thou suffer'd thus for me?
Ah! I hide my blushing face;
How have I requited thee?
Should not I with ardor burn
Some love's token to return?

6 But alas, the spark how small!
Scarcely seen at all to glow;
Lord, thou know'st how short I fall,
And my growth in grace how slow;
Yet when to thy cross I fly,
Soon all strange affections die.

7 In thy death is all my trust,
I have thee my refuge made,
And when once consign'd to dust,
In the tomb my body's laid,
Then with saved souls above
I will praise thy dying love.

8 But while here I'm left behind,
Burden'd with infirmity,
May I help and comfort find,
Visiting Gethsemane,
Calvary and Joseph's tomb,
Till my sabbath's also come.

122. T. 114.

NOW haste, my soul, with awe and deep devotion,
To Joseph's tomb, thy Saviour to behold
Laid in the dust, his body pale and cold.
Ah! in thy stead he drank death's bitter potion:
He as a lamb was wounded, bruis'd and slain,
For thee eternal happiness to gain.

2 For worthless me (O Godlike condescension!)
The Maker of creation's boundless sphere,
Whom all celestial hosts as Lord revere,
Whose pow'r divine is past their comprehension,
Became a man, my guilty soul to save,
And rests from labor in the silent grave.

3 Here is the place where weary souls may tarry;
Tho' near the dead, death can no pow'r assume,
For life, eternal life rests in this tomb.
Come then, my pardon'd soul, with humble Mary [sleep;
Behold thy wearied Master sweetly
Admire his matchless love, adore and weep.

4 I view in thee, thou wan and mangled body,
My Lord, Redeemer, Priest and Sacrifice,
The Bread of life, the Pearl of greatest price,
My soul's Belov'd, the Fairest, white and ruddy,
The promis'd Seed, the Lord our Righteousness,
The long-predicted Lamb and Prince of peace.

5 Here will I stay, engag'd in contemplation
On my Redeemer's agony and death;
This shall increase and fix my wav'ring faith
In thee, the Finisher of my salvation;
Yea, in my soul and body mortify
The sins which did my Jesus crucify.

6 Thou Lord of life! fix thou my soul and senses
On thee, the dearest object of my heart;
That when from this vain world I shall depart,
And when the awful scene of death commences,
I may resign my spirit unto thee,
And in thy presence live eternally.

7 Meanwhile I'll love and thank without cessation
Thee, my Redeemer, who my soul hast bought,
And me a wand'ring sheep in mercy sought!
Accept my tears, my pray'r and adoration;
To thee my life, my all I now resign
In life and death; O keep me ever thine!

123. T. 208.

NOW while I, like Mary,
My best spices carry
To my Saviour's tomb;
I'll behold his body
Mangled, pale, and bloody;
Now my sabbath's come.
But, alas;—what spices has
My poor heart, save tears and crying,
Heart-felt throbs and sighing!

2 Lo! methinks his body,
There stretch'd out already,
Lifeless I behold:
Yes, I view him yonder,
And astonish'd ponder
O'er him dead and cold,
Deep and wide—I see his side,
Livid wounds on ev'ry member
I see without number.

3 Back, the scourges ploughed!
Side, whence blood-streams flowed!
Hands, and feet, and head!
Lips, o'er which death hover'd,
Now with paleness cover'd!
Cheeks, whose color's fled!
Bruised face—still full of grace!
On this scene I gaze ashamed,
Weep whene'er 'tis named.

4 Lamb of God, my Saviour,
Thou shalt be for ever
My most fav'rite theme:
And for thy atonement,
Might I ev'ry moment
Praise thy saving name:
Constantly—thy passion be,
Till my final consummation,
My heart's meditation.

124.* T. 45.

O Deepest grief,—which the relief
Of mankind hath procured!
God's beloved only Son
In a tomb was buried.

2 Ye sons of men,—this doleful plan
Was laid by your transgression;
What Christ suffer'd for your guilt
Is beyond expression.

3 The Lamb of God—shed all his blood,
Which flow'd upon the mountain;
This for all iniquity
Is an open fountain.

4 O Prince of Peace,—thou Source of grace,
And Author of salvation!
Thy unbounded love demands
Humble adoration.

5 How blest he is—who weigheth this,
That God became his Saviour,
To bestow eternal life
Upon him for ever!

6 O Jesus blest!—my heart's true rest,
Be thou my soul's desire,
Till I too can in my tomb
From this world retire.

125. T. 119.

SLAUGHTER'D Lamb, :||:
My Redeemer! while I view
Thee by faith, I'm lost in wonder;
Grateful tears my cheeks bedew:
Blessed Saviour, when I ponder
On the cause of all thy grief & smart,
Melts my heart. :||:

2 Holy Lord, :||:
By thy body giv'n to death,
Mortify my sinful nature
Till I yield my dying breath.
Ah, protect thy feeble creature,
Till I shall in heav'n for ever be,
Lord, with thee. :||:

126. T. 11.

GO my soul, go ev'ry day,
To the tomb where Jesus lay;
Be my members with him dead,
Be his sepulchre my bed.

2 Boldest foes dare never come,
Near my Saviour's sacred tomb;
Evil never can molest
Those who near his body rest.

127.* T. 185.

WHEN I visit Jesus' grave in spirit,
It is never done in vain;
Since 'tis only from his death and merit
I can life and strength obtain:
Jesus' cross, his last hours in his passion,
Jesus' stripes, his wounds and expiration,
Jesus' body and his blood
Shall remain my highest good.

128. T. 205.

RESTING in the silent grave,
Spent with torment, pangs and cries,
See the Lord God, strong to save!
Him, whose thunders shake the skies!
'Twas for me he groan'd, he bled,
And was number'd with the dead;
Sacred body, with amaze,
Thankfully on thee I gaze.

129.* T. 519.

MOST holy Lord and God!
Holy, almighty God!
Holy and most merciful Saviour!
Thou eternal God!
Grant that we may never
Lose the comforts from thy death!
Have mercy, O Lord!

VI. Of the Resurrection of Christ from the Grave.

130.* T. 132.

CHRIST Jesus was to death abas'd
Because of our transgression;
But now for us, by being rais'd,
Hath gain'd life and salvation.
'Tis this should prompt us to rejoice,
To praise the Lord with heart and voice,
In singing Hallelujah!

2 By none of all the human race
Could death and hell be foiled;
Sin render'd all men weak and base,
All ruin'd were and spoiled;
Death having enter'd by the fall,
Bore sway and was entail'd on all;
All sinners are by nature.

3 But Jesus Christ, the Son of God,
In love and great compassion,
To free us from sin's galling load,
Appear'd in human fashion:
He hath destroy'd sin's pow'r & claim,
And left death nothing but the name;
Its sting can't hurt believers.

4 How great and wondrous was the strife,
Life was by death assailed!
But Jesus Christ, the Prince of life,
O'er sin and death prevailed;
He triumph'd over them in death,
And we are conqu'rors too by faith
In Christ our risen Saviour.

5 He is the blessed Paschal Lamb,
By God himself appointed:
The prophets all aloud proclaim
That he is the Anointed.
If on our hearts his blood appear,
We're freed from death's enslaving fear,
Subdu'd is that destroyer.

6 This is the day the Lord hath made
To lively hopes to raise us:
Let heav'n rejoice, let earth be glad,
And join to sing his praises:
For Christ, our everlasting light,
Dispels the clouds of sin's dark night,
And all the pow'rs of darkness.

7 The bread of life we eat in faith
Is Jesus Christ our Saviour,
Who conquer'd Satan, sin, and death,
And liveth now and ever:
Our souls desire no other food,
But our Redeemer's flesh and blood,
Which gives us life eternal.

131.* T. 590.

SING Hallelujah, Christ doth live,
And peace on earth restore!
Come, ransom'd souls, and glory give,
Sing, worship and adore!
With grateful hearts to him we pay
Our thanks in humble wise:
Who ought unto our charge can lay?
'Tis God that justifies.

2 Who can condemn? since Christ was [dead,
And ever lives to God;
Now our whole debt is fully paid,
He saves us by his blood.
The ransom'd hosts in earth and heav'n
Thro' countless choirs proclaim
"He hath redeem'd us; praise be giv'n
To God and to the Lamb!"

3 God rais'd him up, when he for all
Had freely tasted death,
And thus redeem'd us from the fall;
On this we ground our faith.
For God thereby his sacrifice
Declar'd, unto his praise,
An all-sufficient ransom-price
For Adam's fallen race.

4 The God of peace to guilty man
Doth pard'ning grace afford,
Since from the dead he brought again
Our Shepherd, Head, and Lord;
That Shepherd who so freely shed
His blood for sinners poor;
Who dy'd, but now is ris'n indeed,
And lives for evermore.

5 The God of mercies let us praise,
Who saveth fallen men,
And by his pow'r which Christ did raise,
From death begets again
Us to a lively confidence,
That we for Jesus' sake
Shall of that blest inheritance,
Reserv'd for us, partake.

6 His resurrection's pow'r divine,
By grace on us bestow'd,
Renews us, that we dead to sin,
May live alone to God:
Thus we, supported by his might,
'From strength to strength proceed;
And, walking in his truth and light,
Praise him in word and deed.

7 In all we do, constrain'd by love,
We'll joy to him afford,
And to God's will obedient prove
Thro' Jesus Christ our Lord.
Sing Hallelujah! and adore
On earth the Lamb once slain,
Till we in heav'n shall evermore
Exalt his name, Amen!

132. T. 590.

BELIEVING souls, rejoice and sing,
Your risen Saviour see,
And say, "O death, where is thy sting?
O grave, thy victory?"
He dy'd your guilty souls to save;
And, dying, conquer'd death;
Was bury'd in the gloomy grave,
But re-assum'd his breath.

2 Rejoice, your conqu'ring Saviour [lives,
He lives, to die no more;
And life eternal freely gives,
Since he our sorrows bore,
To all who their lost state bewail;
For Jesus' precious blood
Doth for each contrite soul prevail
Before the throne of God.

3 Sing praises to our risen Lord;
Life, immortality,
And lasting bliss are now restor'd
For all; for you and me.
Believe the wondrous deed, my soul,
Adore his saving name;
Rejoice, ye saints, from pole to pole
His love and pow'r proclaim.

4 The Prince of life reclin'd his head,
Expiring on the cross;
But now the Lord is ris'n indeed,
Is ris'n and lives for us.
Rejoice, and in the dust adore
The Lamb for sinners slain;
He liveth now and evermore,
For evermore to reign.

133. T. 50.

REJOICE, O church, the Saviour's bride,
All grief and mourning lay aside:
With cheerful hearts and voices sing
The resurrection of our King. Hal.

2 He, having triumph'd over death,
Now re-assumes his vital breath:
The angels wait with watchful eyes,
And joy to see their God arise.

3 Our gracious Saviour, Head and Lord,
Hath well perform'd his promis'd word;
And now would have his church rejoice;
He loves to hear her cheerful voice.

4 Let us then with the heav'nly throng
Now join in that eternal song:
'Salvation to our God and King,
Whose death did our redemption bring.'

5 Blessing and praise we give to thee,
That thou from death hast set us free;
Thy resurrection from the grave
Proves clearly thou hast pow'r to save.

6 Thy blood shall wash our garments white
Then we, with all the saints in light,
Shall joyful meet our Lord and Head,
We know for us thy blood was shed.

7 Astonish'd, at thy footstool low,
With humble gratitude we bow:
Our words can never fully tell
What in our thankful hearts we feel!

134. T. 595.

CHRISTIANS, dismiss your fear;
Let hope and joy succeed,
The joyful news with gladness hear,
"The Lord is ris'n indeed!"
The promise is fulfill'd
In Christ our only Head;
Justice with mercy's reconcil'd;
He lives who once was dead.

2 The Lord is ris'n again,
Who on the cross did bleed;
He lives to die no more, Amen!
The Lord is ris'n indeed.

He truly tasted death
For wretched fallen men;
In bitter pangs resign'd his breath;
But now is ris'n again.

3 He hath himself the keys
Of death, the grave and hell;
His is the victory and praise,
And he rules all things well.
Death now no more I dread,
But cheerful close mine eyes:
Death is a sleep, the grave a bed;
With Jesus I shall rise.

135. T. 11.

GLORY unto Jesus be!
From the curse he set us free;
All our guilt on him was laid,
He the ransom fully paid.

2 All his glorious work is done;
God's well pleased in his Son;
For he rais'd him from the dead,
Christ now reigns, the church's Head.

3 His redeem'd his praise show forth,
Ever glorying in his worth;
Angels sing around the throne,
"Thou art worthy, thou alone!"

4 Ye who love him, cease to mourn,
He will certainly return;
All his saints with him shall reign;
Come, Lord Jesus, come! Amen.

136. T. 580.

JESUS, who dy'd the world to save,
Revives and rises from the grave,
By his almighty pow'r:
From sin and death he sets us free,
He captive leads captivity,
He lives again, to die no more.

2 Children of God, look up and see
Your Saviour, cloth'd with Majesty,
Triumphant o'er the tomb:
Cease, cease to grieve, cast off your fears,
In heav'n your mansions he prepares,
And soon will come to take you home.

3 His church is still his joy and crown,
He looks with love and pity down
On her he did redeem:
Each member of his church he knows,
He shares their joys and feels their woes,
And they shall ever reign with him.

137.* T. 22.

REJOICE, the Lord in triumph reigns,
Breaks death and hell's infernal chains,
Retakes his life and majesty;
Praise him to all eternity.

2 Behold the great accuser cast,
The hour of darkness now is past;
No right to us can Satan claim,
If we believe in Jesus' name.

138. T. 14.

ON this glad day a brighter scene
Of glory was display'd
By God th' eternal Word, than when
The universe was made.

2 He riseth, who mankind hath bought
With grief and pain extreme:
'Twas great to speak the world from nought,
'Tis greater to redeem.

139.* T. 132.

CHRIST, being risen from the tomb,
To Mary show'd his favor,
And kindly called her by name;
She, when she saw her Saviour,
Directly turn'd about in haste,
His feet with heart-felt joy embrac'd,
And hail'd her risen Master.

2 His holy name for ever be
Adored, bless'd and praised,
That he hath such invariably
To taste his friendship raised,
As Mary Magdalen, and me,
Who nought can boast of, but that he
Hath pardon'd their transgressions.

3 How happy feels a contrite heart,
Enjoying Christ's salvation!
Those who have chosen Mary's part
And fav'rite occupation,
Find in our Saviour, day and night,
A source of comfort and delight;
'Tis this makes life important.

4 He pardon'd me, like Magdalen,
I love him, my Preserver!
I love him, but (it gives me pain)
I love not with such fervor.
When Jesus I shall once behold,
I then shall feel as she of old,
When he to her appeared.

140.* T. 185.

HAIL, all hail, victorious Lord, and Saviour!
Thou hast burst the bonds of death!
Grant us, as to Mary, that great favor
To embrace thy feet in faith:
Thou hast in our stead the curse endured,
And for us eternal life procured;
Joyful, we with one accord
Hail thee as our risen Lord.

2 O thou matchless Source of consolation,
Scarce thy resting moments end
When a heart-enliv'ning salutation
To thy children thou dost send;
We would share thy dear disciples' feeling,
As before their risen Master kneeling;
Thus shall we, with all our heart,
Witness what a Friend thou art!

141.* T. 205.

JESUS, who is always near,
To assuage his children's grief,
Unto Thomas did appear,
To remove his unbelief,
" Come," he said, " my nail prints view,
And my side, the spear pierc'd thro';"
Bold in faith he then avow'd:
" Christ, thou art my Lord, my God!"

2 I would go from pole to pole
To behold my risen Lord;
But content thyself my soul,
Listen to thy Saviour's word:
" They who me by faith receive,
Without seeing who believe,
Trust my word and thereon rest,
They abundantly are blest."

VII. Of the Ascension of Christ; his Sitting at the Right Hand of God, and interceding for us.

142.* T. 83.

SURELY God is present here!
Since the Lord with grace and favor
To my spirit doth appear,
As my Jesus, as my Saviour;
For the holy Trinity
Is to us in Jesus nigh.

2 O might all my wishes tend
Unto Christ without cessation,
He's my best and nearest Friend,
Full of grace, truth and salvation;
I, when he is present, feel
Happiness, no tongue can tell.

3 Holy awe pervades my heart,
When I see my great Creator
Of man's nature taking part,
That he, as my Mediator,
Might lay down his life for me,
And from death might set me free,

4 In the grave for me he lay,
Then arose, with pow'r, and glorious,
Grace triumphant to display,
Proving over death victorious;
And for forty days was seen,
By his foll'wers, God with men!

5 When the Lord's disciples saw
Jesus, gloriously arrayed,
From their longing sight withdraw,
In a cloud to heav'n conveyed;
Sure, alternate grief and joy
Did their hearts and thoughts employ.

6 He ascended up on high,
Glorious and with honor crowned,
Cloth'd in god-like majesty,
Is at God's right-hand enthroned;
And doth still as man appear,
Pleading for poor sinners there.

7 God be prais'd, they who are his,
In this present dispensation,
Nought essential ever miss,
Since they share in his salvation;
Tho' unseen, he's nigh to all,
Who in truth upon him call.

8 O when will the time draw near,
That he, who to heav'n ascended,
Will in majesty appear,
By the heav'nly hosts attended!
But we're silent:—to believe
Is our lot, while here we live,

143.* T. 58.

YE, the Lord's redeemed,
Holy, beloved,
Who as new creatures are in Christ approved, Look heaven-ward!

2 That he, who ascended
For our salvation,
May give you of his grace a sweet sensation, Tho' still unseen.

3 Countenance majestic,
Yet kind and gracious,
Of our once suff'ring, now exalted Jesus! We gaze at thee.

4 Hark! the Father welcomes
His Son beloved:
" Come thou, whose pow'rful arm victorious proved, Come to my throne!

5 Sit thou at my right-hand,
Till for thy passion,
Thy foes shall at thy footstool with prostration Confess thee Lord."

6 At the word of th' Father,
With awe before him
The countless heav'nly hosts fall down, adore him, And homage pay.

7 While on earth we tarry,
His death and passion
We will show forth, and our sanctification From him derive.

8 With his ransom'd people,
Each day that passes
Shall be devoted unto solemn praises For Jesus' death.

9 Lamb of God most holy!
Praise, honor, blessing,
Be giv'n to God, thro' thee, by all possessing Thy saving grace.

10 Everlasting praises
And adoration
To him, who hath himself by Jesus' passion To us made known!

11 Holy, holy, holy!
In earth and heaven,
To God and to the Lamb be glory given By all that breathe!

144. T. 14.

THE Lord ascendeth up on high,
Deck'd with resplendent wounds;
While shouts of vict'ry rend the sky,
And heav'n with joy resounds.

2 Eternal gates their leaves unfold,
Receive the conqu'ring King:
The angels strike their harps of gold,
And saints triumphant sing.

3 Sinners, rejoice; he dy'd for you;
For you prepares a place;
His spirit sends, you to endow
With ev'ry gift and grace.

4 His blood, which did for you atone,
For your salvation pleads;
And seated on his Father's throne,
He reigns and intercedes.

145.* T. 146.

GO up with shouts of praise!
Go up, High-Priest, to heaven!
Who hast the ransom'd race
Upon thy heart engraven;
Though seated on thy throne,
Thou deign'st to hear our pray'r;
Nor art asham'd to own,
That we thy brethren are.

146.* T. 26.

O Comfort, words can ne'er express!
That, by th' angelic hosts attended,
Our gracious Lord to heav'n ascended,
There to prepare for us a place.

147. T. 580.

When thou, dear Saviour, didst ascend,
"My hosts," thy Father said, "attend,
And worship ye the Son."
With loud acclaims of joy they gaz'd,
And cheerful Hallelujahs rais'd,
Adoring humbly at thy throne.

2 Can we thy triumphs e'er forget?
Shall we not worship at thy feet,
For all thy griefs and pain?
Yes, we will join th' angelic throng,
In singing that eternal song;
"Worthy the Lamb, for he was slain!"

3 Th' assembly, which with thee at rest
Appears in spotless garments drest,
Bows down and humbly sings:
We too thy saving name will bless,
And thee, our gracious Lord, confess
The Lord of lords and King of kings!

148.* T. 132.

RAISE your devotion, mortal tongues,
To praise the King of glory;
Sweet be the accents of your songs
To him who went before you:
Lo! angels strike their loudest strings,
For heav'n and all created things
Must sound Immanuel's praises.

2 Ye mourning souls, look upward too,
For Christ is now preparing,
At God's right-hand a place for you;
Shake off all thoughts despairing:
Thence he your gracious Lord will come
To fetch your longing spirits home,
And crown your love and labor.

3 Since he o'er heav'n bears sov'reign sway,
By all it's pow'rs attended;
And hath more graces to display
Than can be comprehended:
Fear not, for he his blessing pours
On such meek humble breasts as yours,
The objects of his favor.

149. T. 22.

TO thee, our Lord, all praise be giv'n,
For thy ascending up to heav'n:
Support us while on earth we stay,
And kindly hear us when we pray.

2 Tho' seated on thy Father's throne
Thou ne'er wilt cease thy flock to own;

For we believe, that thou art near
When in thy presence we appear.

3 For us to heav'n thou didst ascend,
To plead our cause, and to attend
To all our wants, yea, to prepare
A place for us, thy bliss to share.

4 At parting from thy little fold,
Thy second advent was foretold;
Therefore we wait with eagerness,
Lord Jesus, to behold thy face.

150. T. 590.

WE sing thy praise, exalted Lamb,
Who sitt'st upon the throne:
Ten thousand blessings to thy name,
Who worthy art alone!
Thy sacred, bruised body bore
Our sins upon the tree:
And now thou liv'st for evermore:
O may we live to thee!

2 Poor sinners, sing the Lamb that dy'd!
(What theme can sound so sweet!)
His drooping head, his streaming side,
His pierced hands and feet;
With all that scene of suff'ring love,
Which faith presents to view;
For now he reigns and lives above,
Yea lives and reigns for you.

3 Was ever grace, Lord, rich as thine,
Can aught so great be nam'd?
What pow'rful beams of love divine
Thy tender heart inflam'd!
Ye angels, praise his glorious name,
Who lov'd and conquer'd thus;
And we will likewise laud the Lamb,
For he was slain for us.

151. T. 595.

JESUS, who dy'd, is now
Seated upon his throne:
The angels, who before him bow,
His just dominion own.

2 Th' unworthiest of his friends
Upon his heart he bears;
He ever to their cause attends,
For them a place prepares.

3 Blest Saviour, condescend
My advocate to be:
I could not have a better friend
To plead with God for me.

152.* T. 58.

THE man of sorrows, whose most precious blood
Pleads now our cause before the throne of God,
Is in glory seated, and with compassion
Beholds, both far and near, each congregation With looks of love.

153. T. 14.

JESUS, our High-priest and our Head,
Who bear'st our flesh and blood,
And always interced'st for us
Before the throne of God;

2 We know thou never canst forget
Us thy weak members here;
Yea, when we suffer in the least,
Thou part with us wilt bear:

3 Thou with great tenderness art touch'd
At what thy children feel;
When by temptations we are press'd,
Thou know'st well what we ail:

4 Thou hast a tender sympathy
With ev'ry grief and pain;
For when thou wast a man on earth,
Thou didst the same sustain.

5 And tho' in heav'n exalted now,
Yet thou to us art near;
Know'st all our weaknesses and wants,
And list'nest to our pray'r.

6 What shall we say for this thy love,
But 'fore thee prostrate lie;
And thank thee that thou wast a man,
To all eternity.

154. T. 14.

WITH joy, we meditate the grace
Of our High-Priest above;
His heart is fill'd with tenderness,
His bowels yearn with love.

2 In all our griefs he takes a share,
He knows our feeble frame;
He knows what sore temptations are,
For he hath felt the same.

3 He in the days of feeble flesh,
Pour'd out strong cries and tears;
And, in his measure, feels afresh
What ev'ry member bears.

4 He'll never quench the smoking flax,
But raise it to a flame;
The bruised reed he never breaks,
Nor scorns the meanest name.

5 Then let our humble faith address
His mercy and his pow'r;
We shall obtain deliv'ring grace
In the distressing hour.

6 He ever lives to intercede
Before his Father's face;
Give him, my soul, thy cause to plead,
Nor doubt the Father's grace.

VIII. Of God, as manifested in the Creation, Preservation and Government of the World.

155.* T. 234.

O GOD, thou bottomless abyss!
Thee to describe I am not able;
I can't express thy properties, [ble!
Thy heights and depths unmeasura-
Thou'rt an unfathomable sea,
The God of universal nature:
True wisdom is not found in me,
I'm a short-sighted feeble creature.
I'd place thee full in view,
And give thee praises due;
But with mere weakness I'm surrounded;
For all that thou art, knows
Nor origin, nor close;
Ah, here my senses are confounded!

2 All sprung from thine omnipotence,
What now or ever hath subsisted:
No single atom comes by chance;
Wert thou not, nothing had existed.
Whate'er accosts our ear or eye,
Object of knowledge or the senses,
Derives its origin from thee,
Its being at thy word commences:
None can control thy will;
What is impossible
With men, thou to effect art able.
Thou to thyself alone
Art adequately known;
Thy wisdom is unmeasurable.

3 No limits thee can circumscribe,
Thy kingdom ev'ry where extendeth;
Who can thy greatness e'er describe?
Thy praise and power never endeth.
Thou stretchest to infinity,
Beyond the highest heavens seated;
Thy glorious name, thy majesty
Can never be conceiv'd or meted.
Thou art ador'd by all,
Each must before thee fall;
Whoe'er in confidence applied
To thee in his distress,
Prov'd thy unbounded grace,
And all his wants were well supplied.

4 Counsel and deed are one with thee,
And justice in thy court presideth;
Perfection's thine, without degree,
And love thy character abideth.
Mercy and faithfulness most true,
And grace and goodness beyond mea-
Are ev'ry morning to us new, [sure,
According to thy own good pleasure.
Each moment of our days
Thy tender care displays,
And some new pledge of mercy showeth.
What we are or shall be,
Must be deriv'd from thee,
From whom alone each blessing floweth.

5 Ah! who can render thee just praise?
Who? tho' his heart and tongue combined!
No temple is thy dwelling-place,
Thy worship cannot be confined;
By building shrines, where thou shalt be,
No man thy proper aim attaineth;
Thou lovest him, who trusts in thee,
And prostrate at thy feet remaineth;

What man performs for thee,
Shall his own profit be;
Thou of his gifts hast no occasion:
Thou dost on him bestow
Life, and salvation too;
But thou receivest no accession.

6 Thy hand rewards, tho' all is thine,
Thou! by whose fire thy foes must perish;
Altho' its genial warmth and shine
Thy friends meanwhile doth warm and cherish.
The seraphim with sweetest tone
Express their praise and adoration;
The elders, kneeling at thy throne,
Serve thee with deepest veneration.
Thine is the kingdom, pow'r,
And glory evermore!
With humble awe I sink ashamed
Before thy majesty;
Thou art essentially
All that is great and holy named!

156. T. 14.

Almighty God, thou sov'reign Lord,
'Fore thee we prostrate fall,
In heaven and on earth ador'd,
As the great Cause of all.

2 Thou canst not by our eyes be seen,
Thou art a spirit pure,
Who from eternity hast been,
And always shalt endure.

3 Present alike in ev'ry place
Thy Godhead we adore,
Beyond the bounds of time and space
Thou dwellest evermore.

4 In wisdom infinite thou art,
Thine eye doth all things see,
And ev'ry thought of ev'ry heart
Is fully known to thee.

5 Whate'er thou wilt, thou Lord, canst do
Here and in heav'n above,
But chiefly we rejoice to know
Almighty God is Love!

6 Thou lov'st whate'er thy hands have made;
Thy goodness we rehearse,
In shining characters display'd
Throughout the universe.

7 With longing eyes thy creatures wait
On thee for daily food;
Thy lib'ral hand provides them meat,
And fills their mouths with good.

8 Sweet is the mem'ry of thy grace,
My God, my heav'nly King!
Let age to age thy righteousness
In sounds harmonious sing

9 Creatures with all their endless race,
Thy pow'r and praise proclaim:
May we, who taste thy richer grace,
Delight to bless thy name!

157.* T. 22.

Monarch of all, with humble fear
To thee heav'n's hosts their voices raise,
Ev'n earth and dust thy bounties share:
Let earth and dust attempt thy praise.

2 Before thy face, O Lord most high!
Sinks all created glory down:
Yet be not wroth with me, that I
Vile worm, draw near thy awful throne.

3 Of all thou the beginning art,
Of all things thou alone the end:
On thee still fix my wav'ring heart,
To thee let all my actions tend.

4 Thou, Lord, art light: thy native ray
No shade, no variation knows;
To my dark soul thy light display,
The brightness of thy face disclose.

5 Thou, Lord, art love: from thee pure love
Flows forth in unexhausted streams;
Let me its quick'ning virtue prove,
O fill my heart with sacred flames!

6 Thou, Lord, art good, and thou alone:
With eager hope, with warm desire,
Thee may I still my portion own,
To thee in ev'ry thought aspire.

7 So shall my ev'ry pow'r to thee
In love and endless praises rise;
Yea, body, soul and spirit be
Thy ever living sacrifice.

8 Lord God almighty, ceaseless praise
In heav'n, thy throne, to thee is giv'n;
Here, as in heav'n, thy name we bless,
For where thy presence shines, is heav'n.

158. T. 14.

LONG ere the lofty skies were spread,
Jehovah fill'd his throne;
Ere man was form'd, or angels made,
The Maker liv'd alone.

2 His boundless years can ne'er de-
But still maintain their prime, [crease,
ETERNITY's his dwelling-place,
And EVER is his time.

3 While like a tide our minutes flow,
The present and the past,
He fills his own immortal NOW,
And sees our ages waste.

159.* T. 590.

LORD, when thou saidst, "So let it be,"
The heav'ns were spread, and shone,
And this whole earth stood gloriously;
Thou spak'st, and it was done;
The whole creation still records,
Unto this very day,
That thou art God, the Lord of lords;
Thee all things must obey.

160. T. 22.

LORD! I contemplate with delight
Thy various works, both day and night:
What glory shines thro' ev'ry part,
What boundless pow'r, what wondrous art!

2 All things in beauteous form ap-
By thy almighty Fiat rear'd: [pear'd,
At last thou from the dust didst raise
Thine image, Man, unto thy praise.

161. T. 22.

GIVE to our God immortal praise!
Mercy and truth are all his ways;
Give to the Lord of lords renown,
The King of kings with glory crown.

2 He built the earth, he spread the sky,
And fixt the starry lights on high:
He fills the sun with morning light,
He bids the moon direct the night.

3 He sent his Son with pow'r to save
From guilt, from darkness, and the grave:
Wonders of grace to God belong,
Repeat his mercies in your song.

4 Thro' this vain world he guides our feet,
And leads us to his heav'nly seat;
His mercies ever shall endure,
When this vain world shall be no more.

162. T. 166.

HIGH in the heav'ns, eternal God,
Thy goodness in full glory shines;
Thy truth shall break thro' ev'ry cloud
That veils on earth thy wise designs.
For ever firm thy justice stands,
As mountains their foundations keep;
Great are the wonders of thy hands;
Thy judgments are a mighty deep.

2 Thy providence is kind and large,
Both man and beast thy bounty share;
The whole creation is thy charge,
But man is thy peculiar care.
My God, how excellent thy grace!
Whence all our hope and comfort
The sons of Adam in distress [springs,
Fly to the shadow of thy wings.

3 From the provisions of thy house
We shall be fed with sweet repast;
There mercy, like a river, flows,
And we the living water taste.
Life, like a fountain rich and free,
Springs from thy presence, gracious
And in thy light divine we see [Lord,
The glories promis'd in thy word.

163.* T. 214.

I WILL sing to my Creator,
Unto God I'll render praise,
Who by ev'ry thing in nature
Magnifies his tender grace.
Nought but loving condescension
Still inclines his faithful heart
To support and take their part,
Who pursue his blest intention.

All things to their period tend,
But his mercy hath no end.

2 Yea, his Son his heart paternal
Freely did give up for me,
Me to save from death eternal
And from endless misery.
Depth of love past comprehension!
Whence can my weak spirit fetch
Thoughts profound enough to reach
This unfathom'd condescension!
All things, &c.

3 His good Spirit's blest instruction
In his word to me is giv'n,
Whose unerring manuduction
Leads me in the way to heav'n.
He endows my soul and spirit
With the light of living faith,
To o'ercome sin, world and death,
And escape the hell I merit.
All things, &c.

4 My soul's welfare he advances,
For my body he doth care;
Aid and comfort he dispenses,
When I call on him by pray'r;
When my nat'ral strength is shrinking,
In the time of utmost need,
He, my God, draws nigh with speed,
And recovers me from sinking.
All things, &c.

5 As a hen is us'd to gather
Her young brood beneath her wings,
So hath God, my heav'nly Father,
Kept me safe from hurtful things;
Had my God withdrawn his favor,
Had not his protecting grace
Sav'd me in each trying case,
I should have been helped never.
All things, &c.

6 Since nor end, nor bounds, nor mea-
In God's mercies can be found, [sure,
Heart and hands I lift with pleasure,
As a child in duty bound;
Humbly I request the favor:
Grant me grace both day and night,
Thee to love with all my might,
Till I change this infant savor
For that taste of bliss above,
Perfect praise and endless love.

164. T. 14.

WHEN all thy mercies, O my God,
My rising soul surveys,
Transported with the view, I'm lost
In wonder, love, and praise.

2 O how shall words with equal warmth
The gratitude declare,
That glows within my ravish'd heart!
But thou canst read it there.

3 Thy providence my life sustain'd,
And all my wants redrest,
When in the silent womb I lay,
And hung upon the breast.

4 To all my weak complaints and cries
Thy mercy lent an ear,
Ere yet my feeble thoughts had learnt
To form themselves in pray'r.

5 Unnumber'd comforts to my soul
Thy tender care bestow'd,
Before my infant-heart conceiv'd
From whom those comforts flow'd.

6 When in the slipp'ry paths of youth
With heedless steps I ran,
Thine arm, unseen, convey'd me safe,
And led me up to man.

7 Thro' hidden dangers, toils & deaths,
It gently clear'd my way,
And thro' the pleasing snares of vice,
More to be fear'd than they.

8 When worn with sickness, oft hast thou
With health renew'd my face;
And when in sin and sorrow sunk,
Reviv'd my soul with grace.

9 Ten thousand thousand precious gifts
My daily thanks employ;
Nor is the least a cheerful heart,
That tastes those gifts with joy.

10 Thro' ev'ry period of my life
Thy goodness I'll pursue;
And after death, in heav'n with thee,
The glorious theme renew.

11 Thro' all eternity to thee
A joyful song I'll raise:
But, O! eternity's too short
To utter all thy praise.

165. T. 14.

IN thee I live, and move, and am;
Thou number'st all my days:
As thou renew'st my being, Lord,
Let me renew thy praise.

2 From thee I am, thro' thee I am,
And for thee I must be:
'Twere better for me not to live,
Than not to live to thee.

3 Naked I came into this world,
And nothing with me brought;
And nothing have I here deserv'd;
Yet I have lacked nought.

4 I do not praise my lab'ring hand,
My lab'ring head, or chance;
Thy providence, most gracious God,
Is my inheritance.

5 Thy bounty gives me bread with peace,
A table free from strife:
Thy blessing is the staff of bread,
Which is the staff of life.

6 The daily favors of my God
I cannot sing at large;
Yet humbly can I make this boast,
I am th' Almighty's charge.

7 Lord, in the day, thou art about
The paths wherein I tread;
And in the night, when I lie down,
Thou art about my bed.

8 O let my house a temple be,
That I and mine may sing
Hosannas to thy majesty,
And praise our heav'nly King.

166.* T. 192.

HOW well, O Lord, art thou thy people leading,
Tho' oft thy ways seem wonderful and strange!
There can be nothing wrong in thy proceeding,
Because thy faithfulness can never change.
Thy ways seem often crooked, yet are straight,
In which thy children are ordain'd to walk:
Should all to ruin seem to go and wrack,
At last 'tis seen that thou art wise and great.

2 Far as from east to west, thy wisdom scatters
Things, which man's prudence to combine would try:
And that, which some would lay in bonds and fetters,
Is by thy power rais'd to reach the sky.
The contrary of what thou dost intend
Sometimes presents itself to human sight;
Man, while he thought he understood it right,
Is often disappointed in the end.

3 'Fore thee that's nought, which is the admiration
Of all; what's nothing, that thou lov'st, O Lord!
Fine words with thee find no recommendation,
Thy impulse must th' emphatic pow'r afford.
The haughty pharisee thou passest by,
To humble sinners thou dost mercy show;
Thy thoughts are very high, who can them know!
What human mind thy wisdom can descry!

4 We magnify thy name, O God of heaven!
Who, though thou kill'st, dost also quicken us;
When wisdom's treasures unto us are given,
Thy watchfulness, thy heart solicitous
To seek our good, thou dost 'fore us display:
To dwell among us is thy soul's delight;
Love doth thy kind paternal heart excite
To lead thy children on, from day to day.

5 Thou know'st, O Lord, how weak we are and feeble,
Thou clearly canst discern our ignorance;

To help ourselves we're utterly unable,
Our very actions prove our impotence.
Therefore thou tak'st us, thou dost us uphold; [faithfulness
Deal'st father-like, show'st mother's
Those sheep, which that they're thine, no man could guess,
Are ever fed, and kept within thy fold.

6 Sometimes it seems, thou art severely dealing,
Again art tender and compassionate:
Thy chastisement corrects us when we're failing,
Whene'er our minds seek to extravagate.
Then bashfulness forbids us to look up;
Thou pardon'st us, we promise better things;
Thy holy Spirit peace unto us brings,
And puts to all extravagance a stop.

7 O give me heav'nly wisdom's penetration, [shine!
Thou whose eye hateth all deceitful
That I distinguish nature's operation
From grace, that I discern thy light from mine,
Let no strange fire be kindled in my mind,
Which I might bring before thee foolishly,
And vainly think, O Lord, of pleasing thee:
How blest is he who thy true light doth find!

167.* T. 106.

HE that confides in his Creator,
Depending on him all his days,
Shall be preserv'd in fire and water,
And sav'd in many dang'rous ways.
He that makes God his staff and stay,
Builds not on sand that glides away.

2 What gain'st thou by thy anxious car-
What causes thee to pine away? [ing?
Thy rest and health thou art impairing
By sighs and groans from day to day;
Thou art but adding grief to grief,
Instead of getting sure relief.

3 Would we but be resign'd and quiet,
And rest in God's good providence,
Who oft prescribes us wholesome diet,
By methods cross to flesh and sense!
To him, who chose us for his own,
Our wants and cares are fully known.

4 He knows the hours for joy and gladness,
The proper time and proper place;
Are we but faithful 'midst our sadness,
Seek not ourselves, but seek his
He'll come, before we are aware, (praise:
And dissipate our grief and care.

5 God can this hour with ev'ry dainty
The poor man's table amply spread;
And strip the rich of all his plenty,
And send him out to beg his bread;
God can do wonders, if he please,
Humble the one, the other raise.

6 Do thou with faith discharge thy station,
Keep God's commands, and sing his
Rely on him for preservation, [praise;
On whom the whole creation stays.
The man that's truly wise and just,
Makes God, and God alone his trust.

168.* T. 151.

COMMIT thou thy each grievance
Into his faithful hands,
To his sure care and guidance,
Who heav'n and earth commands.
For he, the clouds' director,
Whom winds and seas obey,
Will be thy kind protector,
And will prepare thy way.

2 Rely on God thy Saviour,
So shalt thou safe go on;
Build on his grace and favor,
So shall thy work be done;
Thou canst make no advances
By self-consuming care;
But he his help dispenses,
When call'd upon by pray'r,

3 Thy faithfulness eternal,
O Father, certainly
What's good or detrimental
Doth for thy children see:
Thee all things serve in nature,
According to thy will;
Thou, as the great Creator,
Thy counsel dost fulfil.

4 My soul! then with assurance
Hope still, be not dismay'd;
He will from each incumbrance
Again lift up thy head:
Beyond thy wish extended
His goodness will appear,
When he hath fully ended
What caus'd thy needless fear.

169.* T. 595.

GIVE to the winds thy fears,
Hope, and be undismay'd;
God hears thy sighs and counts thy tears,
God shall lift up thy head;
Thro' waves, thro' clouds and storms,
He gently clears thy way;
Wait thou his time, so shall the night
Soon end in joyous day.

2 He ev'ry where hath way,
And all things serve his might,
His ev'ry act pure blessing is,
His path unsullied light:
When he makes bare his arm,
What shall his work withstand?
When he his people's cause defends,
Who, who shall stay his hand?

3 Leave to his sov'reign sway
To choose and to command,
With wonder fill'd, thou then shalt own
How wise, how strong his hand;
Thou comprehend'st him not,
Yet earth and heaven tell,
God sits as sov'reign on the throne,
He ruleth all things well.

4 Thou seest our weakness, Lord,
Our hearts are known to thee,
O lift thou up the sinking hand,
Confirm the feeble knee;
Let us, in life and death,
Boldly thy truth declare,
And publish, with our latest breath,
Thy love and guardian care.

170. T. 151.

CHILDREN of God lack nothing,
His promise bears them thro';
Who gives the lilies clothing,
Will clothe his people too;
Beneath the spreading heavens,
No creature but is fed;
And he, who feeds the ravens,
Will give his children bread.

2 Tho' vine, nor fig-tree neither,
Their wonted fruit should bear;
Tho' all the fields should wither,
Nor flocks nor herds be there:
Yet God the same abiding,
His praise shall tune my voice;
For, while in him confiding,
I cannot but rejoice.

171. T. 581.

QUIET, Lord, my froward heart,
Make me teachable and mild,
Upright, simple, free from art,
Make me as a weaned child:
From distrust and envy free,
Pleas'd with all that pleaseth thee.

2 What thou shalt to-day provide,
Let me as a child receive;
What to-morrow may betide,
Calmly to thy wisdom leave:
'Tis enough that thou wilt care,
Why should I the burden bear?

3 As a little child relies
On a care beyond his own,
Knows he's neither strong nor wise,
Fears to stir a step alone:
Let me thus with thee abide,
As my Father, Guard and Guide.

4 Thus preserv'd from Satan's wiles,
Safe from dangers, free from fears,
May I live upon thy smiles,
Till the promis'd hour appears,
When the sons of God shall prove
All their Father's boundless love.

IX. Of the Father, Son, and Holy Ghost.

172.* T. 132.

TO God on high all glory be!
And thanks that he's so gracious,
That hence to all eternity
No evil shall oppress us.
His word declares good will to men,
On earth is peace restor'd again
Thro' Jesus Christ our Saviour.

2 We humbly thee adore and praise,
And laud for thy great glory:
Father, thy kingdom lasts always,
Not frail, nor transitory;
Thy pow'r is endless as thy praise,
Thou speak'st, the universe obeys;
In such a Lord we're happy.

3 O Jesus Christ, thou Son belov'd
Of thy celestial Father,
By whom all enmity's remov'd,
And all the lost find succor; [Lord,
Thou slaughter'd Lamb, our God and
To needy pray'rs thine ear afford,
And on us all have mercy!

4 O Comforter, God Holy Ghost,
Thou Source of consolation,
From Satan's pow'r thou wilt, we trust,
Protect Christ's congregation,
The purchase of his bitter smart;
All evil graciously avert,
Lead us to life eternal.

173.* T. 97.

MOST holy, blessed Trinity;
God, prais'd to all eternity!
Lord over all, whose pow'r did frame
The world, and still upholds the same;
All things thou reconcilest unto thee;
With awe we now adore thy Majesty!

2 Father of Jesus, Lord of all,
Thee we our God and Father call,
Since Jesus made us by his blood
Children, and blessed heirs of God;
Eternal praise and thanks are due to thee,
From Christ's redeemed blood-bought property.

3 O Lamb of God, for sinners slain,
Who didst the human race regain,
And claim'st it as thy property;
Worthy art thou eternally!
For all we are and have, is thine alone,
Ah! take and keep us evermore thy own.

4 O Holy Ghost, to thee we raise,
With joyful hearts, our thanks & praise,
For leading us to Christ by faith,
And glorifying Jesus' death;
O grant us all the grace, in him t' abide,
That he may glory in a faithful bride.

5 We all say, Amen! deeply bow'd
In presence of the Triune God,
By whom in Christ we're fore-ordain'd,
To happiness that knows no end;
With grateful hearts we thank and praise the Lord,
His saving name for ever be ador'd!

174.* T. 230.

TO the Father thanks and praises,
Whose love in Christ to life us raises,
And comforts us in all distress;
Glory, thanks and adoration,
Be giv'n to Christ without cessation,
Whose presence yields us joy and peace;
The Spirit magnify
Who doth to us apply—Jesus' merit;
Our God revere,—He's present here,
Come, worship Him, with filial fear.

2 Father of the congregation,
O what abundant consolation
We in thy gracious counsel find
Which by Christ was manifested!
His coming in the flesh attested
Thy tender love to all mankind;
Thy name we magnify—To all eternity;
For thy mercies—unbounded are;
Thy love and care
Exceed our utmost wish and pray'r.

3 Lord, our matchless Friend & Brother,
Thy praises from each day to th' other
I'll sing, while I have breath in me:

God, as man to us related!
The grateful sense thou hast created,
To praise excites me pow'rfully;
Rise, spirit of gladness, rise,
Exalt his sacrifice,—Hallelujah!
In highest strain—To the Lamb slain,
Let heav'n and earth reply, Amen.

4 Holy Spirit, we adore thee,
And to thy name give praise and glory,
For graciously directing us,
To seek pardon, peace and favor
With God, thro' Jesus Christ our Saviour,
From whom alone salvation flows;
O fill us with his love, [honor,
So that our walk may prove—To his
And grant that we—Continually
May to thy voice obedient be.

175. T. 39.

O Father of mercy, be ever ador'd;
Thy love was displayed in sending our Lord [we praise
To ransom and bless us: thy goodness
For sending in Jesus salvation by grace.

2 Most merciful Saviour, who deignedst to die [to buy;
Our curse to remove, and our pardon
Accept our thanksgiving, almighty to save,
Who openest heaven to all that believe.

3 O Spirit of wisdom, of love, and of pow'r,
We prove thy blest influence, thy grace we adore:
Whose inward revealing applies our Lord's blood, [God.
Attesting and sealing us children of

176. T. 206.

O Father! hear—our humble pray'r:
Us kindly own
As children; since thy Son,
Whom thou so graciously—And free
Gav'st up to die,—Did satisfy
For Adam's race;
Procuring truth and grace.

2 Most gracious Lord,—Eternal Word!
Who flesh wast made,
Our Saviour, Friend and Head:
Thou Holy Lamb of God,—Thy blood,
Thy pains and death,—Preserve in faith
Thy church while here,
Till we 'fore thee appear.

3 Dear Comforter!—Receive our pray'r,
Instruct us, Lord,
That we may know thy word,
And thus in love and peace—Increase.
Oh may we all,—Both great and small,
Count all things loss
Save Jesus and his cross.

177. T. 58.

LORD God, Abba Father,
Who didst to bless us
Send thy own Son, our Lord, and call him Jesus, We worship thee.

2 God the Son, Redeemer,
Who by thy bleeding
Hast sav'd us sinners, and for us art pleading, Remember us.

3 Holy Ghost, we praise thee,
That Christ's revealed
Unto our hearts, and that by thee we're sealed Unto his day.

4 Bless'd Three! who bear record
In heav'nly places,
Vouchsafe to hear our fervent pray'rs and praises, For Jesus' sake.

178. T. 14.

OUR heav'nly Father, Source of love,
To thee our hearts we raise;
Thy all-sustaining pow'r we prove,
And gladly sing thy praise.

2 Lord Jesus, thine we wish to be,
Our sacrifice receive;
Made, and preserv'd, and sav'd by thee,
To thee ourselves we give.

3 Come, Holy Ghost, the Saviour's love
Shed in our hearts abroad;
So shall we ever live and move,
And be with Christ in God.

4 Honor to the almighty Three,
And everlasting One;
All glory to the Father be,
The Spirit, and the Son.

179. T. 68.

HOLY Trinity!
We confess with joy,
That our life and whole salvation
Flow from God's blest incarnation,
And his death for us
On the shameful cross:

2 Had we angels' tongues
With seraphic songs,
Bowing hearts and knees before thee,
Triune God! we would adore thee,
In the highest strain,
For the Lamb once slain.

180.* T. 185.

WITH thy presence, Lord, our Head and Saviour,
Bless us all, we humbly pray;
Our dear heav'nly Father's love & favor
Be our comfort ev'ry day;
May the Holy Ghost in each proceeding
Favor us with his most gracious leading;
Thus we shall be truly blest,
Both in labor and in rest.

181.* T. 58.

THAT our Lord's views with us may be attain'd,
We now commend ourselves, with faith unfeign'd,
To the Father's blessing, to the Son's favor,
The holy Spirit's guidance now and ever, The angels' guard.

182. T. 167.

MAY the grace of Christ our Saviour,
And the Father's boundless love,
With the Holy Spirit's favor,
Rest upon us from above!
Thus may we abide in union
With each other in the Lord;
And possess, in sweet communion,
Joys which earth cannot afford.

183. T. 166.

THAT peace which God alone reveals,
And by his word of grace imparts,
Which only the believer feels,
Direct, & keep, & cheer our hearts:
And may the holy Three in One,
The Father, Word, and Comforter,
Pour an abundant blessing down
On ev'ry soul assembled here!

184. T. 185.

THE LORD bless and keep thee in his favor,
As his chosen property;
The Lord make his face shine on thee ever,
And unto thee gracious be;
The Lord lift his countenance most gracious
Upon thee, and be to thee propitious,
And his peace on thee bestow:
Amen, Amen! Be it so!

185. T. 595.

YE angels round the throne,
And men that dwell below,
Worship the Father, love the Son,
And bless the Spirit too.

186. T. 22.

WITH grateful hearts we humbly praise
Our heav'nly Father for his grace,
Our Saviour who for sinners bled,
The Holy Ghost by whom we're led.

187. T. 22.

THE grace of our Lord Jesus Christ,
The love of God so highly priz'd,
The Holy Ghost's communion, be
With all of us most sensibly.

188.* T. 132.

NOW sing, thou happy church of God,
His favor'd congregation,
Redeem'd with Jesus' precious blood
From ev'ry tribe and nation:
Most holy, blessed Trinity,
For the Lamb slain, all praise to thee
Both now and ever! Amen.

X. Of our Heavenly Father.

189. T. 22.

OUR heav'nly Father is not known
To us, but in the Son alone;
His mercy, love, and boundless grace
We see display'd in Jesus' face.

2 O God! how dreadful was thy name,
Until the God-man Jesus came!
We cannot love nor honor thee,
Unless the Son hath made us free.

3 O love, no human tongue can tell!
O love divine, unsearchable!
The Father gave his only Son
For guilty sinners to atone.

4 Can any ill distress my heart,
Since God with his own Son did part?
Whate'er I want can't be deny'd,
Since Christ for me was crucify'd.

190. T. 14.

BEHOLD what love the Father hath
On guilty men bestow'd,
That we who children are of wrath,
Should children be of God!

2 O how beyond expression great
His love in Christ doth shine!
Tis like himself—th' eternal God!
Past knowledge! all divine!

3 Behold! for fallen, guilty man,
The Lord of glory dies;
Lays down his life, us to redeem,
A precious sacrifice!

4 Now doth our Lord, the Son of God,
Who for us liv'd and dy'd,
See of the travail of his soul,
And is well satisfy'd.

5 Peace and good-will are now to man
Most gloriously display'd,
And life eternal we obtain
From God, in Christ our Head.

6 O let us then repeat the theme,
Which always sounds above;
And ever sing, with joyful hearts,
The wonders of his love!

191.* T. 22.

THOU hast the world so greatly lov'd,
Father, that thou by mercy mov'd
Didst give thy well-beloved Son,
By death for all our sins t' atone.

2 That he all who in him believe,
Might in thy family receive;
His sacrifice so great, so dear,
Thou all-sufficient didst declare.

3 As children we are own'd by thee,
Since Christ our Brother deign'd to be;
We feel thy kind, paternal heart
To us who have in him a part.

4 The whole salvation of thy Son,
And all his merits make our own;
Yea, grant us richly, for his sake,
Of heav'nly blessings to partake.

5 Thou art our Father and our God,
Since Christ assum'd our flesh and blood;
Therefore in thee our trust we place,
And give thee never-ceasing praise.

192. T. 341.

THEE, O my God and King,
My Father, thee I sing,
Hear well-pleas'd the joyous sound,
Praise from earth and heav'n receive:
Lost, I now in Christ am found,
Dead, by faith in Christ I live.

2 Father, behold thy son,
In Christ I am thine own.
Stranger long to thee and rest,
See the prodigal is come:
Open wide thy arms and breast,
Take the weary wand'rer home.

3 Thine eye observ'd from far,
Thy pity view'd me near:
Me thy bowels yearn'd to see,
Me thy mercy ran to find,
Empty, poor, and void of thee,
Hungry, sick, and faint, and blind.

4 Thou on my neck didst fall,
Thy kiss forgave me all:

Still the gracious words I hear,
Words that made the Saviour mine,
"Haste, for him the robe prepare,
His best righteousness divine!"

193.* T. 580.

Rejoice, my soul, God cares for thee,
Trust to his word assuredly,
However things may go;
Thy heav'nly Father, for Christ's sake,
Of thy concerns will notice take,
And mercy freely to thee show.

2 My griefs & cares to thee well known,
My God, I cast on thee alone,
In thee is all my trust;
Since thou dost govern, I'll be still,
Into thy hands resign my will,
And thank thee prostrate in the dust.

3 I confidently do believe,
Me, thy poor child, thou wilt not leave,
For thou my Father art:
Fill thou my soul with love and faith,
Thus I am rich in life and death;
And from thy love nought shall me part.

194.* T. 90.

BE of good cheer in all your wants,
And stedfast on God's word rely;
He who the greatest favors grants,
The smallest never will deny:
If God could give his Son for us,
What can he then to us refuse?

195.* T. 132.

WHEN Christ, who sav'd us by his blood,
His foll'wers call'd together,
His farewell was, "I go to God,
To mine, and to your Father;"
Therefore, believing in the Son,
With filial love we humbly own
Thee, God, our God and Father.

196.* T. 96.

DEAR heav'nly Father, we adore
And thank thee for the dreadful pain
Thy Son, when he our sorrows bore,
For our redemption did sustain.

O grant that we may all our days
Live to exalt redeeming grace.

197.* T. 58.

O, SANCTIFY us by thy truth we pray,
Christ's glorious brightness in our hearts display,
We to thy protection ourselves surrender,
With filial confidence and love most tender, O Lord our God.

198.* T. 106.

DRAW me, O Father, to the Son,
That he may draw me unto thee;
Thy Spirit render me his own,
And rule without control in me;
Shed in my heart thy love abroad,
And keep me in thy peace, O God!

199. T. 14.

FATHER of all, almighty Lord!
Our Father, and our God!
Since Jesus Christ th' eternal Word,
Assum'd our flesh and blood.

2 Let all with love and filial fear
Thy sacred name adore;
O may thy kingdom soon appear,
And spread the world all o'er.

3 Help us thy pleasure to fulfil,
As done by heav'nly pow'rs;
Accomplish in us all thy will,
And let that will be ours.

4 Our souls and bodies feed, we pray,
With food which thou see'st best;
We ask our portion for the day,
And leave to thee the rest.

5 Let mercy pardon all our crimes,
Which justice must condemn;
As some have wrong'd us many times,
And we would pardon them.

6 Let not temptation us befall,
While here our race we run;
But rescue and defend us all
From sin, and th' evil one.

7 Thine is the kingdom, thine the pow'r
O'er angels, and o'er men;
The glory too for evermore
Is thine; Amen, Amen!

200. T. 166.

OUR Father, who in heaven art,
Hallow'd be thy most blessed name;
Thy kingdom come; thy will be done
Always in heav'n and earth the same;
Give us this day our daily bread;
Forgive our sins, as we forgive;
Into temptation do not lead,
But full release from evil give.

XI. Of Jesus Christ, the Son of God.

201. T. 22.

BEFORE the heav'ns were stretch'd [abroad,
From everlasting was the Word;
With God he was, the Word was God,
And must divinely be ador'd.

2 By his own pow'r were all things made;
By him supported all things stand;
He is the whole creation's Head,
And angels fly at his command.

3 Mortals with joy beheld his face,
Th' eternal Father's only Son;
How full of truth, how full of grace
Was Christ in whom the Godhead shone!

4 Archangels left their high abode,
To learn new myst'ries here & tell
The love of our descending God,
The glories of Immanuel.

202. T. 22.

MY song shall bless the Lord of all,
My praise ascend to his abode:
Thee, Saviour, by that name I call,
The great, supreme, the mighty God!

2 Without beginning or decline,
Object of faith, and not of sense;
Eternal ages saw him shine,
He shines eternal ages hence.

3 As much, when in the manger laid,
Almighty Ruler of the sky,
As when the six days work he made
Fill'd all the morning-stars with joy.

4 Of all the crowns Jehovah bears,
Salvation is his dearest claim;
That gracious sound well-pleas'd he hears,
And owns Immanuel for his name.

5 A cheerful confidence I feel,
My well-plac'd hopes with joy I see,
My bosom glows with heav'nly zeal
To worship him who dy'd for me.

6 As man he pities my complaint,
His pow'r and truth are all divine;
He will not fail, he cannot faint,
Salvation's sure and must be mine.

203.* T. 172.

THY majesty how vast it is!
And how immense the glory,
Which thou, O Jesus, dost possess!
Both heav'n and earth adore thee.
The numberless heavenly hosts laud thy name
Thy glory & might are transcendent;
Ten thousands of angels thy praises proclaim,
Upon thee gladly dependent.

5 The Father's Equal, God the Son,
With him thou ever reignest;
Thou art partaker of his throne,
And all things thou sustainest.
Both angels and men view their Maker as man,
With joy that is past all expression;
O happy, unspeakably happy who can
Find in him life and salvation!

3 This myst'ry ev'ry throne and pow'r
Admires with adoration;
Th' angelic choirs for evermore
Extol his incarnation:

The angels and elders before him fall
down,
With accents melodious him praising;
Unto the Lamb slain, and to him on
the throne,
They render glory unceasing.

4 The church on earth in humble
Exalteth Christ our Saviour; [strain,
She sings, "The Lamb for us was slain,
Our foe is cast for ever;
For Christ hath redeem'd us by his
precious blood
Out of ev'ry nation and kindred,
And made us thereby kings and priests
unto God,
To him thanksgiving be render'd."

5 When Christ shall come, in majesty,
With all his bright attendance,
And as the Judge in equity
On men pass final sentence: [dread,
Then shall all his enemies quaking with
Wish mountains and rocks them to
cover;
The ransom'd with gladness will lift
up their head,
And live with Jesus for ever.

204. T. 14.

O THE delights, the heav'nly joys,
The glories of the place,
Where Jesus sheds the brightest beams
Of his o'erflowing grace!

2 Sweet majesty and awful love
Sit smiling on his brow,
And all the glorious ranks above
At humble distance bow.

3 Princes to his imperial name
Bend their bright sceptres down:
Dominions, thrones, and pow'rs rejoice
To see him wear the crown.

4 Upon that dear majestic head
That cruel thorns did wound,
See what immortal glories shine
And circle it around!

5 This is the Man, th' exalted Man,
Whom we unseen adore;
But when our eyes shall see his face,
Our hearts shall love him more.

205. T. 341.

WORTHY, O Lord, art thou,
That ev'ry knee should bow,
Ev'ry tongue to thee confess;
Universal nature join,
Strong and mighty thee to bless,
Gracious, merciful, benign!

2 Hail your dread Lord and ours,
Dominions, thrones and pow'rs!
Source of pow'r he rules alone:
Veil your faces, prostrate fall,
Cast your crowns before his throne,
Hail the Cause, the Lord of all!

3 Justice and truth maintain
Thy everlasting reign;
One with thine almighty Sire,
Partner of an equal throne;
King of kings, let all conspire
Gratefully thy sway to own.

4 Jesus, thou art my King,
To me thy succor bring.
Christ the mighty One art thou,
Help for all on thee is laid:
This thy promise claim I now,
Send me down the promis'd aid.

5 Triumph and reign in me,
And spread thy victory:
Sin, and death, and hell control,
Pride and self, and ev'ry foe;
All subdue, thro' all my soul,
Conqu'ring and to conquer go.

206.* T. 97.

THOU reign'st above on heaven's
throne,
The Father's Equal, God the Son;
The Holy Ghost to us displays
Thy majesty and boundless grace,
And in the Scriptures clearly doth ex-
plain,
That thou, Lord, madest, and redeem-
edst man.

2 With awe and reverence 'fore thee,
And at thy name we bow the knee,
As all in earth and heaven join,
T' extol thy majesty divine,
And thee, to God the Father's glory, call
The great Jehovah, mighty Lord of all.

207. T. 595.

JESUS, my Lord, my God!
The God supreme thou art,
The Lord of hosts whose precious blood
Is sprinkled on my heart.

2 Jehovah is thy name;
And thro' thy blood apply'd,
Convinc'd and certify'd I am,
There is no God beside.

3 Soon as the Spirit shows
That precious blood of thine,
The happy, pardon'd sinner knows
It is the blood divine.

4 Yea only he, who feels:
"My Saviour for me dy'd,"
Is certain that the Godhead dwells
In Jesus crucify'd.

208.* T. 58.

OUR gracious God be praised evermore,
That Jesus Christ, who all our sorrows bore,
To our hearts so clearly is manifested,
That with conviction 'tis by us attested
That he is God.

2 O blessed truth which with deep awe is heard,
Truth worthy evermore to be rever'd:
To the man Christ Jesus, a name is given
Above all names; all knees in earth and heaven 'Fore him must bow.

3 Of this great truth we boldly witness bear,
And to mankind this doctrine will declare,
That he, who to save us assum'd our nature
And suffer'd on the cross, is the Creator Of heav'n and earth.

209. T. 595.

PREPARE a thankful song
To the Redeemer's name!
His praises should employ each tongue,
And ev'ry heart inflame.

2 He laid his glory by,
And dreadful pains endur'd,
That rebels, such as you and I,
From wrath might be secur'd.

3 Upon the cross he dy'd,
Our debt of sin to pay;
The blood and water from his side
Wash guilt and sin away.

4 And now he pleading stands
For us, before the throne;
And answers all the law's demands
With what himself hath done.

5 He sees us willing slaves
To sin, and Satan's pow'r;
But with an outstretch'd arm, he saves,
In his appointed hour.

6 The Holy Ghost he sends
Our stubborn souls to move,
To make his enemies his friends,
And conquer them by love.

7 The love of sin departs,
The life of grace takes place,
Soon as his voice invites our hearts
To rise and seek his face.

8 The world and Satan rage,
But he their pow'r controls;
His wisdom, love and truth engage
Protection for our souls.

9 Tho' press'd, we need not yield,
But shall prevail at length,
For Jesus is our Sun and Shield,
Our Righteousness and Strength.

10 Assur'd that Christ our King
Will put our foes to flight,
We on the field of battle sing,
And triumph while we fight.

210. T. 595.

HOSANNA to the Son
Of David, and of God,
Who brought the news of pardon down,
And seal'd it with his blood.

2 To Christ, th' anointed King,
Be endless blessings giv'n;
Let the whole earth his glory sing,
Who made our peace with heav'n.

211. T. 14.

ALL glory to the Saviour's name!
Let angels prostrate fall;
Bring forth the royal diadem,
And crown him Lord of all.

2 Ye saints in glory, who with joy
Have left this earthly ball,
Your most triumphant songs employ,
Extol the Lord of all.

3 Children of God, who walk by faith,
Ye ransom'd from the fall,
Show forth your dear Redeemer's death,
Confess him Lord of all.

4 Let ev'ry tribe, and ev'ry tongue
That hear the Saviour's call,
Unite in one harmonious song,
And hail him Lord of all!

212.* T. 125.

THOU Maker of each creature,
The Father's arm and might,
Thou rulest o'er all nature,
In thy own name and right.
May we in ev'ry station
Enjoy thy great salvation,
And simply follow thee.

2 Lord, let us be increasing
In love and knowledge too;
That we, on thee believing,
In spirit serve thee so,
As in our hearts to savor
Thy matchless grace and favor,
And always for thee thirst.

213.* T. 68.

JESUS, who with thee
Can compared be?
Source of rest and consolation,
Life and light, and full salvation:
Son of God, with thee
None compar'd can be!

2 Life! thou dyd'st for me,
From all misery
And distress me to deliver,
And from death to save for ever:
I am by thy blood
Reconcil'd to God.

3 Highest King and Priest,
Prophet, Lord, and Christ!
Thy dear sceptre is embraced
By me at thy feet abased:
I choose Mary's seat
At thy holy feet.

4 Nigh to thee draw me,
Give me faith on thee
To depend, and daily bolder
Cast all mis'ry on thy shoulder,
Which I feel in me;
Draw me nigh to thee.

5 Grant me steadiness,
Lord, to run my race,
Foll'wing thee with love most tender,
So that Satan may not hinder
Me by craft or force;
Further thou my course.

6 By thy Spirit's light,
Me instruct aright,
That I watch and pray with fervor,
Trusting thee, my soul's Preserver:
Love unfeign'd, O Lord,
Unto me afford.

7 Give me courage good,
That my wealth and blood
I for thee could spend, my Saviour,
Hating world and sin for ever;
Since for me, my God,
Thou didst shed thy blood.

8 When I hence depart,
Strengthen thou my heart,
And into thy realms convey me,
In thy righteousness array me,
That at thy right-hand
Joyful I may stand.

214. T. 583.

THE blessed names of Jesus Christ impart [trite heart:
Strength and rich comfort to the con-
As King, he over those the rule doth bear, [are.
Who in his kingdom faithful subjects

2 He is the Rock, on him we build most sure,
And thus 'midst raging tempests are secure;

The Corner-stone, he of the church is nam'd. [fram'd.
In whom the building's fitly join'd and

3 As Leader, he before his people goes,
And constant vict'ry gains o'er all his foes:
He is our High-priest, having no compeer, [are.
Our names upon his breast engraven

4 Our only Master, who instructs us right; [Prophet's light:
To know God's will we need this
Our Counsellor he is; if we believe
His words, nor flesh, nor world can us deceive.

5 Of all the feeble he the Strength remains,
As Hero in the fight he conquest gains:
Him Everlasting Father,* all must own;
As Prince of peace, he to his church is known. * *Isaiah*, ix. 6.

6 As Lord, none dare his sov'reign will control;
He is thy Lord, be joyful, O my soul!
His name is Wonderful, who can reveal
His thoughts divine, immense, unsearchable!

7 He is the Life, by whom all things subsist;
The Way, which cannot ev'n by fools be miss'd;
The Truth, in which we may confide; the Light [of night.
Which shines resplendent in the shades

8 The Word, by whom all things at first were made,
Who even now to life can raise the dead:
He's our Redeemer, who hath shed his blood,
The world to save, and reconcile to God.

9 Thee, gracious Lord, our Saviour we confess,
Since we're partakers of thy saving grace:
Thou dost our cause before thy Father plead,
As Advocate, and for us intercede.

10 To thee, the Mercy-seat, we may draw nigh,
And confidently on thy name rely:
As Lamb, thou didst become a sacrifice
For us, and pay in blood our ransom-price.

11 As Bridegroom of the soul, the church thy bride
To thee, who purchas'd her, is close ally'd. [sake,
As Head, thy body thou wilt ne'er for-
But of each member special notice take.

12 As Shepherd, thou thy sheep dost richly feed,
Protect from harm, and to green pastures lead:
O Bread of life, whereby alone we live,
Thro' thee we everlasting life receive.

13 O living Fountain, he who drinks of thee
Shall thirst no more to all eternity.
Thou art the Vine, and we the branches are,
Deriving juice from thee, we fruit can bear.

14 Our All in all, sole Source of peace and rest,
Thyself to each more clearly manifest:
O thou who art unchangeably the same,
Grant us to prove the virtue of thy name!

215. T. 341.

O Day-spring from on high!
In mercy hear my cry:
See the travail of thy soul,
Saviour, and be satisfy'd;
Rule in me without control,
May I ever thine abide.

2 Jesus, who art the Tree
Of immortality,
Feed this tender branch of thine;
By thy influence I shall thrive;
Thou the true, the heav'nly Vine!
Grafted into thee I live.

3 Of life the Fountain thou!
I know, I feel it now.
Faint and dead no more I droop;
Thou reviv'st me, thy supplies
Ev'ry moment springing up,
Unto life eternal rise.

4 Thou the good Shepherd art;
From thee I'll never part.
Thou my Keeper and my Guide,
Watch me still with tender care;
Gently lead me by thy side,
Kindly in thy bosom bear.

5 Thou art my daily Bread!
O Christ, thou art my Head!
Countless benefits on me,
As thy body's member flow;
Nourish'd I, and fed by thee,
Up to thee in all things grow.

6 Prophet, to me reveal
Thy Father's perfect will.
Never mortal spake like thee;
Lord, may I by thee be taught,
May I listen eagerly
To thy words, with comfort fraught.

7 High-priest, on thee I call,
Thy blood aton'd for all.
Thou dost still in heav'n above
As the Lamb once slain appear;
There remember me in love,
Plead for me a sinner there.

8 Jesus, thou art my King,
Praises to thee I sing,
Kept by thy almighty hand,
Saviour, who shall pluck me thence?
Faith supports, by faith I stand,
By the faith thou dost dispense.

210. T. [illegible]

COME, worship at Immanuel's feet;
Behold in him what wonders meet!
Words are too feeble to express
His worth, his glory, or his grace.

2 Christ is our Head; each member lives,
And owns the vital pow'r he gives:
The saints below, and saints above,
Join'd by his Spirit, and his love.

3 He is the Vine; his heav'nly root
Supplies each branch with life and fruit:
O may a lasting union join
My soul, as branch, to Christ the Vine!

4 He is the Rock; how firm he proves!
The Rock of ages never moves:
But the sweet streams that from him flow,
Attend us all the desert through.

5 He is the Sun of Righteousness,
Diffusing light, and joy, and peace:
What healing in his beams appears,
To chase our clouds and dry our tears!

6 Yet faintly to us mortals here
His glory, grace and worth appear;
His beauties we shall clearly trace,
When we behold him face to face.

XII. Of the Holy Ghost, and his Gifts and Operations.

217.* T. 203.

COME, Holy Ghost! come, Lord our God!
And shed thy heav'nly gifts abroad
On us, and unto ev'ry heart
True faith and fervent love impart.
O Lord, who by thy heav'nly light,
Hast call'd thy church from sinful night,
Out of all nations, tribes and places;
To thee we render thanks and praises.
Hallelujah! :||:

2 Thou Light divine! most gracious Lord!
Revive us by thy holy word,
And teach thy flock in truth to call
On God, the Father of us all:
From all strange doctrines us preserve,
No other masters may we serve,
But Christ, who is our only Saviour!
In him we will confide for ever.
Hallelujah! :||:

3 O Holy Ghost! kind Comforter!
Help us, with watchfulness and pray'r,

'Midst various trials thee t' obey,
And never from the truth to stray:
O Lord, by thy almighty grace,
Prepare us so to run our race,
That we by thy illumination,
May gain heav'n's glorious habitation.
Hallelujah! :||:

218.* T. 58.

GOD Holy Ghost, in mercy us preserve,
That we from Jesus' doctrine never swerve,
Guide us, till to finish our race permitted
To Jesus' presence we shall be admitted. Have mercy, Lord!

2 O grant us thy divine, thy saving light,
That we may understand Christ's mind aright;
That we may in Jesus abide for ever,
Who gain'd a place in heav'n for each believer. Have mercy, Lord!

3 Thou Source of love, God Holy Ghost, inspire
Our lifeless souls with love's celestial fire:
May we, as Christ's members, be join'd together
In unity, and truly love each other. Have mercy, Lord!

4 O thou our highest comfort in all need,
Grant that we neither shame nor death may dread;
Should we even suffer hard persecution,
O give us grace to stand without confusion. Have mercy, Lord!

219.* T. 22.

TO thee, God Holy Ghost, we pray,
Who lead'st us in the gospel-way,
Those precious gifts on us bestow,
Which from our Saviour's merits flow.

2 Thou heav'nly Teacher, thee we praise
For thy instruction, pow'r and grace,
To love the Father, who doth own
Us as his children in the Son.

3 Thee of ourselves we could not know,
Till thou, O Lord, didst clearly show
The sin of unbelief to us,
Of enmity to Jesus' cross.

4 When this we felt to be our case,
Then Jesus' blood and righteousness
Unto our hearts thou didst reveal,
Imparting thus thy pard'ning seal.

5 Most gracious Comforter, we pray,
O lead us further every day!
Thy unction to us all impart,
Preserve and sanctify each heart.

6 Till we in heav'n shall take our seat,
Instruct us often to repeat,
"Abba, our Father!" and to be
With Christ, in union constantly.

220.* T. 58.

THOU Comforter and Guide of Jesus' train,
Who dost thyself her ministers ordain,
Look on us in mercy, grant us thy favor,
Our souls and bodies we devote for ever, O Lord, to thee.

2 Where'er we look around, both far and near,
The pow'r and glory of the Lord appear,
And such flocks of Jesus are multiplying,
Who only wish to live, themselves denying, Unto thy praise.

3 O thou life-giving Stream! the earth o'erflow,
Whatever would obstruct thy course, break through,
O most gracious Spirit! hear our petition,
Teach all to turn to Jesus with contrition, Thy office 'tis.

4 We pray thee fill us all with Jesus' love,
That we may in his service faithful prove:

Teach us all to deem it the greatest favor,
With humble, contrite hearts to serve our Saviour Till we shall rest.

5 Unto Christ's congregations in each place,
Grant, 'midst all trials, comfort, peace, and grace:
O may all believers, in ev'ry station,
Rejoice in Jesus, and in his salvation,
God Holy Ghost!

221.* T. 9.

HOLY Ghost, thou God and Lord
Of thy Congregation,
We to thee with one accord
Pay our adoration.

2 For thy teachings, heav'nly Guide,
O accept our praises!
Have we thee, we're well supply'd
With good gifts and graces.

3 Thou explainest unto us
Jesus' incarnation,
And how he upon the cross
Purchas'd our salvation.

4 Thou fill'st with the gospel light
Every land and nation,
Aidst thy witnesses, with might,
Under tribulation.

5 Us to Jesus thou hast brought,
And wilt keep us ever
In the faith which thou hast wrought,
Thro' thy grace and favor.

6 With maternal faithfulness
Lead his ransom'd people,
And to please him give them grace,
Bear them up when feeble.

7 Daily Jesus' flock thanks thee
For thy kind tuition;
O may we obedient be,
Thro' thy benediction!

8 Grant, that we may never lose,
Till our dying moment,
The rich comfort which to us
Flows from Christ's atonement.

9 For, our heav'nly Father's love,
Jesus' great compassion,
And thy patience, ever prove
Our strong consolation.

10 Amen, Lord God, Holy Ghost,
Endless thanks and praises
Gives to thee the ransom'd host,
In the name of Jesus.

222.* T. 58.

GOD Holy Spirit, be for ever blest,
That thou to us Christ's death dost manifest,
And of him the Fountain, whence flows salvation,
Dost so distinctly give us information,
And light impart.

2 What of the Father and the Son we know
To thy divine instructions all we owe,
Thro' thy operations we are assured,
That Jesus Christ, who death for us endured, Is Lord and God.

3 Thanks for revealing to us the Lamb slain,
And that his blood would have been shed in vain,
Had to sanctify us ought else availed,
And could our souls have otherwise been healed, Than by his stripes.

4 Christ's meritorious suff'rings are the sum,
And sole foundation of true Christendom;
We enjoy, thro' mercy, those comforts blessed,
Of which, thro' thee, believers are possessed, While here on earth.

5 The blood of Christ alone can joy impart,
Can heal, revive, and cheer the contrite heart;
Therefore show still clearer to us his merit,
And lead us daily more, God Holy Spirit, Into all truth.

6 Have patience with us sinners ev'ry day,
Forgive us all our trespasses we pray;
O instruct & warn us without cessation;
And with thy peace, thy love and consolation, Fill all our hearts.

7 Of Christ we'll gladly testify each hour,
Until his kingdom shall appear with pow'r;
Then will all see clearly, how thou hast trained
God's children, when they once shall have attained To bliss complete.

8 Blest Comforter, vouchsafe us all the grace,
To yield thee joy for thy great faithfulness,
For thy love and patience; from sin protect us,
And in the narrow way to life direct us, Thou heav'nly Guide!

223.* T. 4.

O SPIRIT of grace!
Thy kindness we praise,
In showing to us,
That life and salvation proceed from Christ's cross.

2 In darkness we stray'd,
Until we were led
By thee to believe,
That Jesus, our Saviour, will sinners receive.

3 Our hearts thou didst cheer,
Dispelling all fear;
We humbly could claim [name.
Salvation and pardon in Jesus' dear

4 Grant us to obey
Thy teachings, we pray,
O Spirit of love, [to prove.
And thankful to thee, for thy mercies,

5 We wish to afford
To Jesus, our Lord,
For his bitter pain, [train.
Joy, honor and glory, 'midst his chosen

6 O therefore impart
Thyself to each heart,
That thus we may show,
In our whole behaviour, that Jesus we know.

7 Grant us to increase
In knowledge and grace,
Rejoicing by faith
In Jesus' atonement, wrought out by his death.

224.* T. 22.

O Comforter, God Holy Ghost!
Thou heav'nly gifts on us bestow'st;
The Pledge of our salvation art,
And bear'st thy witness in our heart.

2 The sheep of Jesus, which were lost,
Thou callest, teaching them to trust
For help, forgiveness, peace and grace,
In him, the Lord our Righteousness.

3 Thy unction freely dost impart
To ev'ry poor and contrite heart,
Which Jesus as the Saviour knows,
From whom alone salvation flows.

4 The feeble souls thou dost sustain,
Anointest all the witness train;
Keepest believers in the faith,
And art their Guide in life and death.

5 Who can thy operations trace,
Thy kindness, patience, truth & grace,
Which on God's children thou bestow'st
O Comforter, God Holy Ghost!

225. T. 583.

O Holy Ghost, within my soul repeat
Those blessings which once made this day so great;
Breathe thou upon me with that heav'nly wind,
That it refresh and purify my mind.

2 Kindle within me, and preserve that fire,
Which will with holy love my breast inspire,
And with an active zeal my soul inflame
To do thy will, and glorify thy name.

3 Endow me richly with thy gifts and grace
To fit me for the duties of my place;

So open thou my lips, my heart to raise,
That both my heart and lips may give
thee praise.

4 As in thy temple, keep thou residence
Within my soul, and never part from
thence,
Until I'm fitted and prepar'd by thee
Life to exchange for immortality.

226. T. 582.

COME, Holy Spirit, come,
Let thy bright beams arise;
Dispel the darkness from our minds,
And open all our eyes.

2 Revive our drooping faith,
Our doubts and fears remove;
And kindle in our breast the flame
Of never-ceasing love.

3 Convince us of our sin,
Then lead to Jesus' blood;
And to our stubborn hearts reveal
The hidden love of God.

4 'Tis thine to cleanse the heart,
To sanctify the soul,
To pour fresh life on ev'ry part,
And new-create the whole.

5 If thou, O Comforter!
Thine influence withdraw,
What easy victims soon we fall
To conscience and the law!

6 No longer burns our love;
Our faith and courage fail;
Our sin revives, and death and hell
Our feeble souls assail.

7 Dwell therefore in our hearts;
Our minds from bondage free:
Then shall we know, and praise, and
love
The Father, Son, and Thee.

227. T. 582.

SPIRIT of truth, come down,
Reveal the things of God,
Make thou to us Christ's Godhead
known,
Apply his precious blood.
His merits glorify,
That each may clearly see,
Jesus, who did for sinners die,
Hath surely dy'd for me.

2 No man can truly say
That Jesus is the Lord,
Unless thou take the veil away,
And breathe the living word:
Then, only then we feel
Our int'rest in his blood,
And cry with joy unspeakable,
"Thou art my Lord, my God!"

3 O that the world might know
The all-atoning Lamb!
Spirit of faith, descend and show
The virtue of his name;
The grace which all may find,
The saving pow'r, impart;
O testify to all mankind
And speak in ev'ry heart!

228. T. 14.

COME, Holy Ghost, eternal God,
Proceeding from above,
Both from the Father and the Son,
Thou God of peace and love.

2 Thou art the only Comforter
In all our soul's distress;
Thou showest us our unbelief,
And Christ's redeeming grace.

3 Thou dost thy sanctifying gifts
Unto the church impart;
Writest God's holy, precious law
On each believer's heart.

4 Thy holy unction pow'r affords
The gospel to proclaim:
By thee enabled, we set forth
Salvation in Christ's name.

5 Assist and strengthen us, O Lord!
Thou know'st we all are frail:
Grant, neither Satan, world, nor flesh,
May o'er Christ's flock prevail.

6 Cause all disharmony and strife
In Christendom to cease:
And give to all the flocks of Christ
Love, union, truth, and peace.

229. T. 14.

COME, blessed Spirit, gracious Lord,
Thy pow'r to us make known;
Strike with the hammer of thy word,
And break each heart of stone.

2 Give us ourselves, and Christ, to know
In this our gracious day;
Repentance unto life bestow,
Christ's pard'ning love display:

3 Convince us first of unbelief,
And freely then release;
Fill ev'ry soul with sacred grief,
And then with sacred peace.

4 Show us our poverty, relieve
And then enrich the poor;
The knowledge of our sickness give—
The knowledge of our cure.

5 A blessed sense of guilt impart,
And then remove the load;
Trouble, then lead the troubled heart
To Christ's atoning blood.

6 Vanquish our lusts, our pride remove,
Take out the heart of stone;
Show us the Father's boundless love,
The merits of the Son.

7 The Father sent his Son to die;
The willing Son obey'd;
The witness Thou, to ratify
The purchase Christ hath made.

230. T. 14.

O Holy Ghost, eternal God,
Descending from above,
Thou fill'st the soul, thro' Jesus' blood,
With faith, and hope, and love.

2 Thou comfortest the heavy heart,
By sin and grief opprest;
Thou to the dead dost life impart,
And to the weary, rest.

3 Thy sweet communion charms the soul
And gives true peace and joy;
Which Satan's pow'r can ne'er control,
Nor all his wiles destroy.

4 Let no false comfort lift us up
To confidence that's vain:
Nor let their faith and courage droop,
Who love the Lamb once slain.

5 Breathe comfort where distress abounds,
O make our conscience clean;
And heal, with balm from Jesus' wounds,
The fest'ring sores of sin.

231. T. 14.

COME, Holy Spirit, on us breathe,
With all thy quick'ning pow'rs;
Kindle our love, confirm our faith,
Warm these cold hearts of our's.

2 Assure my conscience of her part
In the Redeemer's blood;
And bear thy witness in my heart,
That I am born of God.

3 Thou art the Earnest of his love,
The Pledge of joys to come:
O lead us, that we may above
Obtain our lasting home.

232. T. 580.

BREATHE on these bones so dry and dead,
God Holy Ghost! thy influence shed
In all our hearts abroad:
Point out the place, where grace abounds;
Direct us to the bleeding wounds
Of Jesus, our incarnate God.

2 Convince us that the Lamb was slain
For us, and to our minds explain
The myst'ry of the cross:
Let us our dear Redeemer see,
And serve and love him fervently;
This be our gain, else all things loss.

233. T. 90.

O That the Comforter would come!
Nor visit as a transient Guest,
But fix in me his constant home,
And keep possession of my breast;
Yea, make my soul his blest abode,
The temple of th' in-dwelling God.

2 Come, Holy Ghost, my soul inspire,
Attest that I am born again;
Come and baptize me, Lord, with fire,
Nor let thy former gifts be vain:
Grant me a sense that I'm forgiv'n,
A pledge that I'm an heir of heav'n.

3 Grant me th' indisputable seal,
That ascertains the kingdom mine!
That pow'rful stamp I long to feel,
The signature of love divine:
O shed it in my heart abroad,
Fulness of love, of heav'n, of God!

234.* T. 230.

THOU great Teacher, who instructest
Christ's flock, and us to bliss conductest,
Who noblest gifts to grant didst deign
To th' apostles, thine anointed,
By thee for that great work appointed
To teach, reprove and comfort men,
And freely offer grace
Unto the Gentile race;
Lord, have mercy!
Grant us to be—Immoveably
Fix'd on their ground, upheld by thee!

XIII. Of God's Call of Grace to the unconverted Sinner.

235.* T. 583.

TEACH us, O Lord! the cross's mystery,
And grant us docile hearts to learn of thee;
Thou art as full of love to fallen man,
As when for our redemption thou wast slain.

2 "I thirst," thou didst upon the cross exclaim,
And on thy throne, thy thirst is still the same;
Not for the blood of foes who scorn thy love,
But that they may thy pard'ning mercy prove.

3 Thou hast no pleasure in the sinner's death,
But callest him to come & live by faith;
Thou sendest messengers of peace abroad,
Beseeching men, "Be reconcil'd to God!

4 "Believe, thou mourning sinner, that for thee
"The Lord did penance on the cross's tree;
"Thereby he triumph'd over sin and hell,
"And gain'd for thee a right in heav'n to dwell.

5 "Tho' then unborn, tho' not in person there,
"Yet in that act of grace thou hast a share;
"Pardon of sin was then for thee procur'd,
"When Jesus death for ev'ry man endur'd.

6 "For all who flee from Sinai's fiery wrath,
"And look to Calv'ry's sacrifice by faith,
"The Judge supreme, to whom all pow'r is giv'n,
"Ordaineth pardon, happiness and heav'n.

7 "Just as thou art, to Jesus come, and live;
"Repenting sinners Jesus will receive;
"Be thou e'er so corrupt and stain'd with sin,
"Fear not, his precious blood can wash thee clean."

8 Who finds that sin hath quite o'erspread his soul,
That his own efforts ne'er can make him whole,
Helpless at Jesus' feet resolves to lie,
Jesus hath sworn that sinner shall not die.

9 Tho' he was dead before, behold, he lives,
The Saviour quick'ning, whom the Father gives;
Henceforth must sin lie vanquish'd at his feet,
Thro' faith in Jesus, he shall vict'ry meet.

10 How pleasing 'tis, a new-born soul to view,
How doth its happiness our own renew!
Might all the pow'r of Christ's atonement prove,
And know the virtue of his dying love!

236.* T. 217.

MY Saviour sinners doth receive,
Whom, with sin's galling load oppressed,
No man nor angel can relieve,
Who have no hope to be redressed;
Who loathe the world and all its ways,
Dread wrath divine, and mourn for grace;
On whom the law pronounceth sentence,
Condemn'd to hell in their own conscience;
Such wretched sinners find reprieve,
Since Jesus sinners doth receive.

2 The fondest mother cannot have
Towards her darling such affection,
As Jesus show'd, vile man to save;
His love exceedeth our conception.
He left his throne and blest abode,
To bear the sinner's heavy load.
Since he now thro' his death & suff'ring
Hath made an all-sufficient off'ring,
Our debt is paid, and we may live;
For Jesus sinners doth receive.

3 Now is his sympathizing heart
A refuge for the most distressed;
He freely pardon will impart;
By him their debt is quite erased.
His blood like th'ocean without ground,
Their sins hath swallow'd up & drown'd,
The Holy Ghost to them is given,
Who leads them in the path to heaven;
And prompts them always to believe,
That Jesus sinners doth receive.

4 They by the Father are esteem'd,
When thus presented by our Saviour;
Heal'd by his wounds, from sin redeem'd
They prove the Father's love & favor;
He owns them as his sons and heirs,
And all he hath their own declares;
Eternal life they now inherit,
Procur'd for them by Jesus' merit;
He dwells in them, in him they live,
Since Jesus sinners doth receive.

5 Might all his loving heart but see,
And know his bowels of compassion
To sinners, straying carelessly,
Or such as mourning seek salvation:
Him, when on earth 'midst sinners trace;
Zaccheus takes his saving grace;
He comforts Magd'len in affliction,
Regards her tears and deep conviction,
Her sins, tho' many, he forgives;
My Saviour sinners poor receives.

6 Behold how he with Peter dealt,
Tho' deep his fall, he show'd him favor.
Not only when on earth he dwelt
Was he a sin-forgiving Saviour;
No, he is still the very same,
Just, good and merciful his name;
As he was in humiliation,
So is he still in exaltation.
Repenting souls, you may believe,
Our Saviour sinners doth receive.

7 Come, sinners, come, tho' vile and base;
Returning prodigals he meeteth;
He freely offers them his grace,
Them with a pard'ning kiss he greeteth.
Why wilt thou stand in thy own way?
Why wilfully be Satan's prey?
Wilt thou sin's drudge remain for ever,
Tho' he appear'd thee to deliver?
Do not delay, sin's service leave,
Since Jesus sinners will receive.

8 Come, ye that heavy laden are,
Come, weary, void of self-assistance;
Tho' doubting, ready to despair,
Come but to him without resistance.
Behold his heart with love replete,
Full of desire the worst to meet;

Long hath he sought for you though
wretched,
You to embrace, his arms outstretched:
O come to him, believe and live;
My Saviour sinners doth receive.

9 Object not, "I'm a wretch too base,
Too oft his goodness I have slighted,
Too often spurned at his grace,
I, who was gen'rously invited."
Is your repentance now sincere?
Your sorrow genuine? Do not fear;
His pow'r and mercy are unbounded,
None, trusting him, was e'er confounded:
He saves whom nought else can relieve;
My Saviour sinners doth receive.

10 Think not, "'tis time enough," nor say,
"God who is gracious beyond measure,
Shuts not the door of grace to-day;
I'll first enjoy some carnal pleasure."
No, God forbid! if you are wise,
Grace, offer'd now, do not despise.
Who slights to-day the invitation,
May ever miss of his salvation.
Come now to Jesus, come and live;
To-day he sinners doth receive.

11 Draw me, a sinner, unto thee,
Thou sinner's Friend, thou gracious Saviour;
Grant I, and all may ardently
Desire thy pardon, grace and favor.
When sin assails, and gives us smart,
Show us thy wounded, loving heart;
May none, who feels sin's condemnation,
Neglect thy gen'rous invitation,
But all experience and believe
That Jesus sinners doth receive!

237.* T. 205.

SINNERS! come, the Saviour see,
Hands, feet, side, and temples view;
See him bleeding on the tree,
See his heart is pierc'd for you!
View awhile, then haste away,
Find a thousand more, and say,
Come, ye sinners, come with me,
View him bleeding on the tree.

2 Who would still such mercy grieve?
Sinners! hear instruction mild,
Doubt no more, but now believe,
Each become a little child;
Artful doubts and reas'nings be
Nail'd with Jesus to the tree;
Mourning souls, who simple are,
Surely shall the blessing share.

3 Thro' his poverty, the poor
May eternal riches gain;
Open'd is heav'n's mercy-door,
None that comes, need come in vain.
Here now freely take who will,
Each poor sinner take his fill;
Rich in grace hereby commence,
Blush no more for indigence.

4 They who search their hearts with care,
And the blame their own confess,
In the Lamb's redemption share,
To his wounds have free access.
They, who deem'd themselves the chief
Of all sinners, and receive
Full forgiveness, peace and rest,
Pard'ning grace can relish best.

5 Cover'd with a holy shame,
Pardon'd sinners they remain:
Yet their freedom they proclaim,
Their adoption they maintain.
Soon as we begin to cease
Trusting in our righteousness,
Ceases the tormenting strife,
All within is peace and life.

238. T. 585.

COME, ye sinners, poor and wretched,
Weak and wounded, sick and sore!
Jesus ready stands to save you,
Full of pity, love and pow'r:
He is able, :||:
He is willing; doubt no more.

2 Ho! ye needy, come and welcome;
God's free bounty glorify:
True belief, and true repentance,
Ev'ry grace that brings us nigh,
Without money, :||:
Come to Jesus Christ and buy.

3 Come, ye weary, heavy-laden,
Lost and ruin'd by the fall,
If ye tarry till ye're better,
Ye will never come at all,
Not the righteous, :||:
Sinners Jesus came to call.

4 Let not conscience make you linger,
Nor of fitness fondly dream;
All the fitness he requireth,
Is to feel your need of him:
This he gives you, :||:
'Tis the Spirit's glimm'ring beam.

5 Agonizing in the garden,
Lo, your Maker prostrate lies!
On the bloody tree behold him,
Hear him cry before he dies;
"It is finish'd!" :||:
Sinner, will not this suffice?

6 Lo! th' incarnate God ascended
Pleads the merit of his blood;
Venture on him, venture freely,
Let no other trust intrude;
None but Jesus :||:
Can do helpless sinners good.

7 Saints and angels, join'd in concert,
Sing the praises of the Lamb;
While the blissful seats of heaven
Sweetly echo with his name:
Hallelujah! :||:
Sinners, here, may sing the same.

239. T. 591.

SINNER, hear thy Saviour's call,
He now is passing by;
He hath seen thy grievous thrall,
And heard thy mournful cry:
He hath pardon to impart,
Grace to save thee from thy fears;
See the love that fills his heart,
And wipe away thy tears.

2 Why art thou afraid to come,
And tell him all thy case?
He will not pronounce thy doom,
Nor frown thee from his face:
Wilt thou fear Immanuel?
Wilt thou dread the Lamb of God,
Who, to save thy soul from hell,
Hath shed his precious blood!

3 Think how on the cross he hung,
Pierc'd with a thousand wounds!
Hark, from each as with a tongue
The voice of pardon sounds!
See, from all his bursting veins,
Blood, of wondrous virtue, flow!
Shed to wash away thy stains,
And ransom thee from woe.

4 Tho' his majesty be great,
His mercy is no less;
Tho' he thy transgressions hate,
He feels for thy distress:
By himself the Lord hath sworn,
He delights not in thy death;
But invites thee to return,
That thou may'st live by faith.

5 Raise thy downcast eyes, and see
What throngs his throne surround!
These, tho' sinners once like thee,
Have full salvation found:
Yield not then to unbelief!
While he saith, "there yet is room;"
Tho' of sinners thou art chief,
Since Jesus calls thee, come.

240. T. 22.

COME, sinners, to the gospel-feast;
Let ev'ry soul be Jesus' guest;
Not one of you need stay behind;
His gospel calleth to mankind.

2 Attend! the gospel trumpet sounds,
Calls sinners from earths farthest bounds;
The year of Jubilee is come!
Return, ye ransom'd sinners, home.

3 Come all ye souls by sin opprest,
Ye wand'rers, who are seeking rest;
The poor, the maim'd, the halt, the blind,
With Christ a hearty welcome find.

4 The message as from God receive;
Ye all may come to Christ and live;
O let his love your hearts constrain,
Nor suffer him to die in vain!

5 His love is mighty to compel;
His conqu'ring love consent to feel:
Yield to his love's almighty pow'r,
And strive against your God no more.

6 See him set forth before your eyes,
A precious bleeding sacrifice!

His offer'd benefits embrace,
And freely now be sav'd by grace.

7 This is the time, no more delay;
This is the acceptable day:
Come in this moment, at his call,
And live for him, who dy'd for all!

241. T. 22.

SINNERS, obey the Gospel word!
Haste to the supper of the Lord:
Be wise to know your gracious day!
All things are ready; come away!

2 Ready the Father is to own,
And kiss his late returning son:
Ready your loving Saviour stands,
And spreads for you his pierced hands.

3 Ready the Spirit to impart
Grace to subdue the stubborn heart;
To shed Christ's love in you abroad,
And witness you are born of God.

4 Ready for you the angels wait,
To triumph in your blest estate:
All heav'n is ready to resound,
"The dead's alive, the lost is found!"

5 Come, sinners, to your gracious Lord,
Incline your ear, and hear his word;
His offer'd grace with joy receive,
Hear sinners, and your souls shall live.

242. T. 22.

HO! ev'ry one that thirsts, draw nigh,
'Tis God invites man's fallen race;
Salvation without money buy,
Buy wine, and milk, and gospel-grace.

2 Come to the living waters, come,
Sinners, obey your Maker's call;
Return, ye weary wand'rers, home,
God's grace in Christ is free for all.

3 Ye heavy laden, sin-sick souls,
See from the Rock a fountain rise;
For you in healing streams it rolls
From Jesus, made a sacrifice!

4 Nothing you in exchange need give;
Leave all you are, and have, behind:
Thankful the gift of God receive,
Pardon and peace in Jesus find.

5 In search of empty joys below,
Ye toil with unavailing strife:
Whither, ah! whither would ye go?
Christ hath the words of endless life.

6 To you he calls, "my goodness prove,
My promises for all are free:
O taste my everlasting love,
And let your souls delight in me."

243. T. 205.

SINNERS, hear the joyful news,
God, your Maker, is your Friend:
Think not, that his wrath pursues,
That his curses you attend.
"As I live," Jehovah saith,
"I do not desire your death,
"Rather, rather would I see
"Each poor sinner turn to me."

2 O then turn to him, and live,
Turn to him with all your woe;
He is ready to forgive,
Ready blessings to bestow.
Outstretch'd see his arms of love,
Haste his tender heart to prove;
Haste, ye sinners, you will find,
Jesus casteth none behind.

244. T. 106.

YE sinners, in the gospel trace
The Friend and Saviour of mankind;
Not one of all th' apostate race,
But may in him salvation find.
His thoughts, his words, & actions prove,
His life and death—that God is love!

2 Behold the Lamb of God, who bears
The sins of all the world away;
A servant's form he meekly wears,
He dwells within a house of clay:
His glory thro' a veil is seen,
And God with God, is man with men.

3 Behold our God incarnate stands,
And calls his wand'ring creatures home;
He all day long spreads out his hands;
Come, weary souls, to Jesus come:
Tho' ye be e'er so much opprest,
Believe, and he will give you rest.

4 Ah, do not of his goodness doubt,
His saving grace for all is free;
He saith, "I ne'er will cast him out,
Who as a sinner comes to me;
I can to none myself deny:"
Come, sinners, come; why will ye die?

245. T. 151.

SINNERS, would ye be healed?
Then come to Jesus Christ;
In him is grace revealed,
Come only undisguis'd;
Come poor and miserable,
Draw nigh just as you are;
You'll find, that he is able
Your losses to repair.

2 His wounds are open fountains
To wash you white all o'er,
Yea, were your sins like mountains,
Or sands on ocean's shore;
Believe in the atonement
By Christ's all-saving blood;
Do not delay one moment,
Come to the Lamb of God!

246. T. 90.

WHERE shall my wond'ring soul begin
While I to heav'nly songs aspire?
A slave redeem'd from death and sin,
A brand pluck'd from eternal fire;
How shall I due thanksgivings raise,
And sound my great Deliv'rer's praise!

2 O how shall I the goodness tell
Saviour, which thou hast shown to me?
That I, a child of wrath and hell
A happy child of God should be;
Should know, should feel my sins forgiv'n,
And that I am an heir of heav'n!

3 Outcasts of men, to you I call,
Harlots and publicans, believe;
He spreads his arms t'embrace you all,
Repenting sinners he'll receive:
No need of him the righteous have,
He came the lost to seek and save.

4 Come, O my fellow sinners, come,
Groaning beneath sin's pond'rous weight;
He calls you now, invites you home!
Come quickly, ere it be too late;
Tho' foes protest, and friends repine,
He dy'd for crimes like your's and mine.

5 For you the healing current flow'd
From the Redeemer's wounded side;
Languish'd for you th' eternal God,
For you the Prince of glory dy'd!
Believe, your sins shall be forgiv'n;
Only believe, and your's is Heav'n.

247. T. 11.

NOW begin the heav'nly theme,
Praise ye Jesus' saving name;
Ye who Jesus' kindness prove,
Triumph in redeeming love.

2 Ye, who see the Father's grace
Beaming in the Saviour's face;
As to heav'n ye onward move,
Praise and bless redeeming love.

3 Mourning souls, dry up your tears,
Banish all your guilty fears;
Jesus will your guilt remove,
Prompted by redeeming love.

4 Ye, alas! who long have been
Willing slaves of death and sin;
Now from bliss no longer rove,
Stop and taste redeeming love.

5 Welcome all by sin opprest,
Welcome all to Jesus Christ;
Nothing brought him from above,
Nothing but redeeming love.

6 He subdu'd th' infernal pow'rs,
His tremendous foes and our's,
From their cursed empire drove,
Mighty in redeeming love.

7 Sing, ye ransom'd, to his praise,
Tune your songs to grateful lays;
Mortals, join the hosts above,
Join to praise redeeming love.

248.* T. 582.

"COME to me," saith the Lord,
"All ye who are opprest,
Weary and heavy-laden souls,
And I will give you rest."

2 "Whoe'er to me will come,
And th' offer'd grace receive,
Him I in no wise will cast out,
He shall be mine and live."

249.* T. 97.

SINNERS, your Maker is your Friend,
He calls you, to his call attend:
"Sure as I live," to you he saith,
"I ne'er desire the sinner's death,
"But that repenting he may turn to me,
"And live for ever." Lord, we come to thee!

XIV. Of Repentance unto Life.

250.* T. 132.

LORD Jesus Christ, my sov'reign Good,
Thou fountain of salvation!
Behold how sin's most dreadful load
Fills me with condemnation.
My sins indeed are numberless;
O Lord, regard my deep distress,
Relieve my guilty conscience.

2 In pity look upon my need,
Remove thou my oppression;
Since thou hast suffer'd in my stead,
And paid for my transgression;
Let me not yield to dark despair,
Nor live in constant dread and fear
Of death and condemnation.

3 When I review my mis-spent days
I feel a heavy burden;
Reflecting on my trespasses,
I scarce could hope for pardon;
But should be hopeless and forlorn,
Uncertain where for help to turn,
If I had not thy promise.

4 But thy reviving gospel-word,
Which leads me to salvation,
Doth joy unspeakable afford,
And lasting consolation.
This tells me, thou wilt not disdain
A broken heart replete with pain,
That turns to thee, O Jesus.

5 Me, heavy-laden sinner, hear,
To thee I make confession;
To my complaints now lend an ear,
Regard my supplication.
My longing is, O wash me clean
From ev'ry spot and stain of sin,
Like David and Manasseh.

6 Lord, I approach thy mercy-seat,
And pray thee to forgive me;
With contrite heart I thee intreat,
Show pity and receive me;
Cast all my sins and trespasses
Into the ocean of thy grace,
And them no more remember.

7 Oh, for thy name's sake, let me prove
Thy mercy, gracious Saviour!
The yoke, which galls me, soon remove,
Restore me to thy favor:
Thy love shed in my heart abroad,
That I may live to thee my God,
And yield thee true obedience.

8 Thy joyful Spirit give me pow'r,
Thy stripes heal my diseases;
Apply thy blood at my last hour
To save me, dearest Jesus!
Then to thy promis'd rest me bring,
That with the ransom'd I may sing
Thy praise above for ever.

251.* T. 132.

OUT of the deep I cry to thee,
My God! with heart's contrition;
Bow down thine ear in grace to me,
And hear thou my petition;
For if in judgment thou wilt try
Man's sin, and great iniquity,
Ah! who can stand before thee?

2 T' obtain remission of our sin,
No work of ours availeth;
We're helpless, guilty and unclean,
Unless God's grace prevaileth;
We're 'midst our fairest actions lost,
And none 'fore him of aught can boast,
We live alone thro' mercy.

3 Therefore my hope is in God's grace,
And not in my own merit;
On him my confidence I place,
Instructed by his Spirit:
His precious word hath promis'd me,
He will my joy and comfort be;
Thereon is my reliance.

4 Tho' sin with us doth much abound,
Yet grace still more aboundeth;
Sufficient help in him is found,
Where sin most deeply woundeth:
He the good Shepherd is indeed,
Who his lost sheep doth seek, and lead,
With tender love and pity.

252.* T. 75.

O Whither shall I fly,
Depress'd with misery?
Who is it that can ease me,
And from my sins release me?
Man's help I vain have proved,
Sin's load remains unmoved.

2 O Jesus, Source of grace!
I seek thy loving face,
Upon thy invitation,
With deep humiliation;
Oh, let thy blood me cover,
And wash my soul all over.

3 I thy unworthy child,
Corrupt throughout and spoil'd,
Beseech thee to relieve me,
And graciously forgive me
My sins, which have abounded,
And my poor soul confounded.

4 Thro' thy atoning blood,
That precious healing flood,
Purge off all sin and sadness,
And fill my heart with gladness;
Lord, hear thou my confession,
And blot out my transgression.

5 Thou shalt my comfort be,
Since thou hast dy'd for me;
I am by thee acquitted
Of all I e'er committed;
My sins by thee were carry'd,
And in thy tomb interred.

6 I know my poverty;
But ne'ertheless for me
Are all good gifts procured,
Since Jesus death endured:
Thus strengthen'd, I may banish
All fears, my foes must vanish.

7 Christ! thy atoning blood,
The sinner's highest good,
Is pow'rful to deliver,
And free the soul for ever
From all claim of the devil,
And cleanse us from all evil.

8 Lord Jesus Christ! in thee
I trust eternally:
I know I shall not perish,
But in thy kingdom flourish!
Since thou hast death sustained,
Life is for me obtained.

9 Lord, strengthen thou my heart,
To me such grace impart,
That nought, which may await me,
From thee may separate me;
Let me, with thee, my Saviour,
United be for ever.

253.* T. 123.

O LORD, afford me light!
I'm straying still in darkness,
And know myself not right.
This I perceive, alas!
Tho' I'm not what I was,
Yet what I ought to be
I find not yet in me.

2 I know 'tis not the same
To be a real christian,
Or only one in name:
To him alone is due
That name, who doth subdue
His lusts thro' Jesus' pow'r,
And lives to self no more.

3 Ah, my defect lies here—
My love to thee my Saviour,
Is not as yet sincere;
Hence grief doth me corrode,
I'm to myself a load,
I'm not inclin'd to part
With things that cause me smart.

4 Resolve my stubborn breast!
I must sincerely venture,
Else I shall find no rest.

If I but bid adieu
To ev'ry fleshly view,
And cleave to Christ alone,
The work at once is done.

5 Vile worm! should'st thou refuse
To Christ to be devoted,
Who dy'd upon the cross
To save thee by his death,
Who gave thee life and breath?
Who Christ hath for his Friend,
His bliss will never end.

6 The language of true faith
Is this: "Lord, my Redeemer,
Oh, by thy blood and death,
Be thou my Help and Shield,
To thee myself I yield.
I'm thine, and thine will be
To all eternity."

7 "Do what thou wilt with me;
If I am but prepared
A vessel fit for thee,
To live unto thy praise,
Cloth'd in thy righteousness,
And sanctify'd by grace;
Then happy is my case."

254. T. 14.

THE Lord first empties whom he fills,
Casts down whom he would raise;
He quickens, when the letter kills,
Exalting thus his praise.

2 All fears and terrors, when he smiles,
At once must disappear;
The bruis'd and wounded heart he heals,
And feeds with heav'nly cheer.

3 When he applies his healing blood
Unto a sin-sick soul;
This balsam pow'rful, precious, good,
Ne'er fails to make it whole.

4 He freely laid his majesty
And all his glory by,
That our wants, thro' his poverty,
He richly might supply.

5 He's full of grace and truth indeed,
Of peace, of life and light;
To all, that helpless sinners need,
He gives thy soul a right.

6 Tho' heav'n's his throne, he came from thence
To seek and save the lost;
Whate'er might be the vast expence,
His love would bear the cost.

7 On us he spent his life and blood,
Our losses to retrieve;
Mankind's redemption now holds good
For sinners who believe.

255. T. 96.

THE Lord descended from above,
Our loss of Eden to retrieve;
O God of mercy, grace and love,
If all the world in thee may live,
In me a quick'ning spirit be,
And witness thou hast dy'd for me.

2 Thou loving, all-atoning Lamb,
By all thy pain and agony,
Thy bloody sweat, thy grief and shame,
Thy cross and passion on the tree,
Thy meritorious death, I pray,
Take all, take all my sins away.

3 I'll be like Magd'len at thy feet,
And humbly bathe them with my tears;
The hist'ry of thy love repeat
In ev'ry mourning sinner's ears;
That all may hear the joyful sound,
That I, ev'n I, have mercy found.

256. T. 14.

IN thee, O Christ, is all my hope,
My comfort's all in thee,
Since I'm assur'd thy mercy's nigh,
And that thou stand'st by me.

2 Me, nor the saints on earth can help,
Nor angels near thy throne;
To thee I run, thy help to find,
In thee I trust alone.

3 I feel the load of sin so vast,
It sinks me to the grave:
But let thy blood wash out my sins,
Since me thou cam'st to save.

4 Cloth'd in thy righteousness divine,
O may I see thy face,
Receive the promise from above,
That I'm restor'd by grace.

5 On me, thy helpless worm, O Lord,
A living faith bestow;
That I thy mercy, truth and love,
May by experience know.

257. T. 205.

LONG I strove my God to love,
Long I strove his laws to keep,
Fain would fix my thoughts above,
Faintly hop'd I was his sheep;
But my striving all prov'd vain,
Still I found my heart in pain;
Yet ne'er all my vileness saw,
Till declar'd accurs'd by law.

2 When with sense of guilt opprest,
All my soul was sunk in fear,
Pain and anguish fill'd my breast;
Then did Jesus Christ appear:
Not with vengeance in his eyes,
No, but as a sacrifice
Acceptable unto God;
Glorious off'ring, precious blood!

3 He was offer'd on the tree,
Jesus the unspotted Lamb:
Worthy truth, great mystery!
By his blood salvation came.
By his stripes my wounds are heal'd,
By his death, God's love reveal'd;
We, once strangers far from God,
Are brought nigh by Jesus' blood.

258. T. 581.

SAVIOUR of thy chosen race,
View me from thy heav'nly throne;
Give the sweet relenting grace,
Soften thou this heart of stone;
Stone to flesh, O God, convert,
Cast a look, and break my heart!

2 By thy Spirit me reprove,
All my inmost sins reveal;
Sins against thy light and love
Let me see, and let me feel;
Sins, that crucify'd my God,
Sins, for which he shed his blood.

3 Jesus, seek thy wand'ring sheep,
Make me restless to return;
Bid me look on thee and weep,
Bitterly as Peter mourn;
Till I can, by grace restor'd,
Say: thou know'st, I love thee, Lord.

4 Might I in thy sight appear,
As the publican, distrest;
Stand, not daring to draw near,
Smite on my unworthy breast;
Utter the poor sinner's plea,
God, be merciful to me!

5 Ah, remember me for good,
Passing thro' this mortal vale!
Show me thy atoning blood,
When my strength and courage fail;
Let me oft in spirit see
Jesus, crucify'd for me!

259. T. 582.

AH! whither should I go,
Burden'd, and sick, and faint?
To whom should I my trouble show,
And pour out my complaint?
My Saviour bids me come,
Ah! why should I delay?
He calls the weary sinner home,
And yet from him I stray.

2 What is it keeps me back,
From which I cannot part?
Which will not let my Saviour take
Possession of my heart?
Some cursed thing unknown
Must surely lurk within,
Some idol which I will not own,
Some secret bosom-sin.

3 Jesus, the hind'rance show,
Which I have fear'd to see:
Yea, let me now consent to know
What keeps me back from thee.
Searcher of hearts, in mine
Thy trying pow'r display;
Into its darkest corners shine,
And take the vail away.

4 I now believe; in thee
Compassion reigns alone:
According to my faith, to me
O let it, Lord, be done!
In me is all the bar,
Which thou wouldst fain remove:
Remove it, then shall I declare,
That thou, O God, art love!

260. T. 582.

O LORD, how vile am I,
Unholy and unclean!
How can I venture to draw nigh
With such a load of sin?
And must I then indeed
Sink in despair and die?
Fain would I hope that thou didst bleed
For such a wretch as I.

2 That blood which thou hast spilt,
That grace which is thy own,
Can cleanse the vilest sinner's guilt,
And soften hearts of stone.
Low at thy feet I bow,
Oh pity and forgive:
Here will I lie, and wait till thou
Shalt bid me rise and live.

261. T. 14.

THE mist before my eyes remov'd
With wonder struck I see,
Dear Lord, the black, the num'rous crimes,
By which I've grieved thee.

2 These were the unrelenting foes,
Which made thee groan and cry;
Caus'd thee to shed thy precious blood,
And bow thine head, and die.

3 Thy love hath thaw'd my frozen heart,
And caus'd my tears to flow;
I now abhor that monster sin,
And find he is my foe.

4 I trust my guilt was done away
By my incarnate God,
Who felt, t' atone for man's offence,
The sin-avenging rod.

262. T. 11.

HEAR, O Jesus, my complaints,
Known to thee are all my wants;
Self-convicted, self-abhorr'd,
I approach thee, dearest Lord.

2 Known to thee, whose eyes are flame.
I thy love and pity claim:
With an eye of love look down,
Help me, Lord, O help me soon.

3 Break, O break this heart of stone;
Form it for thy use alone;
Bid each vanity depart,
Build thy temple in my heart.

4 This be my support in need,
That thou didst so freely bleed:
All my joys and hopes arise
From thy bleeding sacrifice.

5 This confirms me when I'm weak,
Comforts me, when I am sick,
Gives me courage, when I faint,
Well supplies my ev'ry want.

6 Saviour, to my heart be near,
Exercise thy Shepherd-care;
Guard my weakness by thy grace,
Fill my soul with heav'nly peace.

263.* T. 205.

OH, how great, how rich, how free,
Is the grace which Christ bestows!
Only cast your misery
At the foot of Jesus' cross;
Weeping at the throne of grace
Lie, and never quit the place,
Never till your suit's obtain'd,
Never till the blessing's gain'd.

264. T. 16.

NOTHING but thy blood, O Jesus!
Can relieve us from our smart;
Nothing else from guilt release us,
Nothing else can melt the heart.

2 Nothing else can ease our burthen:
Jesus' precious blood alone,
Can produce a sense of pardon,
And dissolve a heart of stone.

265.* T. 66.

BE not dismay'd—in time of need,
Thy Saviour knows thy irksome situation;
His heart is mild,—with pity fill'd,
Can't see thy grief without commiseration.

2 To Christ draw nigh—for help apply,
He will pour out on thee the oil of gladness;
He feels and knows—thy griefs and woes,
Will turn to joy and comfort all thy sadness.

266.* T. 36.

LORD Jesus Christ, if thou wert not my Saviour,
Were not thy blood still pleading in my favor.
Where should I, poorest among all the needy, Find succor ready!

2. What should I do, a sinner vile and wretched,
Were not thy arms of love to me outstretched,
But thou my Refuge art, my Consolation, And whole Salvation.

267.* T. 142.

HERE come I, my Shepherd, athirst after thee;
In mercy receive me, for mercy's my plea:
The word thou hast spoken,
Can never be broken;
Thou know'st I am needy, and greatly distrest,
Thou callest the weary to come and find rest.

XV. Of FAITH.

268.* T. 106.

NOW I have found the ground wherein,
Sure my soul's anchor may remain;
Ev'n Christ, who to atone for sin,
Was as a spotless victim slain;
Whose mercy shall unshaken stay
When heav'n and earth are fled away.

2 O Lord, thy everlasting grace
Our scanty thought surpasseth far:
Thou show'st maternal tenderness,
Thy arms of love still open are,
Thy heart o'er sinners can't but break,
Whether thy grace they slight or take.

3 God in man's death takes no delight;
Each soul may grace and life obtain,
In him, who left his glory bright,
Took flesh, and dy'd, and rose again:
And now he knocks times numberless
At our hearts' door, and offers grace.

4 O Love! thou bottomless abyss!
My sins are swallow'd up in thee;
Cover'd is my unrighteousness,
From condemnation now I'm free;
Since Jesus' blood, thro' earth and skies,
"Mercy, free boundless mercy!" cries.

5 By faith I plunge into this sea,
Here is my hope, my joy, my rest;
Hither, when sin assails, I flee,
I look into my Saviour's breast:
Away, sad doubt, and anxious fear—
"Mercy" is all that's written there.

6 Tho' waves and storms go o'er my head,
Tho' strength, and health, and friends be gone;
Tho' joys be wither'd all and dead;
Tho' ev'ry comfort be withdrawn;
Stedfast on this my soul relies,
Jesus, thy mercy never dies.

7 Fix'd on this ground may I remain,
Tho' my heart fail, and flesh decay;
This anchor shall my soul sustain,
When earth's foundations melt away:
Mercy's full pow'r I then shall prove,
Lov'd with an everlasting love!

269.* T. 22.

IN holy writ it is avow'd
That Christ was Israel's Cov'nant-God,
The Church's everlasting Head,
God of the living and the dead.

2 All things were made by Christ, the Word,
By Christ was man to life restor'd;
The Prophets, strong in faith and bold,
His coming in the flesh foretold.

3 No wonder therefore that we read,
Abra'm to see his day was glad;
Isaiah too his glory saw,
And spoke of him with joy and awe.

4 'Tis sure that by his bitter pain,
He for mankind did life obtain,
Did for his church on earth atone,
And for the ransom'd round the throne.

5 We love the Lamb of God who dy'd:
Whoever seeketh ought beside,
Belongs not to our company;
Christ is our All eternally.

6 Our theme within the church shall be,
Christ's wounds, his griefs and agony!
Our theme when to the world we call,
His blood, the ransom paid for all.

270. T. 22.

FAITH comes by hearing God's record
Concerning Jesus Christ the Lord;
The happy means, which heav'n hath blest
To bring us to the gospel-rest.

2 The joyful sound is news of grace,
Redemption of a fallen race,
Thro' Jesus' righteousness divine,
Which bright from faith to faith doth shine.

3 The promise of immortal bliss
We have in Christ our Righteousness;
By this our righteousness is bought,
Faith pleads that right, but buys it not.

4 True faith receives the offer'd good
And promise seal'd with Jesus' blood:
Faith gives no title to the bliss,
But takes the Saviour's righteousness.

5 In the Redeemer, as my Head,
The cov'nant is established:
In him the promises are Yea,
In him Amen, and not in me.

271. T. 14.

HAIL, Alpha and Omega, hail!
Thou Author of our faith,
The Finisher of all our hopes,
The Truth, the Life, the Path.

2 Hail, First and Last, thou great I AM!
In whom we live and move;
Increase our little spark of faith,
And fill our hearts with love.

3 O let that faith which thou hast taught
Be treasur'd in our breast;
The evidence of unseen joys,
The substance of our rest.

4 Then shall we go from strength to strength
From grace to greater grace;
From each degree of faith to more,
Till we behold thy face.

272. T. 106.

FROM life and grace, (this we are bold
Before an erring world t' assert,)
Nothing one moment doth withhold
A man, but his unwilling heart:
In our dear Lord there's no delay,
Fix'd is his will, and plain his way.

2 Should any one of serious frame,
That long hath seem'd to seek his face,
His tedious tasks and trials name,
Preparatory steps of grace;
We say, "No, Christ requires them not,
And this fine web a false heart wrought."

3 Should any think he's so hemm'd in
With sin, as to be past relief,
Alas! he knows not, that the sin,
Which binds his soul, is unbelief:
If to the cross we lift our eye,
Then sin and Satan soon must fly.

4 Ready our Saviour is indeed,
His glorious work in all to do;
To ev'ry one it must be said,
"Thou hadst been happy long ago,
Hadst thou in faith cast all thy care
On Jesus Christ, who heareth pray'r."

273. T. 22.

BY various maxims, forms and rules,
That pass for wisdom in the schools,
I strove my passion to restrain;
But all my efforts prov'd in vain.

2 But since my Saviour I have known,
My rules are all reduc'd to one;
To keep my Lord, by faith, in view,
This strength supplies, and motives too.

3 I see him lead a suff'ring life,
Patient, amidst reproach and strife;
And from his pattern courage take
To bear and suffer for his sake.

4 Upon the cross I see him bleed,
And by the sight from guilt am freed;
This sight destroys the life of sin,
And quickens heav'nly life within.

5 To look to Jesus as he rose
Confirms my faith, disarms my foes;
Satan I shame and overcome,
By pointing to my Saviour's tomb.

6 Exalted on his glorious throne,
I see him make my cause his own;
Then all my anxious cares subside,
For Jesus lives, and will provide.

7 I see him look with pity down,
And hold in view the conqu'rors crown;
If press'd with griefs and cares before,
My soul revives, nor asks for more.

8 By faith I see the hour at hand
When in his presence I shall stand;
Then it will be my endless bliss,
To see him where, and as he is.

274.* T. 11.

LAMB of God, who thee receive,
Who in thee desire to live,
Cry by day and night to thee,
As thou art, so let us be.

2 Fix, O fix our wav'ring mind,
To thy cross us firmly bind:
Gladly now we would be clean;
Cleanse our hearts from ev'ry sin.

3 Dust and ashes tho' we be,
Full of guilt and misery;
Thine we are, thou Son of God,
Take the purchase of thy blood.

4 Sinners who in thee believe
Everlasting life receive;
They with joy behold thy face,
Triumph in thy pard'ning grace.

5 Life deriving from thy death,
They proceed from faith to faith,
Walk the new, the living way
Leading to eternal day.

6 Blest are they who follow thee,
While this light of life they see;
Filled with thy sacred love
They thy quick'ning power prove.

7 Praise on earth to thee be giv'n,
Never-ceasing praise in heav'n;
Boundless wisdom, pow'r divine,
Love unspeakable are thine!

275. T. 14.

HEAL us, Immanuel, here we are,
Waiting to feel thy touch;
Deep wounded souls to thee repair,
And, Saviour, we are such.

2 Our faith is feeble, we confess,
We faintly trust thy word;
But wilt thou pity us the less?
Be that far from thee, Lord!

3 Remember him who once apply'd,
With trembling, for relief;
"Lord, I believe," with tears he cry'd,
"O help my unbelief."

4 She too, who touch'd thee in the press,
And healing virtue stole,
Was answer'd, "Daughter, go in peace,
Thy faith hath made thee whole."

5 Conceal'd amidst the gath'ring throng,
She would have shunn'd thine eyes;
And if her faith was firm and strong,
Strong were her doubts likewise.

6 Like her, with hopes and fears, we come,
To touch thee if we may;
Oh! send us not despairing home,
Send none unheal'd away.

276.* T. 184.

O JESUS, 'fore whose radiation
The seraphim must cover'd stand,
When, in their awful ministration,
They wait for thy supreme command:
How can this body's eyes, dim-sighted,
Which by sin's gloomy misery
And earthly shadows are benighted,
Endure thy glorious light to see!

2 Yet let by faith my penetration
Reach ev'n within the sanctuary;
Thy mercy be my consolation,
May this uphold and strengthen me.
Reach unto me thy sceptre gracious,
Who low, like Esther, 'fore thee bow,
Say, "I will be to thee propitious,
And loving kindness to thee show."

3 O Jesus, show thy great compassion
Unto the soul that pants for thee;
Hear thou my humble supplication,
My God, be merciful to me!
I know thou art with pity filled
To sinners who thy mercy crave;
My pardon by thy blood is sealed,
I know 'twas shed my soul to save.

4 I recommend myself for ever
To thee, with filial confidence;
I pray, O Lord, regard in favor
My tears, and humble penitence;
I thro' thy death am justified,
No condemnation is in me;
I shall remain to thee allied
Since I am reconcil'd to thee.

5 O let thy Spirit still attend me,
Nor from my soul withdraw his light,
Protect, and graciously defend me,
And order all my steps aright;
That I may, without variation,
By humbly walking in thy ways,
Suit to thy will my conversation,
While here I run my mortal race.

6 Give me the armor of the Spirit,
Support me with thy pow'rful aid,
Then bold in faith, I need not fear it,
When hostile pow'rs would me invade.
Thus will thy kingdom, mighty Saviour,
In which true righteousness is seen,
Be further'd by my weak endeavor;
There grace and truth for ever reign.

7 O yes, above all else I'll love thee;
My heart, tho' worthless, be thine own;
Could infinite compassion move thee
To leave for me thy heav'nly throne?
Then let my heart be dedicated
To thee; fix there thy residence
Till I shall be to heav'n translated,
In joy to see thy countenance.

8 Lord, while my faith to thee ascendeth,
O may thy grace descend to me;
Thou art my joy which never endeth,
O fill my heart with love to thee.
I will adore and love thee longer,
Than while my heart its throbs repeats;
The flame of love shall break forth stronger,
When here my pulse no longer beats.

277. T. 14.

MISTAKEN souls! that dream of heav'n
And make their empty boast
Of inward joys, and sins forgiv'n,
While they are slaves to lust.

2 Vain are our fancies, airy flights,
If faith be cold and dead;
None but a living pow'r unites
To Christ the living Head.

3 'Tis faith that changes all the heart,
'Tis faith that works by love,
That bids all sinful joys depart,
And lifts the thoughts above.

4 'Tis faith that conquers earth and hell,
By a celestial pow'r;
This is the grace that shall prevail
In the decisive hour.

5 True faith obeys its Author's will,
As well as trusts his grace;
A pard'ning God is jealous still
For his own holiness.

6 When from the curse he sets us free,
He makes our nature clean;
Nor would he send his Son to be
The minister of sin.

7 His Spirit purifies the heart,
And seals our peace with God;
True holiness nought can impart
But Jesus' cleansing blood.

278.* T. 37.

THO' ev'ry child of God
Is a new creature,
Yet do we feel the load
Of sinful nature;
Which, if by faith we cleave
To Christ our Saviour,
Can, tho' it cause us grief,
Condemn us never.

2 He's merciful and kind
Past all expression;

If we are but inclin'd
To make confession
Of all our sinfulness,
His great compassion
Prompts him to grant us peace,
And consolation.

3 He grants us, for our tears,
His oil of gladness;
Delivers, heals and cheers,
Dispels our sadness:
Yea, tho' our bodies die,
His resurrection
Proves, they shall certainly
Rise to perfection.

4 My portion is the Lord,
I seek his favor;
And in his name and word
Confide for ever.
Nought in the world to me
Can yield such pleasure,
As to be found in thee,
O Christ, my Treasure!

5 Therefore I'll humbly cleave
To my Creator,
Who, that my soul might live,
Assum'd my nature;
Redeem'd me by his blood,
And bitter passion;
Thanks to the Lamb of God
For my salvation!

279.* T. 184.

WHEN rising winds, and rain descending,
A near approaching storm declare,
With trembling speed their wings extending,
The birds to hollow trees repair;
Thus I, in faith with sin oppressed,
My refuge take, O Christ to thee;
Thy wounds, my hiding-place most blessed,
From ev'ry evil shelter me.

XVI. Of the FORGIVENESS of SINS.

280.* T. 97.

JESUS, our glorious Head and Chief,
Dear Object of our hearts' belief,
O let us in thy nail-prints see
Our pardon and election free;
And, while we view by faith thy pierced side,
Call thee our Lord and God, who for us dy'd.

2 The doctrine of Christ's blood and death,
Imparting life to us thro' faith,
A myst'ry is, which is reveal'd
To babes, but from the wise conceal'd;
Thereby the Saviour's flock on earth is known;
Of this the ransom'd sing before God's throne.

3 While human nature doth exist,
While Jesus reigns as Lord and Christ,
So long of the whole gospel this
From first to last the substance is;
All, to whom God his counsel doth reveal,
To this as truth divine can set their seal.

4 Should any virtuous seem to be,
And blameless from his infancy,
And scarcely ever have been try'd
By avarice, by lust, or pride,
And therefore think, 'I am a child of God'
He's deaf and blind, and quite mistakes the road.

5 All those who, thro' a beam of light,
Can see and own they are not right,
But enter on a legal strife,
Amend their former course of life,
And toil & labor hard from day to day;
Such also miss to happiness the way.

6 But sinners, who, with pungent smart,
Bewail the vileness of their heart,
Mourning because of unbelief,
Of sinners deem themselves the chief,
Despairing of their self-made righteousness,
They may depend on Jesus' saving grace.

7 To such he saith, "Arise and live,
I freely all thy sins forgive,
I have redeem'd thee, thou art mine,
Thyself in faith to me resign;

Obey my voice, and walk in all my ways,
I'll grant to thee in heav'nly realms a place."

8 His Holy Spirit we receive,
And on our Saviour's word believe;
We trust in his atoning death,
As the foundation of our faith,
And in his robe of righteousness array'd,
Are 'midst his chosen richly comforted.

9 The humble sinner's shame we feel,
And pow'r divine to do God's will,
These are combin'd in ev'ry heart
That in Christ's merits hath a part;
No more, for want of strength, good motions die,
Since Jesus gives us constant victory.

10 We rest in Christ, and yet desire,
Because his love our hearts doth fire,
To serve his cause with all our might,
And deem our Saviour's burden light;
Don't we succeed, we think ourselves to blame,
And if we do, we praise his holy name.

11 Should self-complacency take place,
When we review our faithfulness,
We're soon with inward shame bow'd down,
Forget ourselves, and freely own,
That Jesus works in us whate'er is good,
And thank him for the pow'r he hath bestow'd.

12 Grace is the only wish and pray'r,
Of all those who God's children are;
They meditate by night and day,
How they may true obedience pay
To Jesus, who redeem'd us by his death;
And grace unmerited supports their faith.

281.* T. 22.

THE Saviour's blood and righteousness
My beauty is, my glorious dress;
Thus well array'd, I need not fear,
When in his presence I appear.

2 The holy, spotless Lamb of God,
Who freely gave his life and blood,
For all my num'rous sins t' atone,
I for my Lord and Saviour own.

3 In him I trust for evermore,
He hath expung'd the dreadful score
Of all my guilt; this done away,
I need not fear the judgment day.

4 Therefore my Saviour's blood & death
Is here the substance of my faith;
And shall remain, when called hence,
My only hope and confidence.

5 For should I e'er so faithful prove,
Serve my kind Lord with zeal and love,
And spend my life for him I serve,
Nor e'er from his commandments swerve;

6 Yet when my Saviour I shall see,
Then shall I have this only plea:
"Here is a sinner, who would fain
Thro' the Lamb's ransom entrance gain."

7 Thus Abraham was sav'd by grace,
Believing in Christ's righteousness;
And all the ransom'd saints in light,
In this blest song of praise unite:

8 "All pow'r and glory doth pertain
Unto the Lamb, for he was slain;
And hath redeem'd us by his blood,
And made us kings and Priests to God."

9 While here on earth I still remain,
This doctrine firmly I'll maintain;
And both in word and deed proclaim
The pow'r of Jesus' saving name.

10 Lord Jesus Christ, all praise to thee!
That thou didst deign a man to be,
And for each soul which thou hast made
Hast an eternal ransom paid.

11 O King of glory, Christ the Lord!
God's only Son, eternal Word!
Let all the world thy mercy see,
And bless those who believe in thee.

12 Thy incarnation, wounds and death,
I will confess while I have breath,
Till I shall see thee face to face,
Arrayed with thy righteousness.

282.* T. 590.

GRACE! grace! O that's a welcome sound!
A joyful sound to all,
Who clearly see, and deeply feel
The mis'ry of the fall:
Who rightly know the wretched state
Of sinners void of grace,
Ere Christ selects them to enjoy
In heav'nly realms a place.

2 Grace! how exceeding great to those
Who ready to despair,
Asham'd confess, and truly know
How vile and weak they are!
Yet grace, free grace, most sweetly calls,
"Directly come, who will,
Just as you are, for Christ receives
Poor helpless sinners still."

3 All we, who now are his, were first
Deeply convinc'd of sin;
Each felt the plague of his own heart
The leprosy within:
Then life and righteousness divine,
Thro' faith, to us were giv'n;
Thus we a happy people are,
Joint-heirs with Christ of heav'n.

4 Now, dearest Lord, we inly pray,
That in thy service we
May active, true and faithful prove,
Deriving strength from thee:
O may we still in thee abide,
For babes we are most weak,
Poor sinners still, who without thee
Can nought think, act, or speak.

5 We thirst, O Lord; give us this day,
To taste more of thy grace,
More of that stream which from the rock
Flow'd thro' the wilderness.
'Tis grace alone that feeds our souls,
Grace keeps us inly poor;
And Oh! that nothing but thy grace
May rule us evermore!

283.* T. 583.

O WHAT a depth of love and boundless grace
The gospel-light to sinful men displays,
When Christ himself to us doth manifest,
And we in him find comfort, peace, and rest!

2 When in the soul this blessed truth resounds,
That in Christ's death, for sinners life abounds;
Oh, how doth this refresh the fainting heart,
And bid all anxious doubts and fears depart.

3 For such poor sinners, who of nought can boast,
Who think themselves irreparably lost,
Who groan beneath sin's heavy galling load,
The Lamb of God hath shed his precious blood.

4 Virtue goes forth from him, he gives us grace
With confidence his Father to address,
And then we boldly may to all declare,
That we, thro' faith in Christ, God's children are.

284.* T. 16.

WHEN a sinner in affliction
Mourneth on account of sin,
Feels the Spirit's deep conviction,
But no pow'r of faith within;

2 While a flood of tears is gushing,
"Where shall I find Jesus, where?"
While the troubled soul is wishing,
"O that he my Saviour were!"

3 In a moment stands before us
Jesus with his pierced side;
Now we find, that he's desirous
Us from wrath to screen and hide.

4 Thus, the soul at once obtaineth
Pardon from the sinner's Friend;
To true happiness attaineth,
And to life which hath no end.

285.* T. 14.

WHAT joy or honor could we have,
Polluted as we are,
If not the holy Lamb of God
Our joy and honor were!

2 Of nothing we have ever done
To boast could we desire,
When he to judge us shall appear,
Whose eyes are flames of fire.

3 None is so holy, pure and just,
So perfected in love,
That his best plea, or self-defence,
Of any weight could prove.

4 Nor is there any other way
Into the holy place,
But Christ, who took away our sins,
His blood and righteousness.

5. We know the righteousness complete
Which he procur'd for all;
We know the kind reception giv'n,
To the poor prodigal.

6 We know the Shepherd's love, who left
The ninety-nine behind,
And thro' the desart anxious went,
The hundredth sheep to find.

7 To him poor sinners may appeal
With all their misery;
The angels joy to see them come,
Christ calleth: "Come to me."

286.* T. 14.

HAPPY the souls who contrite are,
Them Jesus doth invite,
And gives to everlasting bliss
A never-failing right.

2 Tho' comforted, they still distrust
Their own untoward heart;
And wonder, that the Lord to them
Such mercy could impart.

3 To world and sin they bid adieu,
His pardon daily prove,
Desiring larger draughts to drink
Of Jesus' dying love.

4 When thus the blessings of his blood
And merits we enjoy,
Yea, from the fulness of his grace,
Take daily fresh supply;

5 Then we with pity look on those
Who still in darkness are,
Inviting them to turn to Christ,
And in his mercy share.

6 For we, thro' grace, are taught to think
Each sinner that we see
May pardon, thro' Christ's precious blood,
Obtain, as well as we.

7 For Jesus' pardon, love and grace,
Produce an humble shame,
And us excite with thankfulness
His goodness to proclaim.

287. T. 14.

WITH glorious clouds encompass'd round,
Whom angels dimly see,
Will the Unsearchable be found,
Will God appear to me?

2 Will he forsake his throne above,
Himself to worms impart?
Answer thou Man of grief and love,
And speak it to my heart!

3 In manifested love explain
Thy wonderful design;
What meant the suff'ring Son of man?
The streaming blood divine?

4 Didst thou not in our flesh appear,
And live and die below,
That I might now perceive thee near,
And my Redeemer know?

5 Come then, and to my soul reveal
The heights and depths of grace,
The wounds, which all my sorrows heal,
That dear disfigur'd face.

6 Before my eyes of faith, confest
Stand forth a slaughter'd Lamb;
Array me in salvation's vest,
Declare to me thy name.

7 Jehovah in thy person show,
Jehovah crucify'd:
And then the pard'ning God I know,
And feel his blood apply'd.

8 I view the Lamb in his own light,
Whom angels dimly see:
And gaze, transported at the sight,
To all eternity.

288. T. 90.

O CAN it be that I should gain
An int'rest in the Saviour's blood?
Dy'd he for me, who caus'd his pain?
For me, to make my peace with God?
Amazing love! how can it be,
That Jesus deign'd to die for me?

2 'Tis myst'ry all; my Maker dies!
Who can explore his vast design?
In vain the highest seraph tries
To sound the depths of love divine;
When this became my only plea
He freely pardon'd sinful me.

*3 He left his Father's throne above,
So free, so infinite his grace!
Compell'd by everlasting love,
He bled for Adam's helpless race;
'Tis mercy all, immense and free,
I know that Jesus saved me.

4 Long my imprison'd spirit lay
Fast bound in sin and nature's night;
His eyes diffus'd a quick'ning ray,
I' woke, the dungeon flam'd with light,
My chains fell off immediately,
I rose, went forth, my heart was free.

5 No condemnation now I dread,
Jesus, and all in him, is mine:
Alive in him my living Head,
And cloth'd in righteousness divine,
Now humbly I approach the throne,
And claim the crown thro' Christ my own.

289. T. 14.

IN evil long I took delight,
Unaw'd by shame or fear,
Till a new object struck my sight,
And stopp'd my wild career.

2 I saw One hanging on a tree,
In agonies and blood,
Who fix'd his languid eyes on me,
As near his cross I stood.

3 Sure never till my latest breath
Can I forget that look;
It seem'd to charge me with his death,
Tho' not a word he spoke.

4 My conscience felt, and own'd the guilt,
And plung'd me in despair;
I saw my sins his blood had spilt,
And help'd to nail him there.

5 Alas! I knew not what I did;
But now my tears are vain;
Where shall my trembling soul be hid?
For I the Lord have slain.

6 A second look he gave, which said,
"I freely all forgive;
This blood is for thy ransom paid,
I die, that thou may'st live."

7 Thus, while his death my sin displays
In all its blackest hue,
(Such is the mystery of grace)
It seals my pardon too.

8 With pleasing grief and mournful joy,
My spirit now is fill'd,
That I should such a life destroy,
Yet live by him I kill'd.

290. T. 582.

NOT all the blood of beasts
On Jewish altars slain,
Could give the guilty conscience peace,
Or wash away the stain.

2 Christ, the true Paschal Lamb,
Takes all our sins away;
A sacrifice of nobler name,
And richer blood than they.

3 My faith would lay the hand
On that dear head of thine,
While like a penitent I stand,
And there confess my sin.

4 Lord, I look back to see
The burdens thou didst bear,
When hanging on the shameful tree;
And know my guilt was there.

5 Believing we rejoice
Our curse he did remove;
We bless the Lamb with cheerful voice,
And sing his bleeding love.

291. T. 151.

HOW lost was my condition,
Till Jesus made me whole!
There is but one Physician
Can cure a sin-sick soul!
Near unto death he found me,
And snatch'd me from the grave;
To tell to all around me,
His wond'rous pow'r to save.

2 A dying, risen, Jesus,
Seen by the eye of faith,
At once from danger frees us,
And saves the soul from death:
Come then, to this Physician,
His help he'll freely give,
He makes no hard condition,
'Tis only—look and live.

292. T. 96.

O Thou, who pardon canst impart,
Thy pard'ning grace I wish to feel;
Give life unto my lifeless heart,
And my diseases kindly heal:
Hear, Jesus, hear my feeble moan,
And me as thine in mercy own.

2 Vain are all other helps beside,
Such favours only from thee flow;
Other physicians have I try'd,
Yet only worse and worse I grow:
Give me by faith on thee to lean,
And say unto me: "Be thou clean."

293. T. 151.

MY Lord, how great the favor,
That I a sinner poor,
Can, thro' thy blood's sweet savor,
Approach thy mercy-door!
And find an open passage
Unto the throne of grace,
Then wait the welcome message
That bids me go in peace.

2 In my forlorn condition,
Who else could give me aid?
Where could I meet compassion,
But in the church's Head?
In mercy, O receive me,
Thou God, who hearest pray'r!
From ev'ry evil save me,
Dispel each needless fear.

3 I'll never cease repeating
My numberless complaints,
But ever be intreating
Thee, glorious King of saints,
To form me in thine image,
And fill my soul with love,
Till I to thee my homage
Pay with the saints above.

294. T. 22.

THE one thing needful, that good part,
Which Mary chose with all her heart,
I would pursue with heart and mind,
And seek unweary'd till I find.

2 Hidden in Christ the treasure lies,
That goodly pearl of so great price;
No other way but Christ there is
To endless happiness and bliss.

3 But Oh, I'm blind and ignorant,
Thy Holy Spirit, Lord, I want,
To guide me in the narrow road
That leads to happiness and God.

4 My mind enlighten with thy light,
That I may understand aright
The glorious gospel-mystery,
Which shows the way to heav'n and thee.

5 O Jesus Christ, my Lord and God,
Who hast redeem'd me by thy blood;
By faith unite my heart to thee,
That we may never parted be.

295.* T. 58.

THE more forgiveness thou dost deign t' afford,
The more thou art belov'd, most gracious Lord:
We are all great sinners, before thee, Saviour,
O therefore grant to us the grace and favor To love thee much.

2 How merciful art thou, O God of love!
How doth each needy soul thy comforts prove!
Who to thee can render due compensation?
In heav'n and earth thy mercy and compassion Unequall'd are!

296. T. 14.

THOU, Lord, must for thy sake forgive,
It cannot be for mine;
My pow'r, the pardon to receive,
My faith, is all divine:

2 A sinner on mere mercy cast,
Thy mercy I embrace,
And gladly own from first to last,
That I am sav'd by grace.

XVII. Of the Surrender of the Heart to Jesus.

297.* T. 582.

UNTO the Lamb of God,
Who to retrieve my loss,
Became a man and dy'd for me,
Upon th' accursed cross;
Unto the Prince of Life,
Who felt such racking pain,
While he the vengeance due to me
Did willingly sustain:

2 To him I wholly give
Myself this day anew,
As his reward so dearly gain'd,
His spoil and purchase due;
That with me he may do
What's pleasing in his sight,
And from me take whate'er him grieves,
Whate'er he sees not right.

3 How very weak I am,
My Saviour well can see,
And how exceeding short I fall,
Of what I ought to be:
Compassionate High-Priest,
To thee I must appeal;
My numberless infirmities
O kindly haste to heal!

4 In thy most precious blood,
Which from thy open'd veins,
To heal my soul in plenty flow'd,
I pray wash out my stains:
It is thy daily care,
Thy helpless sheep to feed;
To purify their spotted souls,
And gently them to lead.

5 Redeemer of my soul!
Whene'er thereon I think,
How thy compassion, love and grace,
From sin and hell's dark brink
Have sav'd and rescu'd me;
And how thy cleansing blood,
Apply'd unto my heart by faith,
Hath brought me nigh to God:

6 I in the dust adore,
Amaz'd at grace so free,
Bestow'd on such a wretched worm,
And ask, "How can it be,
That sinners base and vile
Should be so greatly lov'd,
Who cost thee so much pain and grief,
And so ungrateful prov'd?"

7 Me thy all-seeing eye
Hath kept with watchful care;
Thy great compassion never fail'd,
Thou heardst my needy pray'r;
This makes me firmly trust
That thou wilt guide me still,
And guard me safe throughout the way
That leads to ZION's Hill.

8 Dear Saviour, I resign
My worthless heart to thee;
And whether cheerful or distress'd,
Thine, thine alone I'll be:
My only aim is this
(O may I it fulfil!)
Thee to exalt with all my strength,
And do thy holy will.

298.* T. 22.

O GOD of mercy, grace and love!
Thy yearning bowels did thee move,
To call me from death's gloomy night
Into thy own amazing light.

2 I once was wholly dead in sin,
Wholly corrupt and spoil'd within,
The carnal mind still bore the sway,
And hurry'd me a slave away.

3 It caus'd thee pain, O Son of God,
To see the purchase of thy blood
So deeply sunk in misery;
And 'twas thy aim to set me free.

4 Thou drewest me with cords of love,
Till thou at last didst conqu'ror prove;
Till sin's strong pow'r thou hadst supprest,
And till my weary soul had rest.

5 Now, thro' thy wounds my soul hath found
Peace, righteousness, and solid ground;
I've now obtained, thro' thy grace,
Among thy ransom'd flock a place.

6 I thee adore, my gracious King,
And joyful Hallelujahs sing,
My eyes with grateful tears o'erflow,
For all the mercies thou dost show.

7 Faithful to thee I now engage
To be throughout my pilgrimage;
Accept my life and soul, my King,
Pledg'd to thy service these I bring.

8 Nature's reluctance over-rule,
My fleshly tenderness control,
O may I always have in view
Not mine, but thy blest will to do.

9 Thus by thy pow'r I here shall be
Prepared for eternity,
Walk with my God, him serve and love,
Till I shall live with him above.

299.* T. 168.

O! AT last I've found my Saviour
Who laid down his life for me:
He (O undeserved favor)
Own'd me as his property:
Conscious of my imperfection,
I'll rely on his direction:
I will nothing know beside
Jesus and him crucify'd.

2 Others may seek satisfaction
In this poor world's vanity;
Meanwhile shall my heart's affection
On my Saviour fixed be,
On his meritorious suff'ring
And sin-expiating off'ring:
To the world I bid adieu,
Christ alone I have in view.

3 Jesus cur'd my soul's infection
By his suff'rings, stripes and wounds:
From his death and resurrection,
Life and pow'r to me redounds;
I by virtue of his merit
Once shall heav'nly joys inherit,
And ev'n here a foretaste have,
Of that world beyond the grave.

4 Jesus yields me delectation;
When I'm weak he strengthens me,
Sweetens all my tribulation,
And supports me constantly:
His atoning death and passion
Are the cause of my salvation;
Therefore Christ shall ne'er depart
From my sight and from my heart.

5 O! I'm lost in deepest wonder,
To think he shall soon appear
To receive me gladly yonder,
And wipe off my ev'ry tear:
Then my grateful songs and praises
Shall resound in heav'nly places;
Here by faith to him I'll cleave,
Jesus will I never leave.

300.* T. 22.

WE pray thee, wounded Lamb of God!
Cleanse us in thy atoning blood!
Grant us by faith to view thy cross,
Then life or death is gain to us.

2 Take our poor hearts, and let them be
For ever clos'd to all but thee!
Seal thou our breasts, and let us wear
That pledge of love for ever there.

3 What are our works but sin & death,
Till thou thy quick'ning Spirit breathe!
Until we strength from thee derive,
And in communion with thee live.

4 Ah, Lord! enlarge our scanty thought,
To know the wonders thou hast wrought;
Unloose our stamm'ring tongues to tell
Thy love immense, unsearchable.

5 First-born of many brethren thou!
To thee both earth and heav'n must bow;
Help us to thee our all to give,
Thine may we die, thine may we live!

301. T. 580.

DIDST thou, Lord Jesus, me incline,
When I was lost and dead in sin,
To hear thy quick'ning voice?
Have I obtained in thy blood
Redemption, and found peace with God?
And do I in thy name rejoice?

2 O yes, I feel I am forgiv'n,
A foretaste I enjoy of heav'n
Thy Spirit witness bears;
By faith thy righteousness is mine,
I'm well-assur'd that I am thine,
My soul no condemnation fears.

3 Yet 'fore thee, Jesus, I must own,
I have not this salvation known
By tracing legal ways;
No! 'twas thy pow'r rais'd me from sin,
Thou didst the saving work begin;
Thine be the glory, thine the praise.

4 May I be faithful to thy call,
Surrender unto thee my all,
Myself to thee resign;
When dangers threaten me around,
Invincible may I be found,
And never from thy will decline.

5 Me with thy gladd'ning oil anoint;
The destin'd path thou dost appoint
Gladly I then shall tread;
Bedew me with a genial show'r,
Into my heart thy influence pour,
And me with heav'nly manna feed.

302.* T. 106.

O GOD! whose love (immense in height,
In depth unfathom'd) no man knows;
Grant unto me thy saving light,
Inly I sigh for thy repose:
My heart is pain'd, nor can it be
At rest, till it finds rest in thee.

2 Thy gracious call invites me still,
How light thy burden is, to prove;
Yet I'm unsteady; tho' my will
Be fix'd, yet wide my passions rove;
Great hindrances obstruct the way,
I aim at thee, yet from thee stray.

3 Mere mercy 'tis, that thou hast brought
My soul to seek its peace in thee;
Yet while I seek, but find thee not,
At rest my wand'ring mind can't be;
Oh, when shall all my wand'rings end,
And all my wishes to thee tend!

4 Is there a thing beneath the sun,
That strives with thee my heart to share?
Ah! tear it thence, and be alone
The spring of ev'ry motion there:
Then shall my heart from earth be free,
When it hath found repose in thee.

303.* T. 106.

TAKE, Lord, all self from me, that I
No more, but Christ in me may live!
My vile affections crucify,
Let not one darling lust survive:
O may my heart to thee aspire,
And nought on earth but thee desire.

2 Dear Lord, thy sov'reign aid impart,
To save me from low-thoughted care;
O banish self-will from my heart,
From all its latent mazes there;
And grant, that I may never move
From the blest footsteps of thy love.

3 Each moment draw from earth away
My heart, that humbly waits thy call:
Speak to my inmost soul and say,
"I am thy life, thy God, thy all!"
Thy love to taste, thy voice to hear,
Thy pow'r to prove, is all my pray'r.

304. T. 90.

JESUS, thy light again I view,
Again thy loving-kindness prove,
And all within me pants anew
T' enjoy thy all reviving love:
Again my thoughts to thee aspire,
Unto thy name is my desire.

2 But O! what off'ring shall I give
To thee, the Lord of earth and skies?
My soul and body now receive
A holy, living sacrifice;
'Tis all I have to offer thee;
O take me as thy property.

3 O may I never from thee stray,
Or be again subdu'd by sin;
Guide me, my life, my truth, my way,
Thy blood preserve my garment clean,
O let thy blood and righteousness
My beauty be, my glorious dress.

4 Send down thy likeness from above,
Thine image, Lord, on me impress;
Fill me with wisdom, patience, love,
With purity and lowliness:
These precious gifts on me bestow,
That I may in thy knowledge grow.

5 O Lord, be thou my shield and light,
Since I am call'd by thy great name;
In thee my wand'ring thoughts unite,
Of all my works be thou the aim:
Thy grace attend me all my days,
My sole employment be thy praise!

305.* T. 376.

"GIVE me thy heart, my son," thus saith the Lord,
"Give me thy heart, and listen to my word;
Observe my ways,
Walk in the path of grace;
In foll'wing my direction
I'll grant thee my protection."

2 'Tis only this which Christ of us desires;
He to promote our welfare this requires;
How blest are they
Who Jesus' voice obey,
And give their hearts for ever
To him our God and Saviour!

306.* T. 376.

O TAKE my heart, and whatsoe'er is mine,
Beloved Jesus, I'll be only thine;
To thee I'll live,
And soul and body give;
My words and whole behavior
Be rul'd by thee for ever.

2 But give thyself, my Jesus unto me,
And dwell within my heart continually:
O Lord, remain
My joy 'midst grief and pain;
From thee, my soul's beloved,
May I ne'er be removed!

307. T. 14.

LORD, take my heart just as it is,
Set up therein thy throne;
So shall I love thee above all,
And live to thee alone.

2 I thank thee, that in mercy thou
Hast waken'd me from death,
Arous'd me out of sin's deep sleep,
And call'd to walk in faith.

3 Complete thy work, and crown thy grace,
That I may faithful prove,
And listen to that small still voice,
Which whispers only love.

4 Which teacheth me what is thy will,
And tells me what to do;
Which fills my heart with shame, when I
Do not thy will pursue.

5 This unction may I ever feel,
This teaching of my Lord,
And learn obedience to thy voice,
Thy soft reviving word.

308. T. 74.

O LORD in me fulfil
Whatever is thy will;
To thee I now resign
Myself, and all that's mine;
Thine, only thine I'll be
And live alone to thee.

2 Each day unto my heart
New life and grace impart;
For without fresh supply
I languish, droop and die;
Continually I've need
By faith on thee to feed.

309.* T. 155.

LORD, thou mad'st the universe,
I though dust, am yet thy creature,
Spoil'd by nature,
Yet desire to cleave to thee;
Make thou me,
Like the clay thine hand can fashion,
To a vessel of salvation
Fitted for eternity.

2 I resign myself to thee,
With me do whate'er thee pleases,
Gracious Jesus;
May I have to thee always
Free access:
Thus in faith and love proceeding,
I on heav'nly joys am feeding,
Till in thee I end my race.

3 Banish from me what's not right,
In thy blood, O cleanse me wholly,
Make me lowly;
From whate'er displeaseth thee,
Set me free;
And preserve my soul and senses
From all hurtful influences;
Only thine I wish to be.

310.* T. 11.

GRANT, most gracious Lamb of God,
Who hast bought me with thy blood,
That my soul and body be
Quite devoted unto thee.

2 Jesus, hear my fervent cry!
My whole nature sanctify;
Root out all that is unclean,
Tho' it cause me pungent pain.

3 Gracious Lord! I wish alone
Thine to be, yea, quite thine own,
And to all eternity,
To remain thy property.

311.* T. 184.

DEAR Lord, consume, yea dash to shatters
All that, which is not right in me;
While the world holds me by its fetters,
Or silken cords, I cannot be
Partaker of thy full salvation;
For thou requirest such a heart,
As can without equivocation
For thee, O Lord, with all things part.

312.* T. 15.

SEARCHER of hearts, thou know'st, thy love
My heart hath captivated;
My soul is closely to thee join'd,
Ne'er to be separated;

2 All thou demandest I give up,
Lord, without hesitation;
But never, never will I leave
Thee and thy congregation.

313. T. 184.

O MIGHT we all, Lord God our Saviour,
Thy condescending mercy prize,
T' accept of us (O boundless favor!)
As of a holy sacrifice;
Of us, tho' sinful, poor and needy:
Grant that we freely unto thee
May offer up both soul and body,
To love and serve thee faithfully.

313. T. 590.

PRESENT your bodies to the Lord,
A living sacrifice,
A holy off'ring unto him,
And pleasing in his eyes:
This is a service which ye owe,
And reasonably due;
For ye are not your own, ye know,
But Christ hath purchas'd you.

XVIII. Of COMMUNION with CHRIST.

315.* T. 132.

JESUS, thou art my heart's delight,
My joy and my salvation;
Thy presence yields me, day and night,
Abundant consolation;
Thee I desire to love and praise,
Since thy great love and boundless grace
Are ev'ry thing unto me.

2 Thou art the Way, thy Spirit is
As my Conductor given;
In foll'wing thee I cannot miss
The path to life and heaven;
Thy word be my unerring guide;
Preserve me lest I turn aside,
Or stray from thee my Saviour.

3 Thou art the Truth, in thee I've found
All that which is essential;
Without thee, all is empty sound,
In thee is strength substantial:
O Truth! set me at liberty,
That I depend on none but thee,
By whom I can be healed.

4 Thou art my Life, thy pow'r divine
Shall influence ev'ry motion;
O may thy Spirit me incline
To true unfeign'd devotion:
Thus I eternal life shall gain,
And, till my latest breath, remain
A member of thy body.

5 Lord Jesus, thou my Shepherd art,
Who dyd'st for my transgression;
When lost, I caus'd thee pungent smart,
When found, joy past expression:
Ah! best of Shepherds, ever keep
Within thy fold thy helpless sheep,
Protect it from all danger.

6 Thou art my faithful Friend in need,
My flesh and bone, my Brother;
Thy faithfulness and love exceed
That of the fondest mother:
Thou art my Healer when I'm sick,
My Cordial strength'ning me when weak,
My refuge in all trouble.

7 O Lord, how very short I fall,
When on thy praise I enter!
Thou art, indeed, my All in all,
In thee my wishes centre:
Whate'er I want, thou art to me;
O let my heart incessantly
Be by thy love inspired.

316.* T. 58.

WHAT peace divine, what perfect happiness
Our Saviour's presence to our hearts conveys!
Unto us poor sinners, thereby is given
A blessed antepast of bliss in heaven,
And lasting joy.

2 Altho', dear Jesus, we can't see thy face,
We richly may enjoy thy love and grace,
Since thou hast pronounced those souls thrice blessed,
Who, tho' they do not see thee, are possessed Of faith in thee.

3 Were we but all desirous, day and night
Thee to enjoy, O what supreme delight
Would both soul and body taste in thy favor!
We then with all our heart could say,
"Dear Saviour, Who is like thee!"

4 Long suff'ring, merciful and kind to be,
Forgiving daily and abundantly,
To heal, cheer, and comfort, and show'r thy blessing
On us, with looks thy tender love expressing, Is thy delight.

5 Gracious Redeemer, grant to us while here
Of thy salvation constantly to share,
May our souls and senses, without cessation,
Prompted by love and need, for consolation Unto thee look:

6 Thus in communion may we live with thee,
Happy like children, till thy face we see;
Tho', while here we tarry, we're often grieved,
May we apply to thee and be relieved
In all distress.

317.* T. 228.

HOW bright appears the Morning-star,
With grace and truth beyond compare!
The royal root of Jesse;
O David's Son, of Jacob's line,
My soul's belov'd, and King benign,
Thou cam'st from heav'n to bless me.
Precious,—gracious,
Ever glorious,—and victorious,
Is my Saviour,
Nought but he can please me ever.

2 From him descends a beam of joy,
When he, with a complacent eye,
Beholds his needy creature:
Immanuel! my sov'reign good,
Thy word, thy Spirit, flesh and blood
Renew my very nature.
Grant me,—richly,
Thro' thy merit—to inherit
Thy salvation;
Hear my ardent supplication.

3 The Father from eternity
In mercy was inclin'd to me,
Thro' thee his Well-beloved:
I, as a member of thy bride,
In thee, my Jesus, can confide,
Thy love remains unmoved.
Oh! I—have joy,
That in heaven,—with thanksgiving,
Thee my Saviour
I shall love and praise for ever.

4 Tune all your notes to songs of praise,
If you can earthly music raise,
To join celestial concerts;
Be Jesus your delightful theme;
In him, and in his saving name,
Are center'd all our comforts;
Joyful,—awful,
Be the phrases—of our praises,
'Tis our duty,
'Fore the Lord of bliss and beauty.

5 Before the world I make my boast,
That he in whom I place my trust,
Is Lord of light and glory:
At last he'll bring me to that place,
Where wonders of redeeming grace
Shall lie disclos'd before me;
Amen!—Be then
Praise and blessing,—never ceasing
To him given,
Here, and by the hosts of heaven!

318.* T. 185.

THE unbounded love of my Creator
Heart-felt gratitude doth claim;
Why did Christ appear in human nature?
'Twas for me he man became;
While the whole world's Saviour I confess him,
As my own Redeemer oft I trace him,
And his merits I apply
To myself especially.

2 When with him, my Lord, in closest union,
I can all things else forget;
In his fellowship and blest communion,
I heav'n's bliss anticipate;
By his presence he dispels all sadness;
Filling my poor soul with joy & gladness;
Tho' I often am to blame,
Yet his love is still the same.

3 When my mind pursues this meditation,
That the all-creating Word
Hath by his humanity and passion,
To God's image man restor'd;
I regard my body as Christ's temple,
'Tis my aim to follow his example,
And my vessel, thro' his grace,
In due honor to possess.

319.* T. 68.

BLISS beyond compare,
Which in Christ I share!
He's my only joy and treasure;
Tasteless is all worldly pleasure;
When in Christ I share
Bliss beyond compare.

2 Jesus is my joy,
Therefore blest am I.
O! his mercy is unbounded,
All my hope on him is grounded;
Jesus is my joy,
Therefore blest am I.

3 When the Lord appears,
This my spirit cheers;
When his love to me revealing,
He, the Sun of grace with healing,
In his beams appears,
This my spirit cheers.

4 Then all grief is drown'd;
Pure delight is found.
Joy and peace in his salvation,
Heav'nly bliss and consolation.
Ev'ry grief is drown'd
Where such bliss is found.

320.* T. 4.

LORD Jesus, my pray'r
Is while I am here,
In union to be
With thee and thy people inseparably.

2 Concern'd for more grace
And true happiness;
Intent evermore,
'Fore thee to be contrite, & lowly & poor.

3 O were my whole mind
And spirit inclin'd
To show forth thy praise,—To serve thee with gladness, and walk in thy ways.

4 If question'd by thee:
"Say, lovest thou me?"
I own I shall prove—Deficient, O Lord,
yet thou know'st that I love.

5 John's portion so blest
To lean on thy breast,
Be mine, till with thee,
When time is no more, I for ever shall be.

321.* T. 159.

'TIS the most blest and needful part
To have in Christ a share,
And to commit our way and heart
Unto his faithful care;
This done, our steps are safe and sure,
Our hearts' desires are render'd pure,
And nought can pluck us from his hand,
Which leads us to the end.

2 Nought in this world affords true rest,
But Christ's atoning blood,
This purifies the guilty breast,
And reconciles to God:
Hence flows unfeigned love to him
Who came lost sinners to redeem,
And Christ our Saviour doth appear
Daily to us more dear.

3 My only joy and comfort here
Is Jesus' death and blood;
I with this passport can appear
Before the throne of God:
Admitted to the realms of bliss,
I then shall see him as he is,
Where countless pardon'd sinners meet,
Adoring at his feet.

322.* T. 14.

THY child so minded ever keep,
Let me know nought beside
Thee, who wast slain me to redeem,
Thee, Jesus crucify'd.

2 May I to thee in all my wants
Child-like yet closer fly,
Directing still throughout my course,
By faith to thee mine eye.

3 Tho' tis but little I can do,
Yet I would willingly,
Jesus, do that which yields thee joy,
This is enough for me.

323.* T. 206.

THOU slaughter'd Lamb, :||:
Whose love the same—doth still abide,
Tho' oft severely try'd;
I am no longer mine, :||:—But thine,
Bought with a price;—As sacrifice
Accept the whole
Of spirit, body, soul. :||:

2 My King benign! :||:—I'd fain be thine;
Not anything,—No smallest hankering,
Cause me while here I stay,
My dearest Lord, from thee :||:—To stray;
No, may each breath—Exalt thy death,
And sing thy praise
For thy unbounded grace. :||:

324.* T. 86.

O LET thy countenance, most loving Saviour,
Shine on me day and night, and let me ever
Have of thy presence, and thy gracious dealing A tender feeling.

2 That soul and body on thy merit feeding
May daily be from grace to grace proceeding,
With thee at peace, in tend'rest love's communion, And perfect union.

325. T. 14.

JESUS, my Saviour, full of grace,
Be thou my heart's delight,
Remain my fav'rite theme always,
My joy by day and night.

2 Hungry and thirsty after thee,
May I be found each hour;
Humble in heart, and constantly
Supported by thy pow'r.

3 May thy blest Spirit to my heart,
Throughout my future race,
True faith and constancy impart
To live unto thy praise.

4 The myst'ry of redeeming love
Be ever dear to me:
Till I shall once in heav'n above
For ever dwell with thee.

326. T. 14.

O DEAREST Lord, take thou my heart!
Where can such sweetness be,
As I have tasted in thy love,
As I have found in thee!

2 If there's a fervor in my soul
And fervor sure there is,
It shall be quite at thy control,
To serve thee only rise.

3 'Tis vain in earthly things for bliss
To seek, none can be found,
Till Jesus Christ our object is;
In him true joys abound.

4 'Tis heav'n on earth to taste his love,
To feel his quick'ning grace;
And all the bliss I seek above,
Is to behold his face.

327. T. 14.

'TIS heav'n on earth by faith to see
Thy face, my gracious Lord;
The noblest, most substantial joys
Thy cheering smiles afford.

2 Thou say'st, dear Jesus, all thy saints,
Who love thy face to see,
Shall have, while in this vale of tears,
Kind visits oft from thee.

3 O let my soul with thee converse,
Who art my chief delight;
For the whole world can't ease my heart,
If banish'd from thy sight.

328. T. 580.

O JESUS, everlasting God,
Who hast for sinners shed thy blood
Upon mount Calvary,
And finish'd there redemption's toil;
Thus I became thy happy spoil:
All praise and glory be to thee!

2 Fain would I think upon thy pain,
Would find therein my life and gain,
And firmly fix my heart,
Upon thy wounds and dying love;
Nor ever more from thee remove,
Till from this world I shall depart.

3 The more thro' grace myself I know,
The more inclin'd I am to bow
In faith beneath thy cross;
To trust in thy atoning blood,
And look to thee for ev'ry good,
Yea, count all earthly gain but loss.

329. T. 90.

THOU hidden Source of calm repose!
Thou all-sufficient love divine!
My help and refuge from my foes,
Secure I am, for thou art mine:
Thou art my fortress, strength, and tow'r,
My trust and portion evermore.

2 Jesus, my All in all thou art,
My rest in toil, my ease in pain,
The balm to heal my broken heart,
In storms my peace, in loss my gain;
My joy beneath the tyrant's frown,
In shame my glory, and my crown.

3 In want, my plentiful supply,
In weakness, my almighty pow'r:
In bonds, my perfect liberty,
My refuge in temptation's hour;
My comfort 'midst all grief and thrall,
My Life in death, my All in all.

330. T. 580.

O THAT we could for ever sit
With Mary, at our Saviour's feet,
Be this our happy choice!
Our only care, delight and bliss,
Our joy, our heav'n on earth be this,
To hear the Bridegroom's cheering voice.

2 O may his love our hearts inspire,
Nought else on earth may we desire,
Nought else in heav'n above;
Let earth and all its trifles go,
Give us, O Lord! thy grace to know,
Give us to feel thy precious love.

331. T. 22.

'TIS thro' the grace thou dost bestow
O Lord, that I thy goodness know;
Grant that I in humility
For evermore may cleave to thee.

2 The privilege to be with Christ
In union, can't enough be priz'd;
Since I'm the purchase of his blood,
Grant me this privilege, O God!

332. T. 146.

O WHAT is Christ to me!
Who hath for my diseases
Found out a remedy,
And ev'ry grief appeases;
My ever faithful Friend,
My Confident most true,
On whom I can depend,
In joy and sorrow too.

333.* T. 79.

CAN any contemplation
E'er vie with that sensation,
O Christ, that we're thine own!
That our names on the pages
Are written, where the wages
For thy soul's travail are put down!

334.* T. 230.

BE our comfort which ne'er faileth,
When any trial us assaileth,
Or when we're needlessly distrest;
Jesus, show on each occasion
That thou our strength art, and salvation,
Our shield, our hiding-place and rest:
O may we constantly
Look up by faith to thee,
Who redeem'd us,
And daily prove
That thou art love,
Till we shall be with thee above.

335.* T. 244.

THO' we can't see our Saviour
With these our mortal eyes,
Our faith, which tastes his favor,
The want of sight supplies:
Our hearts can feel him near,
So that to us 'tis clear,
His presence is as certain
As if we saw him here.

336.* T. 185.

BETHANY, O peaceful habitation,
Blessed mansion, lov'd abode!
There my Lord had oft his resting station,
Converse held in friendly mood;
With that bliss which Mary highly savor'd,
I could wish this day still to be favor'd;
But thy presence makes to me
Ev'ry place a Bethany.

337. T. 586.

WHEN Christ our Saviour lives and dwelleth
In us, O what consummate bliss!
This from our hearts all gloom dispelleth,
Our life of heav'n a foretaste is.
Lord Jesus, hear our supplication!
Let all of us in ev'ry station,
Be truly join'd to thee
Until eternally
Thy face we see.

XIX. Of the Happiness of Children of God.

338.* T. 114.

JESUS, my King, thy kind and gracious sceptre
Assuageth ev'ry grief that burdens me:
When I, with all my heart, apply to thee,
Then thy peace-giving Spirit's my Preceptor;
Thy gracious looks so warm and melt my heart,
That fear and restlessness must soon depart.

2 The gifts of Christ are so inestimable
That all the world nought equal can afford;

What are the treasures which the worldlings hoard?
To comfort weary souls they are not able,
But Jesus can, and doth abundantly;
All earthly joys will fail, but never he.

3 How highly blest, how happy is the spirit,
Which, weary of self-working, inly mourns,
And unto him for aid and succor turns!
The humble ev'ry good from him inherit,
He to the troubled soul imparteth ease,
Restoring to the wounded conscience peace.

4 That which the law could have imparted never
Is then produc'd alone by Jesus' grace;
This is the source of genuine holiness,
This changes and reforms our whole behavior;
From strength to strength, from grace to grace led on,
We safe proceed, until our race is run.

5 O may I look to Christ without cessation!
Come visit me, thou Day-spring from on high,
That in thy light, the light I may espy,
On grace depending as my sole foundation;
Confirm my faith, grant that no fault in me
May intercept the light that beams from thee.

6 Thou Source of love, I rest in thy embraces
Thou art alone my everlasting Peace!
My only treasure is thy boundless grace;
'Tis heav'n on earth to live upon thy mercies;
And since in thee all happiness I find,
I seek nought else to satisfy my mind.

339.* T. 115.

HOW great the bliss to be a sheep of Jesus!
And to be guided by his Shepherd-staff;
Earth's greatest honors are, howe'er they please us,
To this compar'd, but vain and empty chaff:
Yea, what this world can never give,
May, thro' the Shepherd's grace, each needy sheep receive.

2 Here is a pasture rich and never-failing,
Here living waters in abundance flow;
None can conceive the grace with them prevailing,
Who Jesus' Shepherd-voice obey and know;
He banisheth all fear and strife,
And leads them gently on to everlasting life.

3 Whoe'er would spend his days in lasting pleasure,
Must come to Christ, and join his flock with speed;
Here is a feast prepar'd, rich beyond measure,
The world meanwhile on empty husks must feed:
Those sheep may share in ev'ry good,
Whose Shepherd doth possess the treasuries of God.

340.* T. 164.

O DAYS of solid happiness,
O antepast of heaven!
When, in th' accepted time of grace,
We know our sins forgiven,
Cleans'd in the precious flood
Of Christ's atoning blood,
Enjoying in our hearts by faith
The blessings purchas'd by his death.

2 The peace of God then fills the soul,
And heals the wounded spirit;
The broken heart is then made whole,
By virtue of his merit;
Yea his sweet looks of grace
Convey such happiness,
That we, in his redeeming love,
Anticipate the bliss above.

3 But why do tears, grief and distress
Sometimes allay our gladness,
And tho' we've tasted pard'ning grace,
Still often cause us sadness?

Because we can't forget
Our former wretched state,
And that the grace on us bestow'd
Cost Jesus ev'ry drop of blood.

4 When thus we contemplate the cost,
It fills us with amazement,
We take it prostrate in the dust,
With joy, yet deep abasement;
For all that we possess
Is undeserved grace,
By torments on the cross procur'd,
When he for rebels death endur'd.

5 How pleasant is our lot, yea good
And great beyond expression!
For, having cleans'd us by his blood,
He bears us with compassion,
Applies his healing pow'r,
To us each day and hour,
Yea, we in Him redemption have
In death itself and in the grave.

6 And this at last our theme shall be,
When call'd to see our Saviour,
We join the glorious company,
Around his throne for ever;
Then we in highest strain
Shall praise the Lamb once slain,
Who hath redeem'd us by his blood,
And made us kings and priests to God.

341.* T. 218.

How blest am I, most gracious Saviour,
When filled with thy sacred love!
With grief oppress'd, I seek thy favor,
And thy reviving bounty prove:
The dismal clouds of night must vanish,
When joys divine my heart replenish,
While I recline upon thy breast:
Ah, then I find on earth my heaven;
Such comforts to all those are given,
Who seek in thee their peace and rest.

2 If my sin's burden would oppress me,
Or legal thunders me affright,
Or fear of death and hell distress me,
By faith to thee I take my flight:
In thee I always find protection
Gainst Satan's darts and sin's infection,
Thou art my Shield and Hiding-place;
Tho' foes should join in combination,
Who shall condemn? Lord my Salvation,
My confidence is in thy grace.

3 If thou thro' thorny paths wilt lead me,
I'll simply trust in thee, O Lord;
The clouds at thy command must feed me,
And rocks must drink to me afford:
In thy kind leadings acquiescing,
I'm sure to meet with nought but blessing;
If I have thee, it doth suffice:
I know that souls to bliss created,
Who shall to glory be translated,
Must humbled be before they rise.

4 Friend of my soul! O how contented
Am I, when leaning upon thee!
By sin I am no more tormented,
Since thou dost aid and comfort me.
O may the heart-reviving feeling
I have of thy most gracious dealing,
A foretaste yield of joys above.
I scorn, vain world, thy adulation,
For Jesus is my delectation,
And I'm an object of his love.

342.* T. 582.

JESUS, thou art reveal'd
To my poor heart, by faith,
And hast to me made manifest
Thy wounds, thy blood and death.
Thy name and cross alone
To me can comfort yield,
Since I thereby, as thy reward,
To God am reconcil'd.

2 My soul, tho' deeply bow'd,
Is cheered by thy grace,
Now I no more need toil and strive
In search of happiness;
But am assur'd that thou
Hast all my sins forgiv'n,
And by thy painful death for me
Procured life and heav'n.

3 Thou who didst love me first,
Teach me to trust in thee
Unshaken, till I thee above
Shall praise eternally:
Ev'n here thou art my song,
Thy grace doth richly claim
That thy church militant on earth
Give glory to thy name.

4 Unfeigned thanks receive,
For thy unbounded grace,
From us, who in thy name believe,
And wish to walk thy ways;
And who are bound to thee,
Because thou us hast gain'd,
And for us, by thy precious blood,
Eternal bliss obtain'd.

5 The merits of thy death
Each day to us apply,
And grant, that to the throne of grace
We boldly may draw nigh;
That we may mercy find,
And help in time of need;
Thus shall we, by thy Spirit led,
From grace to grace proceed.

6 Thy cross and saving name
We freely will confess,
Thy gospel we will spread on earth,
And sound thy matchless praise;
To all mankind point out
Thee, our incarnate God,
Who hast redeem'd us from the fall
By thy atoning blood.

343.* T. 11.

BLEST are they, supremely blest,
Who, of Jesus' grace possest,
Cleave to him by living faith,
Till they shall resign their breath.

2 One with Christ their Head they share
Happiness beyond compare;
Since on him their hopes they build,
He is their Reward and Shield.

3 Tho' all earthly joys be fled,
If in him they trust indeed,
He will be their constant Friend,
And protect them to the end.

4 If to Jesus they appeal,
When their faith and courage fail,
He assures them of his love,
Doth their Strength in weakness prove.

5 They who simply to him cleave,
From his fulness grace receive;
And throughout their mortal days,
Their employment is his praise.

6 Jesus wipes away their tears,
And alleviates all their cares;
They in truth, with heart and voice,
Evermore in Christ rejoice.

344.* T. 166.

WITH grateful hearts we all declare,
That in Christ's congregation
We may substantial blessings share,
Since he is our Salvation;
And he requires of us, that we
Deeply abas'd before him,
Stir up each other heartily
To love, and to adore him.

2 The grace is great, unspeakable,
The privilege unbounded,
That we, altho' deserving hell,
By sin most deeply wounded,
Are by the virtue of Christ's death
From sin's pollution cleared,
And, cleaving unto him by faith,
Are one with him declared!

345. T. 590.

JESUS, whose hands once pierc'd with nails
Were stretch'd upon the wood,
Out of whose wounds in plenteous streams
Flow'd the atoning blood:
How safely rests a weary child
Who keeps thee, Lord, in view;
Let unbelief say what it will,
This is for ever true.

2 The more the Lamb of God we view,
The more we walk in light;
His gracious presence doth dispel
Sin's dark and dismal night:
The cheering beams which Christ the Sun
Of righteousness displays,
Enkindle many a lifeless heart,
And love unfeigned raise.

3 Is there a thing that moves and breaks
A heart as hard as stone,
That warms a heart as cold as ice?
'Tis Jesus' blood alone:
This precious balm can truly cheer
And heal the wounded soul;
What multitudes of broken hearts
This stream of life makes whole!

4 Hark, O my soul, what sing the choirs
Around the glorious throne?
Hark! "the Lamb slain" for evermore
Sounds in the sweetest tone;
The elders there cast down their crowns,
And all, in endless day
Sing praise to him who shed his blood,
And wash'd their guilt away.

5 This, while on earth, we will declare
Cheerful in our degree,
That thro' the blood of God's dear Lamb
Each soul may happy be.
But thou, O Lord! make ev'ry day
Thy grace to us more sweet,
Till we behold thy pierced side,
And worship at thy feet.

346. T. 132.

O IF the Lamb had not been slain,
To save us from perdition,
And everlasting life to gain,
What had been our condition?
But since poor sinners favor'd are
To have a Friend so very dear,
We cannot but be happy.

2 With all our errors and mistakes
He bears, and loves us dearly;
A contrite soul He ne'er forsakes,
That acteth but sincerely.
When the whole heart to him is giv'n
We have a foretaste here of heav'n,
In fellowship with Jesus.

3 When we have fail'd and deeply mourn
That we the Spirit grieved,
And to our Lord for comfort turn,
We quickly are relieved:
Whene'er we say, with humble shame,
"Lord Jesus, I have been to blame,"
He saith, "Thou art forgiven."

4 As pardon'd sinners we rejoice,
With Jesus' congregation;
Above all other things we prize
His bitter death and passion;
His wounds, his tears, and bloody sweat,
We bear in mind, and can't forget
His unexampled mercy.

347. T. 14.

AMAZING grace! (how sweet the sound!)
That sav'd a wretch like me;
I once was lost, but now am found,
Was blind, but now I see.

2 'Twas grace that taught my heart to fear,
And grace my fears reliev'd;
How precious did that grace appear
The hour I first believ'd!

3 Thro' many dangers, toils and snares,
I am already come;
'Tis grace hath brought me safe thus far,
And grace will lead me home.

4 The Lord hath promis'd good to me,
His word my hope secures;
He will my Shield and Portion be
As long as life endures.

5 Yes, when this flesh and heart shall fail,
And mortal life shall cease,
I shall possess within the vail,
A life of joy and peace.

348. T. 22.

MY Saviour left his throne, and came
From guilt lost sinners to redeem,
That they might have their sins forgiv'n,
And find in him their peace and heav'n.

2 Daily may I from thee receive
That peace the world can never give,
Since Jesus on the cross's tree
By death procur'd that peace for me.

3 Lord, I am thine, O take me now,
I in the dust before thee bow,
Asham'd, that I no sooner ran
To thee the Saviour of lost man.

349.* T. 4.

DEAR Lord, when I trace
The offers of grace
Received from thee,—Thy drawings of love from my first infancy;

2 I fall at thy feet;
Thy mercy's so great,
I'm lost in amaze:—Thy love and forbearance all thoughts far surpass.

3 I now wish to be
Devoted to thee,
Who for me hast dy'd—Grant that I
may serve thee, and in thee abide.

350.* T. 228.

O HOW enraptur'd is my heart,
That in my Jesus I have part,
He is my only treasure!
May I for evermore abide
A member of his chosen bride,
And live unto his pleasure;
Oh! I—have joy,
At the favor—that my Saviour
Here already
Join'd me to the church his body.

351.* T. 83.

O REJOICE, Christ's happy sheep!
For your Shepherd will for ever
You, his flock in safety keep;
You are objects of his favor:
Only fast unto him cleave,
You he'll ne'er forsake nor leave.

352.* T. 97.

MY All in all, my faithful Friend!
Upon whose mercy I depend;
Than ought in earth or heav'n more dear;
My Paschal Lamb from year to year;
My Shield, my Rock, my Polar-star, my Guide,
Thou art my God, and ever shalt abide!

XX. Of Thankfulness of the Heart for Jesus' Incarnation and Death.

353.* T. 119.

THANKS and praise, :||:
Jesus, unto thee are due;
O accept our adoration,
For the blessings which accrue
From thy human life and passion;
May our hearts and lips with one accord
Praise thee, Lord! :||:

2 For thy death :||:
Thou art worthy, Lamb of God,
That our lives and whole demeanor
Praise thee, yea each drop of blood
Be devoted to thy honor,
And our souls uninterruptedly
Cleave to thee. :||:

3 O how great :||:
Are the blessings we derive
From the fulness of our Saviour!
They who him by faith receive,
And desire to taste his favor,
From this source may freely take always
Grace for grace. :||:

4 Ah remain :||:
Ah remain our highest Good!
In our hearts, dear suff'ring Saviour,
Shed thy dying love abroad;
This will rule our whole behavior,
Us with love inspire, till we shall be,
Lord, with thee. :||:

354. T. 14.

TO our Redeemer's glorious name
Awake the sacred song!
O may his love (immortal flame!)
Tune ev'ry heart and tongue.

2 His love what angel's thought can reach?
What mortal's tongue display?
Imagination's utmost stretch
In wonder dies away.

3 He left his radiant throne on high,
Left the bright realms of bliss,
And came on earth to bleed and die!
Was ever love like this!

4 Dear Lord, while we adoring pay
Our humble thanks to thee,
May ev'ry heart with rapture say:
"The Saviour dy'd for me."

5 O may the sweet, the blissful theme
  Fill ev'ry heart and tongue,
Till strangers love thy charming name,
  And join the sacred song.

355.* T. 14.

O JESUS, for thy matchless love,
  Accept our warmest praise;
Since thou didst leave thy throne above,
  To save a sinful race.

2 Thanks for thy suff'rings, tears, and cries,
  And groans in thy distress;
The source of never-fading joys,
  And endless happiness.

3 Thanks for thy thirst, O Prince of peace,
  When hanging on the tree;
What a divine refreshment this
  To souls athirst for thee!

4 Thanks for thy last heart-piercing cry,
  And meritorious death:
Grant we may all on thee rely,
  And live a life of faith.

356. T. 167.

SING with humble hearts your praises,
  For our Saviour's boundless grace;
Pay due homage to Christ Jesus,
  Come with thanks before his face:
Praise him for his death and bleeding,
  All our happiness lies there;
Praise him for his gracious leading,
  Praise your faithful Shepherd's care.

2 Thou to purchase our salvation
  Didst assume humanity;
Jesus, for thy bitter passion,
  May we ever thankful be:
Fill'd with awe, and humbly bowing,
  At thy feet we prostrate fall,
Gratefully this truth avowing,
  That thou art our All in all.

357.* T. 244.

REDEEMED congregation,
  Extol with one accord
The God of our salvation,
  Sing praises to the Lord:

For us he man became,
  And still abides the same;
To make us all one spirit
  With him, is his blest aim.

358.* T. 155.

ANGELS, principalities,
Thrones and pow'rs in heav'nly places,
Worship Jesus,
As the Author of their frame;
We with them
Praise him for his incarnation,
Human life and bitter passion,
And adore his saving name.

359.* T. 590.

WHAT strikes, O wounded Lamb of God,
  My soul so sensibly?
'Tis when I view the fervent love,
  That urged thee to die;
And feel that from thy precious blood,
  So freely shed for me,
Flows all my happiness in time,
  And in eternity.

2 This grace, as long as life shall last,
  I humbly will proclaim;
I, who a sinner void of good,
  Who dust and ashes am:
'Tis deeply rooted in my heart,
  Eras'd it ne'er shall be,
That by thy meritorious death
  Thou hast redeemed me.

3 Thy mercy may I ne'er forget,
  While here below I stay:
I'm lost in wonder and amaze,
  When I thy goodness weigh,
That I, poor sinner, am become
  A child of thine, thro' grace,
And being thine, a joyful heir
  Of ceaseless happiness.

4 With contrite tears I thee adore,
  And thank for mercy free;
I'll in my walk show forth thy praise,
  Ev'n in my small degree:
If thou support me with thy aid,
  As my most gracious Lord;
Th' imperfect service which I yield,
  Will joy to thee afford.

5 Whenever my frail nature swerves
Beyond the proper bounds, [gives,
Thou know'st, O Lord, what pain it
How grievously it wounds;
With eager haste I therefore flee,
And safely wish to hide
Within thy wounds, O God my Rock,
And in those clefts abide.

6 O thou, who to redeem my soul
Didst on the cross expire,
Grant I may love thee in return,
Be this my fix'd desire:
Henceforth no more to cherish self,
But to thy praise to live,
Who lovedst me, and out of love
Thyself for me didst give.

7 Thy suff'rings then, and bitter death,
My heart shall e'er retain;
And earnestly I'll shun thro' grace,
All that which gives thee pain;
For nothing now which this vain world
Can offer or devise,
Can yield me any further joy,
Nought but my ransom price.

8 For ever then remain engrav'd
Deep in my heart's recess;
Thee whom I wish to love in truth,
O may my mouth confess:
Grant that each sheep within thy fold
Thy seal impress'd may bear,
Until thou, at the judgment day,
In glory shalt appear.

360.* T. 151.

BEHOLD, my soul, thy Saviour
Gives up his life and blood,
Thee to restore to favor,
And reconcile to God;
Thy ev'ry pain he eases,
In him thou find'st relief,
Rise then, and sing his praises,
Who turns to joy thy grief.

2 How is my soul delighted,
Tho' shame o'erspreads my face,
When I, by faith excited,
The Lamb of God can trace,
In all his bitter passion,
Till dying on the tree!
He bare my condemnation,
And gained life for me.

3 I see him in the garden
Shed floods of bitter tears,
Sinking beneath the burden;
I hear his anxious pray'rs;
I see him pine and languish,
As on the ground he lay,
Till, thro' his pores in anguish,
The blood-sweat forc'd its way.

4 I fully am assured
My Saviour loveth me,
By all he hath endured
In his great agony;
His back plough'd o'er with furrows,
His side pierc'd with a spear,
And unexampled sorrows,
His boundless love declare.

5 My fav'rite theme is Jesus,
All else I count but loss;
His love all thought surpasses,
Ah, view him on the cross!
Thence hope and consolation
I freely can derive;
Were he not my salvation,
I could not bear to live.

6 Near Jesus' cross I tarry,
On him I fix mine eyes,
Behold him spent and weary
A bleeding sacrifice;
Once of his heav'nly glory
I shall obtain a sight;
But here, his suff'ring beauty
Remains my chief delight.

7 What undeserved favor
Hath Jesus to me shewn!
Might I recline for ever
Upon his breast, like John.
Tis my heart's inclination,
Like Mary, oft to sit,
Until my consummation,
Lord, at thy pierced feet.

8 In my forlorn condition
Thou, Lord, didst me receive,
Thou savedst from perdition
My soul, and badst me live:
With inward spirit's ardor,
I thank thee for thy grace;
Thyself this heav'nly fervor
Of love to thee increase!

361.* T. 146.

LORD Jesus, who for me
Hast endless bliss obtained,
And as thy property
My soul by blood regained:
Accept a weeping eye,
A warm and grateful heart,
Tho' a thank-off'ring poor,
Yet take it in good part.

2 Jesus, thy dying love
And thy blood-bought salvation,
By day and night shall prove
My fav'rite meditation.
When I commune with thee,
As tho' before mine eyes
I saw thee bodily;
My faith this vivifies.

3 I look to Golgotha,
For me I view thee languish,
And melt like wax away
Before thy pain and anguish;
By faith I see God's wrath
In what on thee did fall,
The fountain too and bath
For my offences all.

4 Most gracious God and Lord!
Mankind's almighty Saviour!
Worthy to be ador'd
By all both now and ever!
Those souls are blest indeed
Who thee embrace by faith,
As thou for us wast laid
Low in the dust of death.

5 In thee I trust by faith,
Jesus, my God and Saviour;
On thy atoning death
My soul shall feed for ever;
Thy suff'rings shall remain
Deep on my heart imprest,
Thou Son of God and man!
Till I with thee shall rest.

362.* T. 149.

WHEN I Christ in spirit trace
As the world's Creator,
And regard the sinfulness
Of my fallen nature;
I revere—him with fear:
But his expiration
Yields me consolation.

2 Heart-reviving is the view
Of our lovely Saviour;
Him our highest Good to know,
Be our whole endeavour;
We're unclean,—full of sin,
But the stripes of Jesus
Heal all our diseases.

3 Lamb of God, all praise to thee!
Thou hast vict'ry gained,
And upon the cross for me
Endless bliss obtained;
Thou art mine,—I am thine;
May my whole demeanor
To thy name give honor.

363.* T. 97.

THANKS to the Man of sorrows be,
To Jesus Christ, who set us free
From sin and death, when on the cross
He suffer'd to retrieve our loss;
Had he not shed his blood our debt to pay,
We still had been the devil's wretched prey.

2 O had not Jesus' blood been shed,
Life would a burden be indeed,
No comfort could we ever find,
No ray of hope to cheer our mind;
But now on earth we may enjoy his grace,
And humbly hope in heav'n to see his face.

3 Rise, brethren, we to all the earth
Our Lord's atonement will set forth,
Will love our Master unto death,
And humbly cleave to him by faith.
Lord Jesus, be thou prais'd eternally,
If there no Jesus were, what should we be!

364.* T. 146.

WE sinners void of good,
Defil'd by sin and stained,
Yet bought with Jesus' blood,
Who our salvation gained,
As helpless, vile and poor,
Appear before his face,
And humbly him adore
For our blest lot of grace.

2 When we thy mercy weigh,
How nails and scourges tore thee,
Our debt immense to pay;
We melt in tears before thee:
Thy pain, thy stripes and wounds,
Thy death, thou slaughter'd Lamb,
Whence all our bliss redounds,
Our grateful praises claim.

3 Eternal thanks be thine,
Author of our salvation!
Thou didst our hearts incline,
T' accept thy invitation;
We are thy property,
O may we thine abide;
This is our only plea,
That thou for us hast dy'd.

365.* T. 15.

THY blood, thy blood the deed hath wrought,
That won me for thee, Saviour;
Else had I never on thee thought,
Nor come to thee for ever.

2 Tho' I'm a sinful creature still,
I have a full exemption
From serving since, since thou didst quell
Its pow'r by thy redemption.

3 I feel how much in debt I am,
This makes me oft ashamed;
Yet as thy purchase, slaughter'd Lamb,
I am thro' grace esteemed.

4 O let me thee behold in faith,
As thou for me wast wounded;
And trust in thy atoning death,
Whereon my bliss is grounded.

5 Thy mercy ne'er from me remove;
But under thy direction,
Let me experience, while I live
On earth, thy kind protection.

6 May this each day be my employ,
The fruits of thy blest passion
Still more completely to enjoy,
And taste thy great salvation.

7 Till I shall once behold thy face,
In endless bliss and glory,
And for the wonders of thy grace,
With humble thanks adore thee.

366.* T. 228.

O LAMB once slain, my Lord and God!
Thy bitter suff'rings, death and blood
Remain my heart's confession;
Thee, the great Author of my frame,
Thankful I call the slaughter'd Lamb,
Thy love is past expression.
For joy—weep I
O'er thy bloody—wounded body,
For thy passion
Hath procur'd for me salvation.

2 Thy blood was shed for me, I know,
For my redemption did it flow;
O sweetest consolation!
Now nothing in the world beside
Can make me truly satisfy'd,
But thy blood-bought salvation:
There is—true bliss,
Virtue healing—all that's ailing,
Strength supplying
Life, altho' my flesh be dying.

367. T. 228.

O HAPPY hour! by faith I see
My suff'ring, dying Lord for me
Upon the cross outstretched;
If from my view this should depart,
I then should feel a piercing smart,
Yea I should be most wretched:
But he—knows me
To be feeble,—and not able
For a moment
To live without his atonement.

2 A sinner I, and full of blame;
But "Saviour" is his precious name;
He nothing will deny me;
His blood was shed for me, I know,
Thence blessings in abundance flow,
Nought else could satisfy me.
My God!—thy blood
Still can wash me—and refresh me;
It is cleansing,
Pardon, life, and grace dispensing.

3 Therefore I'll ever view my God,
His body cover'd o'er with blood,
His soul with grief oppressed;

This sight removes all doubt and fear,
It gives me boldness to draw near,
By whatsoe'er distressed:
Here I—find joy,
Heav'nly pleasure—beyond measure
Near my Saviour
I would fain abide for ever.

368. T. 141.

LAMB of God beloved,
Once for sinners slain,
Thankful we remember,
What thou didst sustain;
Nothing thee incited
But unbounded grace,
To bear condemnation
In the sinners' place.

2 This fills me with rapture,
That thou bar'st my smart,
And thy dying figure
Captivates my heart;
Since thou by thy passion
Didst for me atone,
I myself surrender
To thee, as thine own.

3 In thy wounds, O Jesus!
I have found true peace;
Thou in all distresses
Art my hiding-place;
Unto thee I'll ever
Look with humble faith,
And rejoice, and glory
In thy wounds and death.

4 I unworthy sinner
Lie before thy throne;
Tho' I scarce am able
To express, I own,
All my wants, dear Saviour,
Yet thou know'st them well;
Now in me the counsel
Of thy love fulfil.

369. T. 341.

'TIS done, my God hath dy'd,
My love is crucify'd.
Break, this stony heart of mine,
Pour my eyes a ceaseless flood,
Feel, my soul, the pangs divine,
Catch, my heart, the issuing blood!

2 To love thee, Lord,—ah! this
Ev'n here is heav'nly bliss;
With thy love my heart inspire,
There by faith for ever dwell;
This I always will desire,
Nothing but thy love to feel.

3 He bore the curse of all,
A spotless criminal:
Burden'd with our crimes and guilt,
Blacken'd with imputed sin,
Man to save his blood he spilt,
Dy'd, to make the sinner clean.

4 Join earth and heav'n to bless
The Lord our Righteousness;
Sinn'd we ALL, and dy'd in One;
Just in One we ALL are made:
Christ the law fulfill'd alone,
Dy'd for all, for all obey'd.

5 In him complete I shine,
His death, his life is mine;
Fully am I justify'd;
Free from sin, and more than free,
Guiltless, since for me he dy'd,
Righteous, since he liv'd for me!

6 Jesus! to thee I bow,
Approach thee humbly now.
O the depths of love divine!
Who thy wisdom's stores can tell?
Knowledge infinite is thine,
All thy ways unsearchable.

370. T. 206.

FULL to my view,—In bloody hue,
The Lamb of God
Stretch'd out upon the wood,
With wounds and stripes and scars—
Appears,
The nails and spear—His body tear,
And open wide
The fountain in his side.

2 His matchless worth—None can set forth,
Or duly praise
His mercy, love and grace;
He bore most willingly—For me
God's fiery wrath,
Which caus'd his death,
When on the cross
He died to ransom us.

3 By his blood shed,—The Lamb hath paid
My ransom price,
Offer'd a sacrifice
Well-pleasing unto God;—His blood
For me avail'd,—And never fail'd
To give me peace
And solid happiness.

4 His cries and pray'rs,—His bitter tears,
His bloody sweat,
And all his torments great,
His stripes and ev'ry wound,—Abound
With life and grace,—Yea lasting bliss:
From Golgotha
My soul would never stray.

371. T. 205.

LAMB of God,—thy precious blood,
Healing wounds, and bitter death,
Be our trust,—our only boast,
Blessed object of our faith!
Thy once marred countenance
Comfort to our hearts dispense,
By thy anguish, stripes and pain
May we life and strength obtain.

2 We adore—thee evermore,
Jesus, for thy boundless grace;
For thy cross—whereby for us
Thou hast gain'd true happiness;
For thy death which sets us free
From sin's cruel slavery;
For thy all-atoning blood,
Which hath brought us nigh to God.

3 What can we—now give to thee,
For thy unexampled love!
We're unclean—and full of sin,
Till thou dost our guilt remove;
All that's good in us, we own,
Is not ours, but thine alone;
Unto us belongeth shame;
But all glory to thy name.

4 Thro' thy grace,—may we always
Put our trust in thee by faith,
And rely—eternally
On thy meritorious death:
Fill our hearts with constant peace,
Till in thee we end our race,
And shall thee for evermore,
'Midst the ransom'd hosts adore.

372. T. 159.

I'M overcome with humble shame,
And blushes fill my face,
When I behold the suff'ring Lamb,
And when my faith can trace
How Jesus paid my ransom price,
And gave himself a sacrifice:
My gracious Saviour, near to thee
I ever wish to be.

2 'Tis then, with happy John, I view
His body, mark'd with scars;
Like Mary, I his feet bedew
With floods of sinner-tears;
I'm struck with this most charming sight
The Lamb of God is my delight,
The glory of the Trinity
In him by faith I see.

3 Free from the noisy, busy crowd,
Here would I ever stay,
And live in union with my God,
With Jesus night and day:
Extolling his unbounded love,
Till to his presence I remove,
And there, in higher notes of praise,
My Hallelujahs raise.

373. T. 166.

WHAT praise unto the Lamb is due!
How should this theme our souls inspire
When we his boundless love review,
And see him in his blood expire!
Who can describe how much he lov'd,
Or paint that strong and fervent zeal,
With which his tender heart was mov'd,
When he sustain'd the pangs of hell!

2 While others make the law their aim,
Thence count their gain, thence mourn their loss,
We'll know, and seek no other name
Than Jesus bleeding on the cross;
Jesus, the mourning sinner's feast,
The true believer's only Good;
He longs to give, we long to taste
Our meat and drink his flesh and blood.

3 In lively colors, Jesus, draw
Thy bleeding wounds within my breast;
And make thy dying love my law,
Till sin is wholly dispossest:

By grace alone we wish to live,
Nor from the law seek ease again;
For if thy blood can't vict'ry give,
Legal attempts will all prove vain.

374. T. 16.

SWEET the moments, rich in blessing,
Which before the cross I spend,
Life and health and peace possessing
From the sinner's dying Friend.

2 Here I'll sit for ever viewing
Mercy's streams, in streams of blood;
Precious drops! my soul bedewing,
Plead and claim my peace with God.

3 Truly blessed is this station,
Low before his cross to lie;
While I see divine compassion
Floating in his languid eye.

4 Here it is I find my heaven,
While upon the cross I gaze;
Love I much? I've more forgiven,
I'm a miracle of grace.

5 Love and grief my heart dividing,
With my tears his feet I'll bathe;
Constant still in faith abiding,
Life deriving from his death.

6 May I still enjoy this feeling,
In all need to Jesus go;
Prove his wounds each day more healing,
And himself more fully know.

375. T. 14.

HOW can I view the slaughter'd Lamb,
And all his suff'rings trace,
And not sink down with humble shame,
And give him thanks and praise!

2 This, Lord, I do with many tears,
And own with wonder fill'd,
Thy stripes & shame, thy griefs & pray'rs,
Made me thy pardon'd child.

3 Still be thy wounds to me more dear,
More precious ev'ry day;
Till I at thy pierc'd feet appear,
Dress'd in thy bright array.

376.* T. 14.

TH'impression of what Christ my Friend
Hath done for worthless me,
When he his life and blood did spend,
Attend me constantly.

2 O may I humbly onward move,
While dying here I stay,
And Jesus, whom my soul doth love,
Prepare me for his day.

377.* T. 68.

BE thy wounds and cross
Ever new to us!
From thy suff'ring scenes and merit
Nothing e'er divert our spirit;
With thy blood bedew
All we think or do.

378.* T. 79.

ETERNITY's expansions,
Time's numberless dimensions,
In spirit I have trac'd:
But nothing hath so struck me,
As when God's Spirit took me
To GOLGOTHA: O! God be prais'd!

379.* T. 228.

SING Hallelujah, honor, praise;
Your grateful lauds to Jesus raise,
O favor'd congregation!
For he became a sacrifice,
And paid in blood our ransom price,
Procuring our salvation.
Holy,—happy
Is our union—and communion
With our Saviour,
Blessed be his name for ever!

380.* T. 234.

THANKS be to thee thou slaughter'd Lamb!
For thy eternal love and favor;
We, sinful worms, with humble shame
Acknowledge thee our only Saviour;
For us thy soul was sore dismay'd,
For us thy body was tormented,
For us thou bowd'st thy sacred head,
Thus, by thy death, death's power ended:
Now fix our hearts and eyes
On this thy sacrifice;
O that we may forget it never!
But be it always clear,
God did in Christ appear,
From judgment us to free for ever.

XXI. Of the Love of JESUS.

381.* T. 97.

THOU Source of love, thou sinners' Friend,
Thy mercy who can comprehend?
Who ever can presume to say,
He lov'd, ere thou hadst shown the way?
Thou, who hast lov'd us from eternity,
Doth raise within us genuine love to thee.

2 Such unexampled, boundless grace
Doth fill our souls with deep amaze,
That God, who earth and heaven made,
Should be in human flesh array'd,
Thereby to save lost man from death and hell
Who did so basely 'gainst his Lord rebel!

3 Thy love, which always is the same,
Can ev'n the coldest hearts inflame,
Yea, they must feel a kindling ray,
Dissolve in tears and melt away;
Thy mercy, Lord, is such an endless store,
Man's reason here must silently adore.

4 However weak and helpless we,
However pow'rful sin may be,
Thou art our Strength in ev'ry case;
Thro' thy support and aiding grace
We firmly trust that we shall conqu'rors prove,
Since thou dost give us vict'ry from above.

5 Lo, we fall down with filial fear,
Conscious that thou art present here;
We humbly laud thy saving name,
We sink, abas'd with humble shame,
Almighty God, before thy glorious throne;
And thee our only Lord and Saviour own.

6 Reach out thy sceptre, King of love,
Let us thy royal favor prove,
Who, conscious of our indigence,
Approach thy throne with confidence;
O teach our lips to praise, our hearts to glow,
Our eyes with grateful tears to overflow.

382*. T. 97.

WHOM dear Redeemer, dost thou love?
What doth thy highest pleasure prove?
Whom dost thou favor, cheer, and bless,
And call to endless happiness?
Thou who art holy, great, unchangeable,
The mighty God, yet our Immanuel!

2 The answer humble thanks doth claim,
And fills our souls with conscious shame:
"I love thee, sinner, come to me,
I will receive thee graciously;
Tho' thou be sinful, ready to despair,
Thou shalt my pardon, help and glory share."

3 What wonder in the soul takes place,
When we survey thy boundless grace!
To know our own depraved heart,
And thy great name, and what thou art,
And yet to find thee still so gracious prove;
This makes us sink abas'd with shame and love.

4 We all know who, and what we are,
And all with one consent declare,
That we no good in us could find
To move thee, Lord, to be so kind:
Yet many here with inward rapture feel
Thy Spirit's unction, and assuring seal.

5 O ground us deeper still in thee,
And let us thy true foll'wers be;
And when of thee we testify,
Fill thou our souls with heav'nly joy:
May thy blest Spirit all our souls inspire,
And set each cold and lifeless heart on fire.

6 Our souls and bodies, Lord, prepare,
That we rich fruit for thee may bear;
Grant we may live unto thy praise,
And serve thy cause with faithfulness;
Since grace and truth is our hearts' wish and aim,
O glorify in us thy saving name.

383.* T. 90.

MY Saviour, thou thy love to me
In want, in pain, in shame, hast shown;
For me thou on th' accursed tree,
Didst by thy precious blood, atone:
Thy death upon my heart impress,
That nothing may it thence erase.

2 O that my heart, which open stands,
May catch each drop, that tort'ring pain,
Arm'd by my sins, wrung from thy hands,
Thy feet, thy head, thy ev'ry vein:
That still my breast may heave with sighs
Still tears of love o'erflow mine eyes:

3 O that I, like a little child,
May follow thee; nor ever rest,
Till sweetly thou hast pour'd thy mild
And lowly mind into my breast:
O may I now and ever be
One spirit, dearest Lord, with thee.

4 What in thy love possess I not?
My Star by night, my Sun by day,
My Spring of life, when parch'd with drought,
My Wine to cheer, my Bread to stay,
My strength, my shield, my safe Abode,
My Robe before the throne of God!

5 From all eternity with love
Unchangeable thou hast me view'd;
Ere knew this beating heart to move,
Thy tender mercies me pursu'd:
Ever with me may they abide,
And close me in on ev'ry side.

6 In suff'ring be thy love my peace,
In weakness be thy love my pow'r;
And when the storms of life shall cease,
Jesus, in that important hour,
In death, as life, be thou my Guide,
And save me, who for me hast dy'd.

384.* T. 580.

GRACIOUS Redeemer, who for us
Didst die upon th' accursed cross,
To save our souls from death:
We humbly at thy feet fall down,
And thee thy body's Saviour own,
On whom we firmly trust by faith.

2 Weak, helpless babes, 'tis true we are,
Poor sinners, but from guilt made clear;
The virtue of that blood,
Which did for all our sins atone,
We have experienc'd, and have known
From thence the quick'ning pow'r of God.

3 And now we nothing can reply,
But humbly at thy feet we lie,
Astonish'd at thy grace,
That vile and wretched as we are,
Such undeserved love we share;
To thee is due eternal praise.

4 When we thy boundless love survey,
Our hearts like wax then melt away,
Our eyes with tears o'erflow,
We are determin'd nought beside
To know, but Jesus crucify'd,
And him to follow here below.

385.* T. 580.

CHRIST, my Redeemer, Lord & God,
How came I, sinner void of good,
To that blest company
Of ransom'd souls, who are in faith
United, grounded on thy death,
Why didst thou fix thy choice on me?

2 When I to thee for succor cry'd,
Thy bounty all my wants supply'd;
I brought to thee a heart
So cold, that it seem'd scarcely fit
A spark of love divine t' admit;
But now 'tis kindled by thy smart.

3 Tho' I to mercy had no right,
Yet I found favor in thy sight,
Like Magd'len at thy feet;
So that I now, supremely blest,
In thee have found true peace and rest,
Yea happiness, and joy complete.

386.* T. 132.

THE Lord my Shepherd is and Guide,
Who kindly doth direct me;
For all my wants he will provide,
From dangers will protect me.
He leads me to a pasture-ground,
Where for my soul rich food is found,
The word of his salvation.

2 He guides my soul to living springs,
Where sweetly I'm refreshed;
His Spirit joy and comfort brings
To me whene'er abashed;
He leads me in the blessed way
Of his commandments, day by day,
To his name's praise and glory.

3 A table for me he prepares,
My soul enjoys his favor;
And thus secur'd, no en'my dares
My God and me to sever:
His holy Spirit cheers my heart,
And changes ev'ry grief and smart
To joys unutterable.

4 His goodness and his mercies all
Will follow me for ever,
And I'll maintain my proper call,
To cleave to my dear Saviour,
And to his congregation here;
And when call'd home, I shall live there
With Christ, my soul's Redeemer.

387.* T. 36.

THY thoughts of peace o'er me, my gracious Saviour,
Thy mercy, love, and patience, which ne'er waver,
They are my comfort, prompt me to prostration, And adoration.

2 I am the chief of sinners, yea, the poorest
Of those, whom of thy favor thou assurest;
Thy goodness shown to me can't be expressed, Or duly praised.

3 Hadst thou not sought me first, and follow'd ever,
I had not come to thee, nor known thy favor;
When thou hadst found me, then with arms of mercy
Thou didst embrace me.

4 I thank thee with sincerest heart's affection,
That thou according to thy grace election,
Hast brought me to thy blood-bought congregation, Seal'd my Salvation.

388.* T. 208.

NONE but Christ, my Saviour,
Loves with matchless fervor;
This is surely true!
Souls in him believing,
And his blessings craving,
Taste them daily new;
Yea, his mercy far exceeds
All to think or say we're able;
'Tis incomparable.

2 Weeping or rejoicing,
When from love arising,
He takes in good part;
Whoe'er cannot truly,
Holy, holy, holy,
Sing with cheerful heart,
O might he but contrite be!
Christ regards our mournful crying,
Inward groans and sighing.

3 Yea, his own he guideth,
Faithful he abideth,
Till his thoughts of peace
Fully are accomplish'd,
And our race here finish'd,
We shall see his face.
O rejoice with heart and voice,
Church of God, and praise for ever
His unbounded favor.

389. T. 89.

ONE there is above all others,
Who deserves the name of Friend,
His is love beyond a brother's,
Costly, free, and knows no end:
They who once his kindness prove,
Find it everlasting love!

2 Which of all our friends, to save us,
Could or would have shed his blood!
But our Jesus dy'd, to have us
Reconcil'd in him to God:
This was boundless love indeed!
Jesus is a Friend in need.

3 When he liv'd on earth abased,
Friend of sinners was his name,
Now to heav'nly glory raised
He rejoiceth in the same:
Still he calls them brethren, friends,
And to all their wants attends.

4 Could we bear from one another,
What he daily bears from us?
Yet this glorious Friend and Brother
Loves us, tho' we treat him thus;
Tho' for good we render ill,
He accounts as brethren still.

5 Oh! for grace our hearts to soften!
Teach us, Lord, at length to love;
We alas! forget too often,
What a Friend we have above;
But when home our souls are brought
We will love thee as we ought.

390. T. 14.

JESUS, thy love exceeds by far
Thy love of earthly friends;
Bestows whate'er the sinner needs,
Is firm, and never ends.

2 My blessed Saviour, is thy love
So bounteous, great and free?
Behold I give my sinful heart,
My life, my all to thee.

3 No man of greater love can boast,
Than for his friend to die:
Thou for thy enemies wast slain,
What love with thine can vie?

4 Tho' in the very form of God,
With heav'nly glory crown'd,
Thou wouldst partake of human flesh,
Beset with troubles round.

5 And now, ev'n on thy throne above,
Thy love is still as great;
Well thou remember'st Calvary,
Nor canst thy death forget.

6 O Lord, I'll treasure in my soul
The mem'ry of thy love:
And thy dear name shall still to me
A grateful odor prove.

391. T. 90.

JESUS, Redeemer of mankind,
Sov'reign Creator, Lord of all,
Since I in thee salvation find,
Before thy cross I humbly fall:
My Lord, my God, my soul's desire,
With sacred flames my heart inspire.

2 How couldst thou love such worms as us?
Why didst thou look upon our race?
Why didst thou die upon the cross?
What caus'd all this but boundless grace?
'Twas, dearest Lord, thy matchless love
Which thee to save our souls did move.

3 O let thy pity thee constrain,
Pardon our sin, its pow'r subdue,
May all of us be born again,
Thy image in us all renew:
Let on us shine thy cheering face,
Give us to know thy saving grace.

4 Be thou our strength, be thou our song;
Be our exceeding great reward:
Let ev'ry heart, and ev'ry tongue,
Rejoice and triumph in the Lord:
Jesus, our boast shall be of thee,
In time, and in eternity.

392. T. 14.

COME, Holy Ghost, inspire my song
With thy immortal flame;
And teach my heart, & teach my tongue,
The Saviour's lovely name.

2 The Saviour! O what endless charms
Dwell in the blissful sound!
Its influence ev'ry fear disarms,
And spreads sweet comfort round.

3 Here pardon, life, and joys divine,
In rich effusions flow,
For guilty rebels lost by sin,
And doom'd to endless woe.

4 God's only Son, (stupendous grace!)
Forsook his throne above;
And swift to save our wretched race,
He flew on wings of love.

5 Th' almighty Former of the skies
Stoop'd to our vile abode;
While angels view'd with wond'ring eyes
And hail'd th' incarnate God.

6 O the rich depths of love divine!
Of bliss a boundless store:
Dear Saviour, let me call thee mine,
I cannot wish for more.

7 On thee alone my hope relies,
Beneath thy cross I fall;
My Lord, my Life, my sacrifice,
My Saviour, and my All.

393. T. 74.

SAVIOUR! thro' grace divine
I know, that I was thine
From early infancy;
This by thy calls I see,
And drawings all along
Frequent, distinct and strong.

2 I know, thro' mercy free
Thine I shall ever be,
No separation here
From thee I need to fear;
In thee I can confide,
Thou faithful wilt abide.

3 I know I worthless am,
This fills my soul with shame,
Down in the dust I bow,
Lord, keep me ever low;
In thee alone I trust,
Thy love is all my boast!

394. T. 90.

BEFORE the Father's awful throne
Our High-Priest lifts his pierced hands,
And interceding for his own
His purchas'd property demands;
His people's everlasting Friend,
Who loving, loves them to the end.

2 By faith we claim him as our own,
Our Kinsman, near ally'd in blood,
Flesh of our flesh, bone of our bone,
The Son of man, the Son of God;
We to his mercy-seat draw nigh;
He never can himself deny.

395.* T. 14.

THY mercies and thy faithfulness,
Dear Lord, are daily new,
But who can tell them to thy praise,
Upon a close review?

2 Could I exalt thee worthily,
For thy unbounded grace,
Display'd in various ways to me,
My lauds would never cease.

396.* T. 590.

O LORD, accept my worthless heart,
And keep it ever thine;
Since thou for me, a sinful worm,
Hast shed thy blood divine,
Therewith to save my guilty soul
From endless pain and woe:
What dearest friend in all the world
Could equal kindness show!

397.* T. 56.

THOU, O Jesus, :||: art a gracious Lord,
Ever faithful, :||: keeping to thy word;
None can be so full of grief,
But he soon may find relief,
By the comfort :||: thy kind looks afford.

398.* T. 87.

LORD, had I of thy love
Such an impression,
As to forget all else
In that fruition,
Still would my love fall short
Of thy great mercies;
Nor can eternity
Sing all thy praises.

399. T. 184.

HOW much we're lov'd by God our Saviour,
With warmest gratitude we trace;
His patience, mercy, pardon, favor,
Supported us throughout our race:
To him we trust for future blessing,
He'll lead us till our latest breath:
O may we all, with love unceasing,
Rejoice in him, our Lord, by faith!

XXII. Of Love to JESUS.

400.* T. 206.

THEE will I love, my strength & tow'r,
My soul with love to thee inspire;
Thee will I love with all my pow'r,
Thou art alone my soul's desire;
Thee will I love, my King and God,
Shed in my heart thy love abroad.

2 Ah, why did I so late thee know,
Thou fairest of the sons of men!
Ah, why did I no sooner go
To thee who canst relieve my pain!
Asham'd I sigh, and inly mourn
That I so late to thee did turn.

3 Give to my eyes repenting tears,
Give to my heart chaste, hallow'd fires;
Give to my soul with filial fears,
The love that all heav'n's host inspires:
That all my pow'rs, with all their might,
In thy sole glory may unite.

401.* T. 232.

THEE, Lord, I love with sacred awe,
Thy gracious presence ne'er withdraw
From me, thy feeble creature.
The world is tasteless unto me,
I find no comfort but in thee,
And in thy loving nature:
Yea, when the strings of life are broke,
Thou shalt remain my lasting Rock;
Thou art my comfort and my All,
Whose blood redeem'd me from the fall;
Lord Jesus Christ, :||: thy saving name
Preserve me from eternal shame.

2 All my desires are fix'd on thee,
Lord Jesus, thou art more to me
Than ev'ry earthly treasure;
Were heav'n itself without thee, Lord,
What could all heav'nly bliss afford,
To yield me solid pleasure?
Did I not feel that thou art near,
Whene'er I mourn, my heart to cheer,
Nought in this world could comfort me;
My wishes centre all in thee;
Lord Jesus Christ! :||: if thou art gone,
My ev'ry comfort is withdrawn!

3 With my whole heart I cleave to thee,
And thou wilt come and dwell with me;
This is my consolation!
In joy and pain my soul depends
On thee with humble confidence,
Thou Rock of my salvation!
Thou shalt remain my Portion blest,
My All, by word and deed confest,
Till these mine eyes behold thy face;
Meanwhile support me by thy grace,
O Jesus Christ :||: my God and Lord,
In ev'ry trial help afford.

402.* T. 200.

O CHRIST, my only Life and Light,
Whose loving condescension
Refresheth me by day and night,
Beyond my comprehension:
Grant, that I may return thy love
With grateful heart's devotion,
Thus my notion
Of mercy will improve
With ev'ry thought and motion.

2 Let nothing dwell within my heart,
But thy great love and favor:
May this engage my soul to part
With ev'ry sinful savor:
With all things, whether great or small,
Which breed the least division,
Or Collision,
'Twixt me and God my All,
Who sav'd me from perdition.

3 How blest, how excellent and kind,
Are thy great love and merit!
Were these but fix'd within my mind,
What could disturb my spirit?
O might no thought arise in me,
No object move my senses,
No pretences,
T' obstruct my love to thee;
Thus heav'n on earth commences.

4 O that I were still more possest
Of this great, sov'reign blessing!
O that my cold and lifeless breast
Might glow with love unceasing!

Grant I may watch both day and night,
To keep this heav'nly treasure
From the seisure
Of Satan's secret spite,
Who seeks our woe with pleasure.

5 Thou cam'st in love to my relief,
Bar'st sin's due pain and torment,
Hung'st on the cross just like a thief,
Or murd'rer, without garment,
Scorn'd, spit upon, and sore distrest:
O! let thy suff'rings enter
To the centre
Of this my stubborn breast,
To melt and make it tender.

6 The blood, which thou hast shed for me,
Is precious, pure and holy;
But this my heart, that swerves from thee,
Is hard, replete with folly:
Lord! may the virtue of thy blood
Sink deep into the nature
Of thy creature,
And its kind influences spread
Thro' ev'ry vein and feature.

7 O that my heart with eagerness
Would open wide, and gather
Each drop of blood my sins did press
From thee, my Mediator!
O were mine eyes a well of tears,
To weep for thee my Saviour!
May I ever,
Freed from all needless fears,
Enjoy thy love and favor.

8 O that I with a babe's desire
Came running, weeping, stretching,
So long, till love's celestial fire
My longing soul were catching:
Without thy love there's nought but gall,
Nought else yields satisfaction,
But distraction,
Nought else I joy can call,
Nought else gives me refection.

9 Thy love divine is perfect rest,
The source of all true pleasure:
O Jesus, be my soul thus blest,
T' enjoy thee in full measure!
Shed in my heart thy love abroad;
O let thy blood be healing
All that's ailing,
And that depravity
I am with grief bewailing.

10 Thy love, my Saviour, all supplies
That to my soul is wanting,
'Tis the true light unto mine eyes,
My cordial, when I'm fainting:
My bread and wine, my costly dress,
My joy and delectation,
My salvation,
My comfort in distress,
My refuge 'midst oppression.

11 My dearest Lord, shouldst thou remove,
Nought else could yield me pleasure;
Shouldst thou withdraw thy precious love,
I lose my only treasure.
Thee may I seek and entertain,
With inward joy receive thee,
Never leave thee,
And ne'er henceforth again
Unfaithful prove and grieve thee.

12 Thy love hath always been the same,
And ever did pursue me;
Before I knew thy saving name,
In mercy thou didst view me.
O let thy love, almighty Lord,
Continue to direct me,
And protect me,
Yea, help to me afford,
'Gainst all that would obstruct me.

13 Thy love uphold me, when distrest,
Give strength, when I am feeble;
And when this mortal period's past,
Thou, who to save art able,
Support, and strengthen my weak faith;
Apply thy pow'rful merit
To my spirit,
That I may after death,
Eternal joy inherit.

403.* T. 151.

JESUS, my highest treasure!
In thy communion blest,
I find unsully'd pleasure,
True happiness and rest.
Myself as an oblation
I have to thee assign'd,
Because thou by thy passion
Hast heal'd my sin-sick mind.

2 O joy, all joys exceeding!
Thou Bread most heavenly,
When I on thee am feeding,
Thou dost me satisfy
With marrow and with fatness,
With comfort, joy and peace,
And fill'st my heart with gladness,
Assuaging my distress.

3 Let me perceive thy friendly,
Thy cheering countenance;
Spread thro' my heart its kindly
Enliv'ning influence.
Without thee, gracious Saviour,
To live, is nought but pain;
T' enjoy thy love and favor,
Is happiness and gain.

4 Earth's glory to inherit,
Is not what I desire:
My heav'nly minded spirit
Glows with a nobler fire;
Where Christ himself appeareth
In brightest majesty,
For me a place prepareth,
There, there I long to be.

4 Jesus, thou my only rest,
O my Jesus, let me find thee;
Jesus, take me to thy breast,
With thy cords of love now bind me.
Thou'rt the object of my mind,
I am by thy love inflamed;
Ev'ry good that can be named,
Ev'ry bliss in thee I find.

5 May I of thy chosen bride
Be a member chaste and holy;
Let me quite in thee confide,
Cleave to thee and love thee solely:
Jesus, kindly me receive;
Thine alone may I be called;
Grant, that what hath me inthralled
May no longer me enslave.

6 Thou in grace hast look'd on me,
And with precious gifts hast blessed;
Yet content I cannot be,
Till I am of thee possessed.
Jesus, now upon me shine,
Jesus, be my Sun resplendent,
Jesus, be my joy transcendent,
Jesus, be thou ever mine!

404.* T. 156.

JESUS is my Light most fair,
Jesus yields me solid pleasure;
In his love I have a share,
This I count my highest treasure;
He alone is my delight,
He my soul hath captivated,
With his love I'm penetrated;
He hath overcome me quite.

2 Round his pierced feet I'll cling,
Him I seek with love most tender;
And accurs'd be ev'ry thing,
Which my seeking him would hinder.
Tell me nought of worldly fame,
Tell me nought of earthly treasure,
Would you please in any measure,
Tell me of his lovely name.

3 But himself I must behold,
To him I will make confession:
My defects are manifold,
But I trust to his compassion.
For I cannot, will not rest,
Till I've found my dearest Saviour,
Till he looks on me in favor,
Till he grants me my request.

405.* T. 39.

I'LL glory in nothing but only in Jesus,
As wounded and bruised from sin to release us:
For he is my Refuge, to him I'll cleave solely,
Thus can I, like Enoch, in this world live holy.

2 What tho' the world foameth and rageth with fury,
I in my dear crucify'd Jesus will glory;
Beside him my Saviour I'll know nothing ever,
From whom neither trials, nor death me shall sever.

3 My Saviour takes notice of hearts for him pining,
He soothes their distress who on him are reclining;

All this I've experienc'd, I therefore will hold him,
I never will leave him, my faith shall infold him.

4 My Jesus is always desirous to meet me,
Abounding in love, and in mercy to greet me.
Above all I love him, for he is my treasure,
I humbly adore him and serve him with pleasure.

5 My heart's fix'd on Jesus, whose love is so tender,
My life and my all unto him I surrender;
He is and remaineth my heart's meditation,
My faith's only object, till my consummation.

406.* T. 83.

JESUS will I never leave,
He's the God of my salvation;
Thro' his merits I receive
Pardon, life and consolation:
All the powers of my mind,
To my Saviour be resign'd.

2 Nought on earth can satisfy
One desire which God inspireth,
Only Jesus can supply
All my needy heart requireth;
He all losses can retrieve,
Him I'll therefore never leave.

3 He is mine, and I am his,
Join'd with him in close communion;
And his bitter passion is
The foundation of this union;
Full of hopes, which never yield,
Firm on him, my Rock, I build.

4 O the happy hours I spend
With him in blest conversation!
He's my near and Faithful Friend,
Full of grace, peace, and salvation;
From the look at Jesus' wounds
Pure delight to me redounds.

5 With my Jesus I will stay,
He my soul preserves and feedeth;
He, the Life, the Truth, the Way,
Me to living waters leadeth:
Blessed, who can say with me,
Christ, I'll never part with thee!

407.* T. 22.

DEAR Jesus, when I think on thee,
My heart for joy doth leap in me;
Thy blest remembrance yields delight,
Till faith is changed into sight.

2 When thou art near, I must confess,
I feel a bliss I can't express:
Thy love, my Saviour, ne'er can cloy,
Fountain of bliss, and source of joy.

3 Let me by faith behold thy face,
Still taste thy love, and share thy grace;
Still let my tongue resound thy name,
And Jesus be my constant theme.

4 Thy love and mercies all exceed;
The more I on these dainties feed,
The more my eager soul is bent
To live but in this element.

5 Blest Jesus, what delicious fare,
How sweet thy entertainments are!
Never did angels taste above
Redeeming grace and dying love.

408.* T. 11.

DEAREST Jesus, come to me,
And abide eternally;
Friend of needy sinners, come,
Fill and make my heart thy home.

2 Oftentimes for thee I sigh,
Nothing else can give me joy;
This is still my cry to thee:
Dearest Jesus, come to me!

3 Should I in earth's pleasures roll,
None could satisfy my soul;
Thee, O Jesus! I adore,
Thou'rt my pleasure evermore.

4 Jesus, thee alone I call,
My beloved Friend, my All;
Nothing, whatsoe'er it be,
Shall divide my heart with thee.

409.* T. 15.

GRACIOUS Redeemer, thou hast me
To come to thee invited;
Thy love, to love thee ardently
Hath my cold heart excited.

2 Thy cross, thy shame, thy pangs, thy smart,
Thy wounds, and bitter passion,
Now melt and captivate my heart,
And prompt my adoration.

3 The fire of love that burns within,
Is that divine impression,
That thou didst suffer for my sin,
And die for my transgression.

410.* T. 97.

'TIS evident that Jesus loves,
His death for us this fully proves;
He lov'd the world, a sinful race,
He loves the church, his flock of grace,
He loveth children, yea he loveth me
Who nought deserv'd but endless misery.

2 O may I in his love be blest,
Like John, reclining on his breast;
And oft, like humble Magdalen,
Adore the Friend of sinful men,
With longing heart attending at his feet,
Till with a gracious look from him I meet.

3 I'll weep whene'er he's not to me
What a most cordial friend can be;
Do I not always feel him nigh,
And his reviving grace enjoy,
Do I not in his sweet communion live,
Nought else to my poor soul can comfort give.

411.* T. 4.

WHEN duly I weigh,
How much day by day
Thee, Lord, I have try'd,—My Friend ever faithful, who for me hast dy'd;

2 I own the fault mine:
Thy patience divine,
Which clearly I trace—With tears fills my eyes, with shame covers my face;

3 As Mary ador'd
Her Master and Lord,
When her thou didst greet,
And deeply abas'd she embraced thy feet;

4 As Thomas with awe,
When thy wounds he saw,
His Saviour avow'd,—And cry'd with conviction, "My Lord and my God!"

5 As Peter reply'd,
His love being try'd,
"My heart thou dost prove,—Lord, thou knowest all things, thou know'st that I love;"

6 So may I, each day,
A clearer display
Obtain of thy grace;—Thus my love O Jesus! to thee will increase.

412.* T. 45.

WHAT splendid rays—of truth & grace,
All other lights excelling,
I perceive, when Jesus Christ
Makes my heart his dwelling!

2 He blesseth me—so sensibly,
That spirit, soul and body,
Can in him my Saviour joy,
Tho' quite poor and needy.

3 His looks of grace—insure always
To me my heav'nly calling:
Am I weak, his hand preserves
Me his child from falling.

4 My earnest pray'r—while absent here
From him my soul's Beloved,
Is, that my heart's confidence
In him be unmoved.

5 Could I with him—spend all my time,
In constant love's fruition,
Infinitely happy then
Would be my condition.

6 Whene'er I mourn—and humbly turn
For comfort to my Jesus,
I have never-failing proofs
That he's near and gracious.

7 They who always—our Saviour's face
Seek upon each occasion,
Never fail to be refresh'd
With his consolation.

413.* T. 167.

O COULD we but love that Saviour,
Who loves us so ardently,
As we ought, our souls would ever
Full of joy and comfort be!
If we, by his love excited,
Could ourselves and all forget,
Then, with Jesus Christ united,
We should heav'n anticipate!

2 Did but Jesus' love and merit
Fill our hearts both night and day,
And the unction of his Spirit
All our thoughts and actions sway!
O might all of us be ready
Cheerfully to testify,
How our spirit, soul and body,
Do in God our Saviour joy!

414. T. 14.

TEN thousand talents once I ow'd,
And nothing had to pay;
But Jesus freed me from the load,
And wash'd my debt away.

2 Yet since the Lord forgave my sin,
And blotted out my score;
Much more indebted I have been,
Than e'er I was before.

3 My guilt is cancell'd quite, I know,
And satisfaction made;
But the vast debt of love I owe
Can never be repaid.

4 The love I owe for sin forgiv'n,
For power to believe,
For present peace, and promis'd heav'n,
No angel can conceive.

5 That love of thine, thou sinners' Friend,
Witness thy bleeding heart!
My little all can ne'er extend
To pay a thousandth part.

6 Nay more, the poor returns I make
I first from thee obtain;
And 'tis of grace, that thou wilt take
Such poor returns again.

7 'Tis well—it shall my glory be,
(Let who will boast their store)
In time and in eternity,
To owe thee more and more.

415. T. 12.

HARK, my soul! it is the Lord;
'Tis thy Saviour, hear his word;
Jesus speaks, and speaks to thee,
"Say, poor sinner, lov'st thou me?"

2 "I deliver'd thee, when bound,
"And when wounded heal'd thy wound;
"Sought thee wand'ring, set thee right,
"Turn'd thy darkness into light.

3 "Can a woman's tender care
"Cease towards the child she bare?
"Yea, she may forgetful be,
"Yet will I remember thee.

4 "Mine is an unchanging love,
"Higher than the heights above,
"Deeper than the depths beneath,
"Free and faithful, strong as death.

5 "Thou shalt see my glory soon,
"When the work of grace is done,
"Partner of my throne shalt be;
"Say, poor sinner, lov'st thou me?"

6 Lord, it is my chief complaint,
That my love is weak and faint;
Yet I love thee, and adore,
Oh for grace to love thee more!

416. T. 14.

TEACH me yet more of thy blest ways,
Thou slaughter'd Lamb of God!
And fix and root me in the grace
So dearly bought with blood.

2 O tell me often of each wound,
Of ev'ry grief and pain;
And let my heart with joy confess,
From hence comes all my gain.

3 For thee, O may I freely count
Whate'er I have but loss;
And ev'ry name, and ev'ry thing,
Compar'd with thee, but dross.

4 Engrave this deeply in my heart,
That thou for me wast slain;
Then shall I, in my small degree,
Return thy love again.

5 But who can pay that mighty debt,
Or equal love like thine?
My heart, by nature cold and dead,
To thankfulness incline.

417.* T. 232.

JESUS, I love thee fervently!
As thou upon th' accursed tree
Wast slain for my transgression:
I'm glad, and grateful tears bedew
My cheeks, when I in spirit view
Thy death and bitter passion!
This gives the impulse, Lord that I
In truth can love thee heartily,
My love to thee thou knowest best;
But yet defective 'tis confest;
Thou highest Good! [flood,
Thy precious blood—that cleansing
Claims that my love more ardent glow'd.

418.* T. 58.

They who devoted are to our dear Lord,
And who believe in his most precious word,
Foll'wing the example
Of Christ their Saviour,
In all their actions, words, and whole behaviour,
Show love to him.

419.* T. 228.

WHAT causeth me to mourn, is this:
My warmest love not equal is
To my heart's inclination;
The more I love, the more I feel,
I should far better love thee still,
Thou God of my salvation!
Grant me—daily
More to savor—of thy favor,
Grace and blessing;
Thus my love will be increasing.

XXIII. Of Brotherly Love and Union of Spirit.

420. T. 11.

THEY who Jesus' foll'wers are,
And enjoy his Shepherd-care,
By a mutual, hearty love
Their belief in Jesus prove.

2 From their being join'd in one,
By the faith of God's dear Son,
Boundless blessings they receive,
And to Christ desire to live.

3 None in his own wisdom trusts,
None of his attainments boasts,
Each his brother doth esteem,
And himself the meanest deem.

4 They're delighted, when they all
With one voice on Jesus call;
And when fitly, without strife,
Each his duty doth in life.

5 Meek they are to all mankind,
To good offices inclin'd,
Ready, when revil'd, to bless,
Studious of the public peace.

6 Tender pity, love sincere
To their enemies they bear;
And, as Christ affords them light,
Order all their steps aright.

7 Jesus, all our souls inspire,
Fill us with love's sacred fire,
Thus will all in us perceive
That we in thy name believe.

8 May it to the world appear,
That we thy disciples are,
By our loving mutually,
By our being one in thee.

421. T. 22.

Behold us, Lord, rough stones we are,
Yet for thy building us prepare;
Reject not one of us, we pray,
Thy Spirit's voice may we obey.

2 O may thy flock still more increase
In mutual love, and perfect peace;
In harmony, with fervent zeal,
Serve thee, and do thy holy will.

3 Lord, grant us a forgiving mind,
To patience and to peace inclin'd,
That we may with each other bear;
To cherish love be all our care.

4 Tender compassion may we show,
Share in each others weal and woe,
With those who joyful are, rejoice,
And with the weeping sympathise.

5 At all times may we ready be,
As far as our ability
Permits us, to relieve the want
Of all the poor and indigent.

6 Yea, this be our concern, to seek
In nothing to offend the weak,
But bear with their infirmities,
And thus preserve the bond of peace.

7 Grant us in meekness to reclaim
Those, who have been in ought to blame,
Mindful that we, as well as they,
Are liable from thee to stray.

8 May we, tho' gifts be manifold,
As members of one body, hold
One doctrine, and be ever led
By thee, our Master, Lord, and Head.

9 O make us quite conform'd to thee,
And grant us true humility,
That we, supported by thy grace,
May in our walk show forth thy praise.

422. T. 14.

O LET thy love our hearts constrain,
Jesus, thou God of love;
The bond of peace let us maintain,
All discord far remove.

2 Us into closest union draw,
And in our inward parts
Write thou indelibly thy law;
Let love pervade our hearts.

3 Who would not now pursue the way
Where Jesus' footsteps shine?
Who would not own the pleasing sway
Of charity divine?

4 United firmly by thy grace,
We shall thy foll'wers prove;
The frowning world must then confess:
"See how these christians love!"

423. T. 11.

CHERISH us with kindest care,
Jesus, we thy brethren are,
Of thy flesh and of thy bone;
To the end O love thine own.

2 As our Head us move and guide,
Divers gifts to each divide;
Plac'd according to thy will,
Let us all thy mind fulfil.

3 Sweetly may we all agree,
Useful to each other be,
Each the other's burden bear,
In his weal and woe take share.

4 If one member honor'd be,
All rejoice most heartily;
If one suffers, all a part
Bear with sympathizing heart.

5 Closely join'd to thee, our Head,
Nourished by thee and fed,
Let us daily growth receive,
And with thee in union live.

424. T. 11.

JESUS, we look up to thee,
Let us in thy name agree;
Thou, who art the Prince of peace,
Bid contention ever cease.

2 By thy reconciling love
Ev'ry stumbling-block remove:
Lord, us all in thee unite,
To enjoy thy saving light.

3 Make us all one heart and mind,
Courteous, merciful, and kind,
Lowly, meek in thought and word,
As thou wast on earth, O Lord.

4 Let us for each other care,
Each the other's burden bear;
In our conduct patterns be
Of unfeign'd humility.

425.* T. 155.

NEVER yet hath in this world
Love that highest pitch attained,
Tho' unfeigned,
That it could compared be,
Reas'nably,
To that love our blest Creator
Show'd unto his rebel creature,
While as yet his enemy.

2 Ah! behold the Son of God!
Who for those that crucify'd him,
And deny'd him,
('Mongst whom, to my grief and shame,
Stands my name)
Pardon from his Father craveth,
Yea, ev'n his tormentors saveth;
This his love is still the same.

3 For our brethren we should too,
To lay down our lives be willing,
Thus fulfilling
What he of his flock desires,
Yea requires;
But, with all his flow'ry speeches,
Man in vain this lesson teaches,
Till God's love the soul inspires.

4 Brethren, would you please the Lord,
Copy then, in your behaviour,
Him your Saviour;
That you're his, the world will own
Then alone,
When, preferring each his brother,
Ye show love to one another;
Thus are his disciples known.

5 Yet the warmest mutual love,
That to brethren you're possessing
By his blessing,
When compared with his love,
Weak doth prove;
For, to save us from damnation,
By becoming our oblation,
Love immense our God did move.

426.* T. 167.

FLOCK of Jesus, be united,
Covenant with him anew
By his love divine excited,
Praise and serve him as 'tis due;
O that nothing whatsoever
May relax this blessed tie;
In thy love, most gracious Saviour,
Grant us all stability.

2 With love's ardor to be fired,
Be our aim continually,
So that, should it be required,
For the brethren we could die:
O what boundless love did Jesus
To his enemies display!
May his holy pattern teach us,
How love ought to bear the sway.

3 O that we, his steps to follow,
'Midst affliction, scorn and spite,
And his sacred name to hallow,
Did each other more excite!
Ev'ry one stir up his brother
To keep Jesus still in view,
Thus encouraging each other
His example to pursue.

4 Then the souls he join'd together
Will, according to his pray'r,
Be accepted of his Father,
And his kind protection share:
As thou art with him united,
Lord, may we be one in thee,
And by genuine love excited,
Serve each other willingly.

427.* T. 22.

TH' enjoyment of Christ's flesh & blood,
Which is on earth our highest good,
His members closely should unite,
And them to mutual love excite.

2 Love he most strongly did enforce,
Just ere he finished his course;
For love most fervently he pray'd,
Before in death he bow'd his head.

3 O that the Lord could quite fulfil
In us his testament and will!
To love each other we desire;
Come, sacred love, our hearts inspire;

4 We join together heart and hand,
To walk towards the promis'd land;
For his appearance may with care
Each member day and night prepare.

5 Till we the Lord our Righteousness
Shall see in glory face to face,
Till we shall see the Lamb once slain,
O may we one in him remain!

428.* T. 14.

HOW pleasant is love's harmony,
When brethren truly dwell
Together in heart's unity,
And cordial friendship feel.

2 Lord Jesus, in that very night
Ere thou didst bleed and die,
Thou didst with thy disciples urge
Love's ever sacred tie.

3 Remind thy little flock, too apt
Among themselves to jar,
That all thy members unity
Was ev'n thy dying care.

4 May we this testament fulfil,
One mind and spirit be;
And love with unremitting zeal
Each other fervently.

429.* T. 147.

JEHOVAH! holy Lamb,
Christ, who our hearts hast fired
With love, by thee inspired,
We praise thy saving name.
Thou giv'st us crowns of glory,
Which are not transitory,
Thou, who our flesh and blood
Assumedst, Lamb of God.

2 Thou art the lovliest,
Our only joy and treasure,
Our heart's delight and pleasure,
As long as love shall last:
And love shall ever flourish,
Tho' all things else must perish,
As God himself exprest.
Thou art the lovliest!

3 How fast can love-cords bind!
Thou by thy love hast bound us,
E'er since thy mercy found us,
Thou Shepherd, ever kind!
O let us taste thy favor,
And thy rich bounty savor,
We're closely to thee join'd,
How fast can love-cords bind!

4 O boundless love and grace!
When we shall sing Christ's praises
Above in heav'nly places,
Our voice we'll higher raise.
As Shepherd he will feed us,
Support, protect, and lead us,
Till we shall see his face.
O boundless love and grace!

5 The elder's holy choir,
Who are in the Lamb's presence,
And pay him their obeisance,
Cast down their crowns' attire:
We join their adoration,
And praise him with prostration,
'Fore him we humbly fall,
He is our All in all.

6 Thanks, wisdom, majesty,
His ransom'd congregation
Brings to him for salvation,
And for love's unity.
The Lamb who did deliver
Our souls, be prais'd for ever;
Blessing and honor be
To him eternally.

430.* T. 124.

O IN love what stores of grace
Are contained!
By this band our covenant
Is maintained;
They who strangers are to love
Move our pity,
Love makes living weighty.

2 He, who is to Jesus Christ
Quite resigned,
And to walk his blessed ways
Is inclined,
On his path, by love constrain'd,
Firmly treadeth,
And straight on proceedeth.

431. T. 165.

JESUS, grant me to inherit,
Strengthen'd by thy aiding grace,
Thro' the guidance of thy Spirit,
All the fruits of righteousness.
Grant me true humility,
Faith and zeal to live for thee;
To mankind O make me gracious,
To my friends and foes propitious.

2 Give me grace in all conditions
Firmly to adhere to thee;
And, 'midst all the exhibitions
Of thy boundless love to me,
To let my poor neighbors share
In my plenty, and my pray'r;
By thy love to me imparted
Make me always tender-hearted.

432. T. 159.

WE in one covenant are join'd,
And one in Jesus are;
With voices, and with hearts combin'd
His praise we will declare:
In doctrine and in practice one,
We'll love and serve the Lord alone;
With one accord sound forth his praise,
Till we shall see his face.

XXIV. Of following Jesus, and bearing his Reproach.

433.* T. 230.

JESUS, Lord most great and glorious,
Reward and Crown of the victorious,
Restorer of lost Paradise:
We appear with supplication,
Before thee, God of our salvation,
And send to thee our fervent cries:
O Lord, our Righteousness!
'Tis thy delight to bless,
We desire it;
Come then, for we—belong to thee,
And bless us inexpressibly.

2 O thou Well-spring of salvation!
We thee intreat, to form and fashion
Us all according to thy mind.
We, by nature spoil'd and marred,
Were from that happy life debarred,
Which in thy fellowship we find:
By thy almighty pow'r
Support us evermore,
Thou life's Fountain!
Without thy aid—we can't proceed,
Be thou our help in time of need.

3 Blessed are the poor in spirit,
They shall the realm of heav'n inherit,
Free grace is theirs, and endless bliss;
While all those who place reliance
On their own works, and bid defiance
To grace, will of salvation miss.
O may we all of thee
Learn true humility,
Lowly Jesus,
May we despise—all earthly joys,
For thee, the Pearl of greatest price.

4 They that mourn, blest is their station,
They find abundant consolation,
Since Jesus first that path did tread;
He prevailed while he suffer'd,
And now to us that cup is offer'd,
By which himself was perfected.
We can in no respect
Here constant joy expect,
Here is weeping;
At the Lamb's feast—is perfect rest,
Here, is a vale of tears at best.

5 Blessed are the meek in spirit,
They shall, saith Christ, the earth inherit;
Their life is hid with him while here;
Yet they, by their conversation,
Afford a striking demonstration,
That they in Christ true riches share:
And as the Lamb of God
The greatest meekness show'd,
His disciples
His path pursue,—and as 'tis due
Show in their conduct meekness too.

6 Blessed, who without cessation
Hunger and thirst for that salvation,
Which flows from Christ's pure righteousness
They are fill'd and satisfied,
With richest dainties are supplied,
Who long and pant for saving grace.
Christ's body and his blood
Prove their life-giving food,
Thereby nourish'd,
From year to year—they thrive, and bear
Fruits that to him well-pleasing are.

7 All the merciful are blessed,
For they, when in their turn distressed,
Shall mercy find most certainly,
Water to the poor afforded
Is as an act of love recorded,
And is rewarded gen'rously.
Who to the indigent
Doth prove beneficent,
He is blessed;
But wo to them—who scorn the same,
For God remembers not their name.

8 All the pure in heart are blessed,
Of joys unspeakable possessed,
They shall behold their God in peace.
They who faithful have remained
To Jesus, and preserv'd unstained
The garment of his righteousness,
Shall once obtain the grace,
To see him face to face:
I intreat thee,
Impart to me—that purity,
Dear Jesus, which I trace in thee.

9 They are objects of God's favor,
Who always faithfully endeavor,
Peace 'mongst their neighbors to maintain;
As his children them he owneth,
He with success their labor crowneth,
Such souls the choicest blessings gain.

Love is the character
Of each true follower
Of our Saviour;
May he thro' grace—make us always
Intent upon promoting peace.

10 Blest are they who suffer gladly
For doing good and living godly,
Who Jesus for their pattern take:
Yea, who bear their cross with meekness,
Suff'ring with patience, 'midst all weak-
And earthly joys for him forsake; [ness
For Jesus' help and love
Their consolation prove;
They who freely
For him will bear—reproach, while here,
At last shall in his glory share.

11 Blest are they who are despised,
In scornful manner stigmatized,
And for their Saviour's sake defam'd;
As the bride deems it an honor
To take the bridegroom's name upon her,
Should we of Jesus be asham'd?
Far, far be this from us,
Welcome reproach and cross;
We are Christians,
Who follow thee,—Lord, cheerfully,
Thro' honor, and thro' infamy.

12 Gracious Lord, who by thy passion
And death hast gained our salvation,
O may we all thy name confess:
May we be by faith united
To thee, who hast us all invited
To share eternal happiness.
Constrain us by thy love,
In all we do to prove
Faithful foll'wers,
Dear Lord, of thee;—and grant that we
May ever love thee ardently.

434.* T. 11.

HOLY Lamb and Prince of peace,
Hear my soul implore thy grace:
Let me thro' thy pow'r divine,
In thy lamb-like meekness shine.

2 Grant that faithfully I may
As a lamb thy voice obey;
Valiant, steadfast, may my love
In the hardest trials prove.

3 Keep thou me, a feeble child,
Sober, watchful, undefil'd;
That where'er thy steps I see
Simply I may follow thee.

4 Thou the great victorious Lamb,
Who all hosts of hell o'ercame,
Grant, that by thy blood I may
Conqu'ror be till thy great day.

5 When thou shalt on Zion stand,
May I be at thy right hand;
Clothed in the glorious dress
Of thy spotless righteousness.

435. T. 596.

O TELL me no more
Of this world's vain store;—The time
for such trifles with me now is o'er.

2 A country I've found,
Where true joys abound;—To dwell
I'm determin'd on that happy ground.

3 The souls that believe,
In Paradise live:—And me in that
number will Jesus receive.

4 My soul, don't delay,
He calls thee away!—Rise, follow thy
Saviour, and bless the glad day.

5 No mortal doth know
What he can bestow,—What light,
strength & comfort; Go, follow him, go!

6 Perhaps, with the aim
To honor his name,—I may do some
service, poor dust tho' I am.

7 Yet this is confest,
I count it most blest,—As at the beginning, in him to find rest.

8 And when I'm to die,
"Receive me," I'll cry,—"For life
everlasting thou for me didst buy."

9 So closely in mind
To Jesus I'm join'd,—He'll not live in
glory and leave me behind.

10 Lo, this is the race
I'm running thro' grace,—Henceforth,
till admitted to see my Lord's face.

436.* T. 26.

LORD Jesus, 'tis with us thy aim,
That soul and body should be thine,
O take our hearts, and us incline
To be devoted to thy name.

2 What love can be compar'd with thine!
Who hath to us so just a claim
As thou who didst our souls redeem
And for us leave thy throne divine!

3 Go, all ye wise, without control
Your empty notions still pursue;
Jesus alone I have in view,
This pow'rful magnet draws my soul.

4 A subject I of Christ my King,
And tho' I poor and helpless be,
Yet all around shall plainly see
My Saviour is my ev'ry thing.

5 Thee I adore, most gracious Lord,
Grant that my walk in truth may be
At all times pleasing unto thee,
Directed by thy holy word.

6 My King, thy noble statutes write
Upon the table of my heart,
Thy grace and truth to me impart,
And let thy law be my delight.

437.* T. 56.

BLESSED Jesus :||: all our hearts incline
Thee to follow, :||: where thy footsteps
At all times, and ev'ry where, [shine;
May our words and actions bear
A resemblance :||: gracious Lord, to thine.

438.* T. 83.

JESUS Christ, thou Leading-star,
Thy great name we praise & hallow;
From believers be it far
Any other guide to follow:
Thou, Lord, if we walk in light,
Wilt direct our steps aright.

2 Christians are not here below
To enjoy earth's transient treasure,
After Christ they're call'd to go,
His reproach they count a pleasure;
Under manifold distress,
Thro' the narrow gate they press.

439. T. 26.

THOU meek & patient Lamb of God,
Who can by faith thy suff'rings see,
And not devote himself to thee,
His life, and ev'ry drop of blood!

2 Thy dying love doth justly claim
That I should live unto thy praise,
Yea, gladly share in thy disgrace,
And suffer freely for thy name.

440. T. 22.

IF father, mother, children, wife,
Houses, or lands, or ought in life,
Delude thy heart, that thou desist
From faith and love to Jesus Christ;

2 His words with due attention hear:
"My cross whoever will not bear,
And all forsake to follow me,
He cannot my disciple be."

3 First let us duly count the cost,
And then in Jesus' place our trust,
If we on him alone depend,
He 'midst all trials proves our Friend.

4 If once the plough in hand we take,
Preserve us, Lord, from looking back:
O let us thro' thy aiding grace,
Pursue our course with steadiness.

5 On those who faithful prove to death,
And show by works of love their faith,
A crown of life thou once wilt place,
Before thy Father them confess.

441.* T. 90.

"MY yoke," saith Christ, "upon you take,
Serve me, amidst oppression;
The world, and all its joys forsake,
And shun no tribulation;
Come follow me, and humbly bear
My cross, and in my suff'rings share."

2 Then let us follow Christ our Lord,
Both soul and body off'ring,
Be cheerfully, with one accord,
Partakers of his suff'ring;
For they who show true faithfulness
Shall gain a rich reward of grace.

442. T. 243.

AMIDST tribulation,
We follow our Saviour,
Whose name and profession
We'll honor for ever,
His shame we bear,—and gladly share.

2 We in ev'ry nation
Will boldly confess him,
Make known his salvation,
Yea serve him and bless him,
And him adore—for evermore.

3 Our Lord contradiction
Of sinners endured;
Him, 'midst all affliction,
We follow, assured
That we at last—with him shall rest.

443.* T. 16.

CROSS, reproach and tribulation,
Ye to me are welcome guests,
When I have this consolation,
That my soul in Jesus rests.

2 The reproach of Christ is glorious,
Those who here his burden bear
In the end shall prove victorious,
And eternal glory share.

3 Christ, our ever-blessed Saviour,
Bore for us reproach and shame,
Now as conqu'ror lives for ever,
And we conquer in his name.

4 Bear then the reproach of Jesus,
Ye who live a life of faith;
Sing ye joyful songs and praises,
Ev'n in martyrdom and death.

5 Bonds, and stripes, and tribulation,
Are our honorable crowns;
Shame is our glorification,
Gloomy dungeons are as thrones.

444. T. 22.

JESUS, and shall it ever be,
A sinful worm asham'd of thee?
Forbid it Lord! thee I confess,
Before both friends and enemies.

2 Asham'd of Jesus! of my God,
Who purchas'd me with his own blood!
Of him who to retrieve my loss,
Despis'd the shame, endur'd the cross!

3 Asham'd of Jesus! of that Friend
On whom my heav'nly hopes depend!
It must not be—be this my shame,
That I not more revere his name!

4 Asham'd of Jesus! of my Lord,
By all heav'n's glorious hosts ador'd!
No, I will make my boast of thee,
In time and in eternity.

5 And when I stand before thy throne,
Me 'fore thy heav'nly Father own;
Then shall the holy angels see
Thee, Jesus, not asham'd of me!

445.* T. 54.

THE suff'rings of this life's short day
Can't be compar'd with that display
Of glory, which God's heirs shall prove,
When they who Jesus truly love
Shall shine above.

2 Therefore we'll follow willingly
Our Saviour in adversity;
Then, after having suffer'd here,
We shall in heav'n his glory share,
Beyond compare.

446.* T. 58.

TO follow Jesus, is his people's aim,
Where'er they go, thro' honor or thro' shame,
They themselves thrice happy esteem, if favor'd
In his reproach to share, which is still savor'd
With inward joy.

447.* T. 164.

HOW great at last my joy will be,
If I have faithful proved
To Christ, and 'midst adversity
Till my last breath him loved.
They who reproach here bear,
In heav'n a crown shall wear;
Who follow Christ are truly blest,
For they with him shall ever rest.

448. T. 159.

WE covenant with hand and heart,
To follow Christ our Lord;
With world, and sin, and self to part,
And to obey his word:
To love each other heartily,
In truth and in sincerity,
And under cross, reproach and shame,
To glorify his name.

XXV. Of Growth in Self-knowledge, and Sighing for Grace.

449.* T. 22.

MY soul before thee prostrate lies,
To thee, its Source, my spirit flies;
O turn to me thy cheering face,
I'm poor, enrich me with thy grace.

2 Deeply convinc'd of sin I cry,
In thy death, Saviour, let me die;
O may the world, may self and pride
In me henceforth be crucify'd.

3 Take full possession of my heart,
To me thy lowly mind impart,
Break nature's bonds, and let me see,
He whom thou free'st, indeed is free.

4 My heart in thee, and in thy ways
Delights, yet from thy presence strays;
O keep, I pray, my wav'ring mind
Stay'd upon thee, to thee resign'd.

5 I know, that nought in me avails,
Here all my strength and wisdom fails;
Who bids a sinful heart be clean?
Thou only, Saviour of lost men!

6 Still will I wait, O Lord, on thee,
Till, in thy light, the light I see;
Till thou in my behalf appear,
To banish ev'ry doubt and fear,

7 All my own schemes, each self design,
I to thy better will resign;
Impress this deeply on my breast,
That I in thee am truly blest.

8 Then ev'n in storms I thee shall know
My sure Support, and Refuge too,
In ev'ry trial I shall prove
Assuredly, that God is Love.

450. T. 121.

FOR grace I weep and pant,
'Tis mercy that I want;
How wretched should I be,
Did I not Jesus know!
Who to deliver me,
Suffer'd in my stead,
In a tomb was laid,
And rose from the dead.

2 Could even all the love
In heav'nly hosts above,
And in the church below,
At once united prove,
And in one bosom glow;
Jesus' love outweighs;
Yea his boundless grace
Is beyond all praise.

3 Love is his nature still,
In me he will fulfil
His precious thoughts of peace,
If I am to his will
Resign'd in ev'ry case;
Let him do what's best,
Then, supremely blest,
I enjoy true rest.

4 O my Immanuel,
My wounded spirit heal,
I humbly seek thy face;
Yea pungent sorrow feel,
That I've abus'd thy grace.
Jesus, pardon me,
May I henceforth be,
Faithful unto thee.

5 O Lord, thy grace impart,
Refresh and cheer my heart,
Thy pard'ning love display,
For thou my Saviour art;
To me, poor sinner, say:
"Thy reproach is mine,
All my merit's thine,
Take my peace divine."

6 I know, that thro' thy grace
Thou wilt, my guilt erase,
And banish all my fear;
Wilt grant to me thy peace,
And me with patience bear,
On me grace bestow,
Jesus thee to know,
Amen, be it so!

451.* T. 141.

I AM a poor sinner,
This I surely know;
And if my dear Saviour
Did not love me so,
That my soul, his purchase,
He can ne'er forsake,
He ere now had taken
His grace from me back.

2 Grace, and a sensation
Of my sinfulness,
Keep on each occasion
In me equal pace;
While I own ashamed,
"I deserved wrath!"
I rejoice, reclaimed
From sin's pow'r, by faith.

3 Jesus, when thy blessings
Fill my needy heart,
Fear and anxious doubtings
Then from me depart;
I in thy atonement
My election trace;
And rejoice astonish'd
At my lot of grace.

4 Witness true and faithful,
Christ, the church's Head,
All is Yea and Amen
Thou hast promised;
As I am, so take me
With my worst and best;
Ever thine preserve me
Till with thee I rest.

5 Now what thou art doing
I with joy will view,
For thy tender mercies
Are each morning new;
And thou wilt thy promise,
Lord, fulfil to me,
That 'midst all my weakness,
I thy joy shall be.

452.* T. 141.

JESUS' love unbounded
None can e'er explain;
Yet, alas, how often
Do we cause him pain!
Even such still grieve him,
As enjoy his grace,
And, to him devoted,
Should show forth his praise.

2 Lord, thy body's Saviour,
Comfort us anew,
Ah, regard our weeping,
Thy compassion show;
Pardon our transgressions,
Hear our fervent cry,
And our souls and bodies
Heal and sanctify.

3 All our days, O Jesus,
Hallow unto thee,
May our conversation
To thy honor be;
Let us all experience,
To the end of days,
Thy reviving presence
'Midst thy chosen race.

453.* T. 30.

O MY God, I come oppress'd with sadness,
Fill my troubled soul with joy & gladness
In thy salvation;
No where else I find true consolation.

2 Faithfully thy Spirit me directed,
But his warning I have oft neglected;
Most gracious Saviour,
Pardon and restore me to thy favor.

3 I confess, O Lord, with deep contrition,
My unfaithfulness, hear my petition;
Comfort and bless me,
With thy gracious presence now refresh me.

4 O baptize me with thy fire & spirit,
Grant me from the fulness of thy merit
True heart's compunction,
Prim'tive love, simplicity and unction.

5 Give me grace to walk with circumspection,
Keep me from the world's and sin's infection,
That my behavior
May adorn thy doctrine, gracious Saviour.

454.* T. 16.

O WHAT would be my condition,
Did not Jesus stand my Friend!
But his faithful love and mercy,
Keep me from all danger screen'd.

2 Doth howe'er in my frail nature
Something stir that is not good,
And might to my soul prove hurtful,
Straight I turn to Jesus' blood,

3 Straight to Jesus' wounds and bruises,
With believing confidence;
Thus I always can find shelter
From sin's baneful influence.

4 Lamb of God, display the virtue
Of thy sanctifying blood,
Overstream with life and blessing
Us poor sinners 'fore thee bow'd;

5 Sinners, in ourselves unworthy
Of the smallest crumb of grace,
But who dare of boundless mercy
Boast, to our Redeemer's praise.

455.* T. 4.

WE know that we're poor,
And sinful all o'er,
In us there's no good,—O cleanse us, dear Saviour, in thy precious blood.

2 How wondrous thy love
And mercy do prove,
This plainly our faith—Discerns by thy agony, passion and death.

3 Lord Jesus, receive
The thanks we can give;
O that to thy praise,—Each blood-drop within us were hallow'd always!

4 We all at thy throne
Now humbly fall down;
Praise to thee, our God,—Be brought by us, sinners, redeem'd with thy blood.

456.* T. 244.

WHEN I am conscious truly
Of my great sinfulness,
And that so very slowly
Towards the mark I press;
Nought then can comfort me,
But Jesus' mercy free,
And that he bore with patience
My sins upon the tree.

2 Yea, when I see in spirit
My Saviour shed his blood,
That I might life inherit,
And everlasting good;
Then I true happiness
And joy in him possess,
My eyes with tears flow over
For heart-felt thankfulness.

457.* T. 22.

WHILE here on earth we run our race,
We Jesus' love and kindness trace;
Our faults are more than we can tell,
Yet did his mercy never fail.

2 When we like wand'ring sheep had stray'd,
His boundless goodness he display'd;
He sought us, worthless as we are,
And took us in his tender care,

3 Asham'd we own our great defect,
And did not Jesus us protect,
We should be oft depress'd with fears,
While traversing this vale of tears.

4 But Jesus' blood and death impart
True comfort to the needy heart:
Those who still weak and feeble are,
He kindly in his arms will bear.

458. T. 119.

AT thy feet :||:
At thy pierced feet I lie;
Saviour, mark my heart's contrition,
Listen to each broken sigh;
Ah! refuse not the petition
Of a sinner conscious he's unclean,
Full of sin! :||:

2 Make me clean, :||:
My whole nature purify,
Cleanse me in that precious fountain,
Which by faith I open'd see,
Standing on the blissful mountain,
Where thou bar'st my sin, my guilt and shame,
Slaughter'd Lamb! :||:

3 Look on me, :||:
See each painful wound and sore,
Thou compassionate Physician,
Speak the word, my sickness cure,
Wrest me from the sad condition,
Into which transgression brought my soul;
Make me whole. :||:

4 Bid me live, :||:
Bid a dying sinner live,
Raise, O raise my drooping spirit;
Then to thee myself I'll give,
And, until I heav'n inherit,
Ev'ry moment in thy service spend,
Faithful Friend! :||:

10 Chastise me when I do amiss,
O might no thought arise
Which is displeasing unto thee;
Of grace send fresh supplies.

11 Impress thy wounds upon my heart,
And all thy bitter pain;
Abide in me for evermore,
And constant vict'ry gain.

459. T. 14.

O JESUS, Jesus, my good Lord,
How wondrous is thy love,
Thy patience, pity, tenderness,
Which I each moment prove!

2 I once was wholly dead in sin,
And ignorant of thee,
And liv'd contentedly therein,
Nor knew thy love to me.

3 But thine all-seeing eye then view'd,
And mark'd my ev'ry way,
Me still in tender love pursu'd
Who oft from thee did stray.

4 Yet O! how faithless is my mind,
How apt to turn aside,
And wander in its own deceits
Of reas'ning and of pride!

5 How doth the old corruption strive
And fight to reign again!
There's surely not a heart like mine,
So wretched, dark and vain.

6 Thou Friend of sinners, love me still,
The poorest and the worst;
Where sin abounded, well I know,
Thy grace aboundeth most.

7 Yet let me not thy grace abuse,
And sin because thou'rt good:
But let thy love fill me with shame,
That I so long withstood.

8 On me, my King, exert thy pow'r,
Make old things pass away;
Create all new, draw me to thee,
Still nearer ev'ry day.

9 Thou know'st which way to rectify
Each stubborn ill within,
How to subdue my ev'ry thought,
And conquer all that's sin.

460. T. 58.

O LAMB of God, who wast for sinners slain
That they might pardon, life and bliss obtain,
Give me to experience thy great salvation,
And in my heart O fix thy habitation
For evermore.

2 Thou know'st my inmost soul, I've nought to boast,
And without thee should be for ever lost;
When I am neglectful thou dost reprove me,
Yet I am well assur'd that thou dost love me,
For thou forgiv'st.

3 How glad am I that thou so gracious art,
That thou dost bless my sinful, worthless heart
And canst with such patience bear my behavior,
O wert thou not exactly such a Saviour
What should I do!

461. T. 151.

COME, faithful Shepherd, bind me
With cords of love to thee!
And evermore remind me
That thou hast dy'd for me;
O may thy holy Spirit
Set this before mine eyes,
That I thy death and merit
Above all else may prize.

2 I am of my salvation
Assured, thro' thy love;
Yet ah, on each occasion
Might I more faithful prove!

Hast thou my sins forgiven,
Then leaving things behind,
May I press on to heaven,
And bear the prize in mind.

3. Thou, Lord, wilt not forsake me,
Tho' I am oft to blame;
As thy reward, O take me
Anew, just as I am;
Grant me henceforth, dear Saviour,
While in this vale of tears,
To look to thee, and never
Give way to anxious fears.

462. T. 106.

AH, Lord, how apt am I to stray
From thee! how prone to lust and pride!
Nature oft strives to bear the sway,
And turn my heart from thee aside;
Yet such vile, wretched sinners are
The objects of thy love and care.

2 Forbid, O Lord, each vain desire,
Bind my affections to thy cross;
Quench all the sparks of nature's fire,
May I count all for thee but loss:
Lord Jesus, tear each idol down,
Thy love within my heart inthrone.

3 O Jesus, wipe away my tears,
Be unto me a healing balm;
Warm thou my heart, dispel my fears,
And speak the tempest to a calm:
Remove the maladies of sin,
And in thy blood O wash me clean.

4 I gladly will show forth thy praise,
If thou wilt gird me with thy pow'r,
And sing the glories of thy grace,
Until my pilgrimage be o'er.
With hallow'd fire inspire my tongue,
And love shall be my endless song.

463. T. 22.

VAIN are all efforts made to trace
The way to life and happiness,
Before 'tis on our minds imprest,
That Jesus is our only rest!

2 By my own strength I can't procure
True rest, nor even feel I'm poor;
Strive I great comforts to obtain,
Instead of joy, I've nought but pain.

3 But when He shows me how I rove,
And court my neighbor's praise and love,
How self-will raises discontent
Against my Saviour's government;

4 How soon, when Satan tempts, I start,
Pass by convictions in my heart,
Let my first love and zeal abate,
Fall, and my very falls forget;

5 And at the same time lets me feel,
That he hath patience with me still:
I stand asham'd before his face,
And humbly thank him for his grace.

6 Search out, discover, and erase,
Whatever is not to thy praise,
All that might an obstruction prove
To thy blest purposes of love.

7 Complete thy work, my gracious King,
My heart into subjection bring;
Destroy, I pray, the carnal mind,
And make me quite to thee resign'd.

464. T. 22.

FROM my own works at last I cease,
For God alone can give me peace;
Fruitless my toil, and vain my care,
Of my own strength I must despair.

2 Lord, I despair myself to heal,
I see my sin, but cannot feel
True sorrow, till thy Spirit show
My unbelief, the source of woe.

3 'Tis thine alone to change the heart,
Thou only canst good gifts impart,
I therefore will my heart resign
To thee, O cleanse and seal it thine!

4 With humble faith on thee I call,
My Light, my Life, my Lord, my All;
I wait, O Lord, to hear thee say,
"My blood hath wash'd thy sins away."

5 Speak, gracious Lord, my sickness cure,
Make my infected nature pure;
Peace, righteousness, and joy impart,
And give thyself unto my heart.

465. T. 106.

O JESUS, could I always keep
My eye on thee, the living way,
I then, tho' once a wand'ring sheep
Should no more err, or run astray;
But wheresoe'er thou goest, I
Should follow thee, not asking why.

2 O that I never might forget,
What thou hast suffer'd for my sake,
To save my soul, and make me meet
Once of thy glory to partake:
O might I oft in spirit see
How thou wast crucify'd for me.

3 But, gracious Lord, when I reflect
How oft I've turn'd my eye from thee;
How treated thee with cold neglect,
And listen'd to the enemy;
And yet to find thee still the same,
This fills my soul with humble shame.

4 Astonish'd at thy feet I fall,
Thy love exceeds my highest thought;
Henceforth be thou my All in all,
Thou who with blood my soul hast bought:
May I henceforth more faithful prove,
And ne'er forget thy dying love.

466. T. 580.

WHEN, having been with guilt oppress,
My wand'ring spirit findeth rest
Thro' Jesus' pard'ning grace;
Then I by faith can call him mine,
My needy soul doth then incline
To be in Mary's happy place.

2 My pray'r is: "Jesus, let me hear
Thy voice, which can instruct & cheer
My poor and worthless heart;
For should I cease thy words t' obey,
And from thy blessed presence stray,
Nature would soon its pow'r assert."

3 A single eye, a faithful heart,
Dear Jesus, to thy child impart,
In ev'ry trying hour;
Reason's tormenting thoughts prevent,
Still keep my eye on thee intent,
Till sight my faith & hope o'erpow'r.

467. T. 22.

LORD Jesus, my most faithful Friend,
Thy aid unto thy child extend
In each temptation's trying hour,
That sin may not thy grace o'erpow'r.

2 That spark enkindled in my heart
Remain unquench'd, tho' all the art
Of sin and Satan be combin'd
To make me leave my matchless Friend.

3 O let thy Spirit stay with me,
To groan and speak my wants to thee;
Still let him show my ev'ry need,
And that in thee I'm help'd indeed.

4 Thy faithfulness I oft have prov'd,
In countless trials quite unmov'd;
Thy grace alone can me preserve,
When my frail heart from thee would swerve.

468. T. 14.

GRACIOUS Redeemer, Lamb of God,
I thirst alone for thee,
I long t' enjoy thy saving grace,
And taste thy mercy free.

2 For mercy, mercy, Lord, I ask,
This is the total sum:
Mercy, good Lord, is all my suit,
O let thy mercy come!

3 Search me, O God, and know my heart,
Try me, and know each thought;
On me look down in mercy, Lord,
Whom thou with blood hast bought.

4 My faithless heart, O gracious Lord,
Correct with gentle hand;
In ev'ry danger help afford,
Alone I cannot stand.

5 Without thy favor while I live,
Life but a burden is;
Nought else can satisfaction give,
Experience shows me this.

6 Haste then, O Lord, to thee I pray:
Impart to me thy grace,
That when this life is fled away
In heav'n I may have place.

469. T. 96.

AH give me, Lord, myself to feel,
My inbred misery reveal:
Ah give me, Lord, (I still would say)
A heart to mourn, a heart to pray;
My business this, my only care,
My life, my ev'ry breath be pray'r.

2 Father, I want a thankful heart;
I wish to taste how good thou art,
To plunge into thy mercy's sea,
And comprehend thy love to me
More fully with the saints below,
Till I, as I am known, shall know.

470. T. 159.

WITH what unwearied faithfulness
Lord hast thou followed me!
Tho' I regardless of thy grace
In darkness stray'd from thee;
How heavy hung the dismal cloud,
How did distresses on me crowd!
And I, despairing of relief,
In thee had no belief.

2 But thou my kind, almighty Friend,
Didst sin's dominion quell;
My mis'ry and confusion end,
And ev'ry cloud dispel;
One look into thy pierced heart
Alleviates the keenest smart,
There mercy without bounds I see
Is moving ev'n for me.

471. T. 159.

MY case to thee is fully known,
On thee I cast my care,
Dear Saviour, that thy will be done
In me, is all my pray'r;
O may I harbor in my breast
No thought that cannot bear the test,
When thou discover'st by thy light
To me what is not right.

2 Reality and solid ground,
Firm root in thee to gain;
To feel, thy precious blood hath drown'd
Whatever gives thee pain;
'Tis this I want, nor can I be
Content, till I am one with thee,
Until my life is hid in thine,
Till thou art wholly mine.

472. T. 14.

I KNOW the weakness of my soul,
But Jesus is my stay,
My kind Redeemer hath engag'd
To lead me in his way.

2 For ever he abides the same,
Tho' I to change am prone;
My welfare always he promotes,
Who chose me for his own.

473. T. 22.

THE more of Jesus' love I see,
The more I know the misery,
The pride and treach'ry of my heart,
By which I cause my Saviour smart.

2 Long this was from my sight conceal'd
Till by the Spirit's light reveal'd,
Which shows God's love and Jesus grace,
And fills my troubled heart with peace.

474.* T. 97.

WHATE'ER I am, whate'er I do,
'Tis grace I must ascribe it to;
This can alone my heart preserve;
For I'm so liable to swerve,
That ev'n the grace which thou to-day bestow'st,
If not renew'd to-morrow might be lost.

475. T. 590.

THE worst of evils we can name
Is an unfaithful heart;
May none of us to our dear Lord
Thereby cause pungent smart;
Our human frailty need not lead
Our souls from him astray;
For he the needful strength imparts
To walk the narrow way.

476 * T. 590.

FEAR not, without reserve disclose
The fest'ring sores of sin;
Your case the Lord your Healer knows,
His blood can wash you clean;

There is a balm in Gilead,
To cure the sin-sick soul;
None e'er to Christ for refuge fled
But was by him made whole.

477.* T. 214.

THOUGH by nature I'm defiled,
Jesus' blood hath made me clean;
He my sin-sick soul hath healed,
And whate'er doth still remain
Of my former sad condition,
He alleviates when I cry,
Yea, to sooth my pain is nigh:
Lord, remain my kind Physician,
I, thy patient, then am sure
Thou wilt work a thorough cure.

478. T. 97.

O LAMB of God for sinners slain,
Our souls from mis'ry to regain,
How blest are they, who truly see
Their weakness, who derive from thee
The mercies which thou freely dost dispense,
And look to thee with filial confidence!

479.* T. 79.

LORD, shouldst thou be induced
To ask, how we have used
Thy precious gifts and grace?
And into judgment enter
With us, we durst not venture
To plead: our faults are numberless.

XXVI. Of SANCTIFICATION.

480.* T. 58.

THE Lamb of God, who saves us by his death,
Is made unto us holiness by faith;
None besides availeth, since our Creator
Became a man, assuming our frail nature
To ransom us.

2 To Jesus Christ is due eternal praise,
For our high calling in these gospel days;
What divine enjoyment & consolation
Do we now gain from Jesus' incarnation
And bitter death!

3 If we in Jesus' saving name believe,
And pardon of our sins from him receive;
With his blood besprinkled, and cleansed truly,
In soul and body we are render'd holy,
And have his mind.

4 And thus by faith we live, & yet not we,
But Christ lives in us so effectually,
That, by him renewed and actuated,
We are in him unto good works created,
And grow in grace.

481.* T. 126.

THIS yields true joy and pleasure
To Christ, when with one voice
His people in their measure
Exalt his sacrifice,
And praise him for the wounds which he
Receiv'd for our redemption
Upon th' accursed tree.

2 Of his complete salvation
We witness here below,
And gladly make confession,
Resolv'd nought else to know.
God in his wisdom did ordain,
That lost, repenting sinners
His righteousness should gain.

3 No holiness availeth
With God, but this alone;
The Holy Spirit sealeth
This truth, that in the Son
By faith we're freely justify'd,
And gain sanctification,
Because for us he dy'd.

482.* T. 22.

JESUS, the church's Lord and Head!
O mightst thou o'er thy flock be glad,
Whom thou, while sinners, by thy blood
Hast ransom'd and brought nigh to God.

2 Since thou our wretched, lost estate
In mercy didst commiserate,
And feeble flesh and blood assume,
To save us from the wrath to come;

3 We are, if we in thee believe
And from thy fulness grace receive,
Cleansed and sanctify'd by thee,
And serve thy name acceptably.

4 Renew'd in heart, we're then inclin'd
To live according to thy mind,
Can we do good—with cheerfulness
We do it, and give thee the praise.

5 Whatever honours thee our Lord,
What's called virtue in thy word,
Is honest, lovely, pure and just,
By faith in thee is then produc'd.

6 Preserve, O Lord, our garments pure,
Keep us from ev'ry harm secure;
Our members render, thro' thy grace,
Blest instruments of righteousness.

7 May spirit, soul and body be
A pleasing sacrifice to thee;
Thy name we bear, our hearts thou
know'st
In thee alone we place our trust.

483.* T. 11.

PRAISE to Christ, the Son of God!
Who assum'd our flesh and blood,
Since he death for us endur'd,
And eternal life procur'd.

2 When we see our names enroll'd
'Mongst the sheep of Jesus' fold,
Wond'ring, we ourselves confess
Undeserving of such grace,

3 And when we explore the end,
Why our Lord would condescend
To assume humanity,
Us thereby to sanctify:

4 And reflect on all the pain,
Which for us he did sustain,
On his labors, sorrows, cares,
On his tears, and fervent pray'rs;

5 Poverty, and ev'ry want
To our nature incident,
Which he bore, and which for us
Are all meritorious;

6 Then thro' his enabling grace,
We with joy can run our race,
While we him in mem'ry bear,
Who was tempted as we are,

7 Yea, 'midst failings numberless,
We rejoice that we are his;
And if we his word obey,
Each of us may cleanse his way.

8 Tho' the outward mark and scar
Of the fall doth still appear,
Yet we're freed from sin's hard yoke,
Since our bonds and chains he broke.

9 Mighty God, we humbly pray:
Carry thy victorious sway
In the flesh to such a length,
That we gain thy godlike strength.

10 Grant that all of us may prove,
By obedience, faith, and love,
That our hearts to thee are giv'n,
That our treasure is in heav'n.

484.* T. 14.

HOW can a sinner here below
Be pleasing unto God?
By his own righteousness?—O no:
Alone thro' Jesus' blood.

2 If any thing in us appears
Unlike to Jesus' mind,
To own it with repenting tears
Ah, may we be inclin'd!

3 A child of God for ever pants
More like his Lord to be;
Tho' with conviction still he grants,
That none is good but HE.

4 Oft as in spirit Christ he views
This is his humble cry,
Which he continually renews
"As thou wast, O were I!"

5 "Whate'er is carnal, thro' thy grace
In me be mortify'd;
Thus clothed in thy righteousness
I shall in thee abide."

485.* T. 185.

HE who striveth for sanctification,
And is unrenew'd in heart,
Feeling yet a secret condemnation,
Since with sin he still takes part;
He who hath not yet in Christ believed,
Pardon in his blood and peace received;
Hath not found that holiness
Which adorns a child of grace.

2 But how happy is the soul that cleaveth
To the Friend of sinners poor;
And with humble confidence believeth
"My diseases he can cure;"
Such a one, tho' e'er so vile by nature,
Tho' throughout a spoil'd and wretched creature,
Mourning on account of sin,
Is by Jesus' blood made clean.

486. T. 151.

WHO, thro' Christ's blood, remission
Of all his sins hath gain'd,
And without intermission
With Jesus hath remain'd;
To true sanctification
Attains thro' Jesus' grace,
And in his conversation
Shows forth his matchless praise.

2 Our pleasure and our duty,
Tho' opposite before,
Since we have seen his beauty
Are join'd to part no more;
It is our highest pleasure,
No less than duty's call,
To love him beyond measure,
And serve him with our all.

487. T. 166.

THOU, Jesus! more than thirty years
In deep humiliation
Hast liv'd on earth, thy pray'rs and tears
Have purchas'd our salvation;
Thou hast, till yielding up thy breath,
Unheard-of pains sustained,
In soul and body felt our death,
And life for us regained.

2 O what a privilege is this,
That man; tho' fall'n by nature,
May thro' thy grace know what it is
To be a happy creature;
Heal'd by thy stripes and wounds, from sin
And Satan's pow'r released,
Fill'd with thy love and peace within,
And thus to new life raised!

3 Thou chosest us to show thy praise
In all our conversation,
As witnesses of blood-bought grace,
Each in his call and station:
This is our cov'nant's only ground
To yield thee soul and body,
In life and death to thee we're bound,
And for thy service ready.

4 How precious are thy thoughts of peace
O'er us, if but attained!
O may we steadfast run our race,
Till we the crown have gained.
Grant we may never fall asleep,
But in faith persevering
Our lamps may always burning keep,
Until thy blest appearing.

488*. T. 185.

WITH new life endow'd by Christ our Saviour,
Might we to this world be dead;
That great prize to gain be our endeavor,
Purchas'd when for us he bled;
Filled with his love, may we adore him,
Thinking, speaking, acting, as before him
Being to his gracious mind
Ever willingly resign'd.

2 May we all be ever so disposed
In our hearts, by day and night,
As when this life's period being closed,
We to him shall take our flight;
Or as when, releas'd from condemnation,
We receiv'd the seal of our salvation,
And obtained, thro' his blood,
Happiness and peace with God!

489. T. 126.

DRAW nigh to Christ, your Brother,
Let no distrust take place;
He's lovely as none other,
Draw nigh, receive the grace
Which flows from his humanity,
To all who with full purpose
Like Jesus aim to be.

2 He's yours, with all his merit,
If you are truly his;
And thus become one spirit
With him who holy is,
Who spirit, soul and body heals,
And is that kind Physician
Who for his patients feels.

3 Whoe'er this truth believeth,
With love to Jesus burns,
But none its pow'r perceiveth,
Until to Christ he turns;
O blessed Jesus! grant us grace
To grow into thy likeness,
And live unto thy praise.

490.* T. 22.

LORD Jesus, sanctify thou me,
And make my spirit one with thee;
Thy body torn with many a wound
Preserve my soul and body sound.

2 The blood-sweat trickling down thy face,
My condemnation doth erase;
Thy cross, thy suff'rings, and thy pain
My everlasting strength remain.

3 The water flowing from thy side,
Which by the spear was open'd wide,
Shall be my bath; thy precious blood
Cleanse me, and bring me nigh to God.

4 Dear Jesus, grant this my request,
Be thou my everlasting rest,
Protect me by thy saving arm,
Secure my soul from ev'ry harm.

491.* T. 102.

CHRIST crucify'd! my soul by faith
With thee desires to be united;
For, as the purchase of thy death,
To thy communion I'm invited.
O hear my petition, and let me with thee
Be crucify'd, Jesus, with all that's in me.

2 O that I might still more enjoy
The blessed fruits of all thy passion;
Thy merits to my soul apply,
And let me share thy great salvation;
O hear my petition, &c.

3 Let me in all things conqu'ror prove,
Deliver me from sin's infection;
Preserve me in thy sacred love,
As well in joy as in affliction;
O hear my petition, &c.

492. T. 14.

I ASK not honor, pomp or praise,
By worldly men esteem'd,
I wish from sin's deceitful ways
To feel my soul redeem'd.

2 I wish, as faithful christians do,
Dear Lord, to live to thee,
And by my words and walk to show,
That thou hast dy'd for me.

3 O grant me thro' thy precious blood,
Thy gospel thus to grace;
Renew my heart, O Lamb of God,
Thus shall my works thee praise.

493. T. 14.

BESPRINKLE with thy blood my heart,
O Jesus, Son of God;
And take away whate'er thy grace
Hath hitherto withstood.

2 Earthly affections mortify,
And carnal nature's strife;
O may I henceforth only thirst
For thee, the Well of life.

3 Waters of life hence may I draw,
And never more depart;
My ardent longing is, O Lord,
"Fix at this spring my heart."

4 Alas, with shame I own that oft
I've turn'd away from thee;
O let thy work renew'd to-day
Remain eternally.

494.* T. 580.

JESUS, thyself to us reveal,
Grant that we may not only feel
Some dawnings of thy grace,
But in communion with thee live,
And daily from thy death derive
The needful strength to run our race.

2 O let us always think thee near,
As near unto us as the air
Which constantly we breathe;
Thus will from all we think or do
To thee unfeigned praises flow;
For thine we are in life and death.

3 Jesus, thou fain wouldst have us be
In all things more conform'd to thee;
We're fill'd with conscious shame,
And thank thee for thy care and love;
Thy patience, which we richly prove,
Our heart-felt gratitude doth claim.

495.* T. 237.

O LORD GOD Holy Ghost,
As sure as Christ's I am,
So sure am I in him
With thee in close communion;
Might my whole walk proclaim
With Christ a blessed union,
The pardon'd sinner's frame,
A mind to his conform'd;

2 The genuine mind of Christ,
Proceeding from a heart
Engaged with his cross,
Blest theme of meditation!
Deriving all delight
From Jesus' great salvation;
Supported day and night
With peace and joy divine.

496. T. 16.

JESUS, by thy Holy Spirit
May we all instructed be;
Sanctify us by the merit
Of thy blest humanity.

2 Grant that we may love thee truly,
Lord, our thoughts and actions sway,
And to ev'ry heart more fully
Thy atoning pow'r display.

3 Lead us so that we may honor
Thee, the Lord our Righteousness,
And bring fruit to thee, the Donor
Of all gospel-truth and grace.

497.* T. 28.

TO that Lord, who unconstrained
Death's dire pangs for us sustained,
May we all in our small measure
Willingly give joy and pleasure.

2 May our mind and whole behavior
Bear resemblance to our Saviour,
And his sanctifying merit
Hallow body, soul and spirit.

498. T. 582.

LOVE God with all thy heart, and soul, and mind;
To friend and foe be just, and true, and kind;
Be meek and patient, humble, sober, chaste;
In these good ways be constant to the last.

2 And when thou hast done all, then humbly cry:
"An useless, sinful servant, Lord, am I!
My strength and grace come from the Holy Ghost,
My Saviour's merits are my only boast."

499.* T. 590.

O THOU, whose human life for us
Did happiness obtain;
Thou who, expiring on the cross
God's image didst regain;
Once lost it was, but is restor'd
By thy humanity;
Under thy shadow, Son of Man,
'Tis good for man to be!

500. T. 585.

HOW could I bear to be partaker
Of sinful frail humanity,
Had not the world's almighty Maker
Become a sinless man for me?
But since my God assum'd my nature
I gladly am a human creature;
For now he takes a part,
With sympathizing heart,
In all my smart.

501.* T. 244.

LORD Jesus, thy atonement
Be ever new to us;
Grant we may ev'ry moment
In spirit view thy cross:
O keep our garments pure,
In the the temptation hour,
From sin's infatuation
Preserve us by thy pow'r.

502.* T. 228.

O JESUS, were we thro' thy grace,
In all respects form'd to thy praise,
Like thee in thought and action;
Did we but wake and sleep to thee,
Bear pain and sickness patiently,
Trusting in thy direction.
Where'er—we are;
Might, dear Saviour,—our behavior,
Thro' thy blessing,
Always be to thee well-pleasing.

503.* T. 580.

THY law, O Lord, be my delight,
My gracious King, thy statutes write
In my untoward heart;
Thy pow'r divine afford me grace
To love thee, and to walk thy ways,
And never from thee to depart.

XXVII. Of Humility, Simplicity, and Growth in Grace.

504. T. 590.

O LORD, the contrite sinner's Friend,
Most wretched should I be,
Did I not know thy precious blood
Was shed for worthless me:
Nought could console me in distress,
Or give my soul relief;
When troubles seize my anxious breast,
Nought could appease my grief.

2 O give me, Jesus, give me still
My poverty to know;
Increase my faith; may I in grace
And in thy knowledge grow:
More clearly to me manifest
The myst'ry of thy cross;
And for this precious Pearl may I
Count all things else but dross.

505.* T. 22.

WHOE'ER in Jesus doth believe,
To soaring thoughts no room can give;
The blessed fellowship with Christ,
And nothing else by him is priz'd.

2 Reflecting how our Lord and Head,
When ris'n, his foll'wers visited,
We pray to share that happiness
Which, without sight, we may possess.

3 Communing with the Lamb of God,
With heart-felt gratitude we're bow'd:
And walk in true humility,
As Christ's disciples constantly.

506.* T. 22.

MY Saviour, that I without thee
Can nothing do, rejoiceth me:
For all the grace thou dost bestow,
I fain my gratitude would show.

2 Tho' weak and poor, I am thine own;
All praise to thee is due alone,
That thou, when humbly I appear
'Fore thee in mercy drawest near!

3 When pride would stir within my breast
I find no happiness nor rest;
But, walking in humility,
Have perfect peace and joy in thee.

4 O keep me contrite, low and poor!
Thus shall I praise thee evermore.
Myself thrice blessed I can call,
When I am nought, and thou my All.

507.* T. 14.

NONE God the Father's favor share,
Or heaven's kingdom win,
But those who little children are,
And as such enter in.

2 The high and mighty ones the Lord
Doth from their seats put down;
But to the poor doth grace afford,
And them with blessings crown.

3 O may I with submissiveness,
Dear Lord, be taught by thee;
To thee obedience show thro' grace,
And learn humility.

4 Jesus, I humbly thee implore,
Grant me thy Spirit's light,
That he may teach me evermore,
And guide my steps aright.

5 A lowly mind impart to me,
According to my pray'r;
Since those who know their poverty,
To the Most High are near.

6 Thou, who in heaven art ador'd,
Dost with the contrite dwell,
Revive the humble by thy word,
The broken-hearted heal.

7 Therefore, my soul, delight no more
In this world's vanity;
Look forward; Jesus hath in store
Unfading joys for thee.

8 Lord Jesus Christ, O may I grow
In knowledge and in grace!
Grant that in me, while here below,
Thy likeness each may trace.

508.* T. 583.

THOSE are partakers of our Saviour's grace,
Who, while his gifts they share with thankfulness,
Glory in their infirmities, and boast
Of nothing but his grace wherein they trust.

2 His loving-kindness those shall richly share,
Who at a loss, and ready to despair,
Retire in secret, pray him for relief,
And consolation to assuage their grief.

3 To those the Lord will deign his teaching mild,
Who gladly listen to the meanest child,
And from experience willingly allow,
That they are learners, and but little know.

509.* T. 14.

HAPPY the man whose highest Good
Is Christ invariably;
He shows his love and gratitude
By true humility.

2 In weakness pow'r divine he gains,
He dwells in peace and rest;
And owns with filial confidence:
"Lord, what thou dost is best."

3 "For thou art gracious, wise and good,
Thou know'st how help t' afford,
The time when it should be bestow'd:
Thy goodness be ador'd."

510.* T. 141.

GO, ye flatt'ring visions,
Honors, wealth and lusts:
He who lowly minded
In our Saviour trusts,
Rich in grace, is blessed,
Freed from anxious care;
For the poor in spirit
Heaven's kingdom share.

511.* T. 16.

WHEN simplicity we cherish,
Then the soul is full of light:
But that light will quickly vanish,
When of Jesus we lose sight.

2 He who nought but Christ desireth,
He whom nothing else can cheer
But the joy which he inspireth,
Lending to his voice an ear;

3 Who sincerely loveth Jesus,
And upon his grace depends;
Who but willeth what him pleases,
Simply foll'wing his commands;

4 Who to Jesus humbly cleaveth,
Pays obedience to his word,
Yea, in closest union liveth
With our Saviour, Head and Lord,

5 Who in Jesus Christ abideth,
And from self-dependence free
In nought else but him confideth:
Walks in true simplicity.

6 He who is by Christ directed,
Trusting the good Shepherd's care,
He is graciously protected,
And no danger needs to fear.

512.* T. 184.

O BLEST condition, happy living,
Which true simplicity imparts,
When we to God are wholly given,
And Jesus' mind rules in our hearts!
This ev'ry vain imagination
Casts down, and us subjects to grace.
It shows the ground of our salvation
To be Christ's blood and righteousness.

2 That which is by the world esteemed,
A single mind counts vanity;
What's innocent by others deemed,
Is shunn'd by true simplicity:
Because the love to things terrestrial
We must deny thro' Jesus' grace,
And, to obtain the prize celestial,
Cast off whate'er impedes our race.

3 The simple heart no care perplexeth
That robs the world of all content;
Of envy, which so many vexeth,
Simplicity is ignorant;
And carefully preserves its treasure,
Unruffled by the worldling's spite;
If others ask to share this pleasure,
Simplicity tastes true delight.

4 O Jesus, God of my salvation,
Thy single mind to me impart;
Root out the world's infatuation,
Tho' it be done with keenest smart:
Thrice happy they, who tread unweary'd
The path of true simplicity;
They as wise virgins are prepared
To meet the Bridegroom cheerfully.

513. T. 22.

MEEK, patient Lamb of God, impart
Thy meekness to my stubborn heart;
Grant me to keep thee full in view,
And thy example to pursue.

2 Thy blood preserve my garments clean
From ev'ry spot and stain of sin:
As a wise virgin, to prepare
For meeting thee, be all my care.

3 Bestow on me a simple mind,
To ev'ry hurtful fancy blind;
Thy meekness, true sincerity,
And needful wisdom grant to me.

4 Thou holy, spotless Lamb of God,
My worthless heart make thy abode:
O may I in thy image grow,
And honor thee in all I do.

514. T. 106.

A SINGLE mind to me impart,
Lord, may I sordid lucre flee,
Nor set on earthly gain my heart,
Hate av'rice as idolatry;
Fix my desires on things above,
Rich in possession of thy love.

2 Let neither honors, pomp, nor pride,
Nor this world's gaudy vanity,
Which draw the soul from thee aside,
Beguile me from simplicity:
May this my highest honor be,
To be esteemed, Lord, by thee.

3 Screen me in each unguarded hour,
Lord, under thy protecting care;
Preserve me from seduction's pow'r,
Lest fleshly lusts my soul ensnare:
May I to av'rice, lust and pride
Say, "Christ destroy'd you when he dy'd."

515.* T. 15.

LORD, grant to me a simple mind,
By thee may I be guided,
And as thy blessed will design'd,
Have my whole course decided.

2 With this desire 'fore thee I bow,
Asham'd of my demerit,
Ah, take without exception now,
My body, soul and spirit.

516.* T. 208.

WOULD we, sinners needy,
Here on earth already
Heav'nly joys possess;
Jesus nought desireth,
Or of us requireth,
For our rest and peace,
But that we—like children be;
Since he all our wants redresses,
Soothes all our distresses.

517.* T 151.

AMIDST this world's profaneness,
May I thy truth confess;
In prim'tive way and plainness,
Thy servant be thro' grace;
Nor fear, nor int'rest ever
Cause me to turn aside,
Or my connexion sever
With thy redeemed bride.

518.* T. 22.

CHRIST is the Vine, we branches are;
Without him we no fruit can bear:
For of ourselves we cannot thrive,
'Tis he who gives us pow'r and life.

2 Lord, thou hast chosen us, that we
Should bear well-pleasing fruit to thee.
O make us fruitful to thy praise;
Preserve us from all barrenness.

519. T. 11.

JESUS, who for me hast dy'd,
Grant I may in thee abide:
Set me, Lord, unto thy praise;
Water me with show'rs of grace.

2 Make my heart a garden fair,
Which such pleasant fruit may bear
As affords true joy to thee
And thy Father constantly.

3 In thy garden here below
Water me that I may grow;
When all grace to me is giv'n,
Then transplant me into heav'n.

520.* T. 167.

AS the branches are connected
With the vine, ev'n so thro' grace,
A close union is effected
'Twixt the Lord our Righteousness
And believers, who, tho' feeble,
Life and pow'r from him derive,
And thereby are render'd able
Bearing fruit to grow and thrive.

521.* T. 10.

WOULD we by our behavior
Show that we love our Saviour;
He only can instruct us,
And in the way conduct us.

2 Thro' his atonement's powers
O may we bloom like flowers,
And by his grace and blessing
Bear fruits to him well pleasing.

522.* T 185.

IN thy love and knowledge, gracious Saviour,
May we more and more abound;
Thy complete atonement shall for ever,
Of our doctrine be the ground.
Grant that all may, in thy word believing,
And to thee the Vine as branches cleaving
Thro' thy Father's nursing care,
Fruit unto thy honor bear.

523.* T. 4.

LORD Jesus, be near
Thou seest us here;
Unite us in heart:—Dear Lord, come and bless us; our Brother thou art.

2 Soon make us to be
Well-pleasing to thee;
'Tis time, and 'tis right,—To bring forth some fruit which may yield thee delight.

3 From this very day,
We will not delay
To follow the Lamb,—To serve him with gladness, and honor his name.

524.* T 228.

THIS one thing needful grant to us,
By faith to view thee on the cross,
Bleeding for our salvation;
Then, 'midst all weakness, we indeed
Shall still from grace to grace proceed,
Lord, in thy congregation:
May none—ground on
Empty notions—or good motions
His religion,
Without pow'r and life's fruition.

XXVIII. Of Resignation, Confidence, and Patience in Tribulation.

525.* T. 151.

IS God my strong Salvation?
No enemy I fear;
He hears my supplication,
Dispelling all my care:
If he, my Head and Master,
Defends me from above,
What pain or what disaster
Can part me from his love?

2 Of this I am persuaded,
And boast now openly,
That he, whose love ne'er faded,
Is always kind to me;
He aid to me dispenses,
He stands at my right hand;
Yea, when a storm advances,
'Tis calm at his command.

3 The ground of my profession
Is Jesus and his blood;
He gives me the possession
Of everlasting Good;
Myself, and whatsoever
Is mine, I cannot trust;
The gifts of Christ my Saviour
Remain my only boast.

4 My Jesus and his merit
Are all my aim and care;
Were he not with my spirit,
Ah! I should soon despair;
T' appear 'fore my Creator
I never could desire,
He'd to my sinful nature
Prove a consuming fire.

5 'Tis Jesus Christ who taketh
Away sin, death and woe,
And by his blood he maketh
Each spot as white as snow;
Free from that condemnation
Which sinners else must find,
I joy in his salvation
With an embolden'd mind.

6 His Spirit is the sov'reign
Possessor of my heart;
There he alone shall govern,
And slavish fear depart;
He gives his benediction,
Yea, helpeth me to cry
Abba, when in affliction,
With child-like fervency.

7 His Spirit cheers my spirit
With many a precious word,
That I shall joy inherit,
By trusting in the Lord;
Since after tribulation,
All those who Jesus love
Have that blest expectation
To live with him above.

8 Should earth lose its foundation,
He stands my lasting Rock;
No temp'ral desolation
Shall give my love a shock;
I'll cleave to Christ my Saviour,
No object, small or great,
Nor height, nor depth, shall ever
Me from him separate.

526. T. 14.

GOD is my Saviour and my Light,
Why should I be dismay'd?
'Tis he defends my life; of whom
Then need I be afraid?

2 Hear my requests, O Lord, and give
An answer full of grace:
Thy face thou bidst me seek, and I
Reply, "I'll seek thy face."

3 Lord, do not in displeasure hide
Thyself, nor me reject;
The aid which I have had before,
From thee I still expect.

4 Wait still on God, my soul! from him
All needful strength derive:
Tho' he delay, he will at length
The fainting heart revive.

527.* T. 208.

JESUS, source of gladness,
Comfort in all sadness,
Thou canst end my grief;
I for thee am waiting,
Ardently intreating
Thee for thy relief:
Slaughter'd Lamb,—thy saving name
Yields to me far greater pleasure
Than all worldly treasure.

2 God is my salvation,
Joy and consolation;
With the world I've done;
To pride's vain pretension
I pay no attention,
Av'rice I disown;
Perils, loss,—shame, death and cross,
Suff'rings e'er so keen, shall never
Me from Jesus sever.

3 If the Lord protect me,
Sin cannot infect me,
Nought can do me harm;
Altho' Satan rageth,
Christ the storm assuageth
By his mighty arm:
Would the foe—his malice show,
Since Christ is my strength and tower,
I dread not his power.

4 Gloomy thoughts must vanish,
Jesus doth replenish
Me with heav'nly peace;
Who the Saviour loveth,
By experience proveth
Grief is chang'd to bliss;
Tho' I here—reproach must bear,
Yet he turneth all my sadness
Into joy and gladness.

528. T. 22.

WHO can condemn, since Christ hath dy'd?
I, by his blood, am justify'd:
He ever lives to intercede,
And send me help in time of need.

2 What can from Christ me separate?
Shall trials howsoever great,
Shall tribulation or distress,
Shall peril, sword, or nakedness?

3 O no, in all things I shall prove
Conqu'ror through him, who me did love;
My Lord obtain'd the victory,
Sufficient is his grace for me.

4 O love unbounded! refuge sure!
My helpless soul now lives secure;
Long as in thee, O Lord, I trust,
I know I never shall be lost.

529.* T. 22.

JESUS, my All, my highest Good!
Who hast redeem'd me with thy blood,
When confidence in thee I place,
My soul is fill'd with joy and peace.

2 Where should I turn, or how thee leave?
Jesus, to thee my mind doth cleave;
With thee my heart hath always found
True counsel, comfort, help abound.

3 All who possess true faith and love,
This daily by experience prove,
That they who simply put their trust
In Jesus Christ, can ne'er be lost.

4 None can be so o'erwhelm'd with grief,
But he in Christ may find relief;
All misery, however great,
His comforts can alleviate.

5 Jesus, my only God and Lord,
What comfort doth thy name afford!
No friend on earth can ever be
Compar'd for faithfulness with thee.

6 Were health, and strength, and friends withdrawn,
Were ev'ry earthly comfort gone,
If I have thee, I have howe'er
What me eternally can cheer.

7 O Lord, preserve me sound in faith,
Thine let me be in life and death;
May nothing pluck me from thy hand,
Lead me in safety to the end.

530. T. 590.

NO more with trembling heart I try
  A multitude of things,
Still wishing to find out that point
  From whence salvation springs;
My anchor's cast, cast on a ground,
  Where I shall ever rest
From all the labor of my thoughts,
  And workings of my breast.

2 What is my anchor, if you ask?
  A hungry, helpless mind,
Diving, with mis'ry for its weight,
  Till firmest grace it find:
What is my ground? 'Tis Jesus Christ,
  Whom faithless eyes pass o'er;
A Refuge here each troubled soul
  May find, tho' tempests roar.

531. T. 580.

THAT I am thine, my Lord and God,
Ransom'd and sprinkled with thy blood,
  Repeat that word once more,
With such an energy and light,
That this world's flattery or spite
  To shake me never may have pow'r.

2 From various cares my heart retires;
Tho' deep and boundless its desires,
  I'm now to please but One,
Him, before whom the elders bow;
With him I am engaged now,
  And with the souls that are his own.

3 This is my joy, which ne'er can fail,
To see my Saviour's arm prevail,
  To mark the steps of grace;
How new-born souls, convinc'd of sin,
Yet by his precious blood made clean,
  Extol his name in ev'ry place.

4 With these my happy lot is cast,
Thro' the world's deserts rude and waste,
  Or thro' its gardens fair:
Whether the storm of malice sweeps,
Or all in dead supineness sleeps,
  Still to go on, be all my care.

5 See the dear sheep, by Jesus drawn,
In blest simplicity move on,
  They trust his Shepherd-crook;
Beholders many faults will find,
But they can guess at Jesus' mind,
  Content, if written in his book.

6 O all ye just, ye rich, ye wise,
Who deem th' atoning sacrifice,
  A doctrine weak and slight!
Grant but I may (the rest's your own)
In shame and poverty sit down
  At this one well-spring of delight.

7 Indeed had Jesus ne'er been slain,
Or could ought make his ransom vain,
  That it avail'd no more;
Were his unbounded mercy fled,
Were he no more the church's Head,
  Nor Lord of all, as heretofore;

8 Then, so refers my state to him,
Unwarranted I must esteem,
  And wretched all I do;
Ah! my heart throbs, and seizeth fast
That cov'nant, which will ever last,
  It knows, it knows these things are true.

9 Yes, my dear Lord, in foll'wing thee,
Not in the dark uncertainly
  This foot obedient moves;
'Tis with a Brother and a King,
Who many to this yoke will bring,
  Whoever lives and ever loves.

10 Now then my Way, my Truth, my Life,
Henceforth let sorrow, doubt and strife,
  Drop off like autumn leaves;
Henceforth, as privileg'd by thee,
Simple and undistracted be
  My soul, which to thy mercy cleaves.

11 Let me my weary mind recline
On that eternal love of thine,
  And human thoughts forget;
Childlike attend what thou wilt say,
Go forth and do it, while 'tis day,
  Yet never leave my safe retreat.

12 At all times to my spirit bear
An inward witness, strong and clear,
  Of thy redeeming pow'r;
This will instruct thy child aright,
This will impart the needful light,
  For exigence of ev'ry hour.

13 Now then the sequel is well weigh'd,
I cast myself upon thy aid,
  A sea where none can sink;
Yea, thereon I depend, poor worm,
Believing that thou wilt perform
  Beyond whate'er I ask or think.

532. T. 14.

HOW happy we, when guilt is gone!
This alters our whole frame;
The same occasions still come on,
But we are not the same.

2 The load which caus'd us anxious care
No more doth weigh us down,
For Christ the burden helps to bear,
We bear it not alone.

3 While we at honest labor toil,
Our hearts may be at ease;
For if our Saviour on us smile,
'Midst trouble we have peace.

4 Sick outwardly, or in distress
We may be, 'tis confest:
But the believer ne'ertheless
In trials finds he's blest.

5 Have we thro' dang'rous paths to rove,
The shades of death to pass,
Our shield eternal is his love,
Our light his glorious face.

6 Thy secret hand we bless; on thee
O Lord, we can depend,
Thou betwixt us and misery
Of ev'ry kind dost stand.

533.* T. 212.

THE will of God is always best,
His will be done for ever;
Those who confide in him are blest,
And prove his love and favor.
He helps indeed—in time of need,
'Midst chastisements he saveth;
Those who depend—on God their Friend
He never, never leaveth.

2 His comforts daily me sustain,
He lends me his assistance;
To what he doth for me ordain
I'll yield without resistance:
True is his word,—that ev'n the Lord
My hairs in mercy numbers;
He guards and wakes,—care of me takes,
And all my wants remembers.

534.* T. 14

WHATE'ER our God doth, must be right,
Altho' it cause us pain;
For God is love, and ever will
The source of love remain.

2 The church's Head we thee confess,
Thou of thine own tak'st care;
Jesus, thy will be always done!
This be our wish and pray'r.

535. T. 590.

SINCE we can't doubt God's equal love,
Unmeasurably kind,
To his unerring, gracious will
Be ev'ry wish resign'd;
Good, when he gives, supremely good;
Nor less when he denies;
Ev'n crosses from his sov'reign hand
Are blessings in disguise.

2 Whate'er I ask, I surely know,
And stedfastly believe,
He will the thing desir'd bestow,
Or else a better give;
To thee I therefore, Lord, submit
My ev'ry fond request,
And own, adoring at thy feet,
Thy will is always best.

536.* T. 234.

JESUS, my All, my soul's best Friend,
To thee myself I now deliver;
Whate'er comes from thy faithful hand,
How hard it be, how strange soever,
I'll take it with a passive heart;
And tho' I cannot shout for gladness,
But keenly feel affliction's dart,
O may I not be sunk in sadness!
May I with cheerfulness,
In thy ways acquiesce,
Nor murmur at thy dispensation;
But simply trusting thee,
On thy fidelity
Depend with humble resignation.

537. T. 22.

DESPONDING soul, thou need'st not fear,
Since God thy ev'ry pray'r doth hear,
In his own time he'll surely grant,
As he thinks fit, what thou dost want.

For he thy case doth understand,
Himself will take thy cause in hand,
The scale will turn, and thou shalt be
Asham'd of thy anxiety.

538.* T. 79.

I'LL spare all needless thinking,
Nor shall my mind be shrinking
Concerning what may be;
I'll follow thy kind leading,
Dear Lord, in each proceeding;
That thou'rt my All sufficeth me.

539. T. 9.

WHAT, my soul, should bow thee down,
Perils or temptation?
Is not Christ upon the throne
Still thy strong salvation?

2 Cast thy burden on the Lord,
Thy almighty Saviour;
He, who death for thee endur'd,
Surely will deliver.

3 Mention to him ev'ry want,
Yea, whate'er doth grieve thee,
If for comfort thou dost pant,
Jesus will relieve thee.

4 Turn, my soul, unto thy rest,
Quickly turn to Jesus,
He will do for thee what's best,
Heal all thy diseases.

5 Mourn, whene'er thou hast forgot
Him, whose great compassion
Never fails, whose blood hath bought
Thy complete salvation.

6 Earthly things do not regard,
Trust in Jesus' favor,
He will be thy great reward,
And thy shield for ever.

540.* T. 16.

STORMS of trouble may assail us,
Yea, life's vessel overwhelm;
Yet no danger need appal us,
If our Saviour guide the helm.

2 If with willing resignation,
Free from care, we acquiesce
In his ways, his consolation
Will alleviate our distress.

3 God is mighty to deliver,
None his power can withstand;
In all trials whatsoever
He will be our gracious Friend.

4 When his hour strikes for relieving,
Help breaks forth amazingly,
And to shame our anxious grieving,
Often unexpectedly.

541. T. 22.

WHEN by adversity I'm try'd,
In God, my Rock, I will confide,
'Midst trials, whatsoe'er they be,
Rely on his fidelity.

2 I'll trust my great Physician's skill,
Resign'd obey his blessed will;
For each disease he knows what's fit,
He's wise and good, and I submit.

3 Altho' his med'cine cause me smart,
And wound me in the tend'rest part,
It is with a design to cure,
I must and will his touch endure.

4 Lord Jesus Christ, afford me grace,
In ev'ry trial thee to praise:
O let thy sacred will be mine,
To thee myself I now resign.

542.* T. 83.

MY Redeemer knoweth me,
Both in joy and in affliction;
O my soul, now joyful be,
Trust thy Shepherd's kind direction;
His own sheep he knows by name,
And to bless them is his aim.

2 Unexampled is that love
By which we're with him connected;
If we ought distressing prove,
Jesus is thereby affected;
We his watchful love and care,
In all trials richly share.

543. T. 590.

BY Christ we're screen'd, with tender care,
From vain and worldly noise:
Ye who God's happy children are,
Can in the Lord rejoice,
And walk in union with your God,
Who is your nearest Friend,
Upon life's rough and dang'rous road,
In safety to the end.

544.* T. 90.

THRICE happy are the feeble souls,
Whose strength is only in their God!
Since each the fiercest pow'rs controls,
By faith in Jesus' precious blood:
In combat they maintain the field,
Because Jehovah is their Shield.

545.* T. 195.

DOTH our gracious Saviour,
In so many evils,
Which the foe at christians levels,
Kindly guard and keep us:
Ah, how should we praise him,
In all things extol and bless him!
Love should so—ardent glow,
As to make us ever
Cleave to Christ our Saviour.

546. T. 22.

GOD of my life! on thee I call,
Afflicted at thy feet I fall;
When the great water-floods prevail,
Leave not my trembling heart to fail!

2 Friend of the friendless, and the faint!
Where should I lodge my deep complaint?
Where but with thee, whose open door
Invites the helpless and the poor!

3 Did ever mourner plead with thee,
And thou refuse that mourner's plea?
Doth not the word still fix'd remain,
That none shall seek thy face in vain?

4 That were a grief I could not bear,
Didst thou not hear and answer pray'r;
But a pray'r-hearing, answ'ring God,
Supports me under ev'ry load.

5 Poor tho' I am, despis'd, forgot,
Yet God, my God, forgets me not;
And he is safe, and must succeed,
For whom the Lord vouchsafes to plead.

547.* T. 580.

JESUS, our Guardian, Guide and Friend,
Now thy protecting wings extend,
Thy children save from harm;
Would Satan seek us to devour,
Against his malice, craft and pow'r,
Defend us by thy outstretch'd arm.

548.* T. 68.

THANKS for ever be,
Jesus, unto thee,
That thy strength doth us enable
To adhere to thee, tho' feeble;
That thou hear'st our pray'rs,
And regard'st our tears.

549. T. 149.

'MIDST all trials may I cleave
Unto thee, my Saviour;
Ah, my inmost soul doth grieve
When I miss that favor:
Might thy grace—but always,
And thy constant nearness,
Keep my soul in clearness!

550. T. 167.

THO' by trials strong surrounded
Yet thro' Jesus' gracious care,
This poor heart is not confounded,
He doth all my suff'rings share;
On his pow'rful aid reclining,
Calm I'll ev'ry grief sustain,
Bear the cross without repining,
Till the glorious crown I gain.

551.* T. 15.

ARE we in e'er so great distress,
Our God can us deliver;
And should he not, he ne'ertheless
Shall be our God for ever.

552.* T. 583.

AT last he's blest, who by the Saviour's blood,
Was cleans'd while here, and made an heir of God;
Ev'n now the acceptable year draws nigh,
The day, which turns our sorrows into joy.

2 At last God's servants ceaseless joys shall reap,
Who, bearing precious seed, go forth and weep;
If they, 'midst suff'ring, faithful here abide,
They shall with Jesus there be glorify'd.

3 My soul, tho' here by various trials prov'd,
Believe that by thy Saviour thou art lov'd:
Submit thy will to his; with patience wait,
Soon he to perfect bliss will thee translate.

553.* T. 189.

WHO overcometh shall abide for ever
A pillar in God's temple thro' his grace,
Adorned with the name of God our Saviour,
And of Jerusalem his chosen place;
Lord make the feeble
Watchful and able,
That they be stable,
And vict'ry gain.

XXIX. Hymns of Praise and Thanksgiving.

554.* T. 235.

TE DEUM LAUDAMUS.

LORD GOD, thy praise we sing,
To thee our thanks we bring.
Both heav'n and earth doth worship thee,
Thou Father of eternity.
To thee all angels loudly cry,
The heav'ns and all the pow'rs on high:
Cherubs and seraphim proclaim
And cry thrice holy to thy name:
Holy is our Lord God,
Holy is our Lord God,
Holy is our Lord God,
The Lord of Sabaoth!

With splendor of thy glory spread
Is heav'n and earth replenished.
Th' apostles' glorious company,
The prophets' fellowship, praise thee.
The noble and victorious host
Of martyrs make of thee their boast.
The holy church, in ev'ry place
Throughout the earth, exalts thy praise.
Thee, Father, God on heav'ns throne
Thy only and beloved Son,
The Holy Ghost, who Christ displays,
The church doth worship thank and praise.

O Christ, thou glorious King we own
Thee to be God's eternal Son.
Thou, undertaking in our room,
Didst not abhor the virgin's womb.
The pains of death o'ercome by thee,
Made heav'n to all believers free.
At God's right hand thou hast thy seat,
And in thy Father's glory great;
And we believe the day's decreed,
When thou shalt judge the quick & dead.

Promote, we pray, thy servants' good,
Redeem'd with thy most precious blood;
Among thy saints make us ascend
To glory that shall never end.
Thy people with salvation crown,
Bless those, O Lord, that are thy own:
Govern thy church, and, Lord, advance
For ever thine inheritance.

From day to day, O Lord, do we
Highly exalt and honor thee:
Thy name we worship and adore,
World without end, for evermore.
Vouchsafe, O Lord, we humbly pray,
To keep us safe from sin this day.
O Lord, have mercy on us all;
Have mercy on us, when we call.
Thy mercy, Lord, to us dispense,
According to our confidence.
Lord, we have put our trust in thee,
Confounded let us never be.
Amen!

555.* T. 132.

ALL glory to the sov'reign Good,
And Father of compassion!
To God our help and sure abode;
Whose gracious visitation
Renews his blessings ev'ry day,
And taketh all our griefs away:
Give to our God the glory!

2 The heav'nly hosts with awe show forth
The praise of their Creator;
All creatures, both in heav'n and earth,
Whate'er exists in nature,
Speak their divine Original,
Impress'd most wisely on them all:
Give to our God the glory!

3 What is created by our God
Enjoys his preservation;
He doth extend o'er all abroad
His father-like compassion;
Throughout the kingdom of his grace
Prevail his truth and righteousness:
Give to our God the glory!

4 In my distress I rais'd with faith
To God my supplication;
My Saviour rescu'd me from death,
And gave me consolation;
This makes my heart with thankfulness
Rejoice before the God of grace:
Give to our God the glory!

5 The Lord hath ever to his flock
Kept without separation;
He doth abide our Shield and Rock,
Our peace and our salvation;
He leads us with a mother's care,
Protects from danger, guards from fear:
Give to our God the glory!

6 Yea, when all creatures here deny
Their help and consolation,
Our great Creator then is nigh
With succor and compassion,
And sets the humble souls at rest,
That live forsaken and opprest:
Give to our God the glory!

7 As long as I have breath in me
I will sound forth his praises;
His precious, saving name shall be
Exalted in all places;
My heart, with all thy strength adore
The God of grace, the God of pow'r,
And give him all the glory!

8 Ye who profess his sacred name,
Give to our God the glory!
Ye who his pow'r know and proclaim,
Give to our God the glory!
Rejoice from all vain idols freed,
The Lord is God, he's God indeed,
Give to our God the glory;

9 Now then before his face appear,
With praises and thanksgiving,
With awe his holy name revere,
And join with all the living,
T' extol the wonders he hath wrought,
His mighty deeds, surpassing thought,
Give to our God the glory!

556.* T. 14.

I'LL praise thee with my heart and tongue,
O Lord, my soul's delight,
Declaring to the world in song
Thy glory, praise and might.

2 Thou art th' eternal Source of grace,
The Source of lasting bliss;
From thee unto the human race
Flows ev'ry happiness.

3 What are we? what do we possess,
While here on earth below,
Which thy great love and tenderness
Doth not on us bestow?

4 Who spreads the lofty firmament,
And starry skies around?
Who makes the dew and rain descend
To fructify the ground?

5 Who doth preserve our life and health,
Our ease and safe abode?
Who doth secure our peace and wealth?
Our ever gracious God.

6 On thee, almighty Lord of hosts,
Depends our life and all,
Thou keepest watch around our coasts,
Protectest great and small.

7 Thy chastisements are nought but love;
When we our sins confess,
We thy forgiveness richly prove:
'Tis thy delight to bless.

8 Thou count'st thy children's sighs and tears,
And know'st well why they mourn,
No tear too mean to thee appears
To put into thy urn.

9 Thou, when we are oppress'd with grief,
Dost us with pity view,
Administ'ring thy kind relief,
And lasting comfort too.

10 Why need we mourn, as in despair,
And grieve both day and night?
On him we'll cast our ev'ry care,
Who gave us life and light.

11 Hath he not, from our earliest days,
Us nourish'd and maintain'd?
Safe guarded us in all our ways,
In dangers prov'd our Friend?

12 God never yet mistakes hath made
In his vast government;
No, what he doth permit or aid
Is blest in the event.

13 Then murmur not, but be resign'd
To his most holy will;
Peace, rest and comfort thou wilt find
My soul, in being still.

557.* T. 277.

NOW unite to render praises
To Jehovah, to our God, and magnify
His great name in all your places,
Ye his people, ye who are his property;
For his goodness, love and favor
To his children last for ever;
He is full of truth and grace,
Pard'ning all our trespasses;
Still his name by you be praised,
Who are seed to Abra'm raised,
Spread his acts in ev'ry nation,
Give him praises, give him thanks and adoration!

2 Yea, with joy ourselves addressing
To our gracious, heav'nly Father, we'll proclaim
His great mercy without ceasing,
Join with angels to exalt his glorious name;
They, adoring on their faces,
With thrice "Holy" sing his praises,
We too will extol the name
Of our God, and of the Lamb;
Be his glory ever sounded,
And his works which are unbounded!
We his ransom'd congregation
Thank and praise him, for our blessed destination.

3 To the throne go undismayed,
Go with boldness, and approach the mercy-seat,
Since from God in Christ displayed,
Nought but goodness, grace and favor you can meet;
Full of love, he longs to bless us,
And is ready to embrace us;
Yea, to give his flesh and blood
To us, as our highest good;
To his table we're invited,
And thro' grace with him united,
So that nought which may await us
Can from Jesus, and his love e'er separate us.

4 He hath now his Godhead's treasure
To the needy open'd, and hath stores enough,
Therefore 'tis his sov'reign pleasure,
That no sinner, that not one should stand aloof;
Each may take, as were he named,
Grace for grace, nor stand ashamed,
Hungry souls who but believe,
Of his fulness may receive;
And this fulness never ceaseth,
Our enjoyment still increaseth;
Hence we drink, in richest measure,
From life's fountain, draughts of inexhausted pleasure.

5 These our falt'ring lays, dear Saviour,
Which, tho' feeble, yet our grateful hearts express,
Condescend t' accept in favor,
Till in glory we shall see thee face to face;
Then for all thy works our praises
Shall resound in heav'nly places;
There we shall to thee our King
Joyful hallelujahs sing:
May from ev'ry thing in nature
Praise be given to the Creator,
And our lives and whole demeanor
To Jehovah, to our God give praise and honor.

558.* T. 195.

GOD reveals his presence!
Let us now adore him,
And with awe appear before him;
God is in his temple,
All in us keep silence,
And before him bow with rev'rence;
Him alone,—God we own:
He's our Lord and Saviour;
Praise his name for ever.

2 God reveals his presence,
Whom th' angelic legions
Serve with awe in heav'nly regions,
Holy, Holy, Holy!
Sing the hosts of heaven;
Praise to God be ever given!
Condescend—to attend
Graciously, O Jesus!
To our songs and praises.

3 O majestic Being!
Were but soul and body
Thee to serve at all times ready,
Might we, like the angels
Who behold thy glory,
Deep abased sink before thee,
And thro' grace,—be always,
In our whole demeanor,
To thy praise and honor.

4 Grant us resignation,
Hearts before thee bowed,
With thy peace divine endowed:
As a tender flower
Opens and inclineth
To the cheering sun which shineth:
So may we—be from thee
Rays of grace deriving,
And thereby be thriving.

5 Lord, come dwell within us,
While on earth we tarry;
Make us thy blest sanctuary.
O vouchsafe thy presence,
Draw unto us nearer,
And reveal thyself still clearer.
Us direct,—and protect;
Thus we in all places
Shall show forth thy praises.

559.* T. 341.

THOU, Jesus, art our King!
Thy ceaseless praise we sing:
Praise shall our glad tongues employ,
Praise o'erflow the grateful soul,
While we vital breath enjoy,
While eternal ages roll.

2 Thou art th' eternal Light,
And shin'st in deepest night:
Wond'ring gaz'd th' angelic train,
While thou bow'dst the heav'ns beneath,
Taking thy abode with man,
Man to save from endless death.

3 Thou for our griefs didst mourn,
Thou hast our sickness borne:
All our sins on thee were laid;
Thou with unexampled grace
All the mighty debt hast paid,
Due from Adam's helpless race.

4 Thou hast o'erthrown the foe;
God's kingdom fix'd below:
Conqu'ror of all adverse pow'r,
Thou heav'n's gates hast open'd wide,
Thou thine own dost lead secure,
And to life eternal guide.

5 Above the starry sky
Thou reign'st enthron'd on high!
Prostrate at thy feet we fall:
Pow'r supreme to thee is giv'n,
As the righteous Judge of all,
Sons of earth and hosts of heav'n.

6 The mighty seraphs join,
And in thy praise combine;
All their choirs thy glories sing,
Who shall dare with thee to vie,
Mighty Lord, eternal King,
Sov'reign both of earth and sky!

7 The church thro' all her bounds
With thy high praise resounds:
The confessors fearless here
Boldly praise their heav'nly King;
Children's feebler voices there
To thy name hosannas sing.

8 'Midst danger's blackest frown,
Thee hosts of martyrs own:
Pain and shame alike they dare,
Firmly trusting in their God;
Glorying thy cross to bear,
Sealing thus their faith with blood.

9 Arise, exert thy pow'r
Thou glorious Conqueror!
Help us to obtain the prize,
Help us well to close our race;
That with thee, above the skies,
Endless joys we may possess.

560.* T. 101.

THANKSGIVING, honor, praise and might,
Unto the slaughter'd Lamb be render'd,
Who brought us to his kingdom's light,
And bought us from all tongues and kindred;
Before the world was form'd we were ordain'd
By him to happiness, and life which hath no end.

2 To Him who ever doth abide,
Be ceaseless songs of praise repeated,
By Christendom, his chosen bride,
And those in heav'nly mansions seated;
Th' angelic hosts exalt his saving name,
And we with all created beings do the same.

3 By all the saints around his throne,
And all th' angelic choirs in heaven,
With shouts of glory to God's Son,
Our King and Shepherd, praise be given,
They join with us his goodness to rehearse,
His glorious name be prais'd throughout the universe!

561.* T. 146.

NOW let us praise the Lord
With body, soul and spirit,
Who doth such wondrous things
Beyond our sense and merit;
Who from our mother's womb
And earliest infancy
Hath done great things for us,
Praise him eternally!

2 O gracious God, bestow
On us while here remaining,
An ever-cheerful mind,
Thy peace be ever reigning:
Preserve us in true faith
And christian holiness:
That when we go from hence
We may behold thy face.

562.* T. 206.

ALMIGHTY Lord! :||:
Eternal Word,
Creation's Head,
By whom :||: the worlds were made,
Which in heav'n's spacious sphere :||:
Appear;
Who by thy blood
Brought'st us to God:
Thee we confess :||:
The Lord our Righteousness. :||:

2 Sure as thou liv'st, :||:
To all things giv'st
Both life and pow'r,
Supporting :||: them each hour;
Jehovah, great I AM, :||:
And Lamb:
So sure's thy blood
The highest Good
Of sinners poor, :||:
Till death shall be no more. :||:

* Heb. i. 2.

563.* T. 9.

TILL permitted hence to go,
To behold my Saviour,
Whom ev'n here by faith I know,
There in peace for ever:

2 Till on joys I once shall feast
Without intermission,
Of which here a partial taste
Is my blest fruition:

3 Till that time, mine eyes I'll raise
Unto him in spirit;
And my feeble tongue shall praise
His atoning merit.

564. T. 90.

THE Lamb was slain! let us adore.
With grateful hearts his mercy own,
May all within us evermore
In silence at his feet fall down;
Serve without dread, with rev'rence love
The Lord, whose boundless grace we prove.

2 The Lamb was slain! both day and night
Th' angelic choirs his praises sing;
To him enthron'd above all height,
Heav'n's hosts celestial anthems bring;
While here poor sinners join the song,
And praise him with a stamm'ring tongue.

3 Gladly our own poor works we leave,
For him despise, wealth, pleasure, fame,
To him our souls and bodies give,
His death doth our affections claim;
Henceforth we own him as our Lord,
His name be by us all ador'd.

4 Thro' him alone we live, for he
Hath drowned our transgressions all
In love's unfathomable sea;
Fall prostrate, lost in wonder fall,
Ye sinners, for the Lamb was slain,
Who dy'd that we might life regain.

5 As ground, when parch'd with summer's heat,
Gladly drinks in the welcome show'r,
So may we list'ning at his feet,
Receive his words, and feel his pow'r:
May nothing in our hearts remain,
But this great truth, "the Lamb was slain!"

565. T. 159.

ADORED be the Lamb of God,
That he upon the cross
To God, by his most precious blood,
Hath reconciled us.
All praise be given to him, that we
Were born the day of grace to see,
When he his love to us reveal'd,
And thus our pardon seal'd.

2 To be his priests and witnesses
Is now our happy lot,
To sing in songs of endless praise
To Jesus who us bought,
We now, like Mary, wish to sit
In spirit list'ning at his feet,
Waiting with lamps prepar'd and drest
For Jesus' marriage-feast.

3 Meanwhile his promises we trust,
And join our grateful lays,
In concert with the ransom'd host,
To sing redeeming grace.
While they who round his throne appear
The wonders of his love declare,
And sing, "The Lamb for us was slain";
Our hearts reply, Amen!

566. T. 122.

SING praises unto God on high
To him who us created;
Sing praises to the Lord, so nigh
To sinful man related.
Rejoicing Hallelujah sing,
Jesus Jehovah is our King,
And gracious Meditator.

2 He calls us brethren, not asham'd
To bear our human nature!
Yea, heirs of life we now are nam'd,
Joint heirs with our Creator!
He ever lives our cause to plead,
Grants help in ev'ry time of need,
Praise to his name for ever!

567. T. 39.

YE servants of God, your great Master proclaim,
And publish abroad his most excellent name;
The name all victorious of Jesus extol,
His kingdom is glorious, He rules over all.

2 God ruleth in heaven, almighty to save,
And yet he is with us, his presence we have;
The great congregation his triumphs shall sing,
Ascribing salvation to Jesus, our King.

3 Salvation be brought unto God on the throne,
Let all sing rejoicing, and honor the Son;
The praises of Jesus the angels proclaim,
Fall down on their faces, and worship the Lamb.

4 Then let us adore him and give him his right,
All glory, and power, and wisdom, and might,
And honor, and blessing, with angels above,
And thanks never ceasing for infinite love.

568. T. 11.

BRETHREN, let us join to bless
Jesus Christ, our joy and peace;
Let our praise to him be giv'n,
Who is Lord of earth and heav'n.

2 Jesus, lo! to thee we bow,
Thou art Lord, and only Thou;
Thou the woman's promis'd Seed,
Glory of thy church, and Head.

3 Thee the angels ceaseless sing,
Thee we praise, our Priest and King;
Worthy is thy name of praise,
Full of glory, full of grace.
We thy little flock adore
Thee, our Lord, for evermore!
Evermore show us thy love,
Till we join the choirs above!

569. T. 22.

BLESS, O my soul, the God of grace!
His favours claim thy highest praise;
How can the wonders he hath wrought
Be lost in silence, and forgot?

2 'Twas he, my soul, that sent his Son
To die for crimes which thou hast done;
He paid the ransom, and forgives
The hourly follies of our lives.

3 Our youth decay'd his pow'r repairs,
His mercy crowns our growing years;
He satisfies our souls with good,
And filleth us with heav'nly food.

4 Let the whole earth his pow'r confess,
Let all mankind adore his grace;
Let us with all our powers sing
Praise to our Saviour, God and King.

570. T. 14.

COME let us join our cheerful songs
With angels round the throne;
Ten thousand thousands are their tongues,
But all their joys are one.

2 "Worthy the Lamb that dy'd," they cry,
"To be exalted thus;"
"Worthy the Lamb," our hearts reply,
"For he was slain for us."

3 Jesus is worthy to receive
Honor and pow'r divine;
And blessings more than we can give,
Be, Lord, for ever thine.

4 The whole creation join in one,
To bless the sacred name
Of him that sits upon the throne,
And to adore the Lamb.

571. T. 22.

WE sing to God, whose tender love
Caus'd him to leave his throne above,
To dwell with sinful worms below,
And save them from eternal woe.

2 On fallen men he cast his eye,
In depths of mis'ry saw them lie;
Pity'd their state, resolv'd to come,
And suffer freely in their room.

3 A mortal body he assum'd,
Groan'd, bled and dy'd, and was entomb'd;
At length, the work thus finished,
He rose triumphant from the dead.

4 To heav'n's bright realms he took his flight,
Beyond the reach of mortal sight;
There pleads with God for ransom'd men,
Thence will in glory come again.

5 To Jesus, our exalted Head,
Immortal honors now be paid;
The glory of his saving name
Our tongues shall evermore proclaim.

572. T. 14.

O FOR a thousand tongues to sing
My dear Redeemer's praise!
The glories of my God and King,
The triumphs of his grace.

2 Jesus, the name that charms our fears,
That bids our sorrows cease;
In the poor contrite sinners' ears,
'Tis life, and health, and peace.

3 His grace subdues the pow'r of sin,
He sets the pris'ners free;
His blood can make the foulest clean,
His blood avail'd for me.

4 He speaks, and list'ning to his voice
New life the dead receive;
The mournful, broken hearts rejoice,
The humble poor believe.

5 Hear him, ye deaf; his praise, ye dumb,
Your loosen'd tongues employ;
Ye blind, behold your Saviour come;
And leap, ye lame, for joy.

573. T. 14.

NOT all the angels of the sky,
Nor happy saints above,
Have greater cause to praise than I
The Saviour's dying love.

2 Had I an angel's heav'nly tongue,
Or seraphs melody,
My theme should be his praise, who hung
Upon the cross for me.

3 For thee he hangs! my soul, rejoice;
For thee, my soul, expires;
Then sing his love with thankful voice,
Sing what his love inspires.

4 Till fleeting time shall have an end,
And years shall cease to roll,
Due praise shall from his church ascend,
And spread from pole to pole.

5 How sweet the precious gospel sounds
In the believer's ear!
This balsam heals his cank'ring wounds,
And dries each anxious tear.

6 But tears of joy must ever flow
For Jesus' wondrous love,
And when I leave this world below,
I'll sing his praise above.

574. T. 595.

AWAKE, and sing the song
Of Moses and the Lamb!
Wake ev'ry heart, and ev'ry tongue,
To praise the Saviour's name!

2 Sing of his dying love,
Sing of his rising pow'r:
Sing how he intercedes above
For us whose sins he bore.

3 Ye pilgrims on the road
To Zion's city, sing!
Rejoice ye in the Lamb of God,
In Christ, th' eternal King!

4 Soon shall we hear him say,
"Ye blessed children, come!"
Soon will he call us hence away,
To our eternal home.

5 There shall our raptur'd tongues
His endless praise proclaim;
And sweeter voices tune the song
Of Moses and the Lamb.

575. T. 595.

TO God the only wise,
Our Saviour and our King,
Let all the saints below the skies
Their humble praises bring.

2 'Tis his almighty love,
His counsel and his care,
Preserves us safe from sin and death,
And ev'ry hurtful snare.

3 He will present our souls
Unblemish'd and complete,
Before the glory of his face,
With joys divinely great.

4 Once all the chosen race
Shall meet around the throne,
Shall praise him for his saving grace,
And make his wonders known.

5 To our Redeemer-God,
Wisdom and pow'r belongs,
Immortal crowns of majesty,
And everlasting songs.

576. T. 83.

NOW with joyful songs appear,
And with humble adoration,
'Fore the Lord, he's always near
To his ransom'd congregation.
With the poor he deigns to dwell:
He is nam'd Immanuel.

577.* T. 121.

IN joyful hymns of praise,
Like one man, sweetly raise
Voices quite united;
With your liturgic lays
Your Saviour is delighted;
He'll with gracious ear
Your thanksgiving hear,
Feel that he is near!

578.* T. 58.

WHEN all thy mercies, Lord, to mind we call,
Astonish'd at thy feet we humbly fall.
Grant us still in future, thy kind direction,
Till in us all the aim of thy election
Be quite obtain'd.

579.* T. 155.

THOU, my Light, my Leading-star,
Who hast kindly me directed,
And protected;
When thy mercies, daily new,
I review,
In the dust I fall before thee,
Lost in wonder I adore thee,
They are great, yea numberless.

580. T. 249.

IN humble, grateful lays,
The Lord :||: of hosts we praise,
His saving name confess;
Yea, fill'd with holy awe, revere
The Father, Son and Comforter.
Amen, Hallelujah!
Hallelujah,
Amen, Hallelujah!

2 Praise to the slaughter'd Lamb!
His love :||: we will proclaim,
Who dy'd, us to redeem;
Let ev'ry being that hath breath,
Extol his meritorious death.
From angels and from men,
To the Lamb slain
All honour doth pertain.

581.* T. 89.

O THAT we with gladness of spirit for ever
Adored and praised our crucify'd Saviour!
O might each pulsation thanksgiving express,
And each breath we draw be an anthem of praise!

2 The Lamb, who by blood our salvation obtained,
Took on him our curse, and death freely sustained,
Is worthy of praises, let with one accord,
All people say Amen, O praise ye the Lord!

582. T. 230.

PRAISES, thanks, and adoration,
Be given to God without cessation,
To Jesus Christ, our gracious Lord;
For his mercy, love, and favor,
To us, his flock, endure for ever:
Bless, bless his name with one accord.
To God, the Father, Son,
And Spirit, Three in One,
Hallelujah!
In highest strain
Praise the Lamb slain!
Let heav'n and earth reply, Amen!

XXX. Of PRAYER and SUPPLICATION.

583. T. 583.

THE love of Christ to me is greater far
Than outwardly it doth to man appear;
When I before him my complaints make known,
He sympathizeth with them as his own.

2 I know that in myself I have no pow'r,
But 'tis thro' mercy I must live each hour;
His precious death doth strength to me afford,
Thus I can all things do, thro' Christ my Lord.

3 As oft as I approach the holy place,
And bow 'fore him, by whom I live thro' grace,
Then graciously he answers my request,
And thus my troubled heart is sooth'd to rest,

4 He is my All, my Sacrifice and Priest,
My Lord and God, my Saviour Jesus Christ.
His am I both in body and in soul,
Me neither sin, nor Satan can control.

5 I daily drink the healing streams of grace,
And gain new strength to run my future race;
He sheds abroad in me his love divine,
I know that I am his, and he is mine,

584.* T. 136.

THIS yields me joy,
That God in his compassion,
Doth not reject my pray'r and supplication,
But graciously
Regards my poverty;
That with unweary'd patience he is ready
At all times, to attend to me his child most needy,
And to relieve my wants is nigh,
This yields me joy!

2 Long as I live,
The promises of Jesus
I'll to myself apply, to me they're precious;
When I to him
My faithful Saviour cleave,
And pond'ring on his wonders kneel before him,
Praise him with tears of joy, and in the dust adore him,
I of his love fresh proofs receive,
While here I live.

3 I'm well assur'd
His love to me is tender;
Therefore I now my all to him surrender;
He's merciful,
A kind forgiving Lord;
Tho' I may not immediately experience
The succour which I ask, I'll wait with faith and patience,
For he at last will help afford,
I'm well assur'd,

4 Praise ye the Lord,
Whose kindness, grace and favor
Unto his congregation lasts for ever;
Whose presence cheers
His chosen witnesses;
Where'er we are, to him ourselves addressing
In pray'r, we surely shall not fail to share his blessing;
We therefore sing with one accord:
Praise ye the Lord!

585.* T. 16.

QUITE alone, and yet not lonely,
I'll converse with God my Friend,
Now from worldly cares receding,
I my time in pray'r will spend.

2 O how blessed are the moments,
When the Lord himself draws near,
When I feel his gracious presence,
And he listens to my pray'r!

586. T. 14.

MANY complaints to Christ I can
Ev'n by a sigh relate,
Which I can't represent to man,
They are too delicate.

587. T. 16.

NE'ER dejected—unaffected
May I walk before thee here;
What distresses,—or oppresses,
Pouring in thy faithful ear.

588.* T. 580.

WITH ardent longing, at thy feet,
Lord Jesus Christ, I humbly wait,
O lend a gracious ear
Unto my manifold complaints;
I trust thou wilt relieve my wants,
And deign thy needy child to hear.

2 Grant me an upright simple heart,
A cheerful mind to me impart,
Free from sin's galling load;
O may I of my sinfulness
Always retain a consciousness,
But not serve sin; forbid it, God!

3 Grant me a harmless, dove-like mind,
To true humility inclin'd,
Thy will be mine indeed;
O may I labor constantly
Endow'd with spirit's poverty,
From ev'ry hurtful influence freed.

4 In peace with all may I be found,
Clearly thy gospel-truth propound,
In praying faithful be;
A share in others' welfare take,
The schemes and plots of Satan break,
Fast bound unto thy church and thee.

5 Presence of mind on me bestow,
A readiness O may I show
To execute thy will;
When I enjoy the highest good,
Partaking of thy flesh and blood,
My soul with thy love's ardor fill.

6 May I be serious, childlike too,
In all essentials firm and true;
Give me a trusty ear;
A constant, genuine brother's heart,
To sympathize with ev'ry smart,
And gladly others' burdens bear.

7 In converse make me tractable
And mild, in storms invincible,
And never prone to yield;
May I maintain incessantly
A tender fellowship with thee,
From day to day by grace upheld.

8 Thy unction O may I obey,
And tread the pilgrim's rugged way,
Grant I may shun no toil;
In all my senses render me
Well exercis'd, and let me be
Anointed with thy gladd'ning oil.

9 What for myself I thus request,
That pray I also for the rest
Of those, who cheerfully
Go forth salvation to proclaim
Thro' faith in thy most holy name,
Wherever they are sent by thee.

10 O Father, me with pleasure own
The dear-bought purchase of thy Son;
O Spirit, bless thou me,
Guide and protect me as thy child;
Lord Christ, who me hast reconcil'd,
Preserve me thine eternally.

589.* T. 36.

LORD Jesus Christ, thy body's Head and Saviour,
On us, thy children, deign to look in favor;
Our grateful hearts with thanks are overflowing, Before thee bowing.

2 What peace do we derive, what consolation,
What strength from thy atoning death and passion!
Impress'd with holy rev'rence, we adore thee, And fall before thee.

3 Thy goodness, as thy pow'r, is past expression;
We trust, that thou, whene'er with supplication
We seek thy face, in mercy wilt accept us, And not reject us.

4 O Lord, thou great High-Priest of our profession,
Who at God's right-hand makest intercession,
And by thy pow'rful pray'rs to help the needy Art ever ready.

5 The many drops of blood which from thee flowed,
The streams of tears, which oft thy cheeks bedewed,
Are all in our behalf for mercy pleading And interceding.

6 O may thy church before thee bloom like flowers,
Unto thy praise, thro' thy atonement's powers;
Yea, glorify thy name in us, dear Saviour, Both now and ever!

590.* T. 83.

FLOCK of Christ, in fellowship
Offer fervent supplication,
Whether to rejoice, or weep,
We may now have most occasion;
When the lips no more can pray,
Sighs will find to him their way.

2 O may he so sensibly
Bless us with his grace and favor,
That we, in humility,
May rejoice in him, our Saviour;
May he, in his mercy, grant
All we weep for, all we want.

3 May his presence constantly
Yield us joy and consolation,
In the certain hope that he
Will regard our supplication,
Grant our pray'rs, and much more give
Than we're worthy to receive.

4 This be our supreme delight,
To remain in closest union
With our Lord, both day and night,
And enjoy his sweet communion;
This our heav'n, while here we stay,
Him to love, serve and obey.

591.* T. 580.

O THOU, who in the sanctuary
Dost minister! thy church supply
With incense for her pray'r;
Grant to us all a cheerful heart;
A burning, steady light impart,
Defended from all noxious air.

2 Lord, give us an attentive ear,
Which may thy voice distinctly hear,
An eye to view thee still;
And priestly lips to tell thy praise,
And feet earth's rugged craggy ways
To traverse, without fearing ill.

3 Our hands for blessing hallow'd be,
Our bodies temples be to thee,
Our souls enjoy thy peace;
A breeze divine our spirits cheer,
Grant us, thy still small voice to hear,
Unknown, save to thy flock of grace.

592.* T. 79.

O MAY the God of mercies,
Who perfecteth his praises
Out of the sucklings' mouth,
Grant us so blest a feeling
Of his most gracious dealing,
That we adore his grace and truth!

2 May he give us his unction,
To tell, with heart's compunction,
The wonders of his grace;
A constant deep impression
Of Jesus' wounds and passion,
And simple, childlike cheerfulness.

3 Lord, our High Priest and Saviour!
Pour fire and spirit's fervor
On all thy priestly bands;
When we are interceding,
And for thy people pleading,
Give incense, and hold up our hands.

4 By thine illumination,
Thy church's situation
In the true light we trace;
We rise from pray'r with blessing,
O'ercome what is distressing,
Thro' thee, and run with joy our race.

593.* T. 583.

LORD Jesus, may thy blood-bought church increase
From day to day in knowledge and in grace;
To all her choirs those special blessings grant, [want.
Which they in their degree and measure

2 Thy servants and thy handmaids keep in faith, [death;
And ground them all on thy atoning
Let those, who have the care of souls, by thee [rous be.
Be taught; thus will their labor prosp'-

3 May all our pastors who instruct thy sheep,
Firm to the word of thy atonement keep;
To act as in thy sight, O give them grace,
In word and walk may they show forth thy praise.

4 For all our meetings, for each conference [nance,
We crave the blessings of thy counte-
Keep in the bond of harmony and love
All elders, and their strength in weakness prove.

5 Remain our Lord, our Shepherd, Head and King,
And each to th' other in subjection bring.
Thy flocks preserve in peace and unity,
And walk amongst them with complacency.

6 From grace to grace still farther lead us on, [begun,
And finish the good work thou hast
That we thy saving name may magnify,
And for thy bitter torments yield thee joy.

7 Thy messengers, who storms and waves disdain [to gain,
To teach the nations, and their souls
Bless thou, and touch their lips with hallow'd fire; [inspire.
To witness of thy death, their tongues

8 May thy whole flock by thee, their Shepherd, led,
Afford thee joy and in thy footsteps tread;
Unto eternal life let us, by faith,
Feed on the merits of thy blood and death.

9 May all thy people, far and near, fulfil,
Supported by thy aid, thy holy will;
To thee all praise, all honor doth pertain,
Let all who love thy name, reply, Amen!

594.* T. 583.

THOU hast thy church appointed, Lord, that she [should be;
O'er all the world unto thy praise
A church, who in herself is void of good,
And yet by thee with grace and pow'r endow'd.

2 Teach us to pray for all the ransom'd fold: [withhold,
Lord! from thy church no needful gifts
As Head and Ruler in thy house remain,
And be the Leader of the witness-train.

3 Grant that we all may stedfastly adhere
To those great truths, by thee to us made clear;
Altho' we have but little strength, may we
Abiding in thy word, preserved be.

4 O let thy congregation feel thy peace,
And daily may her joy in thee increase;
Preserve her graciously from ev'ry harm,
Protect her by thy strong and mighty arm.

5 Grant her to thee an ever free access,
That cheerful to the mark she onward press;
And far and near, supported by thy aid,
Extend thy knowledge, and thy gospel spread.

6 Thou know'st her wants, and comfort dost impart [heart:
Unto each needy, poor, and sin-sick
Yea, by thy body and thy precious blood
Thou giv'st to her an ever-strength'ning food.

7 By thee, as Shepherd of the flock, we're led,
Till we shall join the church now perfected:
Till then thy blessed aim with us fulfil,
And teach us in all things to do thy will.

595.* T. 1.

O SON of God, High-Priest & Lamb once slain,
Behold the purchase of thy bitter pain.

2 Thou see'st us here assembled in thy name,
To feel thy gracious presence is our aim.

3 Unto each married pair that favor grant,
Thee and thy church, O Lord, to represent.

4 O may the single men be fill'd with zeal
To serve and follow thee and do thy will.

5 And grant the single women grace to be
True virgin hearts devoted unto thee.

6 O may the children true obedience show,
And as in years, in grace and knowledge grow.

7 Be thou the consolation, help and stay, [pray.
Of widowers and widows, Lord, we

8 Give unto all the needful gifts and grace, [place.
Yea, bless each soul thou hast in ev'ry

596.* T. 11.

LORD, with ev'ry needful grace
Bless thy church in ev'ry place;
Fill her with thy love divine,
And each member own as thine.

2 Grant us all to feel thy peace,
Set each troubled heart at ease;
Purify us by thy blood,
Which hath brought us nigh to God.

597. T. 185.

GRACIOUS Saviour, bless thy congregation,
Richly all her wants supply;
Be our only joy and consolation,
Till we quit mortality:
Of each weight may we be more divested,
Live beneath thy sceptre unmolested,
In thy matchless radiance shine,
Filled with thy love divine.

2 Cheer thy chosen witnesses, O Jesus,
Who thy dying love proclaim,
That with joy they may to distant places
Bear thy great and glorious name:
By thy arm O may they be defended
Till their pilgrimage on earth is ended,
And they are with thee at rest:
Lord, we pray, hear our request.

598.* T. 22.

LORD Jesus, with thy presence bless,
By land and sea, thy witnesses;
In ev'ry danger them defend,
In ev'ry trial prove their Friend.

2 O may thy word in Christendom
Be blest, and may thy kingdom come;
May all thy ministers succeed
In bringing fruit to thee their Head.

3 Preserve in constant love and peace,
And thro' thy blessing, still increase
Thy little flocks, which far and near
In towns and villages appear.

4 Thy thoughts of peace o'er us fulfil,
Incline our hearts to do thy will;
Thy gospel make more fully known,
May all the world thy goodness own.

599.* T. 22.

ACCORDING to thy mercy, Lord,
True christian faith to us afford,
That we thy kindness, love and grace,
May taste throughout our future race.

2 Hold over us thy gracious hand,
Protect and keep us to the end
From earthly noise and misery,
Retir'd and still to walk with thee.

3 O grant that we may thine remain,
And deeper ground in thee obtain;
Yea, give us to our latest breath
T' enjoy the merits of thy death.

600. T. 22.

ATTEND, O Saviour, to our pray'r!
All things by thy appointment are;
The world O govern for the best!
The Lord of all thou art confest.

2 Thou who on earth the sick didst heal,
And to the poor thy love reveal,
O comfort by a look from thee
All who are now in misery.

3 Nearer and nearer draw us still;
Might all but know thy holy will:
Subdue all pride and stubbornness,
O Lord, by thy prevailing grace.

4 Preserve by thy most gracious aid
Those who have thee their Refuge made;
Grant that, in all things free from blame,
In meekness they may praise thy name.

601.* T. 97.

OFT as the church the blessings weighs
Deriv'd from Jesus' saving grace,
And ponders on his faithful care,
Which she each day doth richly share,
By love constrain'd, to pray she is inclin'd
For the prosperity of all mankind.

2 For all put in authority
We supplicate most fervently;
The magistrates thou hast ordain'd
Support by thy almighty hand,
In guarding church and state give them success;
The land in which we live protect and bless.

3 From strife and tumult, God of grace,
Preserve us, bless the land with peace;
May all men willingly obey
Rulers, ordain'd to bear the sway;
And under their protection, grant that we
May live in godliness and honesty.

602.* T. 1.

O LORD, asham'd and blushing we declare,
That we thy poor insolvent debtors are.

2 O lift on us thy gracious countenance,
In mercy look upon our indigence.

3 Grant us each blessing purchas'd by thy blood,
O'erstream our souls with that atoning flood.

603.* T. 151.

AMEN, this the conclusion
Of our petitions be:
Lord, by thy blood's effusion,
Let us belong to thee.
Thus we await, possessing
True bliss while we are here,
The time, when joys unceasing
We once with thee shall share.

XXXI. Of the Christian Church in general, and the Brethren's Congregations in particular.

604. T. 167.

GLORIOUS things of thee are spoken
Zion, city of our God!
He whose words can ne'er be broken,
Form'd thee for his own abode:
On the Rock of ages founded,
What can shake thy sure repose?
With salvation's walls surrounded,
Thou may'st smile at all thy foes.

2 See! the streams of living waters,
Springing from eternal love,
Well supply thy sons and daughters,
And all fear of want remove:
Who can faint while such a river
Ever flows their thirst t'assuage?
Grace, which like the Lord, the Giver,
Never fails from age to age.

3 Round each habitation hov'ring
See the cloud and fire appear!
For a glory and a cov'ring,
Showing that the Lord is near:
Thus deriving from their banner
Light by night and shade by day,
Safe they feed upon the manna
Which he gives them when they pray.

5 Blest inhabitants of Zion,
Wash'd in the Redeemer's blood!
Jesus, whom their souls rely on,
Makes them kings and priests to God:
'Tis his love his people raises
Over self to reign as kings,
And as priests, his solemn praises
Each for a thank-off'ring brings.

5 Saviour, if of Zion's city
I thro' grace a member am;
Let the world deride or pity,
I will glory in thy name:
Fading is the worldling's pleasure,
All his boasted pomp and show;
Solid joys and lasting treasure,
None but Zion's children know.

605.* T. 520.

PRAISE God for ever!
Boundless is his favor
To his church and chosen flock,
Founded on Christ the Rock,
His almighty Son;
On fair mount Zion,
By his Spirit, grace and word:
Blest city of the Lord!
Thou in spite of ev'ry pow'rful foe
Shalt unshaken stand, and prosp'ring grow,
'Midst disgrace—to God's praise,
Both in love and unity,
To all eternity.

2 It plain appeareth,
As God's word declareth,
That the Lord his flock defends,
Thro' mercy which ne'er ends;
As he was of old
With his chosen fold,
Thus his pow'r and faithfulness
We in the church may trace,
For our God his people still protects
And 'mongst them his righteous throne erects.
Praises be—giv'n to thee,
Mighty God, Immanuel,
That thou with us wilt dwell!

3 God our Salvation
Feeds his congregation
With his word and sacrament;
All evil doth prevent,
That the weak and poor
Here may dwell secure;
Order is herein maintain'd
By discipline unstain'd,
And God's servants watch with faithful care
O'er his flock, and offer fervent pray'r.
God our Lord—will afford
Righteousness, and joy, and peace,
Until the end of days.

606.* T. 69.

HOW amiable
Thy habitations are!
Wherein assemble
Thy christian people dear,
O Lord,—Thy praises to record.

2 My heart with fervor
And inward longing, pants
Thy grace and favor
To tell there with thy saints,
Boldly—The truth to testify.

3 For there thou choosest
To dwell, my living Tow'r;
Sweet rest diffusest
From that place evermore,
Which thou—Ordained hast thereto.

4 There is asserted
The new birth spiritual;
Souls are converted
By thy pure gospel's call,
And there—In Christ's church grafted are.

5 For this I'm longing,
To be throughout my days
Thereto belonging,
Thy holy name to praise,
And thee—To serve incessantly.

6 All those are blessed
That come into thine house,
With awe expressed,
Which deep conviction shows,
And pray—And to thee homage pay.

7 Thou dost deliver
Thy church in all distress;
Thou art our Saviour;
Whate'er may us oppress,
Vict'ry—We may obtain thro' thee.

8 One day is better
Spent in the christian church,
Thy praise to utter,
Than thousands spent in search
Of joy—In the broad worldly way.

9 This territory
The Lord, as Sun, doth light,
Gives grace and glory,
And sanctify'd delight
To all—Who on his mercy call.

10 Yea, his condition
How splendid 'tis, O Lord,
Whom thou admission
Dost to thy church afford,
And so—The heav'nly kingdom too!

11 Thro' grace afford us,
Dear Lord, church-liberty,
To each good purpose,
That we our days employ
With care—Thy holy word to hear.

607. T. 161.

HIGHLY favor'd congregation,
Founded firm on Christ the Rock!
Own with thanks and adoration,
He's the Shepherd, we his flock;
He's our Saviour,—whose great favor
We've 'midst many trials proved,
We're unworthy, yet beloved.

2 Most who enter your blest borders
View with awe your Master's aim;
And your government and orders
Prompt them to revere his name.
Lord most holy!—may we truly
Prize our great predestination
In thy chosen congregation.

3 Think, my soul, how great the favor
In Jehovah's courts to dwell!
There poor sinners meet their Saviour;
There the sin-sick souls grow well.
Was not Jesus—always gracious,
When we, conscious how we failed,
To his loving heart appealed?

4 Here by faith we're humbly eying
Our Redeemer on the cross;
We behold him bleeding, dying,
To gain endless bliss for us.
Here is ready—for the needy,
Meat and drink at Jesus' table,
Which t'explain we are not able.

5 In thy family, O Jesus,
Love should more and more abound,
This thy word and Spirit teach us,
As its mark to all around.
May we learning—and discerning
Both thy doctrine and example,
Be in truth thy holy temple.

6 Grant that 'mongst thy chosen people
Each may serve thee evermore,
Foll'wing thee as thy disciple,
And in spirit thee adore,
Gracious Saviour—with heart's fervor;
May we walk as thine anointed,
In the path thou hast appointed.

608.* T 166.

UNFATHOM'D wisdom of our King!
In stillness he collects his flock,
Leads on, doth to perfection bring,
And ground it on himself, the Rock;
With little hurry, noise or show,
He safely guideth ev'ry soul;
No more the blinded world can do,
Than scorn and ridicule the whole.

2 Thy church, great Saviour, bought with blood,
Despis'd of men, but dear to thee,
Esteems thy cross a pleasant load,
An easy yoke, thrice happy she!
When, bearing thy reproach below,
She still partakes of thy free grace,
The grace thou richly dost bestow,
And which affliction's load outweighs.

3 Thou hast, with shepherd's faithfulness,
Brought many souls to thy blest fold,
Made them partakers of thy grace,
Amongst thy foll'wers them enroll'd:
They yield thee pleasure and delight,
When they thy voice hear and obey,
And while they in thy love unite,
Thou guid'st them thro' life's narrow way.

4 We humbly pray, support the weak,
Support thy children by thy grace;
Thou know'st for thee a-thirst we seek,
Kind Master of thy chosen race!
We know thy faithfulness and love,
Thy mercy all our wants supplies;
May spirit, soul and body prove
To thee a pleasing sacrifice.

5 By thee protected, gracious Lord,
O may we ever live secure;
Led by thy Spirit, grace, and word,
Relying on thy cov'nant sure;
Thy work O prosper and defend,
We're feeble but confide in thee;
Let thy true foll'wers to the end
Amidst oppression conqu'rors be.

609.* T. 22.

AS long as Jesus Lord remains
Each day new rising glory gains,
It was, it is, and will be so
With his church militant below!

2 Our only stay is Jesus' grace,
In ev'ry time and ev'ry place;
And Jesus' blood-bought righteousness
Remains his church's glorious dress.

3 All self-dependence is but vain,
Christ doth our Corner-stone remain,
Our Rock, which will unshaken stay
When heav'n and earth are fled away.

4 The Spirit which anointed Christ,
By which th' apostles were baptiz'd,
Proceeding from the church's Head,
Is giv'n to us, and makes us glad.

5 That cause shall never suffer harm
Which rests on Jesus' mighty arm:
What men can do, we need not fear,
No foe shall even touch a hair.

6 For these our God hath number'd all,
Without his leave not one can fall:
If in the least he is so true,
What will he not in greater do?

7 He is and shall remain our Lord,
Our confidence is in his word:
And, while our Jesus reigns above,
His church will more than conqu'ror prove.

610.* T. 68.

CHURCH of Christ be glad,
Praise thy Lord and Head;
Grounded on thy Saviour's merit,
That thour't filled with his Spirit
Is perceiv'd, and this
Proves that thou art his.

2 For the Lamb of God
Fixeth his abode
In his ransom'd congregation,
And true joy and consolation,
Grace and truth, abound
Where the Lord is found.

3 All thy strength and life
From Christ's death derive,
And proclaim his bitter passion
As the cause of man's salvation,
Showing forth his praise
Till the end of days.

611.* T. 114.

BRIDE of the Lamb, thou favor'd congregation, [flock,
Thou fruit of Jesus' cross, dear cov'nant
Securely built on him, th' eternal Rock,
Rejoice in him, the God of thy salvation,
Reap all the blessings he design'd for thee,
Grow in his grace and knowledge constantly.

2 Thy glory be to all the world displayed,
To all mankind his dying love proclaim,
Awake, put on thy strength, Jerusalem,
And in thy beauteous garments be arrayed,
Break forth, extend thyself both far and near [share.
That thousands still thy happiness may

612. T. 14.

HAIL, church of Christ, bought with his blood!
The world I freely leave;
Ye children of the living God,
Me in your tents receive.

2 Bride of the Lamb, I'm one in heart
With thee thro' boundless grace;
And I will never from thee part,
This bond shall never cease.

3 Closely I'll follow Christ with thee,
I'll go thy safest road;
Thy people shall my people be,
And thine shall be my God.

4 And am I, Jesus, one of those
Who in thy fold have place?
Who gather'd round th' erected cross
Enjoy redeeming grace?

5 O yes, nor would I change my lot
For all this world can give,
By grace I'll keep the place I've got,
And only to thee cleave.

613.* T. 26.

REDEEMED souls, adore and praise
Our merciful and gracious God,
For all the blessings he bestow'd,
For all the wonders of his grace.

2 The Lord for us great things hath done,
Our warmest thanks to him are due;
We trace his goodness when we view
His church, where he erects his throne.

3 We humbly take what he'll bestow,
Who would refuse his boundless grace?
O may his church in ev'ry place
His blessed views more fully know.

4 We all in spirit are agreed,
To follow Jesus as his flock,
To build on him, our only Rock,
And on the path of life proceed.

5 And tho' a rugged path it be,
On which we oft with trials meet,
And many dangers us beset;
It leads to true felicity.

6 The Father's garden here below
With patience must be watch'd indeed;
For, as in nature 'tis, the seed
Must die before the plant can grow.

7 Here is our hand; us, Lord, assist
To serve thee 'midst reproach and shame,
And thy atonement to proclaim,
Until we in thy presence rest.

614.* T. 205.

RISE, exalt our Head and King;
Praise the Lord who ever lives!
Glad we are his praise to sing;
He his people's praise receives.
On his pow'rful day they rise,
Off'ring free will sacrifice;
His victorious triumph this,
Since hell's host defeated is.

2 Ye who Jesus' death proclaim,
Service yield to him with joy,
Praise with ev'ry breath his name,
Grace t' extol be your employ;
Grace supports us ev'ry day,
Leads us in the narrow way;
'Tis thro' grace alone that we
Can obtain the victory.

3 Gracious Lord, may we believe,
Venture all on thy free grace,
Boldly things not seen achieve,
Trusting in thy promises;
Faith thy people's strong hold is,
Their employment daily this,
To proceed on paths unknown,
Leaning on thy grace alone.

4 Christ, thy all-atoning death
Is our life while here below;
Strengthen thou our feeble faith,
Constantly thy aid bestow;
In thy mercy we confide,
Safely to the end us guide;
Zion, if thy Head depart,
Void of life and strength thou art.

5 Lord thy body ne'er forsake,
Ne'er thy congregation leave;
We to thee our refuge take,
Of thy fulness we receive:
Ev'ry other help be gone,
Thou art our support alone,
For on thy supreme commands,
All the universe depends.

615.* T. 166.

THY church, O Lamb of God, appears
Before thee, fill'd with humble shame;
Our eyes o'erflow with grateful tears,
With melted hearts we praise thy name,
For the discov'ries of thy grace,
And proofs of all thy faithful care,
Experienc'd in so various ways,
Of which each soul can witness bear.

2 With thanks we call to mind the day
On which the power of thy blood
We felt, when chain'd by sin we lay,
As sinners dead and void of good;
The willing slaves of sin and death
We were, and enemies to thee;
But, granting us a living faith,
Thou from the curse didst set us free.

3 Is there a thing that warms the heart,
That stirs up gratitude and love,
It is the grace thou dost impart,
Thy blood, the pow'r of which we prove:
We sink astonish'd at thy feet,
Thy mercy's an unfathom'd sea,
How can we find expressions meet,
Who but so lately loved thee?

4 The word of Jesus' bloody sweat,
Of his dire passion, wounds & death,
With pow'r our souls doth penetrate,
And quicken with life-giving breath:
The pow'rs of hell this vanquishes,
This doth the church of Christ maintain,
Tho' Satan to the threshold press,
Christ's blood won't let him entrance gain.

5 Who in the Spirit's light can trace
The church of God, he must declare,
It is alone thro' Jesus' grace,
That she abiding fruit can bear:
To him all honor doth pertain,
Who by his blood made her his own,
Her choirs repeat in cheerful strain:
"The Lord for us great things hath done."

6 The church of Christ who views aright,
He sees a glorious master-piece,
And must with wonder and delight
Adore him, who the Author is:
Her beauty plainly doth appear
To those who have discerning eyes;
Her songs delight the ravish'd ear
Of all who know celestial joys.

7 She Christ, her faithful Shepherd, knows,
Attends to his instructive voice,
Amidst adversity she grows,
In her election doth rejoice,
Is by the Holy Spirit led:
The blood of covenant maintains
Her union with the Lord her Head,
In whom she constant vict'ry gains.

616.* T. 155.

CHURCH of Christ, sing and rejoice,
Bring the Lord thro' all thy classes
Thanks and praises,
Glory, honor, might and pow'r,
Evermore;
Since he is our Head and Saviour,
And his mercy, grace and favor
Richly doth on us bestow.

2 When we on his faithfulness,
Love and mercy duly ponder,
Lost in wonder,
We desire his name to praise;
For his grace,
Love and goodness never ceaseth,
He the number still increaseth
Of the church in which he rules.

3 Highly favor'd church, thou art
Still beyond all contradiction,
'Midst affliction;
By the Lord, who thee redeem'd,
Much esteem'd:
Therefore, may thy whole behavior
Be an honor to thy Saviour,
Whose great mercy never ends.

4 Tho' thou hast but little strength,
Let thy faith be manifested,
And attested
By unfeigned love to him;
Serve his name
With true zeal in ev'ry station,
As his feeble congregation,
Which relies on his support.

617.* T. 121.

O LORD, thy church which now
Sits at thy footstool low,
Adores and praises thee;
The worth she well doth know
Of thy election free,
Placing in thy grace
All her happiness.

2 We in thy ways proceed,
Refresh'd and comforted;
With us in mercy bear,
And daily forward lead
Thy flock with tender care,
Yea, at every step,
Us protect and keep.

3 Of thee both far and near
We gladly witness bear;
With joy and humble shame,
To sinners ev'ry where
We publish in thy name,
That thy blood makes clean
From all guilt and sin.

4 O give us that good part,
A sanctified heart,
Each needful gift and grace,
Dear Lord, to us impart;
Form us unto thy praise;
Thro' thy aid may we,
Yield true joy to thee.

5 O Lamb, for sinners slain,
For evermore remain,
Unto thy foll'wers nigh;
Let us thy aim attain,
Daily thy grace enjoy;
Never from us move,
Keep us in thy love.

618.* T. 26.

WHO can the love of Christ express
To those who by his blood redeemed,
Are as the heirs of life esteemed?
He owns them as his chosen race.

2 With thanks before his throne appear,
And praise his name, dear congregation,
For ev'ry proof and demonstration,
That you his favor'd people are.

3 We know his boundless love and grace,
Enjoy his goodness, care and favor,
He keeps his covenant for ever,
Can aught exceed his faithfulness?

4 O might this church of Christ always
Be to the world a bright example,
How by the Holy Ghost, a temple
May be constructed to his praise.

619. T. 155.

JESUS, slaughter'd Prince of life,
Thy remembrance ever raises
Thanks and praises;
And thy love, when shed abroad,
Lamb of God,
Prompts us gather'd here before thee,
With abasement to adore thee
For thy suff'rings, wounds and blood.

2 To redeem us from the fall,
Thou hast death for us endured,
And procured
For all those who trust in thee
Mercy free;
Now thy ransom'd congregation
Hath thee for her sole foundation,
Here and in eternity.

3 Since thou hast deliver'd us
From the yoke of ev'ry stranger
And all danger,
In thee, Saviour of the lost!
Is our boast;
From thy all-sufficient merit
We eternal life inherit,
For thy blood hath paid the cost.

4 May thy ransom'd people, Lord,
To thy inmost courts admitted,
For priests fitted,
Off'ring pray'r and praise to thee
Willingly,
Prize their glorious destination,
Yield to thee their ministration,
And thy faithful foll'wers be.

5 Sanctify us for thyself,
From each thing by thy soul hated
Separated,
Freed from this world's sinful ways;
Grant us grace,
In our walk and whole demeanor,
As new creatures, thee to honor,
And thy holy name to praise.

6 Deep engrave it in our hearts,
How by thee we are esteemed,
Why redeemed!
Ev'n to practise in these days
Heaven's ways,
'Midst all poverty and weakness,
To grow up into thy likeness,
And at judgment be thy praise.

7 O lift up thy countenance
On thy church; in love remember
Ev'ry member;
Might none, who would not be thine
Enter in;
May we all in thee believing,
Grace for grace from thee receiving,
Needful strength and succor gain.

620. T. 79.

THRICE happpy congregation,
For thy predestination
Adore the suff'ring Lamb;
Who, mov'd by love unbounded,
To purchase thee was wounded,
The cross endur'd, despis'd the shame.

2 It ne'er can be expressed
In words, how thou art blessed;
Thy happy lot hold fast;
Thy ransom, so expensive,
Is surely more extensive,
Than barely to be sav'd at last.

3 O yes our grace-election,
By our kind Lord's direction,
Is of a nobler kind;
John's portion to inherit,
To be with Christ one spirit,
Rightly acquainted with his mind.

4 To learn how, with precision,
In each state and condition,
To execute his will;
His ev'ry intimation
Be our heart's inclination
To understand, and then fulfil.

5 To this world crucified,
For his use sanctified,
In body and in soul,
Till we to his full stature
Are grown, and of his nature
Partakers are, throughout the whole.

6 A bow of grace, appearing
To the world, witness bearing
That God is well inclin'd;
A light, whose radiation,
From Christ's illumination
Deriv'd, may shine to all mankind.

7 The Father's kind inspection,
His blessing and protection,
Be daily our support;
The holy Spirit's leading,
And Jesus' pow'rful pleading,
Convey us through this world unhurt.

621.* T. 16.

CHURCH of Christ, thy destination
Is to joy in him by faith;
He hath purchas'd thy salvation,
He hath ransom'd thee from death.

2 Sin-sick souls, repair for healing
To his stripes and bleeding wounds;
Then retain a grateful feeling
Of the grace which there abounds.

3 In all wants, in all distresses,
Thence deriving sure relief;
Looking daily unto Jesus,
Who to gladness turns your grief;

4 Join his church in this confession:
"I am sinful, weak and poor,
But my Saviour's birth and passion
Prove to me the richest store."

5 "Nought but Jesus' grace, his merit,
And his blood-bought righteousness,
Is the cause why I inherit
Life and peace and holiness."

6 Jesus' death thy strength abideth,
Church of Philadelphia;
He who in ought else confideth
Goes Laodicea's way.

622. T. 164.

O THOU, who out of sin's dark night
Hast us, thy children, called;
And hast thy glorious gospel-light
Unto our hearts revealed;
Abas'd with shame we all
Before thee humbly fall,
And render for electing grace
To thee, Lord Jesus, thanks and praise.

2 The patience, love, unweary'd care,
Abundant grace and blessing,
Thou dost bestow from year to year,
Is truly past expressing;
Great mercy thou hast shown
To us, we freely own,
Yet hath thy aim, most faithful Friend,
With us not fully been obtain'd.

3 What rich returns of thankfulness
From us might be expected!
Who, that we might show forth thy praise
Have been thro' grace elected;
But here we blush for shame,
Unworthy of the name
We bear, while of our heav'nly call
As yet so very short we fall.

4 May we show forth continually,
In our whole conversation,
What we to others testify
Of thee and thy salvation;
May all men in us see,
Our words and works agree,
Then shall we of redeeming love
To others a sweet savor prove.

5 But are there such among us still,
Whose hearts thy love ne'er warmed,
Who, tho' their wretched state they feel,
Are not thereby alarmed;
O rouse them from death's sleep,
That they may pray and weep,
And flee as sinners to thy wounds,
Where, for the vilest, grace abounds.

623.* T. 126.

TO God the great Creator,
The Lord of earth and heav'n,
Who rules all things in nature,
Eternal praise be giv'n:
That blessed Lamb, which John once saw
As if it had been slaughter'd,
We now revere with awe.

2 Thou ransom'd church of Jesus,
The Saviour's happy bride,
Arise, show forth his praises
Who for thee bled and dy'd;
Ye, tho' a people poor and mean,
Of God are highly honor'd,
Because the Lamb was slain.

3 In our degree and measure
His love we will proclaim;
In lowliness with pleasure
Yield service to his name;
The church with tender care he'll guide,
And will in ev'ry trial
Our sure Support abide.

624.* T. 58.

O THOU whose goodness words can ne'er express!
Daily lift up thy friendly, loving face
On the congregation, her choirs and classes,
Let us perceive in all our streets and places Thy peace divine.

2 In labor, or at rest, O Lord, bedew
With thy most precious blood whate'er we do; [ever,
Let thy gracious presence surround us
As tho' our longing eyes enjoy'd the favor Thee to behold.

3 With fervor all thy people's hearts inspire,
And to enjoy thy grace be our desire;
May thy love, dear Saviour, to love constrain us,
And closely in the bond of peace maintain us, As one 'for thee!

4 We surely are a work of thy own hand,
Sinners, on whom thou'st deign'd thy blood to spend,
By the Holy Spirit to thee directed,
A cov'nant people, by free grace elected To serve thy name.

5 Grant that we all, both young and old, may prove
True witnesses of thy redeeming love;
Showing forth thy praises, may we adore thee,
And humbly walk in grace and truth before, Till we go hence.

6 May'st thou with us thy gracious aim obtain;
Grant that thy church may constant vict'ry gain; [needy
May we, truly conscious that we are
To look to thee in faith be always ready, And trust thy pow'r.

7 Might ev'ry one who knows us, clearly trace
In all thy people unction, truth and grace; [gation,
That whoe'er approacheth thy congre-
May feel and own it from a clear persuasion, "The Lord is here."

625.* T. 26.

O LORD, lift up thy countenance
Upon thy church, and own us thine;
Impart to us thy peace divine,
And blessings unto all dispense.

2 'Tis our desire to follow thee,
And from experience to proclaim
Salvation in thy blessed name:
O bless thy servants' ministry.

3 Thy mercy is our only stay,
Direct us by thy holy word,
Thy Spirit's light to us afford,
Preserve us, lest we go astray.

4 O Well of life, we pant for thee;
In copious streams thy thirsty flock
Desires to drink of thee, the Rock,
And thirst no more eternally.

5 Thy grace thou freely dost bestow,
This is our only plea and claim,
We blush 'fore thee with conscious shame,
Our many faults and wants we know.

6 To thee, O Lord our Righteousness,
Who by thy blood hast wash'd us clean
From ev'ry spot and stain of sin,
We give unfeigned thanks and praise.

626.* T. 244.

LORD, may the congregation,
Establish'd on thy death,
Enjoy thy great salvation,
And daily live by faith!
Believing in thy blood,
That all-atoning flood;
Grant we may cleave forever
To thee our highest Good!

2 Unfold thy grace's treasure,
And all our hearts prepare,
That we may in full measure
In thy salvation share:
O may thy looks of grace
Insure our happiness;
Uphold us, and forever
Set us before thy face. (*Psalm* xli. 12.)

3 Let us 'fore thee abased,
Be daily more and more
To taste thy friendship raised;
Prepare, we thee implore,
Amidst thy chosen race
Still many witnesses,
Who can from heart's experience
Proclaim redeeming grace.

4 We will of Jesus' passion
And meritorious death
Ne'er cease to make confession,
Till we give up our breath,
Till we in heav'nly light
Shall see his face most bright,
And with the saints in glory
In songs of praise unite.

627.* T. 30.

LIFT up thy pierc'd hands, most gracious Saviour,
O'er thy church, and pour out all that favor,
Which in thy loving
And kind heart for us is ever moving.

2 To thy care ourselves we now surrender,
Of our lives to thee we make a tender,
Protect and lead us,
As our faithful Shepherd daily feed us.

628.* T. 58.

HOLD o'er thy church, Lord, thy protecting hand,
And in thy truth O may she ever stand;
May thy ransom'd people show forth thy praises,
And be devoted to thy name, Lord Jesus, Until thou com'st.

2 Preserve thy church, Lord Jesus, every where,
And grant that she rich fruit for thee may bear;
Build her outward structure, fill her with glory,
And let each member praise thee and adore thee,
And serve thy name.

629.* T. 582.

THE happy church of Christ
Stands to this very day;
Those who are chosen daily find
To her an open way.

2 Lord Jesus, when we trace
Thy gracious call and aim
With us thy flock, we render praise
Unto thy holy name.

3 Thou open'st us a door,
Our little strength thou know'st,
Assist us, Lord, we thee implore,
To call to thee the lost.

630.* T. 583.

HOW bold and vain th' attempt to overthrow
The blessed church of Jesus Christ below!
For Salem's bulwarks, holy walls and tow'rs,
Shall stand in spite of all opposing pow'rs.

631.* T. 56.

THOU whose name is :||: inexpressible
And whose counsels :||: are unsearchable,
Thou, who from eternity
Didst the time and place decree,
Where securely :||: thy dear flock should dwell.

2 Spread thy blessing :||: here and ev'ry where,
Far surpassing :||: all our thoughts and pray'r,
When we have performed all
To fulfil thy gracious call,
After labor :||: we sweet rest shall share.

632.* T. 132.

THE Spirit of the witnesses
Rests on the congregation,
Excites her to proclaim free grace
In Christ's propitiation;
And teacheth her when to rejoice,
When to lift up her cheerful voice,
And when to weep in silence.

633.* T. 79.

THOU know'st, the congregation
Hath thee for her foundation,
Whate'er the world may say;
Grant us to cleave for ever
To thee our faithful Saviour,
May love among us bear the sway.

634.* T. 106.

LORD, may not one among us be
Who trifles with his call of grace,
None who believes not heartily
In thee, the Lord our Righteousness;
But grant, that prompted by thy love
We all to thee may faithful prove.

635.* T. 151.

O JESUS CHRIST, most holy!
Head of the church, thy bride,
Each day in us more fully
Thy name be magnify'd;
O may in each believer
Thy love its pow'r display,
And none among us ever
From thee, our Shepherd, stray.

636.* T. 146.

LORD, teach me how to prize
My great predestination;
And thankful to rejoice
With thy dear congregation,
Redeemed with thy blood;
Grant me a child-like faith
Among thy flock, O God!
Until my latest breath.

637.* T. 208.

LORD, thy body's Saviour,
Shepherd and Preserver,
If times numberless,
We, thy congregation,
Paid our adoration
For electing grace,
Yet should we—great debtors be:
Take us all as an oblation
For thy bitter passion!

638.* T. 161.

JESUS, hear our supplication,
'Tis thy pleasure
Those to bless, who to thee cleave:
Grant us stronger demonstration
Of thy favor,
Than our weak minds can conceive;
Help the feeble—us enable,
In thy blest path of salvation,
Bold and joyful
To go thro' each faith's gradation.

639.* T. 221.

O LORD, let thy countenance friendly and gracious
Shine clearly on thy chosen race;
To thee we commend ourselves jointly, to bless us,
Let ev'ry member feel thy peace:
Thy servants protect, O most gracious Lord,
And always direct by thy holy word,
Yea, grant them with boldness thy death to proclaim,
And life and remission of sins thro' thy name.

640. T. 586.

HIGH-PRIEST of thy church dispensation,
Lift up, we pray, thy pierced hand,
And bless thy ransom'd congregation,
In ev'ry place by sea or land;
Before thy Father's throne remember
By name each individual member;
Thy face upon us shine,
Grant us thy peace divine;
For we are thine!

641.* T. 590.

O THOU, whose mercies far exceed
All we can think or say,
As in thy people thou indeed
Dost daily more display:
Let for our happiness, O God,
On us, while here below,
By virtue of thy death and blood,
Still thousand blessings flow.

2 Lord Jesus, let us be thine own,
And ever thine remain,
We now ourselves to thee commend,
With thy whole chosen train:
Till thou shalt fully have obtain'd
With us thy thoughts of peace,
When, we, in joys which never end,
Shall see thee face to face.

642.* T. 590.

SHELTER our souls most graciously
Within thy open'd side;
Move them from ev'ry harm away,
And in thy safeguard hide:
O let our names in life's blest rolls
Inscrib'd be ever found,
And in life's bundle may our souls
Be fast and firmly bound!

643.* T. 121.

IN Jesus' love and peace,
On earth's extended face,
Dwell our congregations:
Both here, and o'er the seas,
We raise our supplications,
That the God of grace
All of us may bless,
Till the end of days.

644.* T. 121.

LORD Jesus, by thy death,
Whereon we trust by faith,
Thy wounds, thy pierced side,
Thy agony and sweat,
Preserve the church, thy bride,
Till thou com'st again,
Prince of life once slain! :||:

XXXII. Of the Servants and Witnesses of the Lord, and the Spreading of his Kingdom upon Earth.

645.* T. 166.

HIGH on his everlasting throne,
The Lord of hosts his work surveys,
He marks the souls which are his own,
And smiles on his peculiar race;
He rests well pleas'd their toil to see,
Beneath his easy yoke they move,
With all their heart and strength agree
In the sweet labor of his love.

2 His eye the world at once looks thro'
A vast uncultivated field,
Mountains and vallies meet his view,
And all a barren prospect yield;
Clear'd of the thorns by civil care,
A few less dreary wastes are seen,
Yet still they all continue bare,
And not one spot of earth is green.

3 See, where the servants of their God,
A busy multitude appear,
For Jesus day and night employ'd,
The ground for him they toil to clear;
The love of Christ their hearts constrains,
And strengthens their unweary'd hands,
They spend their blood, and sweat, and pains,
To cultivate Immanuel's lands.

4 Where'er the faithful lab'rers are,
The steps of industry we view,
They Satan's seed root up with care,
And in its stead the gospel sow;
This seed they water with their tears,
Then long for the returning word,
Happy if all their pains and cares
Can bring forth fruit to please their Lord.

5 Jesus their work delighted sees,
Their industry vouchsafes to crown,
He kindly gives the wish'd increase,
And sends the promis'd blessing down;
Then plenteous show'rs of grace bedew
And fructify the parched ground,
The plants spring up, they thrive & grow,
The earth looks fruitful all around.

6 He prospers all his servants' toils,
And us his flock in mercy chose,;
Yea on us undeserved smiles,
And choicest blessings he bestows:
We, foll'wers of the bleeding Lamb,
Will firmly to his word adhere,
Of him, amidst reproach and shame,
With joy our testimony bear.

7 Here many faithful souls are found,
With genuine love to Christ endow'd,
Led by the Holy Ghost, and crown'd
As kings and priests to serve their God;
Burning with zeal, by love divine
Constrain'd, themselves they freely give,
Their wealth and life for Christ resign,
For him they gladly die or live.

8 What can we offer thee, O Lord?
How worthily set forth thy praise?
Fain would we preach thy saving word,
And dying love in ev'ry place;
In thee believe, thee love and serve;
To thee our life, our all we owe,
Who dost 'midst danger us preserve,
And mercies numberless bestow.

9 O may our lives thy pow'r proclaim,
Thy grace for ev'ry sinner free,
That thousands still may know thy name,
Humbly adore and worship thee;
Open a door, which earth and hell
Striving to shut, may strive in vain,
Grant that thy word may richly dwell
Among us, and our fruit remain.

646.* T. 590.

IS this indeed our happy lot,
T' exalt thee, slaughter'd Lamb!
Who art thou! who can right describe
Thy great and glorious name!
And who are we, that we should take
This mighty task in hand!
We helpless sinners, base and vile:
Sure we must blushing stand.

2 Therefore hast thou us, most gracious King!
To thee our hearts are bound!
Our knowledge yet extends not far,
O grant us deeper ground:
That each beholder may in us
Thy image clearly trace,
And in our words and walk discern
That we are led by grace.

3 In these our days exalt thy name,
Thy precious gospel spread,
That for the travail of thy soul
Thou may'st behold thy seed;
O may thy knowledge fill the earth,
Increase the number still
Of those who in thy word believe,
And do thy holy will.

4 Thanks, Jesus, for thy sacred blood,
That precious healing stream,
All without this is cold and dead
However good it seem;
That virtue is of no avail,
Which takes not hence its rise:
Thy blood were else of no effect,
That blood of so great price.

5 Lord, by thy Spirit us prepare
To follow thy command;
To execute thy utmost aim,
And in thy presence stand,
As servants willing to be us'd,
Who in thy work delight,
And offer freely praise and pray'r,
As incense, day and night.

6 Hereto we cheerful say Amen!
We have this truth avow'd,
That we in spirit, body, soul,
Are bound to serve our God
Who touch'd, and drew, and woo'd our hearts,
And conquer'd us by love;
To him we have engag'd ourselves,
O may we faithful prove!

647.* T. 90.

PRAISE be to God the Holy Ghost,
Who Jesus in the heart displays,
That he the num'rous faithful host
Of blest departed witnesses,
Who now in heav'n are perfected,
To Christ by his instruction led.

2 Christ crucify'd we own as God,
Tho' we were scorn'd by all mankind,

He is our Motto most avow'd;
To such in spirit we are join'd,
And them as brethren gladly own,
Who by this Shibboleth are known.

3 He, who was scorned on the tree,
He, whom his nation still disown,
Who marks with glorious infamy
All who are as his foll'wers known,
He is the church's Lord and Head,
By whom we graciously are led.

4 We stand unto this very hour
In one firm bond of peace and love;
We are at enmity no more,
But reconcil'd to God above:
As children we by him are own'd,
Since Christ for all our sins aton'd.

5 All ye who gospel-preachers are,
Adhere to Jesus crucify'd,
And watch with unremitting care,
That you in your first love abide;
Whoe'er forsakes it can't but feel
A want of apostolic zeal.

6 Heralds of grace would ye commence,
Of grace first self-experienc'd be;
And by the gospel you dispense
Yourselves be reconcil'd and free:
When pardon, grace and life you find,
Then publish it to all mankind.

7 We join the ransom'd church of God,
His blood-bought, blood-besprinkled train,
To publish the good news abroad,
That only thro' the Lamb once slain
The world may gain a full release
From all their sins and endless grace.

8 Christ's ransom'd people rest enjoy,
Upon his arm they lean in peace,
To follow him is their employ,
In this most blessed time of grace:
They preach their Saviour crucify'd,
Determin'd nought to know beside.

9 In life they witness this, with pow'r
That strikes and fastens in the heart,
And when this mortal period's o'er,
And they in peace to Christ depart,
Their dying looks, serene and fair,
Bears witness that they christians are.

648. T. 90.

THE doctrine of our dying Lord,
The faith he on mount Calv'ry seal'd,
We sign, asserting ev'ry word
Which in his gospel is reveal'd,
As truth divine, and curs'd are they
Who add thereto or take away.

2 We stedfastly this truth maintain,
That none is righteous, no not one;
That in the Lamb, for sinners slain,
We're justify'd by faith alone;
And all who in his name believe,
Christ and his righteousness receive.

3 Our works and merits we disclaim,
Opposing all self-righteousness,
Ev'n our best actions we condemn
As ineffectual, and confess,
Whoe'er thereon doth place his trust,
And not on Jesus, will be lost.

4 He is our Master, Lord and God,
The fulness of the Three in One,
His life, death, righteousness and blood,
Our faith's foundation is alone,
His Godhead and his death shall be
Our theme to all eternity.

5 On him we'll venture all we have,
Our lives, our all to him we owe;
None else is able us to save,
Nought but the Saviour will we know;
This we subscribe with heart and hand,
Resolv'd thro' grace thereby to stand,

6 This now with heav'n's resplendent host
We echo thro' the church of God,
Among the heathen make our boast
Of Jesus' saving death and blood;
We loud like many waters join,
In showing forth his love divine.

649. T. 166.

O GLORIOUS Master of thy house,
Thou know'st the thoughts of ev'ry breast,
To thee each servant gladly goes,
Like Noah's dove, for peace and rest,
Indeed the waters overflow
The world all o'er, and us withstand;
Few will our mind and purpose know,
Few comprehend thy blest command.

2 But we can hope thy word and grace
Will soften many a heart of stone;
What means can help the human race?
The same which our poor hearts have won.
Tho' carnal reason stand to faith
Oppos'd, the wounded conscience flies
To the blest doctrine of thy death,
And all-atoning sacrifice.

3 Thy pow'rful presence, Lord, display,
Or else in vain the sun we see;
Thou art our life, our truth, our way,
We have no comfort, but in thee:
Vouchsafe to us thy unction, Lord,
Where'er obedient to thy call
We go, thy help to us afford,
And ever be our All in all.

650.* T. 22.

SHALL I, thro' fear of feeble man,
The Spirit's fire in me restrain?
Aw'd by a mortal's frown, shall I
Conceal the word of God most High?

2 Shall I, to soothe th' unholy throng?
Soften thy truth, and smooth my tongue?
To gain earth's gilded toys, or flee
The cross endur'd, my God, by thee!

3 No, fearless I'll in deed and word
Witness of thee, my gracious Lord;
My life and blood I here present,
If for thy truth they may be spent.

4 For this let men revile my name,
No cross I shun, I fear no shame;
I no reproach nor suff'rings dread,
Is Christ with me, I'm not afraid.

5 Give me thy strength, O God of pow'r;
Then let winds blow, or thunders roar,
I need not fear by sea or land,
For thou, my God, wilt by me stand.

651.* T. 166.

WE often, in our course thro' time,
Have rugged roads to travel;
Faith's fortitude must sometimes climb,
And paths uneven level;
But Jesus, thro' his tender care,
Which is at all times present,
Revives the weary traveller
Again by ways more pleasant.

2 O thou the sole defence and aid
Of all the weak and feeble,
Thou strong support in time of need,
And Saviour of thy people:
Uphold us, Lord, most pow'rfully,
With thy divine assistance,
And grant us constant victory
When meeting with resistance.

3 We offer gladly unto thee
Our spirit, soul and body;
We promise thee fidelity
And loyalty most steady;
Thou surely wilt thy cause maintain,
Nor leave thy work unfinish'd;
Thy servants many conquests gain,
Tho' in appearance vanquish'd.

652.* T. 58.

REDEEMER of mankind, God of all grace,
Pour fire and spirit on thy witnesses,
Preaching thy salvation, by love constrained:
Thus thousands more for thee shall still be gained, By thy blest word.

2 O may thy ransom'd people ev'ry where
Of this great truth for ever witness bear,
That whoe'er believeth in Christ's redemption
May find free grace, and a complete exemption From serving sin.

3 Our elders and all other servants bless,
To all their undertakings give success;
Gracious Lord, afford them thy Spirit's unction,
That they may faithfully fulfil the function, To which they're call'd.

4 Grant none among us may inactive be,
Enable us to serve thee cheerfully,
Render thou successful each step and action,
Which we perform, Lord, under thy direction, And in thy name.

5 Let more unto thy church collected be,
In ev'ry quarter, to yield joy to thee,
Here, and o'er the ocean, in all her stations;
And, O impart to the most savage nations Thy saving grace!

653.* T. 14.

LORD JESUS, who hast called us
To magnify thy name,
And preach the doctrine of thy cross
Amidst reproach and shame;

2 We thee intreat with one accord:
Thy ministers prepare
To lead thy flock, and preach thy word,
With meekness, zeal and care.

3 Without thy aid we nought can do,
But by thy pow'r we know,
Weak as we are, we're heroes too,
Who conquer where we go.

654. T. 56.

YE who called :||: to Christ's service are,
Join together :||: both in work and pray'r;
Venture all on him our Lord,
Who assures us in his word,
That we're constant :||: objects of his care.

2 Show'rs of blessings :||: from the Lord proceed,
Strength supplying :||: in the time of need;
For no servant of our King
Ever lacked any thing,
He will never :||: break the bruised reed.

3 Lord have mercy :||: on each land and place [of peace,
Where thy servants :||: preach the word
Life and pow'r on them bestow,
Them with needful strength endow,
That with boldness :||: they may thee confess.

4 May we faithful :||: in our service be,
Truly careful :||: in our ministry;
Keep us to thy church fast bound,
In the faith preserve us sound,
Often weeping :||: grateful tears 'fore thee.

655.* T. 146.

LORD, grant thy servants grace,
The needful gifts and unction,
That with due faithfulness
They may discharge their function;
That all things as they ought
May punctually be done;
And with success, when wrought,
Their work vouchsafe to crown.

2 We pray thee, bless them all,
And prosper their endeavor,
In their important call,
To serve thee, gracious Saviour;
Thou list'nest to our pray'rs,
And surely wilt uphold
The faithful ministers
Of thy redeemed fold.

656. T. 22.

BE present with thy servants, Lord,
We look to thee with one accord;
Refresh and strengthen us anew,
And bless what in thy name we do.

2 O teach us all, thy perfect will
To understand, and to fulfil;
When human insight fails, give light,
This will direct our steps aright.

3 The Lord's joy be our strength and
In our employ from day to day; [stay
Our thoughts and our activity
Thro' Jesus' merits hallow'd be.

657.* T. 26.

MOST faithful Lord, thyself reveal;
My eyes with contrite tears o'erflow,
My heart with gratitude doth glow,
But adequate expressions fail.

2 If I were free from all distress,
Had to converse with none but thee,
Were I from ev'ry burden free,
Then nothing could my soul oppress:

3 But I have trials to go thro',
And hardships oftentimes to meet:
And, conscious of my wants, intreat
Thee, Lord, to teach me what to do,

4 Give me what thy own mind decrees,
And what thy children must possess,
If they shall serve thee with success:
A neck which with thy yoke agrees.

5 Give me a lowly, faithful mind,
With patience and undauntedness;
If thou my poor endeavors bless
Action and rest may be combin'd.

6 Give me an inly cheerful heart,
Besprinkled with thy blood, made clean:
O may it in my works be seen
That thou its sole Possessor art!

7 Grant me to know thy blessed ways;
With all both joy and grief to share;
And lips thy mercy to declare
To all that mourning seek thy face.

658.* T. 583.

SINNERS' Redeemer, gracious Lamb of God,
We thy poor children, purchas'd by thy blood,
With gratitude acknowledge, that we share
Thy boundless favor and protecting care.

2 From day to day may we with rapture feel
Thy life, thy unction, and thy Spirit's seal,
The pow'rful drawings of thy love and grace,
And zeal to serve thy cause with faithfulness.

3 With each of us obtain thy gracious aim,
That we, thy servants, may exalt thy name;
Enabled by thy grace, may we declare
The greatness of thy ransom ev'ry where.

4 We feel our insufficiency, to bear
The weighty charge committed to our care;
To thee, who dost thy people's cause defend,
We the concerns of thy whole church commend.

659.* T. 185.

SINCE our Saviour call'd us to inherit
Everlasting happiness,
And without the unction of the Spirit
We the way to him can't trace,
Grant us therefore, Holy Ghost, the favor,
Both in doctrine and in our behavior
By thee to be taught and led,
Till in Christ we're perfected.

2 Faithful Lord, my only joy and pleasure
Shall remain, while here I stay,
Thee, my matchless Friend and highest Treasure,
To adore, serve and obey;
Tho' I in myself am weak and feeble,
Yet I trust thy grace will me enable,
By obedience to thy will
All thy purpose to fulfil.

660.* T. 228.

BODY and soul's at thy command,
And we with gladness ready stand
To serve thy name, Lord Jesus!
Since thy blest Spirit did explain
Unto our hearts, why thou wast slain,
Nought else on earth can please us:
O no,—altho'
We are feeble—and unstable,
Thou'rt our Treasure,
And to serve thee is our pleasure!

2 Unto ourselves no praise is due;
And should we even something do,
That in thy sight were pleasing,
To thee we render all the praise,
Thou giv'st thereto enabling grace,
And grantest us thy blessing.
Unless—thy grace
Sway our nature,—ev'ry creature
Is unwilling
Ought that's good to be fulfilling.

661*. T. 166.

TAKE me into thy hands anew,
Out of which none is plucked,
By which thy children are brought thro',
And servants are conducted:
Lord Jesus, lead and bless thou me
In ev'ry future station,
That I may serve thee faithfully
Until my consummation.

2 With mouth and hand I give to thee
Myself as thy own booty,
T'increase each talent thou gav'st me
Shall be my pleasant duty;
O let my soul ne'er moved be
From thee, my faithful Saviour;
Both late and early show to me
Thy mercy and thy favor.

662. T. 89.

LORD, grant us, tho' deeply abased with shame,
With true christian courage, to act in thy name;
May we in thy blessed work always abound,
And let with success all our labor be crown'd.

2 Give grace, that as brethren we join hands in love,
Engaging to thee ever faithful to prove,
Where'er to thy service appointed we stand,
To sow, or to reap, at thy call and command.

663.* T. 22.

IN mercy, Lord, this grace bestow,
That in thy service I may do,
With gladness and a willing mind,
Whatever is for me assign'd.

2 Grant I, impelled by thy love,
In smallest things may faithful prove;
Till I depart, I wish to be,
Devoted wholly unto thee.

664.* T. 155.

FIT us for thy service, Lord,
Each one in thy congregation,
In his station;
Set thou us in ev'ry place
To thy praise;
Make us in thy service stable,
Willing, lively, faithful, able,
Till in thee we end our race.

665.* T. 166.

O MAY the witness-spirit rest,
Lord, on thy congregation,
May godly zeal inspire each breast
To publish thy salvation;
We gladly promise faithfulness
To do what we are able;
Sufficient is for us thy grace,
Which doth support the feeble.

666.* T. 166.

O LORD, we highly magnify
And bless thy saving Jesus' name:
The love that prompted thee to die
We will to all mankind proclaim;
Thou bidst the sparks of grace arise,
Which kindle many a lifeless heart;
Thou hear'st the needy sinner's cries,
And pardon freely dost impart.

2 If we are to thy cause but true,
Upright, obedient to thy will,
Enabling grace thou wilt bestow,
Thy thoughts of peace in us fulfil.
In all things we may trust thy grace,
And rest on thy almighty arm;
Keep thou our souls in constant peace,
And shelter us from ev'ry harm.

667.* T. 22.

IN our short warfare here below,
May our experience daily show,
That in our weakness, thro' thy aid,
Thy strength divine is perfected.

2 Without thy blessing how could we
Be servants pleasing unto thee?
But we can by experience sing,
Thy word hath pow'r and fruit doth bring.

3 Ah, could we preach in ev'ry place
Our Saviour's boundless love and grace,
That thousands who are yet enslav'd,
Might in these gospel-times be sav'd!

4 There's but a small beginning made,
The earth is still o'ercast with shade:
Break forth, thou Sun of righteousness,
And spread thy all-enliv'ning rays!

5 Whene'er we to mankind proclaim
Thy dying love and precious name,
Support thy servants' weakness, Lord,
By thy blest Spirit, grace and word.

6 Lord of the harvest! lab'rers send,
Who willing are their lives to spend,
In scorching heat and chilling cold,
To bring the heathen to thy fold.

7 When all our labor here is o'er,
And when our light shall burn no more,
When our endeavors have an end,
Then let our souls to thee ascend.

668.* T. 114.

THOU Saviour of the world, great Mediator,
O may'st thou for the travail of thy soul
Behold thy seed extend from pole to pole;
Thy boundless mercy show to ev'ry creature;
With old and young thy gracious aim obtain;
Thy pray'rs and tears can never plead in vain.

2 Thy glorious gospel spread thro' ev'ry nation,
Give us an open door, thy saving name
In the most distant regions to proclaim,
With pow'r and with the Spirit's demonstration;
And grant us joyfully to feed by faith
In peace upon the merits of thy death.

669. T. 74.

THINK on our brethren, Lord,
Who preach the gospel-word
In spirit free and bold,
In hunger, heat, and cold:
Thou art their Strength and Shield,
Help them to win the field.

2 Give us an open door,
And spirit, grace and pow'r,
To tell what thou hast done
For mankind to atone,
That thus in ev'ry place
We may declare thy grace.

3 O Lord, before us go;
To ev'ry sinner show
What need he hath of thee,
And then most pow'rfully
Convince each human heart,
That thou our Saviour art.

4 O let thy strength and might
Subdue the en'my's spite:
Our weakness well thou know'st,
Of nothing we can boast
But that we trust thy word,
And know, thou art our Lord!

5 Let our beginnings be
Aided, O Lord, by thee;
The things which purpos'd are
Help us to bring to bear;
Forgive whate'er is wrong,
'Midst weakness make us strong.

6 Our weak endeavors bless,
And crown them with success.
Thou Workman great and wise!
Who shall thy work despise?
A tool that's us'd by thee
Can wonders do, we see.

670.* T. 97.

THE Lord himself gave forth the word,
We preach most gladly Christ the Lord.
May thousands, Lord, thy voice obey,
And turn to thee without delay;
To those who hear us grant an open ear,
And when we point thee out, do thou appear.

2 'Tis the desire of all our hearts
That, in the earth's remotest parts,
The love of God to all mankind
Be preach'd to heathen base and blind;
For Jesus saves from sin all who believe,
And th' offer'd pardon in his blood receive.

671. T. 97.

AS 'twas of old, we now may trace,
In these most blessed times of grace,
How the reviving gospel-sound
Of blood-bought grace is spreading round;

We see with joy the work of God increase,
And thousands who thro' Jesus find release.

2 We see in hearts as cold as ice
The Sun of Righteousness arise,
And that his all-enliv'ning rays
Of Satan's slaves make sons of grace,
Who are increasing daily more and more,
And who the slaughter'd Lamb with us adore.

3 Great is the harvest, truly great;
Saviour of all! we thee intreat,
To send forth lab'rers, who with joy
Of thy atonement testify,
And to prepare still many witnesses,
Who from experience may proclaim thy grace.

672. T. 22.

LORD, at thy feet asham'd we sink,
When on thy wondrous grace we think,
Which now so strikingly appears;
Lost in amaze we melt in tears.

2 The gospel in these blessed days,
Throughout the earth its beams displays;
Nations, that never heard of thee,
Thy great salvation shout to see.

3 That mystery from ages seal'd
God, by his Spirit, hath reveal'd,
That heav'nly thrones and pow'rs might know
God's wisdom by the church below.

4 Tho' hated, tho' despis'd and mean,
Yet while we on thy mercy lean,
Let nations rage, let devils roar,
We will confess thee evermore.

673.* T. 121.

YE people of the Lord,
Be still, and trust his word,
Bring your supplications
'Fore him with one accord,
That many heathen nations
May his word receive,
And in him believe. :||:

2 O might we clearly trace,
In these blest times of grace,
'Mongst the brethren's people
In each a willingness
To be the Lord's disciple,
To spend life and blood
In the cause of God. :||:

674.* T. 206.

LET the world hear! :||:
God's Son and Heir,
Who to us came,
And bore :||: our sin and shame,
Who liv'd among his own :||:
Unknown,
Despis'd and mean,—and then was slain,
The ransom HE :||:
For all the world and me. :||:

2 Hereby we stand, :||:
With life in hand,
Us help afford
To bear :||: this witness, Lord;
That thousands may embrace :||:
Thy grace;
We will diffuse—the gospel-news
In ev'ry land; :||:
The Lord will by us stand. :||:

675.* T. 583.

O LORD, command us what we are to do,
Where thou wilt call us we desire to go,
Because thy orders do imply success,
To break thro' roads we else could never pass.

2 May many wild uncultivated parts,
Where Satan bears the sway in heathens' hearts,
Bear fruit abundantly to thee, O Lord,
And thousands be converted by thy word.

676.* T. 90.

CHRIST JESUS is that precious grain
Which fell into the ground and dy'd,
Now since he for our sins was slain,
He doth no more alone abide,
But, for the travail of his soul,
His seed appears from pole to pole.

677.* T. 79.

GO, witness of the suff'ring
Of Christ, who as our off'ring
Our guilt and curse did bear;
Proclaim his great salvation
To many a heathen nation,
And spread his gospel far and near.

678.* T. 68.

YE who know the Lord,
And his grace and word,
Publish his complete salvation
Still to many a heathen nation;
Joyfully proclaim
Jesus' saving name.

679.* T. 221.

WITH fire and with spirit endow'd ev'ry moment,
Ye ministers of Christ confest,
Go forth and proclaim ye the word of atonement
Both far and near; and when opprest
By hardships and trials, be bold in God,
And gladly for him spend your life and blood.
'Midst tempests and billows, and thro' deserts go,
The seeds of the gospel 'mongst heathen to sow.

680. T. 590.

LORD, to thy people aid dispense,
Their Shield and Portion be,
And let their lives the world convince
That they belong to thee:
Extend thy help to distant parts,
Thy servants send to call,
Reveal thy grace to heathens' hearts;
Thy grace extend to all.

681. T. 195.

LORD GOD, our Salvation!
Let thy grace and favor
Rest upon thy church for ever:
Jesus, thee to follow
Be our blessed function;
Grant us all thy Spirit's unction,
To declare—ev'ry where
The complete salvation,
Purchas'd by thy passion.

XXXIII. Hymns for Festival Days and solemn Meetings.

682.* T. 22.

LORD Christ, reveal thy holy face,
And send the Spirit of thy grace,
To fill our hearts with fervent zeal,
To learn thy truth, and do thy will.

2 Lord, lead us in thy holy ways,
And teach our lips to tell thy praise:
Revive our hope, our faith increase,
To taste the sweetness of thy grace.

3 Till we with angels join to sing
Eternal praise to thee, our King;
Till we behold thy face most bright,
In joy and everlasting light.

4 To God the Father, and the Son,
And Holy Spirit, Three in One,
Be honor, praise and glory giv'n
By all on earth, and all in heav'n.

683.* T. 141.

OWN thy congregation,
O thou slaughter'd Lamb!
We are here assembled
In thy holy name;
Look upon thy people,
Whom thou by thy blood
Hast in love redeemed,
And brought nigh to God.

2 Thou hast kindly led us
For these many years,
Ah! accept our praises,
And our grateful tears;
Grant us all the favor
To obey thy voice,
Yea, what thou directest
Be our only choice.

3 Church, who art arrayed
In the glorious dress
Of thy Lord and Saviour's
Spotless righteousness,
Be both now and ever
By his blood kept clean,
And in all thy members
May his grace be seen.

684.* T. 155.

SLAUGHTER'D Lamb, Immanuel,
Who hast gained our salvation,
By thy passion,
Ah! we give thee thanks and praise
For thy grace;
Grant, that we may all inherit
The anointing of thy Spirit,
Which instructs us what to do.

2 Let thy spirit, which is truth,
Raise our grov'ling thoughts to heaven,
Us enliven;
Thus adorn'd and beautify'd
As thy bride,
May our walk and conversation
Be a striking demonstration
That thou dwell'st and walk'st in us.

3 Lord, for grace we thee intreat,
Grace, the anchor firm and stable
Of the feeble;
Grace, whereon we must depend
To the end;
Grace, the sinner's consolation,
Sure support in each temptation,
Confidence in life and death.

4 God with us, we vow to thee
Due allegiance now and ever;
Gracious Saviour,
We to serve thee ready stand,
Take the hand,
As a pledge and declaration
Of the grateful heart's sensation,
Which thy dying love excites.

685. T. 583.

LORD JESUS, in thy presence we are blest,
And thou art even now our wish'd-for Guest;
Without thee all our meetings would be cold,
And soon become a custom dead and old.

2 Thou canst alone to us true life impart,
Canst comfort, bless and cheer each needy heart:
We are assembled here before thy face
To take out of thy fulness grace for grace.

3 Lord Jesus, be for evermore ador'd,
We thee confess our Master, Head and Lord;
Thy faithfulness each day and hour we prove,
Grant us to live for thee, constrain'd by love.

686.* T. 161.

CHOSEN souls, who now assemble
Under Christ's protecting care;
Tho' you're weak, your foes must tremble,
If by him you guarded are.
Of his goodness—bear ye witness;
Know ye not your high vocation,
As the Lord's own congregation?

2 To his name give thanks and praises,
Him with deepest awe adore;
May his people in all places
Join t'exalt him evermore;
Christ, our Saviour,—be for ever
Of your building the Foundation,
And the God of your salvation.

3 Hernhut,* the Most High's own structure,
Built upon the grace of God,
May thy walls be without fracture,
Sprinkled be thy gates with blood;
God's election—and protection
Founded and maintain our union,
Christ's the ground of our communion.

4 May this place exist no longer
Than, Lord Jesus, thy own hand,
Uncontroll'd, rules in its border,
And be love our sacred band.
May we by thee—be found worthy,
As a good salt to be used,
That some fruit may be produced.

* The first congregation of the renewed church of the United Brethren.

5 Bless our cov'nanting together;
Make us like a burning torch,
Kindled by our heav'nly Father,
In these last days of the church.
To thee joined—and resigned,
May by each of us be further'd,
What thy holy will hath order'd.

6 Now, dear Brethren, know ye Jesus?
Happy who him truly knows:
He's the Head, and we are members,
From him ev'ry blessing flows.
Who believeth—to Christ cleaveth,
Doth rejoice in ev'ry station,
'Midst reproach and tribulation.

687.* T. 114.

THOU Source of love, we pray, impart thy favor
Each day unto thy house and family,
Who as one man united are in thee;
O grant that ev'ry one thy grace may savor,
And that thy church for ever may rejoice
In thee, and praise thy name with heart and voice.

2 O thou whose love extends beyond all measure,
Thou hearest us already, ere we cry,
No soul that calls on thee thou passest by,
But to relieve thy children is thy pleasure;
Thou art our Light, our Strength, our Shield and Rock,
Our faithful Shepherd, and we are thy flock.

688.* T. 155.

MY soul waiteth on the Lord,
And shall never be ashamed;
He is named
God our Sun, our Shield and Rock,
By his flock;
He is merciful and gracious,
And his goodness doth refresh us
When we long and pant for him.

2 His enliv'ning countenance
To lift up on all the needy
He is ready,
And enricheth evermore
All the poor;
In our peaceful habitations,
O how many demonstrations
Of his favor do we prove!

3 We reply Amen thereto,
For his bounty never ceaseth,
Yea increaseth;
And are filled with amaze
At his grace;
Each himself unworthy deemeth
Of his love; his goodness claimeth
Our unfeigned gratitude.

689.* T. 9.

M. CHRIST our Saviour look on thee,
Ransom'd congregation!
C. We to him belong, for he
Purchas'd our salvation.

M. 2 In electing grace rejoice,
Prize his love and favor;
Then his calling, gifts and choice
He'll maintain for ever.

C. 3 Yea, his sympathizing heart
Yields us consolation;
May we ne'er from Christ depart,
Till our consummation.

M. 4 To his voice attentive be,
Thankfully adore him,
And with heart's fidelity
Humbly walk before him.

C. 5 Thus in number and in grace
We shall be increasing,
Showing forth our Saviour's praise,
And to him be pleasing.

690. T. 185.

GRACIOUS Lord, our Shepherd and Salvation,
In thy presence we appear,
Own us as thy flock and congregation,
Let us feel that thou art near;
May we all enjoy thy grace and favor,
And obey thee as our Head and Saviour;
Who by thy most precious blood
Mad'st us, sinners, heirs of God.

2 Lord, receive our thanks and adoration,
Which to thee we humbly pay,
For our calling and predestination,
Gracious Saviour, on this day.
Give us grace to walk as thine anointed,
In the path thou hast for us appointed;
We devote most heartily
Soul and body unto thee.

691. T. 151.

HEAD of thy congregation,
Kind Shepherd, gracious Lord!
Look on us with compassion,
Met here with one accord;
Accept our thanks and praises
For all thy love and care,
Which we in various cases
Repeatedly did share.

2 Our lips would gladly mention
Thy patience, love and grace,
Our hearts with due attention
Thy loving kindness trace,
Which under thy protection
'Midst trials we have prov'd;
Thy fatherly correction
Show'd us, that we're belov'd.

692.* T. 9.

JESUS CHRIST, who bled and dy'd
For mankind's salvation,
Shows his wounds and pierced side
To his congregation.

2 Yea he, with uplifted hands,
Mark'd with nail-prints bloody,
'Midst his chosen people stands,
Saviour of his body!

3 While he doth himself reveal,
Oh, what consolation
In his presence do we feel!
'Tis beyond expression.

4 Teach us, Lord, to follow thee
With entire devotion;
As thy willing subjects, we
Wait thy Spirit's motion.

5 Jesus, all-creating Word,
King of ev'ry nation,
But especially the Lord
Of thy congregation!

6 To thy name be evermore,
Praise and glory given;
Thee we worship and adore
Lord of earth and heaven!

693.* T. 10.

WHEN we rejoice, that Jesus
From year to year doth bless us,
And that his grace and favor
Towards us never waver;

2 Or he that consolation
Grants to his congregation,
That we shall rest for ever
With him, our gracious Saviour;

3 Then we forget distresses,
And what would else oppress us;
Are we with Christ connected,
We need not be dejected.

694.* T. 166.

HEAD of thy church! behold us here,
Direct and rule us by thy grace;
Hear thou each needy sinner's pray'r,
Confirming thus thy promises;
O help us, that we may fulfil
What in thy name we take in hand,
Concordant with thy holy will,
And may it to thy glory tend.

2 One suit in mercy to us grant:
Let us from all divested be
Which furthers not our covenant,
Or is displeasing unto thee;
All that whence hurt to souls accrues,
Whate'er thy doctrine doth disgrace,
Or counteracts thy blessed views,
Root out and utterly erase.

695.* T. 101.

BOW down, ye foll'wers of the Lamb!
These are your hours of consolation;
With awe adore his saving name!
His cross and wounds are of salvation
The lasting source for sinners who believe;
Come then, and grace for grace freely from him receive.

2 His mercy claims our highest praise,
'Tis by his grace we were elected;
Freed from the world's deceitful ways,
We're to his chosen flock collected;
His faithful heart we know, and search it still:
May thousands more believe, and do his holy will.

3 Ourselves, dear Lord, we now to thee
Resign anew with soul and body;
As thy redeemed property
Accept of us, tho' poor and needy;
Out of the mouths of sucklings perfect praise,
And magnify in us, thy name and saving grace.

4 O let thy love our hearts constrain,
That, in one covenant united,
The bond of peace we may maintain,
And be to mutual love excited;
To God and to the Lamb be praises giv'n
By sinners here below, and by the saints in heav'n!

696.* T. 97.

JESUS, O may we thee obey,
Who art the Life, the Truth, the Way;
Since thou didst for our sins atone,
With right thou claim'st us as thine own:
Thou was obedient unto death, that we
Might not be lost, but live eternally.

2 O let each member of thy fold
Be in the book of life enroll'd;
The Holy Ghost to us impart
To bear the sway in ev'ry heart;
Us with thy gracious presence daily bless
And evermore vouchsafe to us thy grace.

697.* T. 15.

LORD, when before the Father's face
Thou, in thy ministration,
Presentest the redeemed race,
Gather'd from ev'ry nation;

2 In love remember this thy flock
Bought by thy bitter passion:
To thee, who art the church's rock,
We pay our adoration.

3 We here unite in pray'r to thee,
And praise thee, Lord Jehovah!
We join to sighs for mercy free
A joyful Hallelujah!

698. T. 341.

OUR souls with inmost shame
Address thy holy name,
Jesus! in our midst appear
Present to each waiting soul,
Ev'ry contrite sinner cheer,
Breathe thy Spirit thro' the whole.

2 We sinners humbly crave
Thy presence here to have,
In this place to find thee true
To thy promises of grace,
Still to own the gather'd few,
Giving them thy life and peace.

3 From thy majestic throne
In mercy, Lord, look down;
View the souls a-thirst for thee,
Turn to them thy cheering face;
Each adores, with bended knee,
Thee, O Jesus! for thy grace.

699. T. 167.

PEACE be to this habitation,
Peace to ev'ry soul therein;
Peace, which flows from Christ's salvation,
Peace, the seal of cancell'd sin;
Peace, that speaks it's heav'nly Giver,
Peace, to earthly minds unknown;
Peace divine, that lasts for ever,
Here erect its glorious throne!

700.* T. 69.

THIS habitation,
And all who dwell therein,
Fill with salvation;
O may in each be seen
True grace,
And lovely childlikeness.

701.* T. 166.

LORD JESUS, for our call of grace
To praise thy name in fellowship,
We're humbly met before thy face,
And in thy presence love-feast keep.
Shed in our hearts thy love abroad,
Thy Spirit's unction now impart;
Grant we may all, O Lamb of God,
In thee be truly one in heart.

702.* T. 159.

THE Sabbath is for man, that he
Therein may find repose,
And that the soul refreshed be
By Christ, the church's Spouse:
Now doth his ransom'd happy bride,
Fruit of his anguish, when he dy'd,
Enjoy a true sabbatic rest,
In his communion blest.

703. T. 205.

GRACIOUS Lord,—with one accord,
We're assembled in thy name;
Deign to hear—our fervent pray'r,
Mercy is our only claim,
While with tears and blushing face
We our sins to thee confess,
And our hearts with thanks o'erflow
For the grace thou dost bestow.

704. T. 590.

JESUS, knit all our hearts to thee,
Unite us all in one,
And in our meetings ev'ry where
Be thou our aim alone;
Reign thou sole Monarch of our hearts,
Without a rival reign;
Till we with angels join above
To praise the Lamb once slain.

705. T. 185.

GRACIOUS Father, bless this congregation
As the purchase of thy Son;
For his sake behold us with compassion,
And us all thy children own;
Jesus, grant to us thy peace and favor;
Holy Ghost, abide with us for ever,
And to us Christ's love explain;
Hear us, Lord our God, Amen!

706.* T. 79.

O KING of peace, our Sov'reign!
Thou shalt alone us govern,
Come, form us soon to be
T' each other an example,
To th' Holy Ghost a temple,
To th' Father pleasing constantly.

2 O thou our first-born Brother,
Thou Master at the rudder,
Who guid'st thy church, to thee
We hearts and hands deliver,
And promise thee for ever,
That we thy faithful souls will be.

707.* T. 185.

WE who here together are assembled,
Joining hearts and hands in one,
Bind ourselves, with love that's undissembled,
Christ to love and serve alone.
O may our imperfect songs and praises
Be well-pleasing unto thee, Lord Jesus!
Say, "My peace I leave with you."
Amen, Amen! Be it so!

708.* T. 79.

INCLINE thine ear in favor
To us, most gracious Saviour,
Accept our promises:
Thy death, thy wounds and passion
Abide our hearts' confession,
Till we shall see thee face to face.

709. T. 159.

WE now return, each to his tent,
Joyful and glad of heart,
And from our solemn covenant
Thro' grace will ne'er depart;
Once more we pledge both heart and hand,
As in God's presence here we stand,
To live to him, and him alone,
Till we surround his throne.

710.* T. 166.

WELCOME among thy flock of grace
With joyful acclamation!
Thou, whom our Shepherd we confess,
Come, feed thy congregation;
We own the doctrine of thy cross
To be our sole foundation;
Accept from ev'ry one of us
The deepest adoration.

2 Lord Jesus, to our hearts reveal
Thy grace and love unceasing;
Thy hand, once pierced with the nail,
Bestow on us a blessing,
That hand, which to thy family,
With tender love's affection,
Ere thou ascendedst up on high,
Imparted benediction.

3 Tho' thou'rt unseen, yet we by sight
Should not be more assured;
As yet thy glorious heav'nly light
Can't be by man endured:
The time will come, when these our eyes
Shall see thy face for ever;
Faith here the want of sight supplies
In ev'ry true believer.

4 Ye who from Jesus Christ have stray'd,
And his communion slighted,
To him return, be not afraid,
You're graciously invited;
Come all, whatever be your case,
Come without hesitation,
He'll now impart to you, thro' grace,
Peace, pardon and salvation.

5 O thou, who always dost abide
Thy body's Head and Saviour,
Who art the pilgrims' constant Guide,
Direct thy servants ever:
O may they an example be
Unto thy congregation,
And in thy temple faithfully
Perform their ministration.

6 Thy statutes to thy church declare,
Thy truth be our confession;
Take of each member special care,
Bless pilgrims in their station:
In danger constantly defend,
And aid thy chosen people;
Of all contention make an end;
Support the weak and feeble.

7 O thou, the church's Head and Lord,
Who as a shepherd leadest
Thy flock, and richly with thy word
And sacrament them feedest:
What shall we say? we can't express
In words our hearts' sensation;
None thee sufficiently can praise,
Thou God of our salvation.

8 Our heav'nly Father, hear our pray'r:
For th' sake of Jesus' passion,
In whom we all accepted are,
O bring into completion
The hidden counsel of thy love,
Its depth still more unravel;
May we, without exception, prove
The fruit of thy Son's travail.

9 O Spirit in the Godhead's throne,
Accept our adoration;
Thou ever didst attend the Son,
And aid his ministration;
Thou teachest us the way to bliss,
Keep under thy protection
That church of which he Ruler is;
We'll follow thy direction.

711.* T. 230.

JESUS, God of our salvation!
Behold thy church with supplication,
Humbly appear before thy face;
We by fervent love constrained,
Since from thy death we life obtained,
To thee give glory, thanks and praise.
O listen to our pray'r,
To meet thee us prepare,
With due rev'rence;
No tongue can tell
What joy we feel,
When thou, Lord, dost thyself reveal.

2 Thee t'approach with awe we venture,
Intreating thee our gates to enter,
Our souls and bodies are thine own.
Speak to ev'ry church division, [sion,
We'll hear thy voice with deep impres-
For we are bound to thee alone.
To thee in each concern
We'll always humbly turn;
Want we insight,
May we by thee
Instructed be,
Then in thy light the light we see.

3 Be especially intreated
To own thy servants, who are seated
Before thy face, tho' poor they are;
And in all their conferences
Grant them thy Spirit's influences,
Be present with them ev'ry where;
This we request of thee,
O let us constantly
Do thy pleasure;
All our distress,
O Lord, redress,
For without thee there's no success.

4 Ruler of the congregations,
Which thou hast gather'd from all nations,
We thee implore thy church to lead;
Shepherd, who so kindly guidest
Thy flock, and over them presidest,
Thy sheep for ever tend and feed:
What joy, what matchless grace
Will still in future days
Be displayed,
When our good Lord,
Who keeps his word,
To the stray'd sheep will help afford!

5 In the dust we sink before thee,
And for thy boundless love adore thee,
Thee, Lord, our All in all we own;
We, thy people, make confession
Thy love is great, beyond expression,
Tho' to the world it is unknown;
The pow'r which doth abound
In thee, we've always found
Efficacious;
We will proclaim
Thy saving name,
O Lord, who ever art the same.

6 Thus our bliss will last for ever;
While we enjoy thy love and favor,
By thee our Shepherd led, we're blest;
We with joyful acclamation
Adore thee in the congregation,
Whose Head and Lord thou art confest:
To th' Ancient of all days
Might, honor, pow'r and praise
Be for ever!
Lord, grant that we
Eternally
May place our confidence in thee.

712.* T. 185.

HEAD and Ruler of thy congregation,
Whom thou lov'st unspeakably,
And to whom thou often a sensation
Giv'st of thy complacency,
Graciously regard the inward glowing
Of our hearts, and tears our cheeks bedewing;
Lord, we blush with humble shame,
And adore thy holy name.

2 Jesus, great High Priest of our profession,
We in confidence draw near,
Condescend in mercy the confession
Of our grateful hearts to hear!
Thee we gladly own in ev'ry nation
Head and Master of thy congregation,
Conscious, that in ev'ry place
Thou dispensest life and grace.

3 Thy blest people trusting in thy merit
On the earth's extended face,
From each other far, but one in spirit,
Sound with one accord thy praise!
May we never cease to make confession,
That thy death's the cause of our salvation;
We to thee, our Head and King,
Joyful hallelujahs sing!

713. T. 97.

THOU, who so graciously didst lead
Israel of old from bondage freed,
And by thy own almighty hand
Didst guide them to the promis'd land,
A cloud thy brightness veiling in the day,
At night thy pillar'd fire did mark their way;

2 That mighty pow'r thou then didst show
We are assur'd attends us now,
We still thy tender, watchful care,
Tho' undeserving, richly share,
If we thy leadings faithfully pursue,
Foll'wing thy Spirit's teaching, as 'tis due.

3 May we to thee, our Shepherd, cleave,
Thy holy Spirit never grieve,
And love each other heartily,
Thereby the scorning world will see,
That we're the temple of the living God,
A chosen people bought by Jesus' blood.

714.* T. 146.

O MAKER of my soul,
My ev'ry hair's Creator,
Who turn'st my tears to joy,
And heal'st my sin-sick nature;
Chief Shepherd of thy flock,
Thy servants' only Guide;
The church's Lord and Head
Thou ever dost abide.

715. T. 68.

LORD, thy church's Rock,
Who dost rule thy flock,
Elder of this congregation,
We, with humble adoration,
Thee, and thee alone
Our chief Shepherd own.

716.* T. 166.

WHEN our great Sov'reign from on high,
Our Lord and Saviour was aware,
That he his chosen family,
O'er whom he watch'd with tender care,
Would be constrained soon to leave;
He fill'd with love and grief intense,
To them his farewel blessing gave,
Before his suff'rings did commence.

2 Feeling beforehand all the weight
Of those dire scenes of pain and woe,
Which he well knew did him await,
His love towards his own to show,
He water in a bason pour'd,
And washed his disciples' feet;
Their souls already by his word,
Save one, were cleansed ev'ry whit.

3 When he this act of love had done,
He unto his disciples said:
"To you I've an example shown:
Ye call me Master, Lord and Head,
If I as such have wash'd your feet,
To one another do the same."
This solemn act to celebrate,
We're now assembled in his name.

4 Arise then, and with due respect,
With humble shame and willingness,
Do what our Saviour doth direct,
Endowed with disciples' grace!
Since Jesus to release from sin
Unto his people power gave,
We in his name are now wash'd clean,
And with our Lord a part may have.

5 Lord Jesus Christ, we pray, be near,
Forgive us all our trespasses;
With joy divine our spirits cheer,
Impart to us thy pard'ning grace!
As our High-Priest lift up thy hand,
That hand the nail once pierced thro',
Thy mercy unto us extend,
Rich blessings upon all bestow.

6 Inspire our hearts with mutual love,
O may we truly humble be,
Thy faithful servants ever prove,
Who yield in all things joy to thee:
In due obedience to thy word
We now have wash'd each other's feet,
Thy blest example, gracious Lord,
To follow, we find always meet.

7 Sure as thou art the church's Head,
Sure as we dust and ashes are,
So sure we, by thy blood once shed,
Are now, thro' grace, absolv'd and clear:
Sure as thy cross's church remains
To the blind world a spectacle,
So sure in her thy Spirit reigns,
And thou dost in thy temple dwell.

717.* T. 22.

(*Reception Liturgy.* A.)

IN th' name of Jesus Christ our Lord,
The church's Head, by us ador'd,
His brethren's congregation now
Into her fold receiveth you;

2 With us in Jesus to be one,
To follow him, and him alone;
T' enjoy his faithful Shepherd-care,
And his reproach and joy to share.

3 O may our Lord, the God of grace,
While you receive the kiss of peace,
Own you his blood-bought property;
And lead, and bless you constantly.

4 With heart & hand you now we own;
The Lord, to whom your heart is known,
Cause your whole walk 'mongst us to be
His joy, and your felicity.

5 The God of peace you sanctify,
With us to yield him praise and joy;
That spirit, soul, and body may
Be blameless, till his perfect day.

718.* T. 22.

(*Reception Liturgy.* B.)

THIS flock of Christ receiveth thee,
While conscious of her poverty;
She weepeth often contrite tears,
When 'fore her Saviour she appears.

2 But yet she can in truth rejoice,
Because she hears the Shepherd's voice,
And owns that by her Lord and Head
She's gently govern'd, train'd and led.

3 While we the kiss of peace impart,
We own thee one with us in heart,
In Christ, who is the only ground
That in one cov'nant we are found.

4 Enjoy then with the church, Christ's spouse,
The privileges of his house;
And in our joy, and grief, and care,
With us take thy allotted share.

5 As his redeem'd from this world's thrall,
With us make sure thy blessed call:
That when the Bridegroom comes we may
Be found wise virgins in that day.

XXXIV. Of HOLY BAPTISM.

719. T. 58.

WHEN we baptize a sinner in Christ's death,
Then is the blood and water his true bath:
Not with water only came the Lord Jesus;
He came with water and with blood to bless us. Praise be to God!

2 The water is in baptism seen by eyes;
On Jesus' blood not seen our faith relies;
We are well persuaded this fountain cleanseth
Polluted sinners, and true grace dispenseth To live to him.

3 This precious blood is full of energy,
It washeth clean, and cures effectually;
And the Holy Spirit, unto us tender'd,
Bears witness pow'rfully that we are render'd Children of God.

4 O come then Father, Son, and Holy Ghost!
While we of Jesus' bitter passion boast;
While on him relying, we are baptizing
This sinner in Christ's death, that he be rising With Jesus too.

5 Besprinkle him, O Jesus, Son of God,
Now with thy precious all-atoning blood;
Cleanse both soul and body from all pollution,
And grant to him the seal of absolution, Thy peace divine.

720. T. 590.

HEAV'N's kingdom none shall enter in
But he who is a child:
Therefore the children are by God
Heirs of his kingdom styl'd.
Is heaven theirs? none shall forbid
A child to come to him!
Who shall forbid the water-flood
A babe to overstream?

2 O Father Son, and Holy Ghost,
Be present with us here:
We trust in Jesus' saving name,
To us his words are dear.
We now baptize a little child
Into the Saviour's death;
We have no scruple, we perform
This solemn act in faith.

3 The heav'nly hosts rejoice with us!
An infant here they see,
Whom Jesus, by his precious blood,
Hath sav'd from misery.
The children's angels, who behold
The Father on his throne,
For Jesus' sake will surely tend
And guard this little one.

721. T. 590.

LORD Jesus, from thy pierced side
Both blood and water stream'd,
A cleansing laver to provide
For man, from sin redeem'd;
Thou saidst, "Preach pardon to the lost,
Baptize them in the name
Of Father, Son, and Holy Ghost;"
We now will do the same.

2 Be present with us, Lord our God;
This water can't make clean,
But while we pour it, cleanse by blood
This infant from all sin.
Accept this child we now baptize
And here present to thee;
His soul be precious in thine eyes,
Now and eternally.

722. T. 22.

BURY'D in baptism with our Lord,
We rise with him, to life restor'd:
Not the bare life in Adam lost,
But richer far, for more it cost.

2 Water can cleanse the flesh we own;
But Christ well knows, and Christ alone,
How dear to him our cleansing stood,
Baptiz'd with wrath, and bath'd in blood!

3 He by his blood aton'd for sin,
This precious blood can wash us clean,
And he arrays us in the dress
Of his unspotted righteousness.

723. T. 582.

OUR baptism first declares
That we must cleansed be,
Then shows that Christ to all God's heirs
Dispenseth purity.

2 Water the body laves;
And, if 'tis done by faith,
The blood of Jesus surely saves
The sinful soul from death.

3 Baptiz'd into his death,
We rise to life divine;
The Holy Spirit works the faith,
And water is the sign.

724. T. 14.

FATHER of Jesus Christ our Lord!
(In him OUR Father too)
O bless, we pray, with one accord,
The work we have to do.

2 Jesus! as water well apply'd
Will make the body clean;
So in the fountain of thy side
Wash thou this soul from sin.

3 O Holy Ghost! with pow'r apply
The Saviour's cleansing blood;
Own thou this babe, and testify:
"This is a child of God."

725. T. 39.

THOU who in the days of thy flesh didst receive
The children, and to them thy blessing didst give;
Most gracious Redeemer, thy favor bestow
On him we present thee, we pray, bless him now.

2 Receive him, O Christ, as a lamb thou hadst lost,
And think what a price his redemption hath cost!
Thy name on his forehead, thy seal on his heart,
O merciful Shepherd and Bishop, impart.

3 Vouchsafe to be present, thou Father ador'd;
And thou our Redeemer, and merciful Lord;
O Holy Ghost, come with thy unction and fire,
And all with thy love and salvation inspire.

726. T. 22.

O BLEST Redeemer! in thy side
Upon the cross was made a wound:
The fountain by which we are purg'd,
Wherein our sin and guilt are drown'd.

2 Water and blood in streams hence ran,
And on the earth were freely spilt;
Water to sanctify and cleanse;
Blood to atone for heinous guilt.

3 This wondrous grace to represent
Baptismal waters were design'd,
In which thou, Lord, wast bury'd too,
To thy great Father's will resign'd.

4 Thus penitents who die to sin
With thee are bury'd in thy grave,
Thus quicken'd to a life divine
Their souls a resurrection have.

5 And though their bodies turn to dust,
This holy symbol doth assure:
The resurrection of the just
Shall render them once bright and pure.

727. T. 582.

COME, lowly souls, that mourn,
Depress'd with grief and shame,
Wash in your Saviour's cleansing blood,
And call upon his name.

2 Rejoice, ye contrite hearts,
The blood which Jesus spilt,
While we with water you baptize,
Will wash away your guilt.

3 While with repenting tears
Your sins you now deplore,
Christ with his blood will blot them out,
Remember them no more.

4 Ye who in Christ believe,
And to his sceptre bow,
Sing your Redeemer's love, and tell
What he hath done for you.

5 Unspotted robes you wear,
Your sighs to songs are turn'd:
Garments of praise adorn you now,
Who late in ashes mourn'd.

6 Ye with your Lord are ris'n;
Aspire to things above,
Mansions for you your Lord prepares,
In realms of light and love.

XXXV. Of the HOLY COMMUNION.

728. T. 160.

SEE Jesus seated 'midst his own,
With pensive mind oppressed,
Foreboding pangs and griefs unknown,
Amazed and distressed;
Strong fears beset—but stronger yet
Love's pow'r his soul then moved,
And love the conqu'ror proved.

2 With great desire he long'd, before
His final, bitter suff'ring,
To eat the passover once more,
Type of his body's off'ring;
And in a last—farewel repast,
To give a sacred token
Of his love's bond unbroken.

3 In that most dark and doleful night,
When Jesus was betrayed,
And, viewing hell's collected might,
As man felt sore dismayed;
Yet see his face—with matchless grace
Shine on his flock with healing,
Pardon and peace revealing.

4 In bread and wine to them he gave
His sacred body broken,
His blood, shed guilty souls to save;
For thus the Lord hath spoken,
And we believe,—adore, receive,
Yea feel the pow'r mysterious
To heal, revive and cheer us.

5 Lord Christ, I thank thee for thy grace,
Since by thy invitation,
Here at thy table I take place,
And taste of thy oblation;
Now seal me thine—and be thou mine,
That nought on earth me ever
From thy communion sever.

6 'Tis here my needy soul is fed,
But not with food terrestrial;
Thy body is my living bread,
Thy blood my drink celestial:
And at thy feet—my rest how sweet!
Here may I have my station,
A trophy of thy passion.

7 And when I once, of heav'nly bliss
And perfect love possessed,
Shall see my Saviour, as he is,
The Lamb for ever blessed,
Still shall each breath—show forth his death;
My voice shall swell the chorus,
To sing that song most glorious.

729. T. 166.

In that important, doleful night,
In which our Saviour was betray'd,
Before his suff'rings, he took bread,
Bless'd it, and brake it, and then said:
"Take, eat; this is my body giv'n
For you, and offer'd on the tree.
Perform this ord'nance as I do,
And doing it, remember ME."

2 Then after supper took the cup,
And having given thanks, he said:
"'Tis the New Test'ment in my blood,
The blood for you and many shed.
Take this, and drink ye all of it,
Your sins' remission here you see;
Oft as this ord'nance ye perform,
It in remembrance do of ME."

3 Yes, Lord, we will remember thee,
We'll ne'er forget thy love divine:
Thy cross we'll ever bear in mind,
Which made thee ours, and made us thine.
We thus commemorate thy death,
Till thou shalt once again appear:
Meanwhile remember, gracious Lord,
Us thy unworthy foll'wers here.

730.* T. 205.

Happy race—of witnesses!
Whom God's Spirit doth ordain
To make known—what God hath done;
Ye can only vict'ry gain
By that sacred cov'nant blood,
Which the fathers, bold in God,
Wrote in faith on ev'ry door,
That the slayer might pass o'er.

2 Israel's seed—from slav'ry freed
Eat with joy their paschal Lamb;
But the bride—of Christ, who dy'd
Her from bondage to redeem,
Hath another passover;
(There the shadow, substance here:)
She enjoys the flesh and blood
Of the slaughter'd Lamb of God.

3 Here we now—most humbly bow,
Being met in Jesus' name,
Who for us—dy'd on the cross
Bearing our reproach and shame,
'Fore the Father, 'fore the Son,
And the Spirit, Three in One,
With the countless heav'nly host,
And th' assembly of the just.

4 Ere we taste—the rich repast,
Which he offers graciously,
On our food,—his flesh and blood,
Feasting in the sanctuary,
Ere the sacrament t' enjoy,
We with awe to him draw nigh:
We in love and fellowship
This communion love-feast keep.

5 Eat and rest—at this great feast;
Then to serve him freely go,
As it is—for pilgrims fit,
As disciples ought to do;
We, when Jesus we shall see
Coming in his majesty,
Shall the marriage-supper share,
If we his true foll'wers are.

6 Then will be—of ransom'd souls
An innumerable throng:
"Lamb, once slain,—to thee pertain
Thanks and praise" will be their song.
"Hallelujah" will they cry
Singing in sweet harmony,
"'Midst all trials we o'ercame
Only by thy blood, O Lamb!"

731.* T. 594.

JESUS, how great was thy desire,
Once more to eat the paschal lamb
With thy dear flock! O what love's fire
Did here thy sorr'wing soul inflame!
Each precious word thy kindness showeth,
Thereby we are divinely blest:
The love that in thy bosom gloweth
Is herein render'd manifest.

2 Thy love is great beyond all measure,
Thence we derive eternal good;
Thou grantest us, O what a treasure!
Thy holy body, and thy blood;
Lord Jesus, was it not sufficient
That thou shouldst die for our offence,
But, out of love, thou ev'ry patient
Wouldst heal, and make thy residence!

3 O love divine! how strong, how ardent!
More strong than death! our life to gain,
Th' incarnate God, thro' love most fervent,
Was as a Lamb for sinners slain.
Love urg'd the sov'reign great Creator,
'Fore whom the universe doth shake,
By whom all things subsist in nature,
Once in the earth his grave to make!

732. T. 590.

THAT doleful night before his death,
The Lamb, for sinners slain,
Did almost with his latest breath
This solemn feast ordain.
To keep thy feast, Lord, are we met,
And to remember thee:
Help each poor sinner to repeat,
"For me he dy'd, for me."

2 Thy suff'rings Lord, each sacred sign
To our remembrance brings;
We feed upon thy love divine,
Forget all earthly things.
O tune our voices, and inflame
Our hearts with love to thee,
That each may gratefully proclaim,
"My Saviour dy'd for me!"

733.* T. 242.

AS oft as we expect the favor,
That in the sacrament our Saviour
Himself will unto his people give,
We weep for joy and grief:
For joy, that we're thus brought nigh to God
By Jesus' blood;
For grief that we so little honor
Afford to him in word and in demeanor;
Yea, sometimes frustrate his gracious views
And purposes with us:
Ah, then in faith we sigh,
And to our Saviour cry:
O that thy hand, for us once pierced thro',
Might bless all of us now,
And give absolving grace:
Lord, leave with us thy peace!

734. T. 151.

DEAR Lord! this congregation
Is poor, despise her not;
She's taken with thy passion,
As were she on the spot,
When, earning her election,
Thy heart-strings broke in death;
That stirs up her affection,
And gives her life and breath.

2 Shouldst thou desire her beauty,
For shame she hides her face;
And shouldst thou look for duty,
Her only plea is grace:
Tho' we are poor and needy,
Yet we're thy property;
When we enjoy thy body
And blood, how blest are we!

735.* T. 146.

WHERE my Redeemer's blood
And sweat the earth did cover,
May ev'ry sinful thought
Be now interr'd for ever;
Lord Jesus, grant my wish,
That I may thine abide,
And by thy holy flesh
And blood be sanctify'd.

736.* T. 4.

O GLORY'D HEAD,
Since mortals may tread
The holiest of all,
And deeply abas'd 'fore the mercy-seat fall;

2 Admit us, we pray,
On this solemn day,
To thee to draw nigh,
And thy holy body and blood to enjoy.

737. T. 9.

SUFF'RING Saviour, Lamb of God,
How hast thou been used!
With God's sin-avenging rod
Soul and body bruised!

2 We, for whom thou once wast slain,
We, whose sins did pierce thee,
Now commemorate thy pain,
And implore thy mercy.

3 What can we poor sinners do,
When temptations seize us!
Nought have we to look unto
But the blood of Jesus.

4 Pardon all our sins, O Lord;
All our weakness pity;
Guide us safely by thy word
To the heav'nly city.

5 O sustain us on the road
Thro' this desert dreary;
Feed us with thy flesh and blood
When we're faint and weary.

6 Bid us call to mind thy cross,
Our hard hearts to soften;
Often Saviour, feast us thus,
For we need it often.

738.* T. 581.

TO avert from men God's wrath
Jesus suffer'd in our stead;
By an ignominious death
He a full atonement made:
And by his most precious blood
Brought us sinners nigh to God.

2 That we never should forget
This great love on us bestow'd,
He gave us his flesh to eat,
And to drink, his precious blood:
All who sick and needy are
May receive in him a share.

3 Hither each afflicted soul
May repair, tho' fill'd with grief;
To the sick, not to the whole,
The Physician brings relief:
Fear not, therefore, but draw nigh,
He will all your wants supply.

4 He who in self-righteousness
Fixeth any hope or stay,
Hath not on a wedding dress,
And with shame is sent away:
To the hungry, weary heart,
He will food and rest impart.

5 But examine first your case,
Whether you be in the faith;
Do you mourn for pard'ning grace?
Is your only hope his death?
Then, howe'er your soul's opprest,
Come, you are a worthy guest.

6 He who Jesus' mercy knows,
Is from wrath and envy freed;
Love unto our neighbor shows
That we are his flock indeed:
Thus we may in all our ways
Show forth our Redeemer's praise.

739.* T. 58.

CHRIST was revealed in the flesh for us,
To suffer death upon the shameful cross;
Now his holy body, for sinners given,
Is our souls' food, until we shall in heaven Adore his name.

2 With thirsty souls we drink the sacred blood,
Which flow'd from Jesus Christ, the Lamb of God,
To procure for sinners complete salvation,
When he became the full propitiation For all our sins.

3 While we partake thereof in humble faith,
We show forth Jesus' sin-atoning death,
And with deep abasement the congregation
Gives glory, honor, praise and adoration Unto the Lamb.

740. T. 232.

THE holy bread which now we break,
The cup of which we all partake,
Is the participation
Of Jesus' flesh and blood, for us
A ransom giv'n upon the cross,
To purchase our salvation.
He said, "My flesh is truly meat;
This is my body, take and eat:"
He also took the cup, and said,
"This is my blood, for you 'tis shed."
Lord, we draw near
Thy table here
With childlike fear:
Dear Jesus, to our hearts appear.

2 Most holy Lord, thou know'st our wants,
And how each needy sinner pants
For thee, our Lord and Saviour:
O may our hungry souls be fed
With thee, the true life-giving Bread,
And taste thy matchless favor:
O may thy blood, the stream of life,
Our thirst assuage, our souls revive.
Thou living Vine, each branch supply;
Our souls and bodies sanctify:
And grant that we
Abide in thee
Continually;
Yea, bear such fruit as pleaseth thee.

3 O Lord, who dost thyself impart
In mercy to each contrite heart,
Enjoying the communion:
Grant that we may be one in thee,
May love each other heartily,
And thus abide in union.
Let nothing 'mongst thy flock take place
Which tends thy doctrine to disgrace;
By faith and love in all we do,
O may we, to thy honor, show
In all our ways
The boundless grace
Thy love displays,
Which in the sacrament we trace.

4 Now bless and praise the slaughter'd Lamb,
Extol his saving Jesus' name,
Thou favor'd congregation!
Which at the table of our Lord
Hast eat and drank with one accord;
Thou know'st thy destination
Is to abide in Christ by faith,
And to show forth our Saviour's death.
Walk then as children of the light,
Live to his praise by day and night;
O Lamb once slain,
We vow again
Thine to remain:
Confirm our promises. Amen!

741.* T. 126.

IS that my dearest Brother,
(Saith one of low degree,)
Who tho' the Father's equal
Became a man like me,
And on the ignominious tree
Aton'd for my transgressions?—
'Tis he most certainly!

2 Ye who believe on Jesus,
And on account of sin
Have mourn'd with pungent sorrow,
But now feel joy within,
What think ye, that to him on high,
'Fore whom ev'n John did tremble,
Ye dare approach so nigh?

3 He show'rs his choicest blessings
This day upon each heart,
And thus to soul and body
Salvation doth impart.
That blood which on the cross he shed
Our drink is, and his body
Is our true heav'nly bread.

4 He said, "My flesh is truly
Meat, and my blood is drink:"
So did, unto his glory,
The Lord's disciples think.
We with the heart believe it too,
And can with full assurance
Declare it to be true.

5 In spirit we behold him
As dying in our stead;
We may approach with boldness
To him in all our need.
Th' enjoyment of this heav'nly feast
Make us, his congregation,
In soul and body chaste.

6 Thou ransom'd church of Jesus,
Increase in love and faith,
United to thy Saviour;
Be faithful unto death,
And own him God for evermore,
Who took our human nature;
Him in the dust adore.

742.* T. 9.

TILL the hour shall come, with tears
By the church desired,
When our Lord again appears,
Now from sight retired:

2 He hath with a pledge of grace
His dear flock supplied,
Whereby his own witness race
Shows forth that he died.

3 'Tis his body and his blood
Which the soul refreshes;
Church of Christ, this highest good
Claims thy thanks and praises!

4 By this sacrament we are
To our Lord united;
To due watchfulness and pray'r,
And good works excited.

5 With deep rev'rence we draw nigh,
Falling down before thee;
While we this repast enjoy,
We with awe adore thee.

6 Us thy congregation own,
Let us taste thy favor,
And by faith recline, like John,
On thy breast, dear Saviour.

743.* T. 23.

SOUL, at this most awful season,
Soar above thy scanty reason;
To the light approach, where clearest;
Duly mind what dress thou wearest.

2 Jesus, Lord of the creation,
Gives thee now an invitation,
His unbounded love revealing,
He'll take up in thee his dwelling.

3 Hasten, as for brides is fitting,
Give thy bridegroom soon the meeting,
Say, "Dear Lord, let me receive thee,
Hold thee fast, and never leave thee."

4 How do I, with spirit's hunger,
Lord, to taste thy goodness, linger!
Oft I pant with inward sighing
This blest food to be enjoying.

5 O how crave I the fruition
Of thy blood, my soul's nutrition!
Since by sharing this communion,
I'm with God in closest union.

6 Heav'nly joy and holy trembling
I feel in me, past dissembling;
For the food to which I'm bidden
Is a myst'ry deep and hidden.

7 Human reason is too shallow
In this wonder thee to follow,
How thou hast unto us given
Thy own flesh, the bread of heaven.

8 How the blood which from thee flowed,
Is in wine on us bestowed;
O the wonders deep and blessed,
By God's Spirit here expressed!

9 Thy communion's celebration
Bows me down to deep prostration;
May I never unprepared,
To my condemnation share it.

744.* T. 23.

COME, approach to Jesus' table,
Taste that food incomparable,
Which to us is freely given,
As an antepast of heaven.

2 Jesus' bride, his congregation,
Calls to mind her Saviour's passion,
With his body she is nourish'd,
With his blood refresh'd and cherish'd.

3 Far be gone all carnal reason,
At this awful blessed season;
Slaughter'd Lamb! we now desire it
By thy love to be inspired.

4 This mysterious, heav'nly blessing
Is all thought by far surpassing;
Deeply bow'd may we adore thee,
Soul and body sink before thee.

5 Now is come our time sabbatic,
Lord, we feel thy pow'r emphatic;
Ah, draw near to us, dear Saviour,
Let us taste thy grace and favor!

745.* T. 71.

MY soul, prepare to meet
Thy Saviour; at his feet
Fall down adoring;
The Lord of earth and skies
A feast for thee supplies,
Past thy exploring.

2 How vast is here display'd,
In brightest form array'd,
His love's dimension!
O grace! beyond the ken
Of angels or of men,
Past comprehension!

3 How should I, slaughter'd Lamb,
Who dust and ashes am,
A worm, and earthy,
To taste such boundless grace,
And have so high a place
Be counted worthy!

4 Ah, why am I thus blest,
That such an heav'nly Guest
My house will enter;
Dare I, thou highest Good,
To taste thy flesh and blood,
A sinner, venture?

5 Upon thy call I'm here,
I venture to draw near,
Because thou'rt gracious:
I on thy word rely,
Thou wilt my soul supply
With food delicious.

6 Grant me but this firm faith,
That with thee by thy death
I am united.
To cure and make me whole,
Thou hast my sin-sick soul
Freely invited.

7 Thy body slain for me,
My food, my foretaste be
Of heav'n's fruition!
And by its pow'r may I,
While I the world deny,
Gain there admission.

8 Pervade, thou precious flood
Of Christ's all-healing blood,
My soul and senses;
And to my needy heart
Life, peace, and health impart,
Thus heav'n commences.

9 Lord, of thy wondrous love
That brought thee from above
Thou gav'st this token:
O may it constantly
Unite my heart to thee
In bonds unbroken.

10 Didst thou thyself devise
To be my Sacrifice,
My Lord, my Treasure!
Grant that continually
To live alone for thee
May be my pleasure.

11 Cause me, who now am thine,
As branch, to thee the Vine
To cleave unceasing;
Receiving strength and juice,
That I may fruit produce
To thee well-pleasing.

12 Such grace on me is spent,
That none hath its extent
Aright explained;
Grant now that I may show
To fellow-sinners too
A love unfeigned.

13 May ev'ry drop of blood
In me, O Lord my God,
Be sanctified:
Oft as my heart doth beat,
May I his praise repeat,
Who for me died.

746.* T. 22.

THE congregation while below,
Being imperfect, tears must sow;
But we expect once joy to reap,
Since we for Jesus' mercy weep.

2 Meanwhile that we might bear in mind
His dying love to lost mankind,
He hath, as his last testament,
To us bequeath'd the sacrament.

3 He, when this feast was first ordain'd,
Its solemn import thus explain'd:
"This is my body, take and eat,
That you may never me forget."

4 "This is my blood, of which whene'er
Ye drink, my death in mem'ry bear."
The church believes, and thus in faith
Partakes, & showeth forth Christ's death.

5 But words can never fully tell
What in our melted hearts we feel:
We taste, experience, and possess
True joy, and weep for thankfulness.

747. T. 14.

WHEN we before our Saviour's face
Appear with contrite hearts,
He soothes our griefs, and pard'ning grace
To ev'ry one imparts.

2 When we commemorate his love,
He saith "For you I dy'd:
Behold my hands, behold my feet,
And view my wounded side."

3 "These are the wounds I bore for you,
The tokens of my pain:
By which I for your guilty souls
Eternal life did gain."

4 We eat his body, slain for us
And giv'n a sacrifice,
Thirsting we drink his sacred blood,
That precious ransom-price.

5 Ah then we feel, that life divine
From Jesus' death redounds,
Eternal blessings from his cross,
And healing from his wounds.

748. T. 14.

LORD, how divine thy comforts are!
How heav'nly is the place,
Where Jesus spreads the sacred feast
Of his redeeming grace!

2 There the rich bounties of our God,
And heav'nly glories shine;
There Jesus saith, that "I am his,
And my Beloved's mine."

3 "Here," (saith our kind redeeming Lord,
And shows his wounded side)
"Behold the spring of all your joys,
That open'd when I dy'd."

4 What shall we pay our heav'nly King
For grace so vast as this!
He brings our pardon to our eyes,
And seals it with a kiss.

749. T. 14.

TOGETHER with these symbols, Lord,
Thy blessed self impart;
And let thy holy flesh and blood
Feed the believing heart.

2 Let us from all our sins be wash'd
In thy atoning blood;
And let thy Spirit be the seal
That we are born of God.

3 Come, Holy Ghost, with Jesus' love
Prepare us for this feast;
O let us banquet with our Lord,
And lean upon his breast.

750.* T. 141.

CHRIST, thy flock doth hunger
For thy flesh, our food,
Thirsts with ardent longing
For thy precious blood,
Which thou hast bequeathed
As thy testament,
To thy congregation
In the sacrament.

2 Like the king of Salem,
Thou with wine and bread
Com'st to meet thy people,
Them to cheer and feed.
O preserve th' enjoyment
Of thy blood and death
To thy congregation,
While we live by faith.

751. T. 185.

GREAT the feast, to which thou, Lord, hast bidden
Such a worthless guest as me;
'Tis an awful myst'ry, deep and hidden;
'Tis a heav'nly legacy:
Contrite souls howe'er by sin infected,
Are made welcome, not one is rejected,
Else this grace to sinful me
Never could extended be.

2 Thou thy table spreadest for the needy,
Who may feast and take their fill,
Thou to grant thy heav'nly gifts art ready,
And thy goodness to reveal;
Soul and body in this rich fruition
Gain from thee, the Bread of life, nutrition;
And we, as thy flesh and bone,
Lord, with thee are render'd one.

752.* T. 22.

O CHURCH of Jesus, now draw near
With humble joy, and filial fear;
According to his testament,
Enjoy the holy sacrament.

2 Here all our wants are well supply'd,
And we show forth that Jesus dy'd:
May we abide in him by faith,
And cleave to him in life and death.

3 Th' enjoyment of the flesh and blood
Of Jesus Christ, the Lamb of God,
Endoweth us with strength and grace
To love and serve him all our days.

753*. T. 151.

THOSE souls are truly blessed,
Who to our Saviour cleave,
Of living-faith possessed,
And in his name believe;
For what is still denied
To sight, while here below,
Is by our faith enjoyed,
And makes our hearts to glow.

2 Faith on Christ's declaration
With confidence relies:
He now his congregation
With heav'nly food supplies;
Would we as branches flourish
On Jesus the true Vine,
His blood our souls must nourish;
Else they would droop and pine.

3 Draw near to Jesus' table,
Ye contrite souls, draw near;
The hungry, sick and feeble
His choicest dainties share.
Let Jesus' death engraven
Upon your hearts remain;
Thus here, and there in heaven,
Eternal life you gain.

754.* T. 99.

ACT full of godlike majesty!
O Love's abyss! I'm lost in thee,
O myst'ry, all our thoughts surpassing!
Now all our wants are well supply'd,
And we show forth that Jesus dy'd,
As oft as we enjoy this blessing.

755.* T. 119.

BREAD of life, :||:
Christ, by whom alone we live,
Bread, that came to us from heaven!
My poor soul can never thrive
Unless thou appease its craving;
Lord, I hunger only after thee,
Feed thou me. :||:

756.* T. 151.

OWN me, Lord, my Salvation!
Receive my Shepherd, me!
I know, thy bitter passion
Is a rich treasury;
And that thou, Man of sorrows,
Hast by thy death and blood
Procur'd a new heart for us,
And sacramental food.

2 What heav'nly consolation
Doth in my heart take place,
When I thy toil and passion
Can in some measure trace!
Oh, what am I enjoying,
Thy flesh and bone, when I
With thee, my Lord, am dying,
What peace divine, what joy!

757.* T. 22.

O THAT in Jesus' church, his bride,
Sin might henceforth be mortify'd
By him, who us to save was slain,
And underwent such racking pain!

2 O might our souls and bodies be
From sinful influences free,
Might we, while still on earth we live,
To him the Vine as branches cleave.

3 O were we free from strange desire
And from depraved nature's fire,
As dead to all corruption base,
As formerly to righteousness.

4 Lord, by the power of thy death,
Renew in us a living faith,
Whate'er is carnal, quite erase;
And sanctify us by thy grace.

5 O church, rejoice, tho' tremblingly,
The Lord's death now pervadeth thee;
O may his sacred body cure,
And make our souls and bodies pure.

758.* T. 97.

THE breath which can the dead bones raise,
And to Christ's members life conveys,
Pervadeth thee, thou church of God,
And Jesus' sanctifying blood
Is now imparted to each thirsty soul;
It cheers the mourners, makes the wounded whole.

2 O church of God, lift up thy heart,
The Vine its power doth impart;
Take, drink the blood so freely spilt
For thine and ev'ry sinner's guilt;
Take, drink the blood, the blood so freely spilt
For mine, for thine, and ev'ry sinner's guilt.

759. T. 582.

MY Saviour's pierced side
Pour'd forth a double flood;
By water we are purify'd,
And pardon'd by his blood.
Look up, my soul, to him
Whose death was thy desert,
And humbly view the living stream
Flow from his wounded heart.

760. T. 166.

YE foll'wers of the slaughter'd Lamb,
Draw near, and take the cup of God:
Approach unto the healing stream,
And drink of the atoning blood;
That blood for our redemption spilt,
Assuring us of purchas'd grace;
That blood, which takes away all guilt,
And speaketh to the conscience peace.

761.* T. 146.

BY thy sweat mix'd with blood,
Which flow'd in thy soul's anguish
From thee, O Lamb of God,
When thou for us didst languish
In sad Gethsemane;
And with our sins oppress'd,
Didst weep, and groan, and pray,
That sinners might be bless'd;

2 Yea, by thy blood once shed
For us, when scourges wounded
Thy back, and when thy head
A thorny crown surrounded;
Oh, by that blood which flow'd
When nails thy body tore,
Bless us, O Lord our God,
Who humbly thee adore!

3 Lord Jesus, may the blood
Thou shedst for our salvation,
Which is our highest good,
Refresh this congregation,
When in the sacrament
We drink of it in faith,
And by this testament
Show forth thy bitter death.

762.* T. 149.

O WHAT happiness divine!
What a lot most precious,
Confidently to recline
On the breast of Jesus!
Where who will—Takes his fill,
And yet longs for ever
For more grace and favor.

2 Jesus cometh to fulfil
All thy heart desireth,
Doth himself to thee reveal,
Thee with love inspireth;
His blood spilt—All thy guilt
Will erase for ever,
And thy sins will cover.

763.* T. 184.

THAT sacred blood, from Jesus bursting,
Who by his stripes soothes ev'ry smart,
And hastes to us when for him thirsting,
His choicest favors to impart;
That precious blood, life's fountain blessed,
Which flows to me from Jesus' wounds,
Hath often cheer'd me when distressed,
For there eternal life abounds.

764. T. 97.

JESUS, thou Source of life, impart
Thy blood unto my thirsting heart,
Panting I seek that fountain-head,
Whence waters so divine proceed;
Still near this living stream may I abide,
By which my needy soul is satisfy'd.

765. T. 124.

MAY the stream from thee, the Rock,
Gracious Jesus,
Richly bless thy thirsting flock,
And refresh us!
'Tis the source of pow'r, of life,
And salvation,
To thy congregation.

766.* T. 580.

THY precious, all-atoning blood
Is to this hour, O Lamb of God,
An ocean of free grace.
All those who venture to draw nigh
To thee, can witness bear with joy,
They ne'er go empty from thy face.

767.* T. 23.

FLOCK of Christ, with exultation,
View the well-springs of salvation!
Drink, and live,—with an emotion
Of unfeigned heart's devotion!

2 May to Jesus, while we're living,
From our works redound thanksgiving,
And our lowly, meek behavior
Clearly show we love our Saviour.

768.* T. 82.

JESUS makes my heart rejoice,
I'm his sheep, and know his voice:
He's a Shepherd kind and gracious,
And his pastures are delicious.
Constant love to me he shows,
Yea, my worthless name he knows?

2 Trusting his mild staff always,
I go in and out in peace;
He will feed me with the treasure
Of his grace in richest measure;
When athirst to him I cry,
Living water he'll supply.

3 Should not I for gladness leap,
Led by Jesus as his sheep;
For when these blest days are over,
To the arms of my dear Saviour
I shall be convey'd to rest:
Amen, yea my lot is blest!

769.* T. 83.

MORE than shepherd's faithfulness
To his flock our Saviour showeth;
From the treasures of his grace
He the choicest gifts bestoweth:
As his sheep by him we're own'd,
Since his blood for us aton'd.

2 They who feel their want and need,
Thirsting for his great salvation,
On the richest pastures feed,
With true joy and delectation;
Till they shall, when perfected,
With celestial joys be fed.

770.* T. 582.

MY Shepherd is the Lamb,
The living Lord, who dy'd;
With all that's truly good I am
Most plenteously supply'd;
He richly feeds my soul
With manna from above,
And leads me where the rivers roll
Of everlasting love.

2 My table he doth spread
With choicest fare, and I,
Behold the Lamb, the living Bread,
And eat most joyfully;
He makes my cup run o'er,
Anointeth me with oil,
I shall enjoy for evermore
The merits of his toil.

3 When faith and hope shall cease,
And love prevail alone,
I then shall see him face to face,
And know as I am known;
Then I my Shepherd's care
Shall praise, and him adore,
And in his Father's house shall share
True bliss for evermore.

771.* T. 583.

HOW blest are we, when we enjoy thy love,
And in the sacrament thy bounty prove!
When we with humble shame, O Lamb of God,
Feed on thy body and thy precious blood.

2 Whenever we this highest good enjoy,
We promise thee anew fidelity;
Pow'r to perform thou hast for us obtain'd
When, by thy death, life was for man regain'd.

3 Make thou us monuments of grace, to show
What wonders thou on sinners vile canst do;
O were in our whole walk this to be seen,
That of thy feast we have partakers been.

4 We humbly pray that, with thy chosen train,
From this repast we may new strength obtain;
O deaden all that would thy grace withstand,
Or to its influence refuse to bend.

5 We have nought good in us to bring 'fore thee,
Yet thou art ours, and we're thy property,
Preserve to us this grace, we thee implore,
To have our part in thee for evermore.

772. T. 26.

AH! who are we, thou God of love!
That we should hear, thro' grace abounding,
The solemn invitation sounding:
"Prepare for the Lamb's feast above."

2 Prostrate before the mercy-seat
We sinners lie, with holy trembling,
The elders' blissful choir resembling,
Who cast their crowns before thy feet.

3 Here more than Tabor's glories shine;
Heart-captivating meditation!
Ev'n here thou feed'st thy congregation
With heav'nly manna, food divine!

4 Here it is good for us to be!
Our souls imbibe, while here we tarry,
The breezes of the sanctuary,
The atmosphere of Calvary.

5 Rise, and your pilgrim-path pursue
Revived by this rich fruition;
Soon shall the beatific vision,
The Lamb in glory, meet your view.

773.* T. 11.

COULD we sinners fully tell,
How our hearts with rapture swell,
Gladly then we would declare
Ev'n to angels what we share.

2 But since words the happiness
Which we feel, can ne'er express,
We adoring 'fore him lie,
And what he bestows enjoy.

3 Angels sing before his throne,
While we at his feet sink down;
Gracious Jesus, Man and God,
What hast thou on us bestow'd!

774.* T. 583.

SINCE Jesus dy'd, my guilty soul to save,
Heav'n's foretaste I may here already have:
O how unutterably blest am I,
Partaking of him sacramentally!

2 When heav'nly bread he gives my soul to eat,
That I may henceforth never him forget;
When I, a needy sheep of his blest flock,
Drink of the stream that flows from Christ, the Rock!

3 I live now, and to God myself will give,
But yet not I, but Christ in me shall live;
His mercy and his goodness I shall taste
Both here below, and when with him at rest.

775.* T. 11.

JESUS, who to save hast pow'r,
And who livest evermore
For thy flock to intercede,
Helping us in time of need;

2 Thou who a divine repast
For the poor prepared hast,
Giving thy own flesh and blood
As the hungry sinner's food;

3 Let thy pow'r divine, we pray,
Be our strength and only stay,
Till we drop this mortal vest,
And the spirit goes to rest.

776.* T. 22.

FOR that amazing love and grace,
Which doth our thoughts by far surpass,
To eat thy flesh and drink thy blood,
Thanks be to thee, O Lamb of God!

2 Thy sacred body thou didst give
For us, that we thereby might live;
No pledge of love could be so great:
O may we ne'er thy love forget.

3 Thy precious blood for sinners spilt
Cleanseth our hearts, removes our guilt,
The debt is paid which we incurr'd,
And we're to happiness restor'd.

4 Thy Holy Spirit with us leave,
So that we rightly may conceive,
What thou for all believers hast
Prepared in this blest repast.

777.* T. 151.

LORD Christ! I give thee praises;
Thy hand ne'er intermits
To show'r, as each day passes,
On me thy benefits;
Thy name, all names exceeding,
I'll praise, for thou art good,
Art with thy flesh me feeding,
To drink giv'st me thy blood.

778.* T. 185.

PRAISE be giv'n to Christ our soul's [Beloved,
By us sinners; what are we?
Feeble human creatures, far removed
From angelic purity:
Yet when he to his rich pastures leads us,
Where he with his sacred body feeds us,
And we drink his blood once shed,
We are richly comforted.

779. T. 582.

COME, O my soul, and sing
How Jesus thee hath fed;
How Jesus gave himself to thee,
The true and living Bread.

2 For food he gives his flesh;
He bids us drink his blood;
Amazing favor, matchless grace
Of our incarnate God!

3 This holy bread and wine
Confirms us in the faith,
In love and union with our Lord,
And we show forth his death.

780.* T. 26.

THOU slaughter'd Lamb, thy flesh and [blood,
Which thou didst sacrifice for us,
Upon the altar of the cross,
Are to our souls delicious food.

2 This makes us all with one accord
To love each other fervently,
Yea, to be wholly one with thee,
And all that love thee, gracious Lord.

781.* T. 22.

HAPPY, thrice happy hour of grace!
I've seen by faith my Saviour's face,
He did himself to me impart,
And made a cov'nant with my heart.

2 Ah, might in my behavior shine
The pow'r of Jesus' love divine,
His conflict and his victory,
His seeking, and his finding me!

782.* T. 590.

THOU, who art present with thy church
According to thy word,
When to enjoy thy flesh and blood,
We meet with one accord;
O grant us to show forth thy death,
Until thou shalt appear;
And may it in our walk be seen,
That we thy foll'wers are.

2 May we so captivated be
By thy redeeming love,
As to be wean'd from earthly things,
And fix our thoughts above;
May all that's carnal be subdu'd,
And mortify'd in us,
That we may glory in thy name,
And count all else but loss.

783.* T. 96.

SINCE Jesus' body I have eat,
And drank the blood he shed for me,
O may I never him forget!
I know he will remember me;
And I shall, when this life is o'er,
Live in his presence evermore!

XXXVI. Hymns for different Ages, Sexes, and Stations in Life; or, Choir Hymns.

784. T. 33.

EACH division of thy fold,
Freed from this world's vain tradition,
Male or female, young or old,
In thee hath true joys' fruition;
All in their allotted place
Should walk worthy of thy grace.

2 Grant us a contented mind,
That in their peculiar station
Each may be to thee resign'd,
Seeking only thy salvation.
By thy staff we're safely led,
Till in thee we're perfected.

A. *For Children.*

785. T. 22.

THOUGH but a little child I am,
Yet I may praise the slaughter'd Lamb,
He loveth children tenderly,
He also loveth sinful me.

2 Yes, gracious Saviour, I believe,
Thou wilt a little child receive;
For thou didst bless them formerly,
And say, "Let children come to me."

3 Lord Jesus, unto me impart
A humble, meek and docile heart;
O cleanse me in thy precious blood,
Shed in my heart thy love abroad.

4 Save me from liking what is ill,
Teach me to do thy holy will;
Each day prepare me, thro' thy grace,
To meet thee, and behold thy face.

786. T. 14.

THO' Christ was God, and all things made,
Himself he humbled thus:
That he, a Servant in our stead,
Might minister to us.

2 Our Saviour was a lovely child,
His parent's chief delight,
In his behavior meek and mild,
And always acted right.

3 A blessed pattern Christ our Lord
Himself to children gave,
That they to him might joy afford,
And never misbehave.

4 A child true happiness may find,
And humbly ought to pray:
"Lord Jesus, make my heart inclin'd
To love and to obey."

5 "I'm often stubborn, vain and wild,
Self-will'd and hard in heart;
O Lord, to me thy chaste, thy mild,
Thy holy mind impart."

787. T. 14.

O WHAT a wretched heart have I,
How full of sin and shame,
How obstinate continually,
How day by day to blame!

2 Lord, look on me 'midst all my faults;
And, when thou seest my guilt,
My wicked words and foolish thoughts,
Think why thy blood was spilt.

3 In that most precious river cleanse
And wash my crimes away,
My selfishness, and that offence
Which I have done to-day.

4 When thou, dear Jesus, wast a child,
Thou hadst no sin like me;
No wicked words thy lips defil'd,
No faults appear'd in thee.

5 Thou wast more spotless than a dove,
More harmless than a lamb,
Obedient, humble, full of love,
And never once to blame.

6 But I am proud, and headstrong too,
Oft sadly misbehave;
I am not meek, like thee, and low;
Me, Lord, in mercy save!

7 O might I but resemble thee,
That ev'ry one might know,
I love the Saviour, and will be
His foll'wer here below.

8 Imprint thine image in my heart,
Bestow thy Holy Ghost,
And an obedient mind impart;
Then I shall not be lost.

4 Loving Jesus, holy Lamb,
In thy hands secure I am;
Fix thy temple in my heart,
Never from thy child depart.

5 Teach me to show forth thy praise,
Love and serve thee all my days;
Oh, might all around me see
Christ, the holy child, in me!

788. T. 14

O LORD, forgive a sinful child,
Whose heart is all unclean;
How bad am I, and how defil'd,
How prone to ev'ry sin!

2 Oh, change my vile, and stubborn heart,
Like thee, Oh, make me pure;
To me thy love divine impart,
Keep me from sin secure.

3 Self-will, that cruel enemy,
No more I would obey;
Thy Spirit shall my Teacher be,
And guide me in thy way.

4 O may I never speak a word
But what I truly mean,
Nor lie to thee, most gracious Lord,
By whom each thought is seen.

5 I'll make thy wondrous, dying love,
Dear Lord, my daily song!
And joys, like theirs who sing above,
Shall tune my infant tongue.

789. T. 11.

LAMB of God, I look to thee,
Thou shalt my example be;
When thou wast a little child
Thou wast gentle, meek and mild,

2 Due obedience thou didst show,
O make me obedient too;
Thou wast merciful and kind,
Grant me, Lord, thy loving mind.

3 Let me above all fulfil
God, my heav'nly Father's will,
Never his good Spirit grieve,
Only to his glory live.

790.* T. 14.

THOU, gracious Saviour, for my good
Wast pleas'd a child to be,
And thou didst shed thy precious blood
Upon the cross for me.

2 Come take me as thy property,
Take me just as I am,
I know that I belong to thee,
Thy love my heart doth claim.

3 Low at thy feet O may I bow,
Be thine, my Saviour, still;
In nothing bad myself allow,
Nor ever show self-will.

4 Preserve, I pray, my heart secure
From ev'ry hurt and stain;
First make it, and then keep it pure,
And shut to all that's vain.

5 If early thou wilt take me hence
O that no harm will be!
Since endless bliss will then commence,
When I shall live with thee.

6 If thou wilt have me longer stay,
In years and stature grow;
Help me to serve thee night and day,
While I am here beolw.

7 Then, after walking in thy ways,
And serving thee in love,
Receive me to thyself in peace,
To sing thy praise above.

791. T. 11.

OUT of love and boundless grace,
Thou hast brought us to a place,
Jesus, where we oft may hear
Of the suff'rings thou didst bear.

2 Be our Shepherd ev'ry day,
That we little lambs ne'er stray;
Whensoe'er we hear thy voice,
To obey may we rejoice.

3 Thanks to thee for all the care
That's bestow'd upon us here;
May we evermore to thee
For thy goodness grateful be.

792. T. 22.

THOU Guardian of thy lambs, behold
Us little ones of thy dear fold;
Take us into thy special care,
Secure our souls from ev'ry snare.

2 Let nothing in our minds take place,
But what comes from thy blood and grace;
May that sink deep into each heart,
And let nought else have any part.

3 Set on our breasts thy Spirit's seal,
Within our hearts thy love reveal,
And our poor souls securely keep
Among thy flock, thy chosen sheep.

793. T. 14.

LOVER of little children! thee,
O Jesus, we adore;
Our kind and loving Saviour be,
Both now and evermore.

2 O take us up into thy arms,
Then we are truly blest;
Thy new-born babes are safe from harms,
While leaning on thy breast.

3 Still as we grow in years, in grace
And wisdom let us grow,
That daily more we thee may praise,
More of thy mercy know.

4 Strong let us in thy grace abide,
But ignorant of ill;
From malice, subtlety and pride
O Lord preserve us still.

794. T. 14.

JESUS, the Lord our Shepherd is,
And did our souls redeem;
Our present and eternal bliss
Are both secur'd in him.

2 His mercy ev'ry sinner claims;
For all his flock he cares;
The sheep he gently leads, the lambs
He in his bosom bears.

3 If unto us our friends are good,
'Twas he their hearts inclin'd;
He bids our fathers give us food,
And makes our mothers kind.

4 Then let us thank him for his grace,
He will not disapprove
Our meanest sacrifice of praise,
For his unbounded love.

5 When children honor Jesus thus,
And thank him for his grace,
Out of the mouths of babes, like us,
His wisdom perfects praise.

795.* T. 22.

JESUS! the children's dearest Friend,
Who dost to all our wants attend,
Thou wast a child, and knowest well,
How we thy helpless children feel.

2 Grant unto us continually
The blessings of thy infancy;
Let us, thro' each succeeding year,
The merits of thy childhood share.

3 Thee, gracious Lord, we now implore,
To manifest thyself still more,
And thus to teach us by degrees
To live a life of happiness.

4 May we thy mind still better know;
May we in grace and knowledge grow,
And learn all that whereby we may
Adorn thy doctrine ev'ry way.

5 O may we ever feel thee near,
And be employ'd in praise and pray'r,
May we in thy blest fellowship
Wake, do our daily work, and sleep.

6 Thus will our infant tongues record
Thy birth and passion, gracious Lord,
That thou who diedst in our stead,
Art God, by whom all things were made.

796.* T. 22.

EMBRACE us in thy tender way,
Dear Lord, and bless us all, we pray.
As thou on earth didst formerly,
When children once were brought to thee.

2 We are baptiz'd into thy death,
And call'd to praise thee with each breath;
Thou bought'st us with thy blood divine,
O take and keep us ever thine!

3 Thy youth unspotted, full of grace,
Teach us all virtue and all praise;
Thou art our pattern, grant that we
In all things may resemble thee.

4 From year to year, while we increase
In stature, may we grow in grace;
In learning and obedience too,
May we thy blessed path pursue.

5 By day and night our steps direct,
And soul and body, Lord, protect
From ev'ry thing that grieveth thee,
Or unto us might hurtful be.

6 Impart to us that needful good,
A heart besprinkled with thy blood,
Wholly devoted unto thee,
For thy soul's bitter agony.

7 That grace upon us all bestow,
Thee more and more by faith to know,
We then the glories of thy name
In grateful accents shall proclaim.

797.* T. 22.

HERE are we children poor and mean,
Corrupt throughout, defil'd by sin,
But by Christ's purifying blood
We're made acceptable to God.

2 May none of us, while we abide
On earth, be weaned from thy side;
But grant that we be found in thee,
And thou in us eternally.

798. T. 22.

I LOVE the Lord, who dy'd for me,
I love his grace divine and free;
I love the scriptures, there I read
Christ loved me and for me bled.

2 I love his tears and suff'rings great,
I love his precious bloody sweat,
I love his blood, were that not spilt
I could not have been freed from guilt.

3 I love to hear that he was slain,
I love his ev'ry grief and pain,
I love to meditate by faith
Upon his meritorious death.

4 I love mount Calv'ry, where his love
Stronger than death itself did prove;
I love to walk his dol'rous way,
I love the grave where Jesus lay.

5 I love his people and their ways,
I love with them to pray and praise;
I love the Father, and the Son,
I love the Spirit he sent down.

6 I love to think the time will come
When I shall be with him at home,
And praise him in eternity:
Then shall my love completed be.

799. T. 22.

I WILL a little pilgrim be,
Resolv'd alone to follow thee,
Thou Lamb of God, who now art gone
Up to thy everlasting throne.

2 I will my heart to thee resign,
Thine only be, O be thou mine!
The world I leave and foolish play,
To happiness to find the way.

3 My lips shall be employ'd to bless
The Lord, who is my Righteousness;
My pleasure only to pursue
His mind, and him my Saviour know.

4 So long I'll pray below to live,
Till I my pardon seal'd receive;
I then, when Jesus calls, shall die,
Or rather live eternally.

800. T. 14.

JESUS, to thee our souls we raise,
And for a blessing look;
May we, assisted by thy grace,
With pleasure learn our book.

2 Give us an humble, active mind,
From sloth and folly free;
Give us a cheerful heart, inclin'd
To useful industry.

3 A faithful memory bestow,
With solid learning's store;
And still, O Lord, as more we know,
Let us obey thee more.

4 Let us things excellent discern,
Hold fast what we approve;
But more than all delight to learn
The lessons of thy love.

801. T. 14.

STILL may we keep the aim in mind,
For which we hither came,
In search of useful learning join'd,
As foll'wers of the Lamb.

2 Daily to Jesus we'll look up,
As soon as we awake,
And for his constant blessing hope
In all we undertake.

3 His meritorious industry,
His labor, toil and sweat,
Shall our support and pattern be,
Him we will imitate.

4 If he his grace on us confer,
We then shall learn apace,
Live to his glory, and declare
Our heav'nly Father's praise.

802. T. 590.

O THOU, before whose Father's face
The children's angels stand,
Grant me, a helpless child, the grace
That thy angelic band
May watch my ways, and guard my bed,
And minister to me,
Till I in death shall bow my head,
And go to live with thee.

803. T. 159.

HOW heart-affecting Christ to see,
Some days before he bled,
Go to Jerus'lem willingly
To suffer in our stead!
When he approach'd, the multitude
Their garments spread and branches strew'd
Crying "Hosanna" to his praise,
With joy and thankfulness.

2 'Twas then the children join'd the rest,
And hail'd him with a song;
With one accord his name confess'd,
Amidst the joyful throng;
O may we little children, now
Attempt the same, and worship too
The Lamb of God, who dy'd for us
Upon the shameful cross.

804. T. 243.

THE holy child Jesus,
Our God and our Saviour,
Who died to release us,
We'll worship for ever,
God's holy Lamb,—the Lord's his name.

2 In liveliest manner
O let us before him
With joy sing hosanna,
And praise and adore him;
Our childlike cries—he'll not despise.

3 Come then, let us follow
Our Master with praises;
His name let us hallow,
Whose blood us releases:
O Christ, to thee—all glory be!

4 Hosanna! Hosanna!
Thou Son of king David:
Hosanna! Hosanna!
For thou hast us saved:
For ever reign—thou Lamb once slain!

805. T. 39.

LORD Jesus, we bless thee that thou wast a child,
And hast us thereby unto God reconcil'd:
We thank thee for suff'ring and dying in pain,
For thy being bury'd and rising again.

2 We thank thee, that thou wilt the children permit
To offer their praises and songs at thy feet;
That thou, Lord, their pray'rs art inclined to hear,
And always to help them and save them art near.

3 Thou wilt be our Saviour, Redeemer and Friend,
Grant we may abide in thy love to the end:
O render us truly obedient to thee,
That we thy dear children for ever may be.

806. T. 39.

WHEREIN is for children true bliss to be found?
When by Jesus Christ as his sheep they are own'd,
In him they find pasture while here they remain,
And joys everlasting in heaven obtain.

2 We sing and we hear, how our Maker came down
To earth, and for us left his heavenly throne,
Assuming our nature became a poor child,
And us by his suff'rings to God reconcil'd.

3 O myst'ry of godliness! wonder of grace!
May we without ceasing adore him and praise;
May all of us know what a Saviour we have,
Yea love him sincerely, and in him believe.

4 We now, with the angels, unite to declare
The praises of him, who our sorrows did bear,
With hearts and with voices exalting the Lamb,
Who dy'd on the cross our poor souls to redeem.

807. T. 39.

DEAR children, assembled to hear of the Lord,
You're here to be taught by his Spirit and word;
O think what great favors on you are conferr'd!
A. For this may his name by us all be rever'd.

2 The Father in heav'n us as children will own,
And we are beloved by Jesus, his Son,
The spirit of truth will instruct us to pray,
And he will direct us throughout our whole way.

3 Ah! should not the mercies you daily do prove
Excite you our Saviour to praise and to love?
A. Yes, we are desirous to value his grace,
To love and adore him, and live to his praise.

4 O merciful Saviour, so grant it to be,
Nor suffer us ever to wander from thee;
We're poor little children, preserve us, we pray,
And may we our love by obedience display.

808.* T. 14.

HAPPY the children who betimes
Have learn'd to know the Lord!
Who, thro' his grace, escape the crimes
Forbidden in his word;

2 Who early, by a living faith,
Have deep foundation laid
In Jesus' meritorious death;
Such need not be afraid.

3 Should they be early hence remov'd,
He will their souls receive;
For they who Jesus here have lov'd
With him shall ever live.

809. T. 14

HAPPY the children who are gone
To Jesus Christ in peace!
Who stand around his glorious throne,
Clad in his righteousness.

2 The Saviour whom they lov'd when here,
Hath wip'd their tears away;
They never more can grieve or fear,
Or sin, or go astray.

3 In ceaseless happiness they view
Our Saviour's smiling face;
That face once bruis'd, in which below
Men saw no comeliness.

4 Methinks I hear them joyful sing,
(Ten thousands do the same:)
Salvation to th' immortal King!
To God and to the Lamb!

5 O that I may so favor'd be,
With them above to join:
O that, like them, I Christ may see,
And he be ever mine.

6 Grant me but this, thou great High-Priest;
And when I'm here no more,
Convey me safe to endless rest,
Where thou art gone before.

810. T. 587.

THE child sweetly rests,
Whom nothing molests,
Received in mercy among the Lamb's guests.

2 He ne'er shall weep more,
His sighing is o'er,
His travel and dangers, he's got safe on shore.

3 The body is dead,
And in the grave laid,
But shall, again raised, to life be convey'd.

4 The spirit is gone
In peace to God's throne,
To praise God our Saviour, where we shall be soon.

5 He sings now above,
Made perfect in love,
And never, O never, he thence shall remove.

6 He rests now in peace,
Beholds the Lord's face,
Hath happily finish'd thus early his race.

7 For that blessed day
We earnestly pray,
Lord Jesus, come quickly, and make no delay!

811. T. 14.

TO thee, almighty God, to thee
Ourselves we now resign,
'Twill please us to look back, and see
We were in childhood thine.

2 Let the sweet work of pray'r and praise
Employ our infant breath,
Thus we're prepar'd for length of days,
Or fit for early death.

B. *For Boys.*

812.* T. 164.

BELOVED youths, if 'tis your aim
To be like Christ, your Saviour,
And to extol his saving name
In word and in behavior,
With an obedient mind
Be to his will resign'd,
He by his blood will wash you clean,
And free you from the pow'r of sin.

2 O might it be our hearts' delight,
Amidst his flock with pleasure
T' obey him, walk as in his sight,
And serve him in our measure,
For ev'ry thing that's good
And just flows from his blood;
A mind that's virtuous, chaste, unstain'd,
May be by faith in him obtain'd.

3 Yea, an obedient, simple mind,
Faithful in ev'ry station,
To true humility inclin'd,
And perfect resignation,
The blest effect will prove
Of that unfeigned love
To Christ, which is produc'd by faith
In him, and his atoning death.

813.* T. 37.

WOULD our youth grow in grace,
Wisdom, and favor;
As truly was the case
With Christ, our Saviour:
Let them continually
View him in spirit,
To them he will apply
His precious merit.

2 When once the sin-sick soul
For grace hath panted,
By Christ we're render'd whole,
To us is granted,
That we a heav'nly life
May here be leading;
In union with our Lord
Each step proceeding.

3 He who without delay
To Jesus turneth,
With confidence doth pray,
And humbly mourneth,
Doth certainly receive
(O boundless favor!)
Forgiveness of his sins
From Christ our Saviour.

4 If we, with uprightness,
'Fore him discover
Our wants; then our distress
Will soon be over;
He'll cure most graciously
Our worst diseases,
And fill us constantly
With thanks and praises.

814. T. 23.

JESUS hath procur'd salvation
For mankind in ev'ry station:
Ev'ry youth who loves our Saviour
Imitates his chaste behavior.

2 If we, when by guilt oppressed,
Look to Christ, our Pattern blessed,
He will graciously direct us,
And from ev'ry sin protect us.

815. T. 22.

DEAR youths, O that ye all but knew
How Jesus burns in love to you,
Is deeply mov'd by your distress,
And pities your great sinfulness!

2 His ears are open night and day,
He hears whene'er to him you pray:
He watcheth closely all you do,
Yea, all your thoughts and reas'nings too.

3 Whene'er a youth bemoans his case,
And weeps to him for saving grace,
He's wash'd in Jesus' precious blood,
And made a happy child of God.

4 Oh if your hearts but upright are,
Not one among you need despair;
Your sinfulness is great 'tis true,
But grace can conquer sin in you.

816. T. 185.

ALL of us, we know, not one excepted,
Are by nature, vile and base;
If we feel it not that we're corrupted
And quite spoil'd, the worse our case;
But doth sin, in thought or deed committed,
Make us mourn and pray to be acquitted,
We, because the Lamb was slain,
Pardon in his blood may gain.

817.* T. 79.

MIGHT we unto our Saviour
Lift up our hearts with fervor,
Each day, and pray for grace
T' obtain a true sensation
Of Jesus' great salvation,
And of our fall and sinfulness!

818.* T. 166.

O MIGHT we all Christ's name confess
In our whole conversation,
And each one through our Saviour's grace,
Be faithful in his station;
Might in our very looks be seen
That we, thro Jesus' merit,
Are humble, steady, chaste and clean,
And guided by his Spirit!

819. T. 58.

WHAT glorious pattern for the heart and mind,
O Jesus, doth each true believer find
In thy words and actions, and whole behavior!
We pray thee, grant unto our youth the favor
To follow thee.

C. *For unmarried Men.*

820. T. 590.

HOW shall a young man cleanse his way?
By foll'wing close his word
Who once on earth a young man was,
Jesus, our God and Lord:
His word is spirit, and is pow'r;
True life doth flow from him;
Our food his sacred flesh, our drink
His blood, that healing stream.

2 We now no longer need remain
Fast bound in chains of sin;
Whoe'er believes, is free indeed,
And by his word made clean:
Since Jesus on th' accursed cross
The pow'r of sin did quell,
When sin disorders us, we look
To him, and soon grow well.

3 Ye chosen people of the Lord,
Which Jesus' pow'r displays,
If in obedience to his word
You're render'd clean through grace;
His dying love be yet impress'd
More clearly on each heart!
And whether you're at work or rest,
To love him be your part!

4 Ye purchas'd souls, Christ's happy flock,
Be to his will resign'd,
And gladly offer up to him
Your body, soul and mind.
O! if the bleeding Lamb of God,
Who dy'd us to redeem,
But calls, who can his call withstand!
Who would not follow him!

821.* T. 217.

BRETHREN, by Jesus Christ belov'd,
First with attention be it weighed,
Whether his mind ours always prov'd,
And how our conduct this displayed;
Whether we have in thought and word,
Shown forth the praises of our Lord;
If countless gifts from him received
So undeserv'd, have this achieved,
That in the world we know of none
To cheer our hearts, but him alone;

2 O let us all press, from this day,
Towards the mark before us placed:
With tears beseech him, that he may
Imprint in us his image blessed;
To look to him be our employ,
That soul and body in him joy;
May his death's pow'r us so replenish,
That sin and its allurements vanish;
In joy and pain we then shall find
In him alone true peace of mind.

822. T. 185.

BRETHREN, 'tis but meet to render praises
To Immanuel, our Lord;
Who to bless his children never ceases,
Since to favor they're restor'd;
'Midst a sense of our own imperfection,
We can magnify that free election
Of his grace, by which we stand
'Mongst his flock, his chosen band.

2 Yes, we feel indeed our own demerit
And our imperfections great;
Had we not been led by Jesus' Spirit,
Never could we thus have met:
We deserv'd eternal condemnation,
But his death procured our salvation:
And since we've experienc'd this,
We're determin'd to be his.

823.* T. 166.

DEAR brethren, let us take to heart
The teaching of the Spirit;
He'll ev'ry grace to us impart,
Which Jesus Christ did merit;
Who, by all he hath done and said
In his humiliation,
Hath boundless blessings merited,
And sanctify'd our station.

824. T. 45.

THEE God's own Son—with joy we own
To be our dearest Brother;
Heav'n and earth do not afford
Like to thee another.

2 But, Oh! might we—such brethren be,
Of whom thou'rt not ashamed;
Might, by all we do, thy grace
Loudly be proclaimed.

825.* T. 166.

JESUS, we now devote to thee
Our body, soul, and spirit,
Since thou to us prosperity
Impartest thro' thy merit.
In thought and deed we wish to be
Like thee, that each who sees us
May in us some resemblance see,
Of our great Pattern, Jesus.

826. T. 56.

DEAREST brethren :||: be this our desire
That our Saviour :||: us with love inspire,
By his cross, his wounds and pain
May we all true freedom gain,
Then to serve him :||: he'll of us require.

2 Chains of darkness, :||: wherewith men are bound,
Now are broken, :||: and a help is found;
They who gladly would be free
May by Christ deliver'd be;
This to sinners :||: is a joyful sound.

3 Nought but blessings :||: he for us intends
And his mercy :||: never, never ends;
Let us look unto the cross,
Where he dy'd to ransom us,
On that off'ring :||: faith alone depends.

4 As thy chosen, :||: blood-bought property,
We'll know nothing, :||: slaughter'd Lamb, but thee;
Thou shalt be our Lord and God,
And redemption in thy blood
Shall our doctrine :||: to all nations be.

827. T. 97.

YE brethren, sav'd by Jesus' blood!
Let us prepare to serve our God,
Remember our Redeemer's toil,
Supply our lamps of faith with oil;
To him devote ourselves each day anew
With soul and body, for they are his due.

2 Then let us rise and serve the Lord,
Go when he calls, proclaim the word
Of his atonement far and near,
Count not our lives for him too dear,
Declare to negros, savages and slaves,
That Jesus' blood the vilest sinners saves.

828. T. 185.

TO thy brethren ever be propitious,
In our hearts thy love reveal.
Grant that we may follow thee, Lord Jesus;
Fill our souls with ardent zeal,
To proclaim to many a heathen nation
Thy atoning death for our salvation:
Grant us, Jesus, to increase
Both in number and in grace.

D. *For Girls.*

829.* T. 14.

OUR Lord and Saviour doth attend
To all our tears and sighs,
And us his maidens will defend
From vain perplexities.

2 Blest Mary, with a cheerful voice,
To all around declar'd:
"In God my Saviour I rejoice,
For he my sighs hath heard.

3 "The Lord hath highly favor'd me;
His handmaid's low estate
He hath regarded graciously,
The poor he doth elate."

4 Thus all who wait upon the Lord,
And seek for peace and rest,
In him, according to his word,
Shall be consol'd and blest.

5 We're poor and needy; but thro' grace,
His Spirit teacheth us
To look, with all our sinfulness,
In faith to Jesus' cross.

6 When simply we obey his voice,
And to our Lord appeal,
In God our Saviour we rejoice,
Since pard'ning grace we feel.

7 Most gracious Saviour! to confide
In thee, O grant us grace;
Preserve us all from self and pride,
That bane of happiness.

8 Meekness, and true humility
Unto us all impart;
Yea, by thy merits sanctify
And render pure each heart.

830. T. 16.

BLESS'D are they whose meditation
Is directed oft by faith
To their Saviour's incarnation,
Human life and painful death.

2 Bless'd are they, who as poor sinners
Gain from Jesus life and grace;
Tho' they be but young beginners,
And by nature vile and base.

3 Blessed, who are ever ready
Him to follow cheerfully,
Who took, in a virgin's body,
For our sake, humanity.

4 Blessed they, who live to Jesus,
Who to him their hearts devote,
Wishing to show forth his praises;
Truly blessed is their lot!

831.* T. 168.

UNTO thee, most gracious Saviour,
We ourselves anew commend!
Look on us in grace and favor,
To our pray'rs and wants attend;
Grant us all a tender feeling
Of thy love and gracious dealing,
That our hearts may truly be
Fill'd with fervent love to thee.

2 This alone can keep us steady
In the simple path of grace,
And when any thing seems ready
To disturb our happiness,
Lord, in mercy us deliver,
Yea protect and keep us ever
From the world and sin secure,
And in soul and body pure!

832. T. 185.

WHEN bemoaning our undone condition,
Weeping for redeeming grace,
We with heart-felt and sincere contrition
Pant for peace and happiness,
Which is only found by faith in Jesus,
Who was slain, from sorrow to release us,
We find then most certainly
Life, and true felicity.

2 Then, renew'd by grace, the heart desireth
To be Jesus' property;
Yea his dying love our souls inspireth
Him to love most fervently;
We remain his maidens poor and needy,
Yet to give him joy are ever ready,
Thinking always how we may
Love unfeign'd to him display.

833. T. 56.

O BE mindful :||: of us gracious Lord,
'Midst our weakness :||: aid to us afford;
Human frailty well thou know'st;
We of nothing else can boast
But the blessings :||: which thy death procur'd.

2 Lord, assist us :||: in the needful hour,
In temptation :||: grant us help and pow'r;
We in thee alone confide,
In this world be thou our Guide,
Keep us humble, :||: and in spirit poor.

3 From each rival :||: O deliver us,
Make us willing :||: to take up our cross;
Our diseases kindly heal;
To our hearts thy love reveal;
All besides thee :||: may we count but dross.

834. T. 168.

BLESSED are we, if believing
In the Lord our Righteousness,
And in lowliness receiving
From his fulness grace for grace;
When we find in him salvation,
Happiness and consolation,
And obey the Shepherd's voice;
Then we truly can rejoice.

2 Tho' we feel that soul and body
Are corrupt and void of good,
Yet the Lord is ever ready
To apply his cleansing blood;
With our weaknesses he beareth,
All our pray'rs he kindly heareth,
And we daily may increase
In his knowledge and in grace.

E. *For unmarried Women.*

835.* T. 185.

WOULD you know the grace and peace enjoyed
By a child of God, thro' faith;
See a virgin, who alone employed
With her Saviour and his death,
Vanity and worldly ways despiseth,
While the converse with her Lord she prizeth,
And thus, on this side the grave,
Foretaste sweet of heav'n may have.

2 Therefore, this be our concern for ever,
Since we're with this knowledge blest,
To have our eternal Bridegroom's favor,
Then we find true peace and rest;
But indeed it is from each expected,
That the heart be by his grace directed,
Nor have any other aim,
Than to love the slaughter'd Lamb.

3 Happy they who feel the healing power
Of Christ's blood in ev'ry case!
May we follow him, and seek each hour
To preserve ourselves thro' grace;
May the virtue of our Saviour's passion,
Sanctify our walk and conversation;
We ourselves to him commend,
May his aim with us be gain'd.

836.* T. 583.

WE virgins, who enjoy our Saviour's grace, [express:
Are happier far than words can e'er
Jesus, the Bridegroom of our souls, supplies
Our wants, and soul and body sanctifies.

2 His love produceth love; constrain'd thereby,
Our sole intention is to yield him joy.
When in our hearts his love is shed abroad, [God.
We then, like Mary, favor find with

3 Lord, may thy love with gratitude inspire
Our souls, and to thy name be our desire!
We thee intreat to form us to thy praise,
And all that's carnal wholly to erase.

4 If we thy rich forgiveness daily prove,
This will unite us, Lord, to thee in love,
O make us all devoted unto thee;
Let us thy chaste and faithful virgins be.

837. T. 16.

HAPPY they, who oft for Jesus
Weep, from need as well as love,
They experience him propitious,
And his favor richly prove.

2 Happy they, who are excited,
Him to follow ev'ry where,
And are with his ways delighted,
He to such is truly dear.

3 Happy is each virgin's station
Whom he kindly owns as his,
And, who counts his great salvation
As her highest good and bliss.

4 Happy she, who finds in Jesus
All her wishes satisfy'd;
Ah, to her how dear and precious
Is that Friend who for her dy'd!

838. T. 16.

BLEST are they, who human nature
Feel as vile, corrupt and base,
But who know each fallen creature
May be heal'd by Jesus' grace.

2 Mourning souls are truly blessed,
They that seek will surely find;
Jesus comforts the distressed,
To the contrite he is kind.

3 Christ the Bread, that came from hea-
Doth the hungry soul revive, [ven,
Unto those who thirst, is given
Water from the well of life.

4 Blest are they, who, thro' his favor,
Are in heart here purify'd;
They shall once behold our Saviour
Who by faith in him abide.

5 Blest are they, who in his merits
Have a share, tho' here despis'd,
All is theirs; what flesh inherits
They renounce, he's only priz'd.

6 Blest are they, who, foll'wing Jesus,
Virgins are in deed and truth;
They have cause to give him praises;
Both the aged and the youth.

839. T. 22.

THE source, whence ev'ry sin doth spring,
Is that we turn from Christ our King;
And hence it is, the giddy eye
Imagines bliss in vanity:

2 Pleasure in things producing smart,
And cleanness in an impure heart;
Knowledge in blindest ignorance,
And plenty in deep indigence;

3 We virgins have great cause to praise
Thee, Lord, and grateful songs to raise,
That, from the world's delusion free,
We wish to be made clean by thee;

4 That they, who weep because of sin,
May be absolv'd and washed clean;
Since thou wast in the flesh reveal'd,
That by thy stripes we might be heal'd.

840. T. 56.

WE thy virgins :||: claim thy special care,
O preserve us, :||: Lord, from ev'ry snare;
May our hearts and senses be
Fix'd, in true simplicity,
On the suff'rings :||: thou for us didst bear.

2 Us deliver :||: from the world and sin,
Let thy Spirit :||: rule alone within,
Ev'ry vain desire control,
And in spirit, body, soul,
Sanctify us :||: by thy grace divine.

3 In temptation :||: may we firmly stand,
Ever watchful :||: as thou dost command:
Without thee we nought can do,
Strengthen and support us too
In all trials, :||: by thy mighty hand.

4 Fix thy temple :||: Saviour in each breast,
Undisturbed :||: be our peace and rest!
Let us on thy merits feed,
In the path of grace proceed,
Be, in union :||: with thee, ever blest.

841. T. 585.

WE thy virgins, Lord, implore thee:
Let us, cleans'd and purify'd,
Walk in grace and truth before thee,
And in thee, our Lord, abide;
Sanctified :||:
Both in body and in mind.

2 Unto us thy name's sweet savor
Is as ointment poured forth;
In thine eyes we have found favor,
Tho' deprav'd and void of worth;
And thy banner :||:
Over us is love divine.

3 Now the conflict is decided,
We count all things else but loss,
What with thee our hearts divided
Now is nailed to thy cross,
Nought can please us :||:
But the wounded Lamb of God.

4 We will dwell on Calv'ry's mountain,
Where the flocks of Zion feed;
Oft resort unto the fountain,
Open'd when the Lord did bleed,
Thence deriving :||:
Grace, and life, and holiness.

5 There with trimmed lamps we'll tarry,
Till the Lord comes from on high,
Watch in pray'r and ne'er be weary,
But await the midnight cry:
Haste to meet him, :||:
Lo! the Bridegroom draweth nigh.

6 On that day of consummation,
May we sinners mercy find,
Saved with complete salvation,
And not one be left behind,
As wise virgins :||:
May we then before thee stand!

842. T. 26.

THY virgins, Lord, 'fore thee appear,
Conscious of their depravity,
Yet longing to be heal'd by thee;
Each mourning sinner deign to cheer.

2 From all false love cleanse ev'ry soul,
And us with sacred love inspire,
O quench in us each base desire,
And bear the sway without control.

3 In mutual love and harmony,
Our virgin-cov'nant we renew,
Say thou in grace Amen thereto;
We give our hearts and hands to thee.

843. T. 22.

THOU Bridegroom of the soul! behold
This part of thy beloved fold;
Thy virgins, who before thee met
Here to perceive thy presence wait.

2 Give us, O Lord, to feel thy peace,
And let the sanctifying grace
Which flows from thy humanity,
Make us well-pleasing unto thee.

3 O may we feel thy healing pow'r
And influence, ev'ry day and hour;
Thus all thy mercies which we prove,
Will us excite to praise and love.

F. *For married People.*

844. T. 22.

LORD, who ordain'dst the married state,
When thou didst man at first create,
Thou who thy body's Saviour art,
To all of us thy grace impart.

2 The husbands sanctify and bless,
Thy mind upon their hearts impress,
Teach them thy Spirit to obey
In all they do, we humble pray.

3 Unto the wives that grace dispense,
To cleave to thee with confidence,
Grant they may love thee fervently,
And walk in true humility.

4 Wisdom and faithfulness afford,
To train our children, gracious Lord,
That in thy knowledge they may grow,
Themselves & thee their Saviour know.

5 Lord Jesus! may each married pair
In all their walk thy praise declare;
O may their rule in all things be,
The union of thy church with thee.

845. T. 159.

THE love which Jesus Christ displays
Towards the church, his bride,
None can describe, it far outweighs
All other love beside:
Believing husbands are to prove,
By holy and unfeigned love
Towards their wives, that they indeed
Resemble Christ our Head.

2 The church submits to Christ, her Lord;
"Thy will be done," we pray:
This teacheth wives, who love God's [word
With meekness to obey;
Adorned with humility
They aid their husbands willingly;
Are clothed with the beauteous dress
Of Jesus' righteousness.

846. T. 590.

WE humbly thee adore, O Lord,
For thy unbounded grace;
Astonish'd, in thy sacred word
Thy love divine we trace:
Thou hast the church in love redeem'd,
Thou gav'st thyself for us;
We know we are by thee esteem'd,
When we behold thy cross.

2 Grant unto ev'ry married pair,
By chaste unfeigned love,
By meekness, patience, faith and pray'r,
And all we do to prove,
That we, united unto thee,
Are truly one in heart;
Thus we shall live eternally
With thee, and never part.

847. T. 580.

TO marry, led by fleshly schemes,
And poison'd nature's foolish dreams,
Christians a curse esteem;
They wish to marry in the Lord,
Direct their marriage by his word,
And in this state to live to him.

848. T. 166.

TO be a happy married pair,
Approv'd by Jesus in their course,
Comes not from nature e'er so fair,
But love to him must be the source;
Good sense and prudence, with a mind
To lead a virtuous life, is far
From answering God's purpose kind,
For which we all ordained are.

2 His Spirit teacheth us to know,
That we are sinners vile and base,
And Jesus doth on us bestow
Remission of our sins, thro' grace:
Thus we in all things richly prove
The Shepherd's care, and faithfulness,
And, actuated by his love, [praise.
In our whole walk show forth his

849. T. 341.

O MAY our married state,
In duties small and great,
In relations far and near,
In its trials numberless,
In all cases whatsoe'er,
Serve Christ's holy name to bless.

2 May we, by Jesus' love
Constrained, clearly prove,
That we are his flock indeed,
Living branches in the Vine,
Heav'nly plants, a holy seed,
Lights who in Christ's image shine!

850. T. 16.

HEAD of thy blest congregation,
Look on ev'ry married pair,
Be our strength and our salvation,
Keep us from all needless care.

2 For our sake, most gracious Saviour,
Thou thy life and blood hast spent;
May we now in our behavior
Thee and thy church represent.

3 No spoil'd creature had been able
E'er to guide his steps aright
In this state so venerable,
Or to act as in thy sight;

4 Hadst thou not life and salvation
By thy suff'rings for us gain'd,
And thereby sanctification
For the married state obtain'd.

5 Bless, O Lord, thy married people,
In thy blood, O wash us clean;
Help us, for we're weak and feeble,
And preserve us from all sin.

851. T. 114.

HEAD of thy church! thy fatherly correction
We have deserv'd: but pardon now impart,
Give each of us a clean and docile heart;
O grant that we may weigh with due reflection
The duties of the holy married state,
While we for thy instruction humbly wait.

852.* T. 9.

LOOK on ev'ry married pair,
Jesus! with compassion,
Grant that each may richly share
In thy great salvation.

2 Be thou with us, then indeed
We shall lack no blessing,
But with thee, O Christ, proceed,
To meet joys unceasing.

3 O may we in all we do
Follow thy direction;
We commend ourselves anew
To thy kind protection.

4 Let our children, gracious Lord,
Share with us thy favor,
Grant they may be a reward
Of thy death for ever.

853. T. 22.

O LORD, who number'st all our days,
Who guardest us in all our ways,
In whom we live, and move, and are,
Who know'st our wants, and hearest pray'r;

2 To this thy handmaid grant thy peace,
Who comes to offer thanks and praise
To thee, her faithful cov'nant-God,
For the support thou hast bestow'd.

3 Thy pow'rful aid thou, gracious Lord,
In travail didst to her afford;
Her sorrows now are turn'd to praise,
Her sighs and tears to grateful lays.

4 O Shepherd of thy chosen sheep!
Both child and mother bless and keep,
May they enjoy in their degree
The fruits of thy humanity.

5 Endow the parents with thy love,
And give them wisdom from above
To educate this child for thee,
As thy redeemed property.

6 Grant us, and all our children, grace,
So here on earth to run our race,
That we in heav'n may meet, and sing
Eternal praise to thee, our King.

854. T. 581.

PARENTS, weigh before the Lord
The importance of your state;
Learn from his most holy word,
Your whole walk to regulate,
That each to his family
May a blessed pattern be!

2 All your children are his own,
He hath bought them with his blood!
Unto him their souls are known,
Full of sin and void of good!
Yet he saith most graciously,
"Suffer them to come to me!"

3 'Tis by you they should be led
In the way that leads to bliss;
Grace is not inherited
As a worldly fortune is,
'Tis free mercy, we must own,
And the gift of God alone.

4 In this vain and wretched world
Children are expos'd and try'd;
Many are to ruin hurl'd,
Few in Jesus Christ abide;
And no human prudence can
Save the soul of fallen man.

5 Here's a task, may parents think,
Far beyond the reach of art;
But let not your courage sink,
Grace and wisdom he'll impart:
Your sincere endeavors bless,
Hear your pray'rs, and grant success.

6 Hear, O Lord, a parent's pray'r,
Let my tears prevail 'fore thee!
How should I in heav'n appear,
If my child were not with me!
Therefore thou my steps direct,
Lest my duty I neglect.

7 In thy grace my children keep,
That when once, on that great day,
Thou shalt come to seek thy sheep,
I may gladly to thee say:
"Here am I, thro' mercy free,
And each child thou gavest me!"

855. T. 166.

OUR children, gracious Lord and God,
With fervor we to thee commend,
Thou hast redeem'd them by thy blood;
They are by thee to bliss ordain'd.
Kind Shepherd, take each little lam.
Into thy faithful arms of love;
Cause them to know thy saving name,
And thy redeeming grace to prove.

2 On us, their parents, grace bestow,
That we, with care and faithfulness,
May lead them thee, our Lord to know,
T' obey thy word, and seek thy face.
Teach us the duties of our state,
To love each other heartily,
Our children so to educate
That they may love and follow thee.

856. T. 83.

IN this world, so full of snares,
Take our children in thy keeping;
Hear the parents' sighs and pray'rs,
When for them before thee weeping:
Mercy for our children we,
Gracious Lord, implore of thee.

857. T. 586.

MOST holy Lord, mankind's Creator,
Who, to redeem us by thy death,
Assumedst feeble human nature,
We call on thee in humble faith:
O hear our fervent supplication,
Let all our children thy salvation,
Thy tender love and care,
In largest measure share;
For thine they are.

G. *For Widowers.*

858. T. 22.

IN God, the mighty Lord of hosts,
A happy wid'wer gladly boasts;
No trials need oppress the mind,
For we in Christ may comfort find.

2 Whene'er by faith our Lord we see
Clothed with frail humanity,
Bearing our griefs and sicknesses,
This doth alleviate all distress.

3 He is our Saviour and High-Priest,
Who, when we suffer in the least,
Sustains us by his pow'r and grace,
And in each hard and trying case.

...pports us ev'ry day,
...fort, Help and Stay;
...his boundless love and pow'r
...our happy dying hour.

859.* T. 22.

JESUS, accept the thanks and praise,
We wid'wers offer for the grace
Which thou so richly hast display'd
Unto us, as the church's Head.

2 Grant that we all, with heart and voice,
In thee, our Saviour, may rejoice;
Let us, in our sabbatic state,
The joys of heav'n anticipate.

3 Fill us with peace, and joy and love,
And our support in trials prove;
When weaknesses of age appear,
Keep thou our mind and senses clear.

4 This be our aim on earth, thy will
To seek in all things to fulfil;
And, when thou call'st, prepar'd to be
To leave this world and go to thee.

5 Then, at the end of all distress,
We shall depart to thee in peace:
Meanwhile thy coming we await,
Like Simeon, ready thee to meet.

860. T. 14.

JESUS, our Helper in all need,
And comfort in distress,
Thou art the wid'wer's only Stay
And Hope in loneliness.

2 A foretaste of eternal joys,
O Lord, to us dispense,
And 'midst our weakness bear us up,
Till we are called hence.

861. T. 167.

THEY who for true consolation,
Like old Simeon, humbly wait,
Shall behold the Lord's salvation,
Then their joy will be complete.
May we follow his example,
Trusting in God's promises,
Wait for Jesus in his temple,
Daily offer pray'r and praise.

862. T. 11.

ON our God we will rely;
Boldly unto him draw nigh;
And the Lord our Righteousness
Both with hearts and voices bless.

2 We can from experience trace,
That, in ev'ry trying case,
Jesus truly can impart
Joy and comfort to the heart.

3 May we fix the eye of faith
On our Lord's atoning death,
Till we shall in heav'nly bliss
See our Saviour as he is.

H. For Widows.

863. T. 22.

'TIS true the lonely widow'd state
With various trials is replete,
But Christ, the widow's faithful Friend,
Will guide us safely to the end.

2 He saith to us repeatedly:
"Cast all your burden upon me,
For I in all things kindly care
For you, and in your troubles share."

3 Therefore whate'er our trials be,
Or weaknesses, or poverty,
Sickness of body, soul's distress,
Or sorrows which we can't express;

4 Our comfort is, he knows and feels
Whate'er his needy children ails;
He sympathizeth with the weak,
Relieves the poor, and heals the sick.

5 He graciously regards our pray'rs,
And counteth all our sighs and tears;
Afflictions, whether small or great,
His comforts can alleviate.

6 Might we, like Anna persevere,
By day and night, in constant pray'r,
And thus for his appearing wait,
In joyful hope the Lord to meet.

864.* T. 22.

GOD will the widows ne'er forsake,
To him we may our refuge take,
And on his care and faithfulness
Our whole dependence firmly place.

2 A widow, who her son belov'd
With tears bemoan'd, his pity mov'd;
His mother he did recommend,
When on the cross, to John, his friend.

3 Widows are objects of his care,
Since scripture plainly doth declare,
That to the church this charge he gave,
Widows to honor and relieve.

4 To Christ, O may we closely cleave,
And in communion with him live;
To love the Lord, be our first care,
The next, to serve his people here.

5 Till we, who here must often weep,
In heav'n eternal joys shall reap;
Till he shall say to us, "Ye blest,
Enter into my joy and rest."

865. T. 185.

WE with joy confess, beloved Saviour,
Thee, the widow's special Friend,
We are objects of thy love and favor:
Thou on us thy life didst spend;
Thou with more than husband's love dost lead us,
Thy all-bounteous hand doth daily feed us;
All our wants thou dost supply;
Thus our cruise is never dry.

2 Thou hast promis'd for our consolation,
That we shall not come behind
In the gifts, which to thy congregation
Thou dispensest, of each kind;
May we, to thy service dedicated,
And for thee our Bridegroom decorated,
For thy blest appearing wait;
Then our bliss will be complete.

866. T. 74.

CHRIST is the widow's Friend,
Our cause he doth defend,
All our complaints he hears,
And listens to our pray'rs,
His care and faithfulness
We prove in ev'ry case.

2 The feeble he makes strong,
With us he beareth long,
On him the weak can lean,
The youthful he keeps clean;
Each may in him confide
Whate'er may them betide.

867. T. 74.

O LORD, the widow's Friend,
To us thy Spirit send,
Be in our husbands' place,
Revive us with thy grace,
Give us whate'er we need
Widows to be indeed.

868. T. 121.

BEHOLD us widows here,
Lord Jesus, hear our pray'r:
Fill our hearts with gladness,
O wipe away each tear,
Dispelling all our sadness;
Make thy face to shine
On us, we are thine.

869. T. 184.

THOU art our comfort in all cases,
Jesus, to thee O may we cleave!
For all thy mercies give thee praises,
In happy union with thee live!
Whene'er we call, thou, Lord, wilt hear us,
And blessings on us all bestow,
Yea for that awful time prepare us,
When we in peace to thee shall go.

2 The needy share thy consolation,
The poor are objects of thy love,
Thou on the weakly hast compassion,
Thy sure support the aged prove:
Thou helpest us in our distresses,
Suppliest kindly all our wants;
We'll cast each burden that oppresses
On thee, who hearest our complaints.

870. T. 168.

'MIDST the trials we experience,
Let us not give way to fears,
But possess our souls in patience,
While here in this vale of tears;
Wean'd thereby from things terrestrial,
Let us look for joys celestial,
Waiting for that time, when we
From all sorrow shall be free.

2 Meanwhile God the holy Spirit
Is our pledge of joys to come,
Of the bliss we shall inherit
When above with Christ at home;
O! this blessed meditation
Yields us solid consolation,
That we shall, when time is o'er,
With the Lord be evermore!

XXXVII. Hymns for sundry Occasions.

A. *For the New Year.*

871.* T. 10.

YEAR after year commenceth,
And as our life advanceth
We, strength from Christ deriving,
Each year by faith are thriving.

2 As, in tempestuous weather,
A kind and tender mother
Her babe from harm protecteth,
And safely home conducteth;

3 So shelters Christ our Saviour
His children by his favor,
And proves in each temptation
Their refuge and salvation.

4 Lord, grant thy benediction
To ev'ry thought and action;
On youth and age declining,
Thou Sun of grace be shining.

5 O keep our souls and senses
Under the influences
Of thy most holy Spirit,
Until we heav'n inherit.

6 O God of our salvation,
Withhold no kind donation
From us, but let us savor
In this new year thy favor.

872. T. 14.

AGAIN another fleeting year
Of my short life is past;
I cannot long continue here,
And this may be my last.

2 Much of my dubious life is gone,
Nor will return again;
And swift my passing moments run,
The few that yet remain.

3 Now a new scene of time begins,
Pursue the way to heav'n;
Seek pardon of thy former sins,
By Christ it will be giv'n.

4 Devoutly yield thyself to God,
And on his grace depend;
Unweary'd walk the heav'nly road,
Nor doubt a happy end.

873. T. 97.

WHO can rehearse, most gracious Lord,
The mercy which thou dost afford
Unto thy people ev'ry year?
We thy poor congregation here [more,
Desire to thank and praise thee ever-
And humbly in the dust thy name adore.

2 For we, unworthy as we are,
Enjoy'd the faithful Shepherd's care;
Thou always comfort didst impart
To ev'ry needy contrite heart;
Thou didst to us thy dying love display,
And wast our help and refuge ev'ry day.

3 The hearing of thy precious word,
Thy gracious presence, holy Lord,
Have cheer'd our hearts abundantly,
When met in fellowship 'fore thee:
But, O what blessings were on us be-
stow'd [blood!
When we enjoy'd thy body and thy

4 Lord Jesus we would fain express
To thee our cordial thankfulness,
For all thy boundless love and grace;
But how imperfect are our lays! [give,
O take our hearts, to thee ourselves we
In future more unto thy praise to live.

874. T. 166.

LORD Jesus, 'mongst thy flock appear,
And thy poor congregation bless;
We're met to close another year,
Accept the thanks our hearts express.
We are not able to record
The boundless favors we have prov'd,
They show that we, most gracious Lord,
'Midst our defects, by thee are lov'd.

875. T. 184.

THEE we approach, most gracious Saviour!
We pray thee, mark our sighs and tears,
Accept our thanks for all thy favor,
Bestow'd on us these many years;
We conscious are of our transgression,
Ah! cleanse us with thy precious blood,
Seal with thy pardon our confession,
Thine are we, and thou art our God.

2 Thou God of mercy! thy salvation
Remain'd throughout this year our stay;
Thy care of us, thy congregation,
Was manifested ev'ry day;
Yea, even trials and affliction
Prov'd thee our gracious God and Lord;
In all we felt thy benediction:
Thee, we now praise with one accord!

3 O gracious Lord, thy name be blessed
By us, for all thy proofs of grace!
For all the gifts by us possessed.
Thou crownest all our years and days.
Tho' we with deep humiliation
Own, that we basely thee requite:
Yet will we joy in thy salvation,
Thou art our Lord, and Help, and Light.

876. T. 595.

LET hearts and tongues unite
And loud thanksgivings raise;
'Tis duty mingled with delight,
The Saviour's name to praise.

2 To him we owe our breath,
He took us from the womb,
Which else had shut us up in death,
And prov'd an early tomb.

3 When on the breast we hung,
Our help was in the Lord;
'Twas he first taught our infant tongue
To form the lisping word.

4 When in our blood we lay,
He would not let us die;
Because his love had fix'd a day
To bring salvation nigh.

5 In childhood and in youth
His eye was on us still;
Tho' strangers to his love and truth,
And prone to cross his will.

6 E'er since his name we knew,
How gracious hath he been!
What dangers hath he led us thro',
What mercies have we seen!

7 Now thro' another year
Supported by his care,
We raise our *Ebenezer here,
"The Lord hath help'd thus far."

8 Our lot in future years
We cannot, Lord, foresee,
But kindly, to prevent our fears,
Thou say'st, "Leave all to me."

9 Yea, Lord, we wish to cast
Our cares upon thy breast;
Help us to praise thee for the past,
And trust thee for the rest.

* 1 Sam. vii. 12.

B. *Morning and Evening Hymns.*

877. T. 22.

AWAKE, my soul, and with the sun
Thy daily stage of duty run;
Shake off dull sloth, and early rise
To pay thy morning sacrifice.

2 Thy former mispent time redeem,
Each present day thy last esteem;
Thy talents to improve take care,
For the great day thyself prepare.

3 Thy conversation be sincere,
Thy conscience as the noon-day clear;
For God's all-seeing eye surveys
Thy secret thoughts, thy works and ways.

4 Glory to God, who safe hath kept,
And hath refresh'd me while I slept!
Grant, Lord, when I from death shall wake,
I may of heav'nly bliss partake.

5 Direct, control, suggest this day,
All I design, or do, or say;
That all my pow'rs, with all their might,
In thy sole glory may unite.

6 Praise God, from whom all blessings flow!
Praise him, all creatures here below!
Praise him above, ye heav'nly host!
Praise Father, Son, and Holy Ghost!

878.* T. 10.

MY soul, awake and render
To God thy great Defender
Thy pray'r and adoration
For his kind preservation.

2 With joy I still discover
Thy light, O Lord my Saviour!
My thanks shall be the spices
Of morning sacrifices.

3 Bless me this day, Lord Jesus,
And be to me propitious,
Grant me thy kind protection
From ev'ry sin's infection.

4 Bless ev'ry thought and action;
Afford me thy direction;
To thee alone be tending
Beginning, middle, ending.

5 Be thou my only treasure,
Fulfil in me thy pleasure,
May I in ev'ry station,
Give thee due adoration.

879. T. 22.

BE with me, Lord, where'er I go, [do;
Teach me what thou wouldst have me
Suggest whate'er I think this day,
Direct me in the narrow way.

2 Prevent me lest I harbor pride,
Lest I in mine own strength confied;
Show me my weakness, let me see
I have my pow'r, my all, from thee.

3 Enrich me always with thy love,
My kind Protector ever prove;
Lord, put thy seal upon my breast,
And let thy Spirit on me rest.

4 Assist and teach me how to pray,
Incline my nature to obey;
What thou abhorrest, let me flee,
And only love what pleaseth thee.

880. T. 582.

TEACH me, my God and King,
In all things thee to view;
And what I do in any thing,
For thee alone to do.

2 To scorn the senses' sway,
While still to thee I tend;
In all I do be thou the way,
In all be thou the end.

3 All may of thee partake;
Nothing so small can be,
But draws, when acted for thy sake,
Greatness and worth from thee.

4 If done t' obey thy laws,
Ev'n servile labors shine;
Hallow'd is toil, if this the cause,
The meanest work divine.

881. T. 26.

THAT favor grant to us, O Lord,
That we maintain our part in thee,
Unto thy voice attentive be,
And seek instruction in thy word.

2 Tho' often of encumb'ring care,
With busy Martha, we complain;
Yet, gracious Lord, we wish to gain
In Mary's happy lot a share.

882.* T. 79.

MAY Jesus' grace and blessing
Attend me without ceasing:
Thus I stretch out my hand,
And do that work with pleasure,
Which, in my call and measure,
My God for me to do ordain'd.

883.* T. 89.

GOD, omnipotent Creator,
Who mad'st all things by thy might,
Rulest ev'ry thing in nature,
And commandest day and night,
Who the universe so wide
By thy pow'r alone dost guide:

2 Let my life and conversation
Be directed by thy word!
Lord, thy constant preservation
To thy erring child afford:
No where but alone in thee
From all harm can I be free.

3 Lord, my body, soul, and spirit,
Keep in thine almighty hand;
Strengthen'd by thy pow'rful merit,
Let me follow thy command:
Thou my glory and renown,
I would fain be all thy own.

884. T. 580.

O GOD, my gracious God, to thee,
My morning pray'r shall offer'd be,
For thee my soul doth pant;
To me th' enjoyment of thy love
Than life itself doth dearer prove;
Renewed strength from thee I want.

2 Thou, Lord, art present to my mind,
When I lie down sweet sleep to find,
And when I wake at night:
Since thy arm to me succor brings,
Beneath the shadow of thy wings
I rest with safety and delight.

885. T. 14

MY God, the spring of all my joys,
The life of my delights;
The glory of my brightest days,
And comfort of my nights!

2 In darkest shades if thou appear,
My dawning is begun:
Thou art my soul's bright Morning-star,
And thou my rising Sun.

3 The op'ning heav'ns around me shine
With beams of sacred bliss,
When Jesus shows his mercies mine,
And whispers I am his.

886.* T. 14.

LORD, in the morning when I rise,
Accept my humble praise:
And when at night I close mine eyes,
Grant me thy pard'ning grace.

2 Lord Jesus Christ, who is like thee!
Thou art, both day and night
The Source of my felicity,
And only true delight.

3 Thanks, dearest Jesus, for thy love,
And great fidelity,
O may I truly thankful prove,
To all eternity.

887.* T. 22.

LORD Jesus, may I constantly
Both day and night be near to thee,
Both when I close at night my eyes,
And in the morn from sleep arise.

2 Lord Jesus Christ, my life and light,
I wish to love thee day and night;
Preserve my steps and guide my ways,
And let me live unto thy praise.

888. T. 106.

O JESUS, may our whole behavior
Rejoice thine heart and please thine
eyes;
In thy communion, gracious Saviour,
May we retire to rest, and rise;
Be present with us constantly,
Then shall we sleep, and wake, to thee.

889.* T. 580.

IN lying down to take my rest,
In rising, and in being drest,
In all I think or do,
In eating, drinking, on the way,
In sickness, and in health, I pray,
Thy blessing, Lord, on me bestow.

890.* T. 36.

LORD Jesus, thro' all temp'ral variation,
Thy loving kindness be my consolation,
By night and day, whene'er I rest am
taking, Or when I'm waking.

891.* T. 22.

ANOTHER day is at an end,
And night doth now its shade extend;
To thee, O Lord, our hearts we raise,
And thee for ev'ry mercy praise.

2 Yet we are of defects aware:
Forgive them, Lord; thy children spare;
O Christ, our souls from guilt acquit,
Take us into thy care this night.

3 Now I'll lie down and safely sleep,
Lord Jesus, in thy fellowship;
Thus under thy protection blest
Will soul and body sweetly rest.

892. T. 14.

THE hour of sleep is now at hand,
My spirit calls for rest;
O that my pillow may be found
The dear Redeemer's breast!

2 This night my longing soul with Christ
Would take up her abode,
I gladly would myself divest
Of ev'ry thing but God.

3 The nightly watches would I spend
In fellowship above;
Would hold communion with my Lord,
And feast upon his love.

4 Dead to the world when I'm asleep,
I'd be alive to God;
My soul would rest at peace with him
Who bought me with his blood.

5 O may I then of Christ this night
Be happily possest,
With holy angels round my bed,
And Jesus for my Guest.

893. T. 22.

THE hours' decline and setting sun
Show, that my course this day is run;
The ev'ning shade and silent night
My weary limbs to rest invite.

2 I now my soul and frail abode
Humbly commit to Israel's God,
To him who slumbers not nor sleeps,
And who his own in safety keeps.

3 Where'er I thee this day did grieve,
O Lord, me graciously forgive;
And, with a mind from trouble freed,
Let me sleep in thy peace indeed.

894. T. 22.

ALL praise to thee, my God, this night,
For all the blessings of the light;
Keep me, oh keep me, King of kings,
Under thy own almighty wings.

2 Lord, for the sake of thy dear Son,
Forgive the ill that I have done,
That with the world, myself, and thee,
I, ere I sleep, at peace may be.

3 Teach me to live, that I may dread
The grave as little as my bed;
Teach me to die, that so I may
Triumphant rise at the last day.

4 O may my soul on thee repose,
And may sweet sleep my eye-lids close,
Sleep that may me more vig'rous make
To serve my God when I awake.

5 When in the night I sleepless lie,
My soul with heav'nly thoughts supply;
Let no ill dreams disturb my rest,
No pow'rs of darkness me molest.

895. T. 14.

IN mercy, Lord, remember me,
Be with me thro' this night,
And grant to me most graciously
The safeguard of thy might.

2 With cheerful heart I close my eyes,
Thou wilt not from me move:
Lord, in the morning let me rise,
Rejoicing in thy love.

3 Oh, if this night should prove my last,
And end my transient days;
Lord, take me to thy promis'd rest,
Where I may sing thy praise.

896.* T. 165.

AUTHOR of the whole creation,
Light of light, eternal Word!
Soul and body's preservation
I commit to thee, O Lord!

My Redeemer, dwell in me,
Let me sleep and wake with thee,
And perceive thy benediction,
Both in joy and in affliction.

2 Ere I close my eyes in slumber,
While to rest I lay me down,
Let my grateful heart remember
All the mercies thou hast shown;
Fill me with thy sacred love,
That I dream of things above,
And bestow on me the favor
Of thy presence, gracious Saviour.

3 Pardon, Jesus, each transgression,
Whether open or unknown,
Thus removing that oppression
Under which I else should groan:
I confess the guilt of sin,
But thy blood can make me clean;
Hear, O Lord, my supplication,
Grant me joy and consolation.

897.* T. 164.

IN peace will I lie down to sleep;
O faithful Lord and Saviour,
Me under thy protection keep,
Let me enjoy thy favor!
Ev'n death I need not fear,
If thou to me art near;
For who with Jesus shuts his eyes,
He also doth with Jesus rise.

2 As oft this night as my pulse beats
My spirit would embrace thee;
Oft as my heart its throbs repeats
May I adore and praise thee;
Thus I can go to rest
In thy communion blest,
United unto thee by faith;
Thou art my joy, in life and death.

898. T. 157.

ERE I sleep, for ev'ry favor,
Which my God—hath bestow'd,
I will bless my Saviour:
O my Lord! what shall I render
Unto thee?—Thou shalt be,
This night my Defender.

2 Thou my Rock, my Strength and Tower!
While I sleep,—deign to keep
Watch from hour to hour;
Visit me with thy salvation;
Be thou near,—that thy care,
Guard my habitation.

899. T. 14.

REFRESH me, Lord, with grace divine,
Unto thy cross I flee,
And to thy care my soul resign,
To be renew'd by thee.

2 Besprinkled with thy precious blood
May I lie down to rest,
As in th' embraces of my God,
Or on my Saviour's breast.

900.* T. 14.

CHRIST's precious bloood, which from each vein
Our sin and curse forth press'd,
When overwhelm'd with grief and pain
His soul was sore amaz'd;

2 May that refresh us while we sleep,
And sanctify our rest,
And while we dream our spirit keep
With him in union blest.

901. T. 580.

NO farther go to night, but stay,
Dear Saviour, till the break of day,
Turn in, my Lord, with me;
And in the morning when I wake
Me under thy protection take,
Thus day and night I spend with thee.

902.* T. 580.

TO rest I now again retire,
Thou know'st thy presence I desire,
Of thee I wish to dream;
Still near to thee by faith to keep,
And taste thy goodness while I sleep,
Who didst my soul by blood redeem.

...T. 68.

...US, hear our pray'r,
For thy children care,
While we sleep, protect and bless us,
With thy pardon now refresh us;
Leave thy peace divine
With us, we are thine.

Cradle Hymn.

904. T. 16.

HUSH, dear child, lie still and slumber,
Holy angels guard thy bed!
Heav'nly blessings without number
Gently falling on thy head.

2 Sleep, my babe; thy food and raiment,
House and home, thy friends provide,
All without thy care and payment,
All thy wants are well supply'd.

3 How much better thou'rt attended
Than the Son of God could be,
When from heaven he descended,
And became a child like thee.

4 Soft and easy is thy cradle,
Coarse and hard thy Saviour lay,
When his birth-place was a stable,
And his softest bed was hay.

5 Was there nothing but a manger
Cursed sinners could afford,
To receive the heav'nly Stranger,
Did they thus neglect our Lord?

6 See the joyful shepherds round him,
Telling wonders from the sky!
Where they sought him, there they found him,
With his virgin-mother by.

7 'Twas to save thee, child, from dying,
That thy blest Redeemer came;
He by groans and bitter crying
Saved thee from burning flame.

8 May'st thou live to know and fear him,
Trust and love him all thy days;
Then go dwell for ever near him,
See his face, and sing his praise.

Cradle Hymn.

905.* T. 22.

SLEEP well, dear child! sleep safe and sound,
The holy angels thee surround,
Who always see thy Father's face,
And never slumber nights nor days.

2 God fill thee with his heav'nly light,
To steer thy christian course aright;
Make thee a tree of blessed root,
That ever bends with godly fruit.

3 Those children are to God most dear,
Who him with rev'rence, love and fear;
And infants are by Jesus Christ
Most kindly bless'd, and highly priz'd.

4 Are not the joys of God above
Giv'n to the children of his love?
He who desires to see his face,
Must here become a child of grace.

5 Be thou, dear child, in thy degree
Like Jesus, in his infancy:
He soon did ev'ry grace display,
Tho' he was God, he learnt t' obey.

6 He hath, by all he did and said,
For thee rich blessings merited;
'Twas thine entailed misery
Made him become a child like thee.

7 If thou partakest of his grace,
Thou wilt enjoy that happiness,
Which our incarnate God regain'd
For all whom Adam's sin had stain'd.

8 Soon in this world will finish'd be
The task God may design for thee;
May'st thou, when this short life is o'er,
With Jesus live for evermore.

9 Sleep now, dear child, and take thy rest;
If thou with riper years art blest,
Increase in wisdom and in grace,
Till thou shalt see thy Saviour's face.

C. *Before and after Meals.*

906. T. 14.

FOUNTAIN of being, Source of good!
By thy almighty breath
The creature proves our bane or food,
Dispensing life or death.

2 Thee we address in humble pray'r,
Vouchsafe thy gifts to crown;
Father of all, thy children hear,
And send a blessing down.

3 May we enjoy thy saving grace,
Thy goodness taste and see,
Athirst for blood-bought righteousness,
And hungry after thee.

907.* T. 10.

TO God the Lord be praises
For all the gifts and graces
He hath to us dispensed,
E'er since our lives commenced.

2 No blessing he denieth,
Us all with food supplieth,
Grants us his preservation
In ev'ry age and station.

908. T. 90.

THOU sov'reign Author of all good,
Whose providence for all doth care,
Giver of life, of health, and food,
Be present with thy children here,
And to our use oh sanctify
The gifts thy bounty doth supply.

2 All creatures, Lord, on thee depend,
And by thy pow'r and bounty live;
May we each blessing thou dost send
With truly grateful hearts receive,
In ev'ry gift thou dost dispense
Admiring thy wise providence.

3 We can't thy boundless mercies share,
And thee, the Spring of life, forget;
For all thy goodness, love and care,
Our thanks we offer at thy feet.
Lord, may we always taste thy grace,
Until we end our mortal race.

909. T. 595.

SURE God is present here,
His gifts demand our praise;
The present instance of his care
Speaks him a God of grace.

2 In him we live and move,
In him our being have;
We thank thee, Jesus, Source of love,
Who cam'st our souls to save.

910. T. 11.

JESUS' mercies never fail,
This we prove at ev'ry meal;
Lord, we thank thee for thy grace,
Gladly join to sing thy praise.

2 Lord, the gifts thou dost bestow,
Can refresh and cheer us too:
But no gift can to the heart
Be what thou our Saviour art.

3 Praise our God! it is but just,
He hath rais'd us from the dust,
Gave us being, gave us breath,
Saves us from eternal death.

911. T. 79.

WHAT praise to thee, my Saviour,
Is due for ev'ry favor,
Ev'n for my daily food!
Each crumb thou dost allow me,
With gratitude shall bow me,
Accounting all for me too good.

912. T. 22.

BE present at our table, Lord!
Be here and ev'ry where ador'd;
From thy all-bounteous hand our food
May we receive with gratitude.

2 We humbly thank thee, Lord our God,
For all thy gifts on us bestow'd;
And pray thee, graciously to grant
The food which day by day we want.

913. T. 22.

LORD, bless what thou provided hast!
Give grace, that we at this repast
May have, in all we think or do,
The glory of our God in view.

2 Thy name be hallow'd evermore,
O God, thy kingdom come with pow'r,
Thy will be done, and every day
Give us our daily bread, we pray.

3 Lord, evermore to us be giv'n
That living Bread which came from heav'n;
Water of life on us bestow,
Which doth from thee, the Fountain, flow!

D. *For Travellers.*

914. T. 580.

A STRANGER and a pilgrim I
With thy command, O Lord, comply,
I go where thou dost send:
My high commission I obey,
The toil and dangers of the way
Shall all in lasting comforts end.

2 Attend me, Lord, in all my ways;
Open my lips to sing thy praise
For blessings freely giv'n:
In all my journies here below
Let thy kind presence with me go;
Yea, grant me once to rest in heav'n.

915. T. 580.

THE Lord be with me ev'ry where,
And screen me with paternal care
By his almighty arm.
No trav'ller needs to faint or fear,
If he believes the Lord is near,
Who can protect him from all harm.

2 By sea and land, by night and day,
O Lord, in safety me convey,
Tho' winds and thunders roar.
Bring me, when ev'ry peril's past,
Safe to the destin'd place at last,
There to extol thy help and pow'r.

916. T. 157.

JESUS, thou art my salvation!
Bow thine ear,—hear my pray'r,
Grant my supplication:
Lo! thou seest me here a stranger;
Unto me—gracious be;
Lord, avert all danger.

2 In distress be thou my Saviour;
Hear my pray'rs,—see my tears,
Show thy servant favor.
Thro' life's journey safely lead me;
Guide my way,—lest I stray
From the hand that made me.

917.* T. 22.

LORD, in thy name we go our way;
Be thou our Guide, Support and Stay,
Protect us by thy mighty hand,
Where'er we go by sea or land.

918.* T. 26.

LORD, let thy presence with us go,
Throughout our journey us direct,
Thy angels guard us and protect,
Yea, prosper thou whate'er we do.

919. T. 583.

PRESERVE this ship and company, O Lord,
And thy protecting aid to them afford;
Be their support when waves and tempests roar,
And bring them safely to their destin'd shore.

920. T. 97.

WHEN Jesus calls we ready stand,
Our future life is in his hand;
Tho' separated for a time,
We yet continue one in him;
And therefore, while we part, need not complain,
As if we never were to meet again.

921. T. 14.

BLEST be that sacred cov'nant love,
Uniting tho' we part;
Our bodies may far off remove,
We still are one in heart.

2 Join'd in one spirit to our Head,
Where he appoints, we go,
And still in Jesus' footsteps tread,
Show forth his praise below.

3 Oh, may we ever walk with him,
And nothing know beside,
Nought else desire, nought else esteem,
But Jesus crucify'd.

4 Nor joy nor grief, nor time nor place,
Nor life nor death can part
Those, who enjoying Jesus' grace,
In him are one in heart.

5 Soon will he wipe off ev'ry tear,
On Canaan's blissful shore,
Where all, who friends in Jesus are,
Shall meet to part no more.

E. *For the Sick.*

922. T. 166.

WHEN pining sickness wastes the frame,
Acute disease or weak'ning pain;
When life fast spends its feeble flame,
And all the help of man proves vain;
Joyless and flat all things appear,
Languid the spirits, weak the flesh,
No med'cines ease, nor cordials cheer,
Food can't support, nor sleep refresh;

2 Then, then to have recourse to God,
To pray to him in time of need,
And feel the balm of Jesus' blood,
This is to find a Friend indeed.
And this, O christian, is thy lot,
Who cleavest to the Lord by faith,
He'll never leave thee (doubt it not)
In pain, in sickness, or in death.

3 When flesh decays, when vigor fails,
He will thy strength and portion be;
Support thy weakness, bear thy ails,
And softly whisper, "trust in me."
Himself will be thy helping Friend,
Thy good Physician, yea thy Nurse,
* To make thy bed will condescend,
And from affliction take the curse.

* Psalm xli. 3.

923. T. 22.

THO' I'm in body full of pain,
My soul doth heav'nly comfort gain;
And, should I die, I'm not afraid,
Since Jesus suffer'd in my stead.

2 Yet one thing will I ask of thee;
Never, O Lord, forsake thou me;
But bless me often, keep my mind
Stay'd on thy help, to thee resign'd.

3 Then I shall be supremely blest,
Nor ask, tho' sick, to be releas'd;
I'll wait thy time, thy love I feel,
I know thou rulest all things well.

924. T. 22.

MY body's weak, my heart unclean,
I pine with sickness, and with sin;
My strength decays, my spirits droop,
Bow'd down with guilt, I can't look up.

2 To thee, O Lord, in faith I turn,
Who all my sicknesses hast borne;
Sin thou hadst none, and yet didst die
For guilty sinners, such as I.

3 Sin's rankling sores my soul corrode,
Oh, heal them with thy precious blood;
And if thou wilt my health restore,
Lord, let me ne'er offend thee more.

925. T. 22.

OH, HOW I long to go and see
The Lamb of God, who dy'd for me;
How do I languish, night and day,
To hear him bid me come away!

2 He loves and values me; I him;
Therefore I all things dross esteem
But my dear Jesus, whom I prize
Above my life, or earth, or skies.

3 With pining sickness I decay,
Diseases wear my flesh away;
But I shall soon his leave obtain
To be releas'd from all my pain.

4 Quickly, O Lord, thy angels charge
To set my longing soul at large;
Quickly thy blessed hosts command
To carry me to thy right hand.

5 My loving friends, farewel, farewel,
I go with Jesus Christ to dwell,
Welcome my heav'nly country now,
Parents and brethren, all adieu!

F. *Concerning the holy Angels.*

926.* T. 22.

TO God let all the human race
Bring adoration, thanks and praise;
He makes his love and wisdom known
By angels who surround his throne.

2 The angels, whom his breath inspires,
His ministers, are flaming fires,
With joy they in his service move,
To bear his vengeance or his love.

3 With gladness they obey his will,
And all his purposes fulfil;
All those who Jesus' children are,
Are special objects of their care.

4 Our God defends us day by day
From many dangers in our way,
By angels, who for ever keep
A watchful eye, when we're asleep.

5 O Lord, we'll bless thee all our days,
Our souls shall glory in thy grace;
Thy praise shall dwell upon our tongues,
All saints and angels join our songs.

6 We pray thee, let the heav'nly host
Be guardians of our land and coast,
Bid them watch o'er thy flock of grace,
That we may lead a life of peace.

927. T. 22.

NOW let us join our hearts and tongues,
And emulate the angels' songs;
For sinners may address their King
In songs that angels cannot sing.

2 They praise the Lamb who once was slain,
But we can add a higher strain;
Not only say, "He suffer'd thus:"
But, that "He suffer'd all for us."

3 When angels by transgression fell,
Justice consign'd them all to hell;
But mercy form'd a wondrous plan
To save and honor fallen man.

4 Jesus, who pass'd the angels by,
Assum'd our flesh to bleed and die;
He who redeem'd us by his blood,
As man, still fills the throne of God.

5 Immanuel, our Brother now,
Is he 'fore whom the angels bow;
They join with us to praise his name,
But we the nearest int'rest claim.

6 But, ah, how faint our praises rise!
Sure, 'tis the wonder of the skies,
That we, who share his richest love,
So cold and unconcern'd should prove.

7 O glorious hour, it comes with speed,
When we from sin and darkness freed,
Shall see our God who dy'd for man,
And praise him more than angels can!

928.* T. 70.

THE holy angels,
When they to Christ draw near,
Fall down before him,
Their God, with holy fear,
And with profound humiliation,
Exceeding all our representation.

2 Heirs of salvation,
Redeemed with Christ's blood,
Their ministration
Demands our gratitude;
They'll guard us till we shall assemble,
Where our joint voices shall fill the temple.

929.* T. 249.

THE seraphim of God
Exalt :||: their voices loud,
With joy 'fore him they shout;
Their holy choirs in heav'nly blaze
Sing constantly with cover'd face,
Holy, Holy is God,—Holy is God,
The Lord of Sabaoth!

2 Thereto the church of Christ,
His flesh :||: and bone confess'd,
Sings, Amen! God be prais'd!
Above and here one voice doth sound:
Praise him who hath for us aton'd!
To God in highest strain!
To the Lamb slain!
All glory be! Amen.

3 When Christ, once crucified,
Returns :||: with his pierc'd side
In glory, to his bride,
And all the world shall quake with fear,
Then will with joy 'fore him appear
The countless ransom'd race,
And sing his praise
In never-ceasing lays.

930. T. 14.

YE angels, who excel in pow'r,
Praise ye and bless the Lord!
Ye who delight to do his will,
Laud him with one accord.

2 Yea, all his works, in ev'ry place,
Extol his holy name!
My thankful heart, my mind and soul,
Unite to praise the same!

931.* T. 583.

THANKS to our Lord for all the faithfulness [race;
Wherewith his angels guard his chosen
Whene'er they ask for his supreme commands, [hands.
He gives them charge to bear us in their

932. T. 166.

ANGELS astonish'd view their God
As Son of man to sinners giv'n;
With awe they saw his streaming blood,
Were struck, and silence was in heav'n;
Now they with all the saints in light
Worship the Lamb enthron'd above,
And praise the length, the breadth, the height,
And depth of God's stupendous love.

933. T. 141.

HOLY, holy, holy,
Sings th' angelic choir;
Might we, sinners, truly
Glow with heav'nly fire;
Praising all together
Deeply bow'd in dust,
God, Jehovah, Father,
Son, and Holy Ghost.

XXXVIII. Of our Departure unto the Lord, and the Resurrection of the Body.

934.* T. 132.

THANK God, towards eternity
Another step is taken,
My heart with longing turns to thee:
Tho' not by thee forsaken,
I long and pant for my release,
When I shall hence depart in peace,
To be with thee for ever.

2 I tell the hours and days and years,
And think them tedious ages,
Until the wish'd-for time appears
Which all my grief assuages;
Meanwhile with haste I forward press,
Till I arrive with thankfulness
At my desired haven.

3 Come, saith thy bride, who longs for thee,
Of all else she is weary,
And prays to thee incessantly,
Come, come, and do not tarry;
Jesus, my Bridegroom, come to me,
Thou know'st, O Lord, my soul to thee
Already is betrothed.

4 I am assur'd, nor life nor death
Me from thy love can sever,
While I abide in thee by faith,
And taste thy love and favor;
What though this time seem long to me,
A foretaste of eternity
I have in thy communion.

935.* T. 151.

FAREWEL henceforth for ever,
All empty worldly joys;
Farewel, for Christ my Saviour
Alone my thoughts employs;
In heav'n's my conversation,
Where the redeem'd possess
In him complete salvation,
The gift of God's free-grace.

2 Counsel me, dearest Jesus,
According to thy heart;
Heal thou all my diseases,
And ev'ry harm avert:
Be thou my consolation
While here on earth I live,
And at my expiration
Me to thyself receive.

3 May in my heart's recesses
Thy name and cross always
Shine forth, with all their graces,
To yield me joy and peace;
Stand 'fore me in that figure,
Wherein thou bar'st for us
Justice in all its rigour,
Expiring on the cross.

936.* T. 146.

THE grace enjoy'd by faith
In Jesus' incarnation,
His wounds and bitter death,
Assures us of salvation;
Engageth our whole heart,
Prompts us to sing his praise,
Until we hence depart
To see him face to face.

2 If Jesus should appear
Now at this very moment,
What think ye, should ye fear?
No, we with deep abasement,
Yet joyful, would adore
The Lamb who shed his blood,
And own him evermore
Our Saviour, Lord and God.

3 Ah, might the time soon come,
When thou, our soul's Beloved,
Shalt fetch thy children home;
Our inmost soul is moved,
To think we shall behold
Him whom by faith we know,
Chief Shepherd of his fold,
In whom we're one, and grow,

4 Hear thou our hearts' desire,
Most gracious Lord and Saviour,
Let us in peace expire,
And rise to meet thy favor;
And when thou shalt assign
His doom to ev'ry one,
Thy righteousness divine
Shall be our boast alone.

937.* T. 74.

THE Lord my Portion is,
I know no other bliss,
Here nor eternally,
But that which flows to me
From Jesus' blood and death,
Whereon I trust by faith.

2 Thou know'st, O God, that I,
Were I just now to die,
No Saviour have beside,
But Christ who for me dy'd;
He is my faithful Friend,
Whose mercies never end.

3 I shall, when time is o'er,
Behold for evermore
My Saviour, Lord and God,
Who bought me by his blood,
And view the wounds which he
Received once for me.

4 The time to time is known,
Meanwhile be this alone
My care, that thro' his grace
I so may run my race,
That I in faith may die,
And live eternally.

938.* T. 149.

YE who Jesus' patients are,
Let your hearts be tending
Thither, where ye wish to share
Bliss that's never ending;
O may ye—constantly,
Wean'd from things terrestrial,
Look for joys celestial.

2 Fixing all our thoughts above,
Where each true believer
Will, for his redeeming love,
Praise the Lord for ever,
Here, by faith—in his death,
We find consolation
And complete salvation,

939.* T. 244.

HOW soon, exalted Jesus,
Thou wilt to us reveal
Thy countenance most glorious,
That none as yet can tell;
So as thou didst appear
To thy disciples here;
Meanwhile, by frequent visits,
Us thy poor foll'wers cheer.

2 Till then, thou wilt call over,
Out of thy family,
Now one, and then another,
To be at rest with thee:
O grant us needful grace,
That we may run our race
Relying on thy mercy,
Till we shall see thy face.

940. T. 11.

LORD, my times are in thy hand,
Be they then at thy command;
Let me live to thee alone,
Then the sting of death is gone.

2 Whither should I, sinner, flee,
Lord, for shelter, but to thee?
Thou hast gone before, in grace,
To prepare a resting-place.

3 Bearing my sin's heavy load,
All thy steps were mark'd with blood,
From the garden to the cross,
Suff'ring to retrieve our loss.

4 By thy bitter agony,
By thy life pour'd out for me,
Oh, let me, a sinner, find
In my God a Friend most kind.

941.* T. 14.

WHETHER the period of this life
Be long or short, we know,
'Tis in itself of no great weight,
We're pilgrims here below.

2 Thrice happy they, who in this time
In Jesus Christ believe,
And as a living sacrifice
To him their bodies give.*

* Rom. xii. 1.

3 He is, as long as life shall last,
The Source of all their bliss,
And when they from this world depart,
They see him as he is.

4 Lord, may I live to thee by faith,
To thee O may I die,
For thine I am in life and death,
Thine, thine eternally.

942. T. 97.

ALTHO' a pardon'd sinner's mind
To be with Christ is most inclin'd,
Yet, long as he remaineth here,
Be it a day, a month, or year, [grace,
If but his heart be daily cheer'd by
With patience he can run his destin'd
race.

2 We in this world no city have
Where we to fix our dwelling crave;
For as a trav'ller on the road
Oft rests, but hath no fix'd abode,
Life's comforts thus we welcome, not
pursue, [view.
But keep our heav'nly mansion still in

943. T. 166.

LORD, whither can I sinner flee,
When I go hence but to thy breast?
For I have sought no other home,
For I have found no other rest.
When earthly cares engross the mind,
And turn my thoughts aside from thee,
Then the successive days and nights
Seem long and wearisome to me.

2 My God, and can a needy child,
That loves thee in humility,
From thy dear presence be exil'd,
Or ever separated be?
O no, for in thy wounded hands
By faith my name engrav'd I see;
Firm and secure thy promise stands,
That where thou art thy friends shall be.

944. T. 96.

IN age and feebleness extreme,
Who shall a helpless worm redeem!
Jesus, my only hope thou art,
Strength of my failing flesh and heart!
O could I catch a smile from thee,
And drop into eternity!

945.* T. 168.

MAKE my calling and election,
Jesus, ev'ry day more sure;
Keep me under thy direction,
Till I, thro' thy godlike pow'r,
Unto endless glory raised,
In thy mansions shall be placed:
When in thee I end my race
Weeping shall for ever cease.

946.* T. 37.

MY happy lot is here
The Lamb to follow;
Be this my only care
Each step to hallow,
And thus await the time
When Christ my Saviour
Will call me hence, with him
To live for ever.

947.* T. 124.

THEE we love and long to see,
Yea, dear Saviour,
We desire to be with thee;
But the favor
To have thee, tho' still unseen,
Ever near us—doth revive and cheer us.

948. T. 590.

OUR conversation is in heav'n,
Whence also we expect
The Lord our Saviour Christ to come,
And gather his elect.
Then shall he our vile body change,
And fashion it like his,
A glorious body, form'd for realms
Of everlasting bliss.

949.* T. 83.

CHRIST, my Rock, my sure Defence,
Jesus, my Redeemer liveth!
O! what pleasing hopes from thence
My believing heart deriveth!
Else death's long and gloomy night
Would my guilty soul affright.

2 Christ is risen from the dead,
Thou shalt rise too, saith my Saviour;
Of what should I be afraid!
I with him shall live for ever.
Can the HEAD forsake HIS limb,
And not draw me unto him?

3 No, my soul he cannot leave,
This, this is my consolation;
And my body in the grave
Rests in hope and expectation,
That this mortal flesh shall see
Incorruptibility.

4 Closely by love's sacred bands
I am join'd to him already,
And my faith's outstretched hands
To embrace my Lord are ready;
Death itself shall never part
Mine and my Redeemer's heart.

5 Flesh I bear, and therefore must
Unto dust be once reduced,
This I own, but from the dust
I shall be to life produced,
And, convey'd to endless bliss,
Live where my Redeemer is.

6 In my body, when restor'd
To the likeness of his body,
I shall see my God, my Lord,
My Beloved in his glory;
In my flesh eternally
My Redeemer I shall see.

7 These mine eyes most certainly
Shall behold and know my Saviour,
I, no stranger, no, ev'n I,
Him to see shall have the favor:
Grieving, pining in that day
Ever shall be done away.

8 What here sickens, sighs, and groans,
There o'er death shall prove victorious;
Earthly here are sown my bones,
Heav'nly they shall rise, and glorious:
What is natural, sown here,
Shall once spiritual rise there.

9 Let us raise our minds above
This world's lusts, vain, transitory,
Cleave to him ev'n here in love,
Whom we hope to see in glory:
May our minds tend constantly
Where we ever wish to be.

950.* T. 22.

MY life I now to God resign,
At his decree I'll not repine,
Will he prolong my mournful days,
He'll help me, well to end my race.

2 I go hence at th' appointed hour,
Nor would I wish to go before,
My hairs the Lord hath number'd all,
Without his will not one can fall.

3 Lord, what is man! a clod of earth,
A needy mortal from his birth,
Brought nothing with him when he came,
And naked leaves this earthly frame.

4 Teach us to number so our days,
That we apply to wisdom's ways,
Knowing how swift our moments fly,
That all, both young and old, must die.

5 This is the fruit of Adam's fall;
Death, like a conqu'ror, seiz'd on all;
Sin gives him pow'r, there is no place,
Exempt from his continual chace.

6 Evil and few, as Jacob says,
Alas! I count my pilgrim-days;
When God shall call his servant home,
In hope of joy I'll meet the tomb.

7 How could I bear the guilt of sin,
Assailing me without, within,
Did I not know, God gave his Son,
Who did for all my sins atone!

8 'Tis he, my Saviour Jesus Christ,
Who for my sins was sacrific'd,
And rose triumphant from the grave,
That he my soul from death might save.

9 To him I yield my life and breath,
His love will guide my soul thro' death,
And bring me to that blissful place,
Where I shall see him face to face.

10 My flesh meanwhile doth rest in hope,
Till in his likeness raised up;
Out of his hands no dust shall fall,
My body he'll to life recall.

11 This gives me comfort and relief,
In all my greatest pain and grief;
He'll wipe away my ev'ry tear,
When he in glory shall appear.

12 Humbly, Lord Christ, I thee address;
Ah! clothe me in thy righteousness;
Within thy wounds I crave a place,
There is my only happiness.

13 Amen! thou sov'reign God of love,
O grant that when we hence remove,
Our souls, redeemed by thy blood,
May find in thee their sure abode!

951.* T. 22.

LORD Jesus, Fountain of my life!
Sole comfort in this world of strife!
I come both weary and opprest,
And pray, Lord, take my soul to rest!

2 When I shall yield my dying breath,
Support me by thy bitter death;
Thy mercy is my only plea;
Thy bonds have gain'd my liberty.

3 By all thou hast for me endur'd,
Thou hast eternal life procur'd;
Thy shame, reproach and thorny crown,
Gain'd for me glory and renown!

4 Thy stripes have me, a sinner, heal'd;
My pardon with thy blood is seal'd;
Thy agony, thy dying breath
Redeem'd me from eternal death.

5 Unto my heart when speech I want,
The utt'rance of thy Spirit grant:
O that my soul to heav'n may rise,
When death in darkness seals my eyes.

6 What songs of everlasting joy
Shall mine and angel's tongues employ!
How shall we to eternity
Exalt thy love and mercy free!

952. T. 22.

CHRIST's bitter death shall sweeten mine;
My soul I to his care resign;
Since he laid down his life for me,
He'll keep me to eternity.

2 How glad am I, that I have known
What he to ransom me hath done!
How glad am I, that I believe,
Die when I will, he'll me receive!

3 Thanks be to thee, my gracious Lord,
That thou hast all my curse endur'd;
Nor doth the grave to me appear
A terror, since thou restedst there.

953.* T. 132.

JESUS, by thy almighty pow'r
My soul from death deliver,
In that important awful hour,
When soul and body sever;
Into thy ever faithful hand
My spirit will I then commend,
I trust thou wilt receive it.

2 Tho' guilt would fill my soul with dread,
Despair and consternation,
I know I need not be afraid,
Since Christ is my salvation [death,
His precious blood, his wounds and
Shall, when I draw my latest breath,
Be my support and comfort.

3 I of his body am a limb,
This is my consolation;
And death between my soul and him
Shall make no separation;
He in me, I in him abide,
In him, who for me liv'd and dy'd,
I've found life everlasting.

4 Since he did from the dead arise,
And then ascend victorious,
I likewise in the hope rejoice,
To rise again more glorious;
Thus free from fear, I can in peace
Depart to see him as he is,
And live with him for ever.

954. T. 582.

THE spirits of the just,
Confin'd in bodies, groan,
Till death consigns the corpse to dust,
And then the conflict's done.

2 Jesus, who came to save,
(The Lamb for sinners slain,)
Hath sanctify'd the gloomy grave,
And made ev'n death our gain.

3 Why should we fear to trust
The place where Jesus lay?
He'll raise our bodies from the dust,
And unto life convey.

4 Sin's pardon'd—I'm secure;
Death hath no sting beside:
The law gives sin condemning pow'r,
But Jesus for me dy'd.

5 God gives the victory;
To him due thanks be paid;
For we are conqu'rors when we die,
Thro' Christ our living Head.

955.* T. 151.

WHEN I shall gain permission
To leave this mortal tent,
And get from pain dismission,
Jesus! thyself present;
And let me, when expiring,
Recline upon thy breast,
Thus I shall be acquiring
Eternal life and rest.

956.* T. 232.

LORD, let thy blest angelic bands
Convey my soul into thy hands,
When soul and body sever;
My body, tho' reduc'd to dust,
Thou wilt (O Lord, I firmly trust)
Once raise to live for ever.
Then shall I see thee face to face,
In everlasting joy and peace,
And sing, with all the saints above,
The wonders of redeeming love.
O Christ, my Lord, :||: I'll thee adore
Here, and above, for evermore.

957. T. 582.

CONFIDING in thy name,
Jesus, the church's Head,
We give to earth the breathless frame,
Rememb'ring thou wast dead:
A bitter death indeed
Was thine, O Lamb of God;
But from the curse thou hast us freed,
By thy atoning blood.

2 O death where is thy sting?
O grave, thy victory?
He that believes in Christ can sing:
"He hath redeemed me!"
Trusting in him by faith
We now the vict'ry gain;
In him we triumph over death,
Who for us rose again.

958. T. 102.

WHERE is this infant? It is gone!
To whom? To Jesus who redeem'd it.
It now appears before his throne,
Where he continues still to tend it,
His favor—for ever
It proves, he doth bear [care.
This lamb in his bosom, 'tis safe in his

2 He took such in his arms on earth,
And show'd to them peculiar favor;
Hence we may know, that from their birth
He is their ever gracious Saviour!
He gave them,—he takes them,
Whene'er he sees best
For them to come to him, and with him to rest.

3 This infant rests now happily
In Christ the Source of our salvation!
Rejoicing to eternity,
Join'd to the perfect congregation.
The body,—we bury;
We know, that from pain
Released we once shall behold it again.

959.* T. 39.

WHEN children, released from all that's distressing,
Are called to heaven, O that's a great blessing!
Removed from danger and woe, they for ever
Rejoice in the presence of Jesus their Saviour.

960. T. 14

HOW sweetly this our *brother* sleeps,
Enjoying endless peace,
The grave, wherein *his* Saviour lay,
Is now *his* resting-place.

2 Nought can disturb this heir of life,
All worldly cares are fled;
To be with Christ was *his* desire,
And *he's* now perfected.

961.* T. 14.

BLEST soul, how sweetly dost thou rest,
From ev'ry toil and care,
Enjoying now, on Jesus' breast,
Bliss far beyond compare!

2 His suff'rings have deliver'd thee
From mis'ry, woe and death;
His word, "'Tis finish'd!" prov'd to be
The triumph of thy faith.

3 Now to the earth let these remains
In hope committed be!
Until the body chang'd obtains
Blest immortality.

962.* T. 483.

NOW rest in peace;
Our pray'rs, when dying, thee attended,
Thou'st ended
Thy mortal life, and now always
Beholdest Jesus face to face;
The holy angels did convey
Thy soul to realms of endless day,
There bless thee, God the Father, and the Son,
And Holy Ghost, Jehovah Three in One,
Thou there ador'st the Lamb that sitteth on the throne.

XXXIX. Of Christ's Coming to Judgment.

963.* T. 132.

'TIS sure that awful time will come,
When Christ, the Lord of glory,
Shall from his throne give men their doom,
And change things transitory:
This will strike dumb each impious jeer,
When all will be consum'd by fire,
And heav'n and earth dissolved.

2 The wak'ning trumpet all shall hear,
The dead shall then be raised,
And 'fore the judgment-seat appear,
On th' right and left hand placed;
Those in the body at that time
Shall, in a manner most sublime,
Endure a transmutation.

3 Woe then to him, that hath despis'd,
God's word and revelation,
And here done nothing but devis'd
His lust's gratification;
Then how confounded will he stand,
When he must go, at Christ's command,
To everlasting torment!

4 When all with awe shall stand around
To hear their doom allotted,
O may my worthless name be found
In the Lamb's book unblotted;
Grant me that firm, unshaken faith
That thou, my Saviour, by thy death
Hast purchas'd my salvation.

5 Before thou shalt as judge appear,
Plead as my Intercessor;
And on that awful day declare
That I am thy confessor,
Then bring me to that blessed place
Where I shall see, with open face,
The glory of thy kingdom.

6 O Jesus, shorten the delay,
And hasten thy salvation,
That we may see that glorious day
Produce a new creation:
Lord Jesus, come, our Judge and King,
Come, change our mournful notes, to sing
Thy praise for ever! Amen.

964. T. 581.

HARK! the trump of God is heard,
And th' archangel's voice on high;
Yea, the Lord himself descends
With a shout that rends the sky;
Lo! the bars of death are burst,
See the dead in Christ rise first;

2 His blest people, still on earth,
In a moment chang'd, all rise
In the clouds, caught up with them,
Meet their Saviour in the skies;
Fears and doubts are far remov'd,
Him they see, whom here they lov'd.

3 See this transient mortal life
Swallow'd up eternally!
Death, O death, where is thy sting?
Where, O grave, thy victory?
Thanks to God, thro' Christ we have
Vict'ry over death and grave.

4 Now all tears are wip'd away;
Free from curse and free from pain,
All Christ's people now with him
Kings and priests for ever reign.
Henceforth his unbounded grace
Is their theme of endless praise.

5 In the hope of all this joy,
Brethren, let us still be found;
Stedfast in the faith of Christ,
May we all in love abound,
Till we shall, when time is o'er,
Live with him for evermore.

965. T. 585.

LO! he cometh! countless trumpets
Christ's appearance usher in!
'Midst ten thousand saints and angels
See our Judge and Saviour shine!
Hallelujah! :||:
Welcome, welcome, slaughter'd Lamb!

2 Now the song of all the saved,
Worthy is the Lamb! resounds:
Now resplendent shine his nail-prints,
Ev'ry eye shall see his wounds!
They who pierc'd him :||:
Shall at his appearing wail.

3 Ev'ry island, sea, and mountain,
Earth and heaven flee away;
All his enemies confounded
Hear the trump proclaim his day:
Come to judgment! :||:
Stand before the Son of man!

4 All who love him view his glory,
In his bright, once marred face:
Jesus cometh, all his people
Now their heads with gladness raise:
Happy mourners! :||:
Lo, on clouds he comes! he comes!

5 See redemption, long expected,
On that awful day appear;
All his people, once despised,
Joyful meet him in the air:
Hallelujah! :||:
Now the promis'd kingdom comes!

966. T. 590.

MY faith shall triumph o'er the grave,
And trample on the tombs;
My Jesus, my Redeemer lives,
My God, my Saviour comes:
Ere long I know he shall appear
In pow'r and glory great;
And death, the last of all his foes,
Lie vanquish'd at his feet.

2 Then, tho' the worms my flesh devour,
And make my corpse their prey,
I know I shall arise with pow'r,
On the last judgment-day:
When God shall stand upon the earth,
Him these mine eyes shall see,
My flesh shall feel a second birth,
And ever with him be.

3 Then his own hand shall wipe the tears
From ev'ry weeping eye;
And pains, & groans, & griefs, and fears,
Shall cease eternally;
How long, dear Saviour, O how long
Shall this bright hour delay?
Oh, hasten thy appearance, Lord,
And bring the welcome day.

967. T. 14.

WHEN rising from the bed of death,
O'erwhelm'd with guilt and fear,
I see my Maker face to face,
Oh, how shall I appear?

2 If yet while pardon may be found,
Thy mercy I've not sought,
My heart with inward horror shrinks,
And trembles at the thought:

3 That thou, O Lord, wilt stand disclos'd
In majesty severe,
And sit in judgment on my soul;
How then shall I appear?

4 But thou declarest in thy word,
That sinners who to thee,
While here they live, repenting turn,
Shall live eternally.

5 Grant that I never may despair
Full pardon to obtain,
Since Jesus Christ, to save my soul,
Upon the cross was slain.

968. T. 166.

ACCORDING to my state on earth
Will the decisive sentence be;
They who have felt the second birth,
The second death shall never see;
But if from hence I take my flight
A captive to the tyrant sin,
Farewel to ev'ry cheering light,
A scene of darkness must begin.

969.* T. 592.

THIS transient world is not our home.
No soul finds here or rest, or bliss;
The man by this vain world o'ercome
Will of salvation surely miss:
Jesus alone yields comfort true,
Jesus is pleasure void of pain;
His mercies ev'ry day are new,
His friendship's fire doth still remain.
The scorn'd selected few thrice happy are
Who have in Jesus' love & grace a share.

2 His shame to all will be display'd,
However specious here his dress,
Who is not in the robe array'd
Of Jesus' perfect righteousness;
Who of Christ's fulness ne'er receiv'd,
Will tremble at the judgment-day;
However righteous here believ'd,
Then naked must he go away:
Haste then to Jesus Christ; thrice happy they
Who to the mercy-seat have found their way!

970.* T. 22.

REJOICE, thou happy little flock,
Which grounded firm on Christ the Rock,
Shalt dwell with him in lasting day,
When heav'n and earth shall pass away.

2 Who doth not turn to him while here,
And love him truly, shall with fear
And trembling, seek a shelt'ring place,
To hide himself from Jesus' face.

3 May Christ continue still to keep,
To feed and tend his dear-bought sheep,
Until his ransom'd flock shall be
Gather'd to him eternally.

4 Help us, O Lord, to watch and pray,
That we be ready ev'ry day,
To stand before thee thro' thy grace,
And in thy kingdom have a place.

971.* T. 16.

JUDGE me now, my God and Saviour,
Ev'n before the judgment-day;
Then to me, a worm, thy favor
Thro' eternity display.

972.* T. 205.

ARE you form'd a creature new,
Cleans'd by Jesus' precious blood,
Can you Christ in spirit view,
Reconcil'd by him to God;
Rise, to meet the Bridegroom, go,
Mingle with the virgin-row,
Have you oil, you need not fear,
Tho' this moment he appear.

2 Rise, go forth to meet the Lamb,
Slumber not, 'midst worldly care;
Let your lamps be all on flame,
For his coming now prepare:
Then whene'er ye hear the cry,
Lo, the Bridegroom draweth nigh,
You will not confounded be,
But can meet him cheerfully.

3 Let us walk the narrow way,
Watchful, cheerful, free from toil,
Trim our lamps from day to day,
Adding still recruits of oil;
Doubly doth the Spirit rest
On his happy, peaceful breast,
Who himself to praying gives,
Who a life of watching lives.

973.* T. 588.

YE virgins, be
Girt with alacrity;
At midnight cometh he:
Cease all your mourning,
The Lord will be returning,
Him ye shall see
In majesty.

2 Now ready stand,
Yea, always ready stand;
The Bridegroom is at hand;
Sleep not, nor slumber,
Let nothing you encumber,
But ready stand;
He is at hand.

974.* T. 244.

PREPARE your lamps, stand ready,
Your vessels fill with oil;
Be clean in soul and body,
Your wishes then can't fail:
Hark, 'tis the midnight cry,
"The bridegroom draweth nigh,"
Arise, go forth to meet him,
With songs of praise and joy.

975.* T. 580.

O LORD of glory, grant, we pray,
That each with ardent longing may
At all times ready be;
In faith and love preserve us sound,
O let us day and night be found
Joyful to meet and welcome thee.

XL. Of the Church Triumphant, and the Glory of Eternal Life.

976. T. 159.

MOUNT Zion, where the Lamb of God
Who for our sins aton'd,
And bought us by his precious blood,
For ever is enthron'd;
Where his redeem'd and chosen bride
Thro' endless ages shall reside;
Is here thro' faith in Jesus' name,
Our joy and final aim.

2 Jerusalem, the church above,
Now triumphs over death,
And when we, perfected in love,
Shall once resign our breath,
We shall, with all the saints in light,
In cheerful songs of praise unite,
And with his chosen evermore
His saving name adore.

3 Deliver'd from this mortal clay,
From sorrow, sin, and pain,
We shall with Christ, in lasting day,
True holiness obtain.
Lord Jesus, hear our fervent pray'r,
Us needy sinners all prepare,
By faith in thee to end our race,
And to behold thy face.

977.* T. 97.

HOW greatly doth my soul rejoice,
That by my faithful Shepherd's choice,
My name is certainly enroll'd
Among the sheep of his blest fold!
May I by nothing e'er be drawn aside,
But be a happy member of his bride.

2 My faith victorious now doth rise
Above all earthly vanities,
And hath Jerus'lem full in view,
That holy city, fair and new;
Thro' faith in Christ I am God's child and heir.
And shall the glories of his kingdom share.

3 Then all old things will pass away,
And a new scene itself display;
We wait for thee, Immanuel,
Come soon, thy majesty reveal:
Our voices then in higher strains shall raise
A joyful Hallelujah to thy praise.

978. T. 14.

THERE is a house not made with hands,
Eternal, and above;
And here my spirit waiting stands,
Till it shall hence remove.

2 My Saviour by his saving grace
Prepareth me for heav'n;
And, as an earnest of the place,
Hath his own Spirit giv'n.

3 We walk by faith of joys to came,
Faith lives upon his word;
But while the body is our home,
We're absent from the Lord.

4 'Tis pleasant to believe thy grace;
But we had rather see:
We would be absent from the flesh,
And present, Lord, with thee.

979.* T. 585.

JESUS' life of grief and sorrows,
All his suff'rings, death and pain,
Prove in life our consolation,
And in death our joy remain,
Hallelujah! :||:
Christ's our Life, hence death is gain.

2 On his precious death and merit
All our hopes are safely built;
We rejoice in his salvation,
Freed from sin's condemning guilt,
Sing his triumphs, :||:
'Twas for us his blood was spilt!

3 Jesus yieldeth up his spirit,
Lo, he bows his head and dies!
From his death we life inherit,
Hence our happiness takes rise;
We now glory :||:
Only in this sacrifice.

4 Jesus' body, once interred,
Sanctifies his brethren's rest,
And the place which keeps their bod ies
Since earth lodg'd that heav'nly Guest,
Now is hallow'd; :||:
We lie down in hope most blest.

5 Our Redeemer rose victorious,
O what joy doth this afford!
Lasting bliss awaits us yonder,
Rais'd to glory, like our Lord;
Blessed Saviour, :||:
Ever be by us ador'd!

6 Conqu'ring Lord, to heav'n ascended
To prepare for us a place,
Pleading thine own blood and merit;
Here, our faith rests on thy grace,
There, in glory, :||:
We shall see thee face to face.

7 Jesus! at thy blest appearing,
Freed from weakness, grief and pain,
We, restored to thy likeness,
Once shall join thy happy train;
Make us ready, :||:
Lord, thy glory to obtain!

980.* T. 58.

HAPPY I am, yet o'er my happiness
Can ne'er rejoice but with a blushing face
For it is mere mercy, remains a wonder
Of Christ's long suff'ring, when thereon I ponder, Now and always.

2 In the glorious presence
Of God my Saviour,
Tho' with abasement, this great truth I'll ever Own to his praise:

3 That his incarnation,
His bitter passion,
And meritorious death procur'd salvation, And life for me.

4 In his great atonement
I'll trust unshaken,
Until I once to see him shall be taken, Whom here I love.

5 Grant to me, Lord Jesus,
The special favor,
Depending on thy grace both now and ever, To look to thee;

6 In that ever lovely,
Heart-piercing figure,
As for us bearing justice in its rigor, Upon the cross.

7 What ecstatic pleasure
Shall I then savor,
When face to face beholding thee forever, So as thou art!

8 On what joys celestial
Shall I be feasting,
When, in thy presence from all labor resting, I sabbath keep!

9 O! what songs of praises
Will then in heaven
Resound, when all the ransom'd souls thanksgiving To Jesus bring!

10 Lamb, once slain for sinners,
Receive our praises,
Honor and glory from all choirs and classes, To thee they're due.

11 Now let all say Amen,
The Lord be praised,
In heav'n and earth his name for ever blessed By all that breathe!

981.* T. 205.

O EXALT and praise the Lord,
Laud his name for evermore,
Gratefully with one accord,
With the angels him adore;
Thank him for the faithfulness
Wherewith he his witnesses,
Who in heav'n are perfected,
Thro' great tribulation led.

2 Here by Jesus' precious blood,
Cleans'd from sin and render'd chaste,
They, as ministers of God,
Him by word and deed confest;
In their Lord's reproach a share,
Hated by the world, they bare,
Now they, with th' angelic train,
Praise the Lamb for sinners slain.

3 They with patience having run
Their appointed race, in hope
Of the prize, at last the crown
Have obtain'd, for them laid up;
Now they serve the Lamb of God,
(Having in his precious blood
Wash'd their robes & made them white,)
In his temple day and night.

4 In fine, spotless linen drest,
Palms of victory they bear,
By no sorrows e'er opprest,
Unmolested now by care,
Free from hunger, thirst and heat,
They, possessing joys complete,
Unto living fountains led,
By the Lamb himself are fed.

5 Since we likewise may attain
To this happiness thro' grace,
And by foll'wing Jesus, gain
With the saints in heav'n a place;
May we tread the narrow path,
Not unfruitful in the faith,
And unto the end endure,
Making our election sure.

6 May we always have in view
The example of our Lord,
Faithfully his steps pursue,
Giving heed unto his word;
In our bodies, while we've breath,
May we bear about his death,
That his life may even here
In our mortal flesh appear.

7 Let us call to mind with joy
Those who have before us gone,
Who obtain'd the victory
Thro' the blood of Christ alone;
That we all may zealously
Imitate their constancy,
Till we too the prize receive,
And with them in glory live.

982.* T. 166.

UNTO ourselves with deepest awe
The spirits of the righteous
We represent, and comfort draw
From hence, when trials fright us;
Rejoicing, we behold them now,
In Jesus' presence blessed,
From the church militant below
To the triumphant raised.

2 There sits the princely company
Of those, who did surrender,
For Jesus' sake, most willingly
Their lives and worldly grandeur:
Undaunted meeting fire and sword,
No toils too great esteemed,
If they to preach his precious word
By him were worthy deemed.

3 All who in Jesus' presence live
Remov'd from mortal vision,
The crown of righteousness receive,
In endless life's fruition;
They are now with the Lord at home;
Our humble expectation
Is, that he'll let us also come
To join that congregation.

983.* T. 71.

WHAT shall I feel, when I
The glorious choirs espy
In bliss unceasing!
Already in my heart
Rays from bright Salem dart,
With hopes most pleasing.

2 I hear th' enraptur'd song
Rais'd by the blessed throng
Of the redeemed:
Seated upon the throne,
The Lamb once slain, alone
Is worthy deemed.

3 Rejoice, my soul, thou soon,
When here thy race is run,
Shalt have the favor
To go and join the blest,
And there at home to rest
With Christ, thy Saviour.

4 Then shall our woe and grief
Find a most sure relief
In joys unbounded:
Triumphant songs shall be
To the blest Trinity
For ever sounded.

5 How blest when we can say,
All else is fled away,
And love prevaileth!
No longer faith and hope
We need to bear us up,
Love never faileth.

6 See, how the victors go
In raiment white as snow,
With glory crowned!
He grants to them, thro' grace,
Around his throne a place,
On whom death frowned.

7 The Bridegroom now appears,
He wipes off all our tears,
And ends all sadness;
To him I had resign'd
Myself, and now am join'd
In perfect gladness.

8 O Lord, grant my request,
To be in heav'n at rest,
When 'tis thy pleasure;
Then, to eternity,
I ne'er shall parted be
From thee, my Treasure.

9 At thy thro'-pierced feet
I'll humbly take my seat,
There's heav'n's enjoyment:
To give thee thanks and praise,
For all thy love and grace,
Be my employment.

10 While here, I live by faith,
Relying on thy death,
For thou'rt my Saviour;
There I shall sweetly rest,
Reclining on thy breast,
In peace for ever.

984. T. 136.

MY Lord and God!
Who hast for me atoned, [ed;
And in death's agony for me hast groan-
I weep for joy,
And raise my feeble song,
For both in life and death this meditation
Proves unto me a sweet and strength'-
ning consolation;
My pardon's sealed with thy blood,
My Lord! my God!

2 The time will come,
When endless consolation [salvation.
Will be their lot, who wait for Christ's
"I am redeem'd,"
Saith a believing heart; [endeth,
"Ev'n here the Lord, whose mercy never
Wipes oft my tears away, and all my
steps attendeth;
The time, to be with him at home,
At last will come."

3 Come soon, O come,
Ye hours, wherein for ever, [favor
With hosts of saints I too shall have the
To see my Lord!
With joy I for him wait;
Who knows but I this day may leave
the body,
Call'd forth to meet the Bridegroom:
may he find me ready;
I long to be with him at home;
Come soon, O come!

4 O happy lot!
To live with Christ, our Saviour,
There to behold his countenance for
In songs of joy [ever;
His holy name to praise;
To thank him for our blessed consum-
mation,
And view his wounds, those pledges
of complete salvation,
All pain and sorrow then forgot;
O happy lot!

985.* T. 149.

O HOW excellent and fair,
Great beyond all measure,
Will to us our lot appear,
And how rich our treasure,
When we see—bodily
Our beloved Saviour,
As he is for ever!

2 Countless hosts before God's throne,
(Where the Lamb resideth,
And, as God and Man, his own
To life's fountain guideth,)
Now possess—perfect bliss,
Which to us is wanting,
And for which we're panting.

3 What here sickness, sighs and groans,
There will prove victorious;
Earthly here are sown our bones,
They shall rise most glorious;
Death and woe—ev'ry foe
Which us here annoyed,
There will be destroyed.

4 May this ever blessed hope
Fill our hearts with gladness,
And, 'midst weakness, bear us up,
Till from sin and sadness
We shall be—wholly free,
And above for ever
Praise our gracious Saviour.

986.* T. 594.

WHEN, O when shall I have the favor
To see th' approach of those blest days,
When I shall welcome my dear Saviour
With solemn strains, with joyful lays?
How blest will then be my condition,
When in my flesh I Christ shall see!
Tho' happy in his love's fruition
Ev'n here, I long with him to be.

2 What heav'nly joy and consolation
This hope affords unto my heart,
That Christ, the God of my salvation,
Will me receive, when I depart!
Then in his presence I for ever,
With the redeem'd shall sing his praise;
O Lord, I long to have that favor,
To leave this world and see thy face.

987.* T. 83.

WHEN departed once in peace,
I shall have the grace and favor
To behold him face to face,
Whom I love, ev'n God my Saviour:
Then I shall for evermore
Him in endless joy adore.

2 When I once shall favor'd be,
To enjoy in fullest measure,
What his suff'rings gain'd for me,
And salvation's blood-bought treasure,
With what rapture shall I sing
Hallelujah to my King!

988.* T. 119.

O WHAT joy, :||:
O what joy awaiteth me!
I rejoice in expectation,
That I in my flesh shall see
Him, the God of my salvation,
And behold the Lord in endless bliss,
As he is. :||:

2 Yea, Amen! :||:
Pardon'd sinners here rejoice
In this hope and consolation,
Till we shall with sweeter voice,
Sing in the great Congregation, [God
Thou, O Lamb, hast brought us nigh to
By thy blood! :||:

989.* T. 45.

MY lot of grace—will be always
Beyond description blessed;
Yea, the bliss I shall enjoy
Cannot be expressed.

2 Him I shall see—whose love to me
My heart hath captivated;
From his presence I no more
Shall be separated.

990.* T. 208.

WHAT hast thou, Lord Jesus,
To redeem and bless us,
For us undergone!
Here we know but partly,
But there will be shortly
More of this depth known;
When above—we shall remove,
And shall live with thee for ever,
Our beloved Saviour.

2 I am lost in wonder,
When I duly ponder,
Jesus, on thy grace;
That I shall in glory
Evermore adore thee;
And that, face to face,
I shall see—eternally
Thee, the God of my salvation,
O what consolation!

991. T. 14.

COME, Lord, and warm each languid
Inspire each lifeless tongue; [heart,
And let the joys of heav'n impart
Their influence to our song.

2 Sorrow and pain, and ev'ry care,
And discord there shall cease;
And perfect joy, and love sincere,
Adorn the realms of peace.

3 The soul, from sin for ever free,
Shall mourn its pow'r no more;
But, cloth'd in spotless purity,
Redeeming love adore.

992. T. 14.

HAPPY the souls to Jesus join'd,
And sav'd by grace alone;
Walking in all his ways, they find
Their heav'n on earth begun.

2 The church above no other theme
But Jesus' love doth know;
In joyful hymns they praise his name,
We do the same below.

3 Him in his glorious realm they praise,
And bow before his throne;
We in the kingdom of his grace:
The kingdoms are but one.

993. T. 14.

THERE where my blessed Jesus reigns,
In heav'n's unmeasur'd space,
I shall a long eternity,
Spend in ne'er-ceasing praise.

2 Dear Jesus, ev'ry smile of thine
Will fresh endearments bring;
And thousand tastes of new delight
From all thy graces spring.

3 Haste, my Beloved, fetch my soul
Up to thy blest abode;
Haste, for my spirit longs to be
With thee, my Lord and God.

994. T. 14.

GOD hath laid up in heav'n for me
A crown which cannot fade;
The righteous Judge, at that great day,
Will place it on my head.

2 Nor hath the King of grace decreed
This prize for me alone,
But all that love and long to see
Th' appearance of his Son.

995.* T. 205.

AMEN, yea, Hallelujah!
Jesus, praise to thee be giv'n,
That a place for me, thro' grace,
Is by thee prepar'd in heav'n:
Ah, how blest will be my case,
When I shall behold thy face,
And, from pain and sorrow free,
Live for evermore with thee!

996. T. 114. [seated

THE just made perfect, who in glory
Around God's throne enjoy eternal bliss
Behold our God and Saviour as he is, [ted
Ah, when shall I poor trav'ller be permit-
To join that happy num'rous company,
And my Redeemer face to face to see!

997. T. 244.

WHEN we shall see our Jesus,
And thankful him adore,
What rapture then will seize us!
We meet to part no more;
Our Lord, with matchless grace,
Will to his glory's praise,
'Midst joys unutterable,
Us as his own confess.

998. T. 588.

WHAT happiness,
What joy and happiness
Shall we above possess,
When we adore him,
With angels bow before him,
And see his face—what happiness!

999.* T. 159.

NOW, Lord, who in this vale of tears
Dost lift thy gracious face,
Upon thy church which thee reveres,
And givest us such peace,
That sweetly we anticipate
The heav'nly bliss, for which we wait,
In thee rejoicing here below,
Ev'n while in tears we sow:

2 O form us all, while we remain
On earth, unto thy praise!
That each one fully may obtain
Thy blessed aim, thro' grace:
Till we in heav'n thy face shall see,
May spirit, soul and body be
Preserv'd by thee, till thy great day,
Blameless, O Lord, we pray.

Conclusion.

1000. T. 159.

SING Hallelujah! praise the Lord!
Sing with a cheerful voice;
Exalt our God with one accord,
And in his name rejoice:
Ne'er cease to sing, thou ransom'd host,
Praise Father, Son and Holy Ghost!
Until in realms of endless light
Your praises shall unite.

2 There we to all eternity
Shall join th' angelic lays;
And sing in perfect harmony
To God our Saviour's praise:
"He hath redeem'd us by his blood,
And made us kings and priests to God;
For us, for us the Lamb was slain."
Praise ye the Lord!

AMEN.

INDEX.

Showing by every first line of each verse, where it is to be found. Those lines marked thus * begin a hymn.
The verses occurring in the Liturgy only, are distinguished by the letter L.

INDEX.

INDEX.

INDEX.

C

INDEX.

G

INDEX.

INDEX.

INDEX.

I

INDEX.

INDEX.

INDEX.

INDEX.

INDEX.

INDEX.

M

INDEX.

INDEX.

N

INDEX.

INDEX.

INDEX.

INDEX.

INDEX.

INDEX.

INDEX.

T

INDEX.

INDEX.

INDEX.

INDEX.

INDEX.

INDEX.

U

INDEX.

INDEX.

INDEX.

INDEX.

TABLE OF TUNES.

NOTE. The number affixed to every line in this Table, corresponds with the Tune-book, which is an extract from the Tune-book used in our congregations abroad, except a few original English tunes.

As several of our Tunes are adapted to the same metre (as 22 *a*. 22 *b*. &c.) an attempt is here made to assign to each hymn an appropriate Tune.

TUNE.

1. No. 595, 602.
4. No. 223, 320, 349, 411, 455, 523, 736.
9. No. 221, 539, 563, 689, 692, 737, 742, 852.
10. No. 521, 693, 871, 878, 907.
11*a*. No. 15, 42, 43, 135, 247, 424, 434, 519, 568, 773, 789, 791, 862, 910.
11*d*. No. 63, 65, 112, 126, 262, 310, 343, 408, 415, 483, 596, 775, 940.
14*a*. No. 10, 24, 26, 64, 66, 67, 71, 101, 102, 103, 104, 106, 109, 116, 153, 154, 229, 230, 256, 261, 275, 289, 296, 307, 322, 325, 326, 355, 375, 376, 390, 414, 416, 422, 428, 459, 468, 472, 484, 493, 507, 526, 532, 534, 586, 724, 747, 748, 749, 786, 787, 788, 790, 809, 829, 860, 872, 886, 892, 895, 899, 900, 921, 941, 960, 961, 967, 993.
14*b*. No. 50, 52, 138, 144, 204, 211, 271, 354, 392, 570, 572, 573, 930, 991, 992, 994.

TUNE.

14*c*. (593*a*.) No. 53, 59, 60, 156, 158, 164, 165, 178, 190, 199, 228, 231, 254, 277, 285, 286, 287, 327, 347, 395, 492, 509, 556, 612, 653, 793, 794, 800, 801, 808, 811, 885, 906, 978.
15. No. 312, 365, 409, 515, 551, 697.
16. No. 7, 47, 264, 284, 374, 443, 454, 496, 511, 540, 585, 587, 621, 830, 837, 838, 850, 904, 971.
22*a*. No. 2, 72, 186, 187, 294, 331, 421, 427, 449, 473, 482, 490, 505, 513, 518, 599, 656, 663, 722, 726, 752, 757, 776, 785, 796, 798, 815, 839, 844, 853, 859, 879, 887, 905, 913, 925, 952.
22*b*. No. 31, 44, 45, 46, 49, 191.
22*d*. No. 27, 107, 348, 457, 463, 464, 467, 506, 537, 717, 718, 746, 792, 797, 858, 863, 891, 923, 924, 950.
22*e*. No. 5, 8, 9, 28, 68, 105, 110, 157, 161, 189, 201,

Table of Tunes.

TUNE.	
22*e*.	202, 216, 240, 241, 242, 269, 270, 273, 281, 298, 300, 440, 571, 600, 682, 795, 864, 877, 893, 894, 912, 926, 951.
22*f*.	No. 6, 137, 149, 569, 598. 609, 650, 672, 927, 970,
22*l*.	No. 22, 160, 219, 407, 444, 528, 529, 541, 546, 667, 781, 799, 843, 917,
22*o*.	No. 224.
23.	No. 497, 743, 744, 767, 814.
26.	No. 146, 436, 439, 613, 618, 625, 657, 772, 780, 842, 881, 918.
30.	No. 453, 627.
36.	No. 77, 86, 266, 324, 387, 589, 890.
37.	No. 278, 398, 813, 946.
39*a*.	No. 57, 405, 581, 662, 806, 807, 959.
39*c*.	No. 175, 567, 725, 805,
45.	No. 124, 412, 824, 989.
50.	No. 34, 133.
51.	No. 96.
54.	No. 78, 445.
56.	No. 397, 437, 631, 654, 826, 833, 840.
58.	No. 12, 37, 56, 61, 69, 143, 152, 177, 181, 197, 208, 218, 220, 222, 295, 316, 418, 446, 460, 480, 578, 624, 628, 652, 719, 739, 819, 980.
66.	No. 265.
68.	No. 179, 213, 319, 377, 548, 610, 678, 715, 903.
69.	No. 606, 700.
70.	No. 928.
71.	No. 745, 983.
74.	No. 308, 393, 669, 866, 867, 937.
75.	No. 252.
79 or 580.	No. 21, 29, 41, 70, 74, 88, 136, 147, 193, 232, 301, 328, 330, 333, 378, 384, 385, 466, 479, 494, 503, 531, 538, 547, 588, 591, 592, 620, 633, 677, 706, 708, 766, 817, 847, 882, 884, 889, 901, 902, 911, 914, 915, 975.
82	No. 768.
83.	No. 14, 142, 351, 406, 438, 542, 576, 590, 769, 784, 856, 949, 987.
84.	No. 3.
89.	No. 19, 389, 883.
90.	(see 96 and 106.) No. 194, 233, 288, 304, 329, 383, 391, 394, 441, 544, 564, 647, 648, 676, 908.
96.	No. 75, 111, 196, 246, 255, 292, 469, 783, 944.
97.	No. 11, 13, 30, 173, 206, 249, 280, 352, 363, 381, 382, 410, 474, 478, 601, 670, 671, 696, 713, 758, 764, 827, 873, 920, 942, 977.
99.	No. 76, 754.
101.	No. 560, 695.
102.	No. 491, 958.
106.	No. 4, 167, 198, 244, 268, 272, 302, 303, 400, 462, 465, 514, 634, 888.
114.	No. 73, 122, 338, 611,

TUNE.	
114.	No. 668, 687, 851, 996.
115.	No. 339.
119.	No. 1, 62, 125, 353, 458, 755, 988.
121.	No. 450, 577, 617, 643, 644, 673, 868.
123.	No. 253.
124.	No. 430, 765, 947.
125.	No. 212.
126 or 597.	No. 39, 92, 481, 489, 623, 741.
127.	Liturgy, page 24.
132*a*.	No. 139, 172, 188, 195, 250, 315, 346, 386, 555, 632, 953, 963.
132*b*.	No. 17.
132*d*.	No. 130, 148, 566, 934.
132*e*.	No. 251.
136.	No. 584, 984.
141.	No. 368, 451, 452, 510, 683, 750, 933.
142.	No. 267.
146.	No. 58, 145, 332, 361, 364, 561, 636, 655, 714, 735, 761, 936.
147.	No. 429.
149.	No. 362, 549, 762, 938, 985.
151*a*.	No. 80, 85, 117, 360, 461, 635, 734, 753, 756, 777, 955.
151*g*.	No. 33, 170, 403, 525.
151*i*.	No. 168, 245, 291, 293, 486, 517, 603, 691, 935.
152*a*.	No. 87.
152*b*.	No. 95.
155.	No. 51, 309, 358, 425, 579, 616, 619, 664, 684, 688.

TUNE.	
156.	No. 404.
157.	No. 35, 898, 916.
159.	No. 321, 372, 432, 448, 470. 471, 565, 702, 709, 803, 845, 976, 999, 1000.
160.	No. 728.
161.	No. 607, 638, 686.
164.	No. 340, 447, 622, 812, 897.
165.	No. 89, 91, 431, 896.
166.	No. 18, 36, 162, 183, 200, 344, 373, 487, 608, 615, 645, 649, 651, 661, 665, 666, 694, 701, 710, 716, 729, 760, 818, 823, 825, 848, 855, 874, 922, 932, 943, 968, 982.
167*a*.	No. 182, 356, 413, 426, 520, 550, 604, 699, 861.
167*e*.	No. 82, 93.
168*a*.	No. 90, 945.
168*b*.	No. 97, 98, 299, 831, 834, 870.
169.	No. 40.
172.	No. 203.
184 (see 594.)	No. 276, 279, 311, 313, 399, 512, 763, 869, 875.
185.	No. 79, 127, 140, 180, 184, 318, 336, 485, 488, 522, 597, 659, 690, 705, 707, 712, 751, 778, 816, 822, 828, 832, 835, 865.
189.	No. 553.
192.	No. 166.
195.	No. 545, 558, 681.
200.	No. 402.
203.	No. 217.
205.	No. 128, 141, 237, 243,

TABLE OF TUNES.

TUNE.	
205.	No. 257, 263, 371, 614, 703, 730, 972, 981, 995.
206.	No. 176, 323, 370, 562, 674.
208.	No. 120, 123, 388, 516, 527, 637, 990.
212.	No. 16. (*a*) 533 (*b*).
214.	No. 163, 477.
216.	No. 94.
217.	No. 99 (*a*), 236, (*b*), 821 (*a*).
218.	No. 341.
221.	No. 23, 639, 679.
227.	No. 557.
228.	No. 317, 350, 366, 367, 379, 419, 502, 524, 660.
230.	No. 174, 234, 334, 433, 582, 711.
232.	No. 114, 401, 417, 740, 956.
234.	No. 155, 380, 536.
235.	No. 554.
337.	No. 495.
240.	No. 54, 119.
242.	No. 733.
243.	No. 83, 84, 442, 804.
244.	No. 335, 357, 456, 501, 626, 939, 974, 997.
249.	No. 580. 929.
341.	No. 192, 205, 215, 369 559, 698, 849.
376.	No. 305, 306.
483.	No. 962.
519.	No. 129.
520.	No.. 605.
580.	(see T. 79.)
581.	No. 121, 171, 258, 738,
581.	No. 854, 964.
582.	(see 595.) No. 25, 108, 151, 226, 227, 248, 259, 260, 290, 297, 342, 629, 723, 727, 759, 770, 779, 880, 954, 957.
583.	No. 113, 118, 214, 225, 235, 283, 498, 508, 552, 583, 593, 594, 630, 658, 675, 685, 771, 774, 836, 919, 931.
585.	No. 48, 238, 841, 965, 979.
586.	No. 55, 337, 500, 640, 857.
587 or 596.	No. 435, 810.
588.	No. 115, 973, 998.
590	(see 593*b*.) No. 20, 32, 38, 159, 282, 314, 345, 359, 396, 475, 476, 499, 504, 535, 641, 642, 646, 680, 704, 720, 721, 722, 782, 802, 820, 846.
591.	No. 239.
592.	No. 969.
593*a*.	(see T. 14*c*.)
593*b*.	(see T. 590.) No. 131, 132, 150, 530, 543, 948, 966.
594.	(see T. 184.) No. 81, 100, 731, 986.
595.	(see T. 582.) No. 134, 169, 185, 207, 209, 210, 574, 575, 876, 909.
596.	(see T. 587.)
597.	(see T. 126.)

Deans, Printers, Manchester.

SUPPLEMENT

TO THE

HYMN-BOOK

FOR

THE USE OF THE PROTESTANT CHURCH,

OF THE

United Brethren,

PUBLISHED IN 1809.

Ashton-under-Lyne:

PRINTED BY T. CUNNINGHAM, SCOTLAND-STREET.

1819.

THIS collection like the Hymn Book of 1801, of which it is designed to be a continuation, consists partly of translations from the German, and partly of original English compositions. The former are marked with an asterisk.

Nearly the same order has been followed in the arrangement of the Hymns.

An index, containing the first line of every verse, and a table of the tunes is subjoined.

May our Saviour, Jesus Christ, lay his blessing on this publication, and render it subservient to the promotion of that liturgical spirit of singing and making melody unto the Lord, which has always peculiarly characterized the Congregations of the United Brethren!

Fairfield, June 1st, 1808.

CONTENTS.

SUPPLEMENT

1. Of the BIRTH and LIFE of CHRIST.

1001.* T. 22.

REJOICE, our nature Christ assumes,
Born of a virgin, lo! he comes,
God had this birth for him ordain'd;
Adore and wonder ev'ry land.

2. He left his bright, his glorious throne,
He bow'd the heav'ns, to earth came down,
And thus his wondrous race began,
As God with God, and man with man.

3. To save mankind from ruin, sent
From God he came, to God he went,
He stoop'd to death and to the tomb,
Ere he his glory did resume.

4. Behold a great, a heav'nly light,
From Bethle'm's manger shining bright
Around those, who in darkness dwell,
The night of evil to dispel.

5. Incarnate God, exert thy pow'r,
Arise, thou glorious Conqueror,
Subdue sin, death, and ev'ry foe,
Erect thy kingdom here below.

1002.* T. 10.

THE Sun of grace is rising,
Man with his beams rejoicing;
He renders undone sinners
Life's glorious heirs and winners.

2. He, grace and truth revealing,
With man takes up his dwelling,
Assumeth, cloth'd in weakness,
Of sinful flesh, the likeness.

3. What welcome shall I give thee,
Or how shall I receive thee,
Thou long predicted Saviour,
In whom the lost find favor?

4. Accept our pray'rs and praises,
O lovely infant Jesus,
When at thy manger waiting,
For mercy thee entreating.

5. By all in earth and heaven,
To God be glory given,
Who by compassion moved,
Gave up his Son beloved.

6. Here, of Christ's incarnation,
And death, we make confession,
There, shall his love unbounded
In nobler strains be sounded.

1003.* T. 83.

TRULY that eventful day,
When the God of our salvation
Helpless in a manger lay,
Of our bliss laid the foundation,
Centuries had never gain'd
What He then for man obtain'd.

2. But why do we Jesus see,
Thus assuming human nature?

Ah! 'twas done for me, for me,
To redeem a wretched creature,
Even me, yea thousands more,
Yet as mine, I him adore.

3. Of such love what mortal can
Fathom the unbounded ocean?
God, the Holy One, loves man;
Sink, my soul, in deep devotion!
First in love the plan He laid,
And man in his image made.

4. When this favor'd creature fell,
Forfeiting his Lord's communion,
And with Satan, sin and hell
Formed a rebellious union,
Still with love lost man He sought,
And with blood and torments bought.

5. Stronger far his love, than death!
Yea before the world's foundation,
Ere first creatures drew their breath,
Or the elements took station,
Worms or seraphs had their place,
Fixed stood his scheme of grace.

6. Who would venture to explain,
With what holy exultation
He foretold his blood-bought gain,
What the heav'nly hosts' sensation,
When with joy and wonder mix'd,
They beheld his purpose fix'd?

7. Scarce had Adam fall'n from grace,
Ev'n in paradise insnared,
When with parent's tenderness
God his will to save declared;
Should not such great mercy move
All to praise, adore and love?

8. See th' almighty God descend,
At the time by him directed,
Thirty years on earth to spend,
As a man despis'd, rejected,
As a victim to be slain,
His love's purpose to obtain.

9. What sure prophecies foretold,
And mysterious types depicted,
Sacred covenants of old,
Solemn promises predicted,
All was made Amen and Yea,
On that great eventful day.

10. What shall I now give to thee?
Take my heart as a thank-off'ring:
What hast thou not done for me,
By that life of woe and suff'ring?
This to man restoreth all
He had lost by Adam's fall.

1004. T. 585.

HEAR, ye sinners, peace and pardon,
Freely offer'd, glad receive;
Nor your hearts yet longer harden,
Hear his voice, and ye shall live;
" To God glory in the highest,
" On earth peace, good will to men!"

2. Meek and lowly see your Saviour,
Meet returning prodigals;
He receives them into favor,
Therefore come, 'tis God who calls;
" Unto us a Son is given,
" Unto us a Child is born."

3. Now to Bethle'm we're invited,
Or to Calv'ry him to know,
But ere long we shall be cited,
When the trump of God shall blow,
'Fore the presence of his glory,
As the Judge of quick and dead.

4. Then on clouds in glory seated,
He'll pronounce their final doom,
Who, while here, tho' oft entreated,
For Immanuel found no room.
Gracious Saviour! since thou callest,
May not one of us refuse.

5. May we all once stand before thee,
Giv'n unto thee without loss,
As thy saints, who here adore thee,
In the manger, on the cross;
" To God glory in the highest,
" On earth peace, good will to men."

1005. T. 585.

PEACE on earth! heav'n is proclaiming,
Peace, descending from above,
Peace, good will, lost man reclaiming,
Peace from God, God who is love!
Peace in Jesus :||: Peace, that never shall remove.

2. Glory to our great Creator,
Glory in the highest strain,
Glory to the Mediator,
Both from angels and from men:
To Immanuel :||: Praise and glory doth pertain.

1006. T. 582.

REJOICE in Jesus' birth,
To us a Son is giv'n,
To us a Child is born on earth,
Who made both earth and heav'n.

2. His arm supports the sky,
The universe sustains;
The God supreme, the Lord most high,
The King Messiah reigns.

3. His name, his nature soar
Beyond the angels' ken,
Yet He, whom heav'nly hosts adore,
Still pleads the cause of men.

4. Our Counsellor we praise,
Our Advocate above,
Who daily in his church displays
His miracles of love.

5. Th' Almighty God is He,
Author of life and bliss,
The Father of eternity,
The glorious Prince of peace.

1007. T. 16.

WELCOME, blessed, heav'nly stranger,
Holy Spirit, ope mine eyes,
Lead me to my Saviour's manger,
Show me where my Jesus lies.

2. O most Mighty, O most Holy,
Far above the seraphs' thought!
Zion, view thy King, as lowly
As inspired prophets taught.

1008. T. 205.

GRACIOUS Saviour, mov'd by love,
Thou the lofty heav'ns didst bow,
Thou did'st leave thy throne above,
With lost man to dwell below;
Here among us thou wilt be,
We rejoice alone in thee,
Here thy name we will record,
O Immanuel, our Lord.

1009. T. 159.

WISDOM and pow'r to Christ belong,
Who left his glorious throne,
The new, the blessed gospel-song
Is due to him alone;
Join all on earth in Jesus' praise,
Join with the highest seraphs' lays,
To us, to us God's Son is giv'n,
The Lord of earth and heav'n.

1010. T. 583.

WHEN with the eye of faith I Jesus see,
Array'd in feeble, frail humanity,
As toiling, resting, sleeping, or awake,
Deeply abas'd I own, 'twas for my sake.

1011.* T. 168.

MAN of sorrows and acquainted
With our griefs, what shall we say?
Never language yet hath painted
All the woes, that on thee lay:
Had I seen thee cloth'd in weakness,
Bearing our reproach and sickness,
To attend thee day and night
Would have been my heart's delight.

2. O that to this heav'nly stranger
I had here my homage paid,
From his first sigh in the manger,
Till He cried: "*Tis finished:*"
That first sigh had consecrated
Me his own, and I had waited
On him from his infancy,
In a constant liturgy.

3. Walking, speaking, in devotion,
Far to fields or forests stray'd,
I had watched ev'ry motion,
And my Lord my pattern made:
More have angels ne'er desired,
Than on him, or far retired,
Or at home, awake, asleep,
Fix'd, their wond'ring eyes to keep.

4. Tell me, little flock beloved,
Ye, on whom shone Jesus' face;
What within your souls then moved,
When ye felt his kind embrace?
O disciple, once most blessed,
As a bosom friend caressed,
Say, could e'er into thy mind
Other objects entrance find!

5. Oft to pray'r, by night retreated,
See him from all search withdrawn;
Tearful eyes, and sighs repeated
Witness'd still the morning dawn;
There, where He made intercession,
I had pour'd forth my confession,
And where for my sins he wept,
Praying, I the watch had kept.

6. Should I thus to thee have cleaved,
'Midst thy poverty and woes,
On thee, as my Lord, believed,
Or perhaps have join'd thy foes?
Ah! thy mercy I had spurned;
But thyself my heart hast turned;
Now thou know'st, beneath, above,
Nought compar'd with thee I love.

II Of the SUFFERINGS and DEATH of CHRIST.

1012. T. 167.

JESUS to thy garden lead us,
To behold thy bloody sweat,
Tho' thou from the curse hast freed us,
Let us ne'er the cost forget;
Be thy groans and cries rehearsed
By thy spirit in our ears,
Till we, viewing whom we pierced,
Melt 'fore thee in grateful tears.

1013.* T. 99.

I smite upon my guilty breast,
And stand myself the cause confest
Of all my Saviour hath sustained;
On Olivet and Golgotha
Deeply abas'd I gaze with awe,
There, there He bliss for me obtained!

2. O that my sins might find their grave,
There, where my God, my soul to save,
In sweat and blood lay agonizing!
I weep, and feel both joy and pain;
Saviour, till sight of thee I gain,
May I this scene be oft revising!

3. Behold, He sinks in death! 'tis done,
See drops of blood still trickling run,
From head and feet, and hands extended;
Mark that last groan! He bows his head!
The tortur'd soul at length hath fled,
His heart-strings break! the conflict's ended.

4. Look up, my soul, by faith and see,
His heart was pierc'd, was pierc'd for thee;
Thence blood and water freely streamed!
Blood to atone for heinous sin,
Water, to wash the sinner clean;
Our debt is paid; we are redeemed.

5. Heart-piercing sight! He bleeds, He dies,
For guilty man a sacrifice,
The earth the sacred trust receiveth;
Soon shall he rise triumphantly,
And then with shouts ascend on high,
Where He to God for ever liveth.

1014*. T. 124.

JESUS, till my latest breath,
May I ponder
On thy agony and death;
As thou yonder
Barest my sins' heavy load,

Suff'ring Saviour,
Me regard in favor.

2. Looking to Gethsemane,
In that garden,
Both the guilt of sin I see,
And its pardon;
Mercy, truth, and righteousness
Here combined,
Man's release have signed.

3. Jesus, on thy dol'rous way
I would meet thee;
With what cruel mockery
Sinners treat thee,
While a crown of pointed thorns
Meekly wearing,
Thy sore temples tearing!

4. From the cross look down at me,
Blessed Saviour!
As at John complacently!
Grant that favor,
That I, by thy dying love,
Be inspired,
And with ardor fired.

5, In thy hands and feet I see
Tokens bloody
Of thy love to worthless me;
From thy body
Drops of blood successively
Now are streaming,
All with blessings teeming.

6. Jesus bows His head and dies!
Dark'ning heaven,
Lo the sun his beams denies,
Rocks are riven!
While earth's pillars shake, I find
In His passion
Cause for exultation,

7. Blood and water from his side
Freely floweth:
Hence I'm fully certified,
My heart knoweth,
That eternal life for me
Was acquired,
When my Lord expired.

8. Now to Joseph's tomb convey'd,
He's interred,
Be my members with him dead,
With him buried
Here, here is my resting place,
Here with Mary,
Weeping I will tarry.

9. Yes I give my heart to thee,
Faithful Saviour!
Living, dying I will be
Thine for ever;
From the tomb I once shall rise,
Freed from weakness,
In thy glorious likeness.

1015.* T. 22.

ROUND Tabor heav'nly glories
shone,
But what on Olivet was done,
What signaliz'd mount Calvary,
Calls forth my praise:—'twas done
for me.

1016. T. 166.

WHEN I survey the wondrous cross,
On which the prince of glory died,
My richest gain I count but loss,
And blush, ashamed of my pride;
Forbid it, Lord, that I should boast
In ought besides my ransom price,
All the vain things which charm'd
me most
For Christ I freely sacrifice.

2. Behold the dying Lamb of God,
And say, was grief like His e'er
known;
See from his wounds in streams of blood
Sorrow and love flow mingled down;
What can I offer, that's not thine?
My thanks, O Lord, how short
they fall!
Love so amazing, so divine,
Demands my soul, my life, my All.

1017.* T. 126.

WITH grateful heart's sensation
At Jesus' feet I fall;
Him with deep adoration
My Lord and God I call.
Since he sustained death for me,
Procuring my redemption,
Upon th' accursed tree,

2. His stripes, whereby I'm healed,
Are precious to my soul,
His blood is now revealed,
The balm to make me whole;
His cry: "My God, my God, Ah! why,
"Why hast thou me forsaken?"
To God now brings me nigh.

3. In holy contemplation
I day and night review
The theme of Christ's salvation
And find it ever new;
My pulse shall to his honor beat,
And till his blest appearing,
Each breath his praise repeat.

4. Myself I now deliver
Into his faithful hand,
He will support me ever,
Till I before him stand;
Till then I never can forget
That his atoning passion
Hath cancell'd all my debt.

1018. T. 244.

THE slaughter'd Lamb, my Saviour,
Remains my sole delight,
My fav'rite theme for ever,
My object day and night;
The incense of his pray'rs,
His cries and bitter tears,
For me to God ascendeth,
My plaintive cry He hears.

2. With God my habitation
Upon mount Calvary,
I'll fix without cessation;
Here it is good to be!
Thus from my Saviour's death
Deriving life by faith,
Of heav'n I have a foretaste,
Until my latest breath.

1019.* T. 14.

WHENEVER I my matchless friend
In spirit suff'ring see,
Again those stripes I call to mind,
Which He endur'd for me.

2. Thereby inflam'd, my heart doth burn
In love to the Lamb slain,
And grateful tears are the return
I make him for his pain.

1020. T. 136.

I WEEP for joy,
And tender love's emotion,
When I Christ's suff'rings trace with deep devotion,
From Olivet
To Calv'ry's bloody brow;
When him with scoffing multitudes surrounded
I view from head to foot for my transgressions wounded,
Ah! then it is my blest employ,
To weep for joy.

2. He died for me,
For me became an off'ring,
My sin-sick soul He healeth by His suff'ring,
His precious blood,
For my redemption shed,
An open fountain is for my transgression,
I in his sacred wounds, those pledges of salvation,
Discover my election free.
He died for me.

1021.* T. 151.

HERE am I blushing, weeping,
A breeze of heav'nly bliss
From Jesus' cross perceiving,
Rejoicing that I'm his;
To Him what shall I render,
My grateful heart to show?
Did but my love more tender,
More ardent for him glow!

2. I was defil'd all over,
Depraved and unclean;
His blood my guilt did cover,
And wash'd my soul from sin;
The time I well remember,
When fill'd with deepest awe,
My name among the number,
In the Lamb's book I saw.

3. My Saviour's death and passion,
His anguish, grief and pain,
Until my consummation,
My fav'rite theme remain;
Himself hath sanctified
The grave, my resting place,
And since for me He died,
I shall lie down in peace.

1022.* T. 168.

THOU hast cancell'd my transgression,
Jesus, by thy precious blood,
May I find therein salvation,
Happiness and peace with God;
And since thou, for sinners suff'ring,
On the cross wast made an off'ring,
From all sin deliver me,
That I wholly thine may be.

2. All the pain thou hast endured,
All thy wounds, thy crown of thorn,
Hands and feet, with nails thro'-bored,
The reproach, which thou hast borne;
Thy back, ploughed with deep furrows,
Cross and grave, and all thy sorrows,
Thy blood-sweat and agony,
O Lord Jesus, comfort me!

1023.* T. 36.

LAMB, for thy boundless love I praises offer,
That love, which urg'd thee in my stead to suffer,
While all the wrath, which I should have endured,
On thee was poured.

2. How highly is poor man by thee esteemed!
Thou gav'st thyself, that he might be redeemed,
Take soul and body, Lord, as an oblation,
For all thy passion.

3. Thou richly dost deserve, that each pulsation
Thy praises should express without cessation.
And that each drop of blood be hallow'd ever,
To thee, my Saviour.

1024. T. 582.

WAS ever grief like thine,
Jesus, thou man of woe?
The visage and the form divine,
Why was it marred so?
That man by thee restor'd,
God's image might regain,
And by the sorrows of his Lord,
In joys eternal reign.

1025.* T. 185.

UNTO Jesus cross I'm now retiring,
There my Saviour's pierced feet,
(Dying love a grateful sense inspiring)
Bath'd in tears I humbly greet;
Might I never lose this blest impression,
But in spirit fix my happy station
On those heights so dear to me,
Golgotha, Gethsemane.

2. Might thy dying look, dear suff'ring Saviour,
Which subdu'd my stubborn heart,
Me engage, and rule my whole behaviour,
Till I from this world depart;
Thus my mortal body I shall cherish,
And as thine, with holy rev'rence nourish,
Watching, praying, that I now
May into thine image grow.

3. With a mind, from earthly cares divested,
Let me dwell by day and night,
Where the body of my Saviour rested,
Here I find supreme delight;
Here 'tis good for me with pardon'd Mary,
At his sepulchre in faith to tarry,
Thus in blessed fellowship
With my Lord I wake and sleep.

1026. T. 598.

BELOVED, white and ruddy,
Of thousands none so fair;
I with thy wounded body
No beauty can compare;
Here to thy care consigned,
Within thy tomb enshrined,
Might but my body lie;
To thee my soul would fly.

2. But while on earth I tarry,
Wrapt in this mortal vest,
Within thy sanctuary,
My troubled soul finds rest.
Here die all strange affections;
O might 'midst imperfections,
Ev'n in my looks be seen,
That I with God have been.

3. In this sepulchral Eden,
The tree of life I've found,
Here is my treasure hidden,
I tread on hallow'd ground;
Ye sick, ye faint and weary,
Howe'er your ailments vary,
Creep hither and make sure
Of a most perfect cure.

4. Here lies in death's embraces
My Bridegroom, Lord and God;
With awe my soul retraces
The bloody, dol'rous road,
That leads to this last station;
Here in sweet meditation
I'll dwell by day and night,
Till faith is chang'd to sight.

III. Of the FATHER, SON and HOLY GHOST.

1027.* T. 58.

GLORY to the Father,
Who in Christ Jesus,
Doth as dear children own, and richly bless us, World without end.

2. Glory unto Jesus,
The man of sorrows,
Who suffer'd, died, rose and revived for us, That we might live.

3. Glory and obedience,
To th' Holy Spirit,
Who glorifies Christ Jesus, and his merit, To us applies.

4. Lamb of God, once wounded
For our salvation,
Let all who breathe, proclaim thy bitter passion, For evermore.

1028. T. 14.

TILL God in human flesh I see,
My thoughts no comfort find,
The holy, just and sacred Three
Fill with dismay my mind:

2. But when Immanuel's face appears,
My hope, my joy begins,
His name forbids my slavish fears,
His grace removes my sins.

1029. T. 590.

FATHER of angels and of men,
Saviour, who us hast bought,
Spirit, by whom we're born again,
And sanctified and taught;
Thy glory, holy Three in One,
Thy people's song shall be,
Long as the wheels of time shall run,
And thro' eternity.

1030. T. 249.

WITH holy awe we cry,
Glory :||: to God on high;
To the blest Trinity,
Blessing and praise be ever giv'n,
By all on earth and all in heav'n;
Amen. Hallelujah,
Hallelujah.
Amen, Hallelujah!

1031.* T. 58.

LORD God, Abba Father,
The whole creation
With us unites in praise and adoration, To thy great name.

2. Unto thee we render
Eternal praises,
For having manifested in Christ Jesus
Thy love to us.

1032.* T. 125.

OUR Father, great and glorious,
On heav'n's exalted throne,
Thy kingdom prove victorious,
That Jesus Christ, thy Son,
May for his death and passion,
From ev'ry tongue and nation,
Receive a rich reward.

1033.* T. 68.

O eternal Word,
Jesus Christ, our Lord!
While the hosts of heav'n adore thee,
We with awe fall down before thee,
And with rapture raise
Songs of love and praise.

2. God and man indeed,
Comfort in all need,
Thou becam'st a man of sorrows,
To gain life eternal for us,
By thy precious blood,
Jesus, man and God.

1034. T. 22.

LORD Jesus, praise to thee be giv'n,
Creator both of earth and heav'n,
Who wast from everlasting Lord,
And art as God and man ador'd.

2. Praise be to thee in Christendom,
Who was, who art, and art to come;
Thy lauds shall dwell upon our tongues,
All saints and angels join our songs.

3. Thy incarnation claims our praise,
We thank thee for thy boundless grace,
We love thee, since thou man wast made,
And hast as man our ransom paid.

4. Receive our thanks, O Lamb of God,
Who hast redeem'd us by thy blood;
Might all mankind thy name adore,
For thy atonement evermore.

1035.* T. 22.

GOD Holy Ghost, how gloriously,
In Christs' redeemed property
Is thy almighty pow'r display'd,
The same that earth and heaven made.

2. When thou thy unction dost impart,
And breath'st new life into the heart,
When thy all-penetrating light
Dispels the thickest gloom of night,

3. When thou revealest Christ to us,
And guid'st our eyes unto his cross,
Thy pow'r divine both far and near,
In countless wonders doth appear.

1036. T. 341.

THOU promis'd Comforter,
Fruit of the Saviour's pray'r,
Thee the world cannot receive,
Thee they neither know nor see,
Dead is all the life they live,
Dark their light, while void of thee.

2. Yet I partake thy grace,
Thro' Christ, my righteousness,
Mine the gifts thou dost impart,
Mine the unction from above,
Pardon written on my heart,
Light and life and joy and love.

3. Thee I exult to feel,
Thou in my heart dost dwell,
There thou bear'st thy witness true,
Shed'st the love of God abroad,
I, in Christ, a creature new,
I, ev'n I, am born of God.

4. Thy gifts, blest Comforter,
I glory to declare,
Sweetly sure of grace I am,
Pardon to my soul applied,

Int'rest in the spotless Lamb,
Dead for all, for me he died.

5. Thou art thyself the seal,
I more than pardon feel,
Peace, unutterable peace,
Joy, that ages ne'er can move,
Faith's assurance, hope's increase,
All the confidence of love.

6. Pledge of the promise giv'n,
My antepast of heaven,
Earnest thou of joys divine,
Joys divine on me bestow'd,
Heav'n and Christ and All is mine,
I'm through thee, an heir of God.

7. Thou art my inward guide,
I ask no help beside;
Holy Ghost, on thee I call,
Weak as helpless infancy;
Weak I am, yet cannot fall,
Stay'd by faith, and led by thee.

1037*. T. 155.

PRAISE the Spirit's mighty work,
For he proves himself most glorious,
And victorious,
Ruling by his influence
Heart and sense:
Doth he not from Jesus' merit,
Truth and comfort, life and spirit,
Grace and health to us dispense?

IV. Of FAITH in CHRIST.

1038.* T. 167.

ERE we know our lost condition,
Ere we feel our inbred woe,
And exclaim, with deep contrition,
"To be sav'd, what must I do?"
Nought can yield true consolation,
Vain is all our righteousness:
Faith alone in Christ's oblation
Gives the conscience rest and peace.

2. Living faith, with clearest vision,
Sees the Lamb upon the throne,
And in him a full provision,
Righteousness and peace, our own:
Then our days are mark'd with blessing,
Then our hearts with rapture glow;
Streams of comfort, rich, unceasing,
From the wounds of Jesus flow.

1039. T. 167.

AS the serpent, rais'd by Moses,
Heal'd the fiery serpent's bite,
Jesus thus himself discloses,
To the wounded sinner's sight;
Hear his gracious invitation:
"I have life and peace to give;
"I have wrought out full salvation,
"Sinner, look to me and live."

2. Dearest Saviour, we adore thee,
For thy precious life and death,
Melt each stubborn heart before thee,
Give us all the eye of faith;
From the law's condemning sentence
To thy mercy we appeal:
Thou alone can'st give repentance,
Thou alone our souls can'st heal.

1040.* T. 121.

THE Lamb of God was slain,
Salvation to obtain;
No sinner need to die,
Those only who disdain
His grace, in ruin lie,
Since they will not flee
To the treasury
Of his mercy free.

2. His people now confess
With joy unto his praise;
"Tho' we by one man fell,
"By whose unrighteousness,
"We all are sinners still;
"Yet thro' the Lamb slain,

"Thro' his toil and pain,
"We true life obtain."

1041.* T. 22.

WHEN shall I gain the glorious dress,
Prepar'd to clothe my nakedness?
I need it, Lord, without that vest,
I cannot be a wedding guest.

2. When thus I cried in deep distress,
Christ cloth'd me in his righteousness;
And now, thank God, the work is done:
I've put my Lord and Saviour on.

3. When Christ our life shall once appear,
It will be manifest and clear,
That is atoning blood from sin
Hath wash'd and kept our garments clean.

1042.* T. 4.

DEAR Lord, when I trace
Thy mercy and grace,
Upon me bestow'd,
'Fore thee with abasement, I sink, deeply bow'd.

2. How blind have I been,
A vile slave of sin,
Till thy gospel-light [not right,
Arous'd me from death, yet I knew it

3. Myself I could feel
Deserving of hell,
And such was my case, [was.
As if I too one of Christ's murderers

4. Then whisper'd the foe,
Still plotting our woe,
"To sin, death, and me
"A slave thou yet art, and for ever shalt be."

5. For refuge I fled
To Jesus, and pray'd:
"Dear Saviour, thy will,
"And purpose of grace in me, sinner, fulfill!"

6. To me he drew near,
His voice I could hear;
"Come, sinful and base,
"Receive, tho' unworthy, my pardon and grace."

7. Behold, Lord, how we
Most gladly would be
Made clean by thy blood,
The robe of thy righteousness deck us, O God.

8. Altho' we are vile,
Yet are we thy spoil,
Since we can by faith,
Joy in the atonement, wrought out by thy death.

9. All they who believe,
And in Jesus live,
Obtain free access, [holy place.
Thro' him our High Priest, to the most

10. Lord Jesus, to thee
We all bow the knee,
At thy feet we fall, [our all.
Accept of our homage, for thou art

1043. T. 14.

THOU Friend of sinners, hear my cry,
And grant me my request,
May I in thy atonement find
My everlasting rest.

2. May I no more resist thy love,
No more thy Spirit grieve;
But as a little child become,
And simply thee believe.

3. Faith is thy gift, thou slaughter'd Lamb,
Gain'd by thy death for me,
Therefore the privilege I claim,
A child of God to be.

4. Impress this truth upon my breast,
That thou for me hast died,
That I in thee with confidence,
For ever may abide.

1044. T. 96.

I TO my God am reconcil'd,
With joy his pard'ning voice I hear,
He owns me his adopted child,
His love forbids all anxious fear;
With confidence I now draw nigh,
And Abba! Abba Father! cry.

V. Of Thankfulness for Christ's Birth and Death.

1045.* T. 147.

IMPRESS'D with filial fear,
A breeze divine perceiving,
Its influence receiving,
With awe we thee revere;
Our eyes with tears o'erflowing,
Our souls devoutly glowing,
That thought absorbs us now:
"Thou, Jesus, only thou!"

2. Who can thy kindness prove,
Or know thy great salvation,
And not with exultation
Confess, that God is love?
Thou Messenger anointed,
The Lamb, by God appointed,
By all in earth and heav'n,
To thee be praises giv'n.

1046.* T. 126.

TO earth no longer cleaving,
I look to Jesus' cross,
All this world's trifles leaving,
For Him count all things loss,
Who underwent such racking pain,
Distress of soul, and anguish,
Vile sinners to regain.

2. I'm lost in deepest wonder,
When I am led to trace
His dying love, and ponder
On his amazing grace;
How he, by giving up his breath,
Procur'd life and salvation,
For rebels doom'd to death.

3. Grace thro' the blood of Jesus,
The contrite soul's delight!
Nought else on earth could ease us,
Should we of this lose sight,
And could we not, thro' mercy free,
Our worthless names engraven
In Jesus' nail-prints see.

4. O were his death impressed
On us indelibly!
Our lot would be most blessed;
How can we happier be,
Then when his rod and staff impart
True joy and consolation
Unto the needy heart?

1047.* T. 126.

O what complete salvation
In Jesus I possess!
In his atoning passion
I find true happiness;
I'm now content on earth to live,
Since to my unseen Saviour,
Thro' grace by faith, I cleave.

2. In him I can completely
Rejoice, ev'n when in pain,
And would ought dissipate me,
He leads me back again;
By him protected, I'm secure,
From every dart of Satan,
From ev'ry thought impure.

3. Nought but my Saviour's passion,
Can purify the heart;
And bid the infatuation
Of world and sin depart:
The very thought is then abhorr'd:
That I those things should cherish,
Which crucified my Lord.

4. O Lamb of God tormented!
Thy pain and anguish sore
Have me to thee cemented,
And bound for evermore;
Who'er relies thereon alone,
Will safely be conducted,
Until his race is run.

5. I trust in Jesus' merit,
My life flows from his death,
And doth his Holy Spirit
Before the eye of faith
My crucified Redeemer paint,
I am thro' grace establish'd,
Firm in his covenant.

1048. T. 185.

IF to me experience had not proved,
What surpasseth human thought,
That my Saviour, by compassion moved,

With his blood my pardon bought,
I had spent my days in anxious grieving,
But, to him be thanks, I now believing
In my Lord, by faith receive
Comforts, which the world can't give.

2. O what blessings are from Jesus' passion,
And atoning death deriv'd!
I refuse all other consolation,
If of these I am depriv'd;
But no sooner doth his blood bedew me,
And impart its healing virtue to me,
Than my soul, tho' sunk in grief,
Is restor'd, and finds relief.

3. When my Jesus from the cross complacent,
Casts on me a look of love.
Grateful tears flow down my cheeks incessant,
All my soft affections move;
Could I with a mind from earth divested,
By the cares of this life unmolested,
Be engag'd with him alone,
Then were heav'n on earth begun.

1049.* T. 10.

HEAR, while I am revealing,
The kind and gracious dealing
Of my benign Creator,
With me a worthless creature.

2. By faith to Jesus cleaving,
And in his wounds believing,
Like Thomas I can trace him,
And as my Lord confess him.

3. With grateful heart's sensation
I own, that when his passion,
His cross and death are named,
My soul is then inflamed.

4. From death to life he raised
My soul—his name be praised,
Now I'm regenerated,
And all is new-created.

5. The eye of faith he giveth,
Which seeth him and liveth,
An ear, to hear with pleasure
His word, that sacred treasure.

6. He graciously conducts me;
The Holy Ghost instructs me;
To understand more fully
His mind, and know him truly.

7. From Jesu's blood and merit,
I gain new life and spirit,
Forgiveness, grace, salvation,
Strength, joy, and consolation.

8. My spirit him embraces,
He all my wants redresses,
I in his love's fruition,
Am happy without vision.

9. Am I, of him possessed,
Already here so blessed;
What joys shall I be tasting,
When in his presence resting.

10. While, lost in deepest wonder,
On my blest lot I ponder,
Tears down my cheeks are stealing,
These best declare my feeling.

1050.* T. 205.

ALL the bliss, which we possess,
Is deriv'd from Jesus' cross;
He to God, hath by his blood,
Reconcil'd and saved us;
Now his righteousness is found
Our salvation's only ground;
Hence all our felicity
Springs here and eternally.

2. Amen yea, Hallelujah!
Lord, our comfort, joy and peace,
By thy cross thou gain'dst for us
Everlasting happiness!
Since th' effects we richly prove
Of this wondrous act of love,
With what gratitude should we
Raise our hearts and eyes to thee!

1051.* T. 58.

PRAISE be to Christ! for us he vict'ry gain'd,
In judgement he our cause by right obtain'd,
We are his thro' mercy: to him our Saviour

We'll humbly cleave, till we shall have the favor, To see his face.

2. While saints in glory praise their heav'nly King,
Let his church militant thanksgivings bring,
Since 'tis solely owing to Jesus' passion,
That no believer needs a separation,
From God to fear.

3. Thy saving name be hallow'd evermore,
Lord Jesus, let thy kingdom come with pow'r;
Might all nations render to thee the glory,
Since not one sinner is despis'd before thee, Saviour of all.

1052. T. 167.

PRAISE for ev'ry scene distressing,
Praise for all thou didst endure,
Praise for ev'ry gift and blessing,
Which thy griefs for us procure;
In thy ransom'd congregation
Shall thy death our theme remain,
Till thou com'st, with full salvation,
Lord of glory, Lamb once slain.

1053.* T. 146.

MIGHT with an iron pen
This truth divine be graven;
For sinners Christ was slain,
To purchase life and heaven;
Unwearied we prolong,
And joyfully repeat
The blessed gospel song;
'Tis ever new and sweet.

VI. Of BROTHERLY LOVE.

1054.* T. 583.

HOW good and pleasant is it to behold
The favour'd sheep of our good Shepherd's fold,
By grace upheld, in love and knowledge grow,
Each sharing in the other's weal and woe.

2. Fullness of grace in him, our Head abounds,
Hence ev'ry blessing to his church redounds;
He dwells among us and his Spirit's light,
To love each other, teacheth us aright.

3. The word of God like plenteous rain descends,
And fructifying pow'r its course attends,
Unto our souls it richest food supplies,
And to salvation makes us truly wise.

4. If love unfeign'd we in our actions show,
The God of peace his blessing will bestow;
O Lord preserve thy church, for Jesus' sake,
And bless what in thy name we undertake!

1055.* T. 167.

GRANT, Lord, that with thy direction:
"Love each other:" we comply,
Aiming with unfeign'd affection,
Thy love to exemplify:
Let our mutual love be glowing,
Thus it will to all appear,
That we, as on one stem growing,
In thee living branches are.

2. Oh! that such might be our union,
As thine with the Father is,
And not one of our communion
Might forsake the path of bliss!

May our light 'fore men with brightness
From thy light reflected shine,
Thus the world will bear us witness,
That we, Lord, are truly thine.

1056. T. 79.

DEAR Lord, my soul desireth,
In all thy word requireth,
By works t'adorn thy grace;
O might my conversation
Display, on each occasion
That holy mind, which in thee was.

2. The tent to me allotted,
In honor and unspotted,
I'll cherish and respect;
But if of me required,
Then by thy love inspired,
Comfort and ease for thee neglect.

3. May I esteem my neighbors,
Fair qualities or labors
Of their's retain in mind;
Yea be myself their servant,
Thro' unbid impulse fervent.
As tho' some contract me did bind.

4. In my degree and measure
To aid men be my pleasure,
To edify, my care;
Since thou art ever ready,
Friend of the poor and needy,
All the disconsolate to cheer.

1057.* T. 124.

WHEN the true believer's mind
Grace o'erfloweth,
Then all labor doth succeed,
No hurt groweth;
Pilgrims trav'lling Zion-ward,
Cheer each other,
Each stirs up his brother.

2. By Christ's dying love constrain'd,
None can ever
Him to serve a burthen deem;
'Tis a favor;
Looking unto Christ, what else
Were distressing,
Will become a blessing.

1058. T. 39.

WHAT brought us together? what joined our hearts?
The pardon, which Jesus, our High Priest, imparts:
'Tis this, which cements the disciples of Christ,
Who are into one, by the Spirit baptiz'd.

VII. Of FOLLOWING CHRIST.

1059. T. 83.

WHEN in Jesus' nail-prints blest,
We behold our grace-election,
When in his sweet peace we rest,
Shelter'd under his protection,
We with joy to him resign'd,
Serve him with a willing mind.

2. Would we inward peace enjoy,
We must first be poor in spirit,
At the feet of Jesus lie,
Trusting only in his merit,
Then our kind and loving Lord
Will to us his strength afford.

3. None from God too distant are,
None too sinful, none too wretched;
But they may his mercy share,
For his arms are still outstretched,
Yet we must, while we apply,
Lay all self-dependence by.

4. In this humble, happy frame,
And from grace to grace proceeding
We press forward in his name,
And have cause to bless his leading;
Cheered by his looks of grace
We run our appointed race.

1060.* T. 11.

O my soul, mark ev'ry word
Of thy kind and gracious Lord,
When he calls, without delay,
Willingly his call obey.

2. When he beckons, haste along,
In his power divine be strong,
Should he e'er thy work commend,
Lowly at his foot-stool bend.

3. Hath he ought to say to thee,
An attentive scholar be,
Doth he chasten thee, as son,
"Tis deserved:" humbly own.

1061.* T. 166.

THRICE happy I esteem my lot,
To feel true spirit's poverty,
This portion from the Lord I've got,
It yields content and peace to me:
He gave me this inheritance,
My soul's salvation to advance;
To him eternal thanks and praise
Be render'd for my call of grace.

2. O how exceeding rich and great
The grace of Jesus Christ appears!
He left his heav'nly Father's seat,
To share our sorrows, griefs and tears;
No wordly pomp, or dignity
The sons of men in him could see
When they th' Eternal Word beheld,
His Godhead in our nature veil'd.

3. For us from heav'nly realms exil'd,
A life of pain and woe he led,
By sinners mocked and revil'd
He freely suffer'd in our stead;
That he those, who in him believe
Might as his property receive,
Since by his anguish, death and blood
He reconcil'd us into God.

4. Yea, the world's Saviour, Jesus Christ,
Th' eternal Son of God, became
A man rejected and despis'd,
An object of contempt and shame;
The Maker of creation's sphere
Did in an abject state appear,
That by his poverty the poor
Might be enriched evermore.

5. While here on earth, no place he had,
Where he his weary head could lay,
Oft hungry, thirsty, spent and sad,
He learnt by suff'ring to obey;
His meat and drink was to fulfil
His Heav'nly Father's holy will,
And to seek out the sons of woe,
That he to them might kindness show.

6. Say, O thou love's eternal Source,
What prompted thee this step to take?
Compassion was the mighty force,
O'er sinful man thy heart did break;
Uncall'd thou cam'st to set him free
From sin, from curse and misery,
Yea to enrich and crown his days
With thy salvation, joy and grace.

7. My body, mind and soul combine,
To laud and magnify the Lord,
My Shepherd and my Guide divine,
Who leads me by his holy word,
Preserves me in the narrow way,
Works wonders for me day by day,
Whose staff to comfort never fails,
When any trial me assails.

8. Nought can such pleasure yield to me,
While in this vale of tears I stay,
As that his glory I shall see,
And live with him in endless day;
Ev'n here of everlasting rest,
I of a foretaste am possess'd,
While in sweet union I abide,
With him and with his chosen bride.

9. Most gladly I to others leave
Their worldly treasure, pomp and fame,
Since of Christ's fulness I receive,
I glory only in his name;
In his reproach I freely share,
Who for my sake the cross did bear,
And joy in shame and poverty,
Since Jesus poor became for me.

1062.* T. 14.

GLORY to God, whose witness-
Those heros, bold in faith, [train,
Could smile on poverty and pain,
And triumph, ev'n in death.

2. Scorn'd and revil'd as was their Head,
When walking here below,
Thus in this evil world they led
A life replete with woe.

3. With the same faith our bosom glows,
Wherein these warriors stood,
When in the cruel gripe of these,
Who thirsted for their blood.

4. God, whom we serve, our God can save,
And damp the scorching flame,
Can build an ark, or smooth a wave,
For such as fear his name.

5. Yea should it ev'n to man appear
At times, as tho' our Lord
Forsook his chosen people here,
At last, he'll help afford.

6. If but his arm support us still,
Is but his joy our strength,
We shall ascend the rugged hill,
And conqu'rors prove at length.

1063.* T. 11.

RISE, ye foll'wers of the Lamb,
Serve him midst reproach and shame,
His example keep in view,
And the narrow path pursue.

2. O all wise, sublime decree!
He assum'd humanity,
Liv'd on earth despis'd and poor,
Died, salvation to procure.

3. See his faithful witness-train,
They endur'd the cross and pain;
(Men, the world deserved not)
Hard and cheerless was their lot.

4. Should we not rejoice to see
Our names in heav'ns registry,
With the names of those enroll'd,
Who shall reap an hundred-fold.

1064.* T. 16.

IN that glorious vest arrayed,
Wherein we 'fore God can stand,
We will Jesus undismayed
Follow, joining heart and hand.

2. If our lives for him we venture,
And depending on his grace,
On the hardest trials enter,
This gives courage and success.

3. Of our lives we will be careful,
While reserved for his use,
But, when he demands, unfearful,
Wealth and life for Jesus lose.

1065.* T. 79.

AS thy will, O my Saviour,
Unto thy Father's ever
Was subject and resign'd;
Grant that in deep subjection,
To follow thy direction,
I may be cheerfully inclin'd.

1066.* T. 14.

O MAY we, Saviour, step for step,
Bear thee sweet company,
Thus will, whate'er we undertake,
An act of worship be.

1067.* T. 14.

TO belong to Christ our Saviour
Christian, what doth this imply?
Constantly to seek his favor,
Ever watching faithfully;
To implore his kind direction,
Day by day, in all we do,
To confide in his protection,
Freed from ev'ry earthly view,

1068.* T. 155.

AMEN yea, Head of thy church,
Grant, we pray, this our petition,
In submission
To thy will, with steady pace,
In thy ways
To proceed: if thou attend us,
Cross or shame shall not offend us,
Thee we boldly will confess.

VIII. Of SELF-KNOWLEDGE.

1069.* T. 22.

TO God our Saviour let us pray,
That he would fashion us like clay,
His mind into our hearts infuse,
And teach us all his blessed views.

2. Detach'd from ev'ry earthly thing,
O might we cleave to Christ our King;
Might our whole walk resemble his,
And witness, where our treasure is.

1070.* T. 228.

ALAS! we're sinful, vile and base,
Yet freely justified by grace,
A myst'ry this, concealed
From all, but those, who gladly own:
"This truth to me had ne'er been known,
"By flesh and blood revealed;
"O no—I owe
"My experience:—And assurance
"Of salvation
"To the Spirit's operation."

2. Whoe'er himself of sinners chief
Esteems and burthen'd seeks relief
From the reproach he feareth,
The evil knows, which in him lies,
However hidden from man's eyes
It fair and good appeareth,
Mourning—Turning
To the Victim—For man's ransom
Finds exemption
From sin's yoke and full redemption.

3. Now guilty blushes him o'erspread,
Again, like John, he falls as dead,
Before Jehovah Jesus,
And worships him with humble fear,
'Fore whom, when they to him draw near,
The angels veil their faces:
"Ah! why—do I;
Saith the sinner—"From my Saviour
"Life inherit?
"Tis all owing to his merit."

4. He, who in Jesus' death believes,
From thence all righteousness receives,
And all sanctification;
Tho' stripp'd of ev'ry self-made good,
Is by the virtue of his blood
Freed from sin's condemnation:
Its voice— Still cries
In his favor—Christ, our Saviour
For him pleadeth,
This is all the plea he needeth.

5. But why is not my wav'ring mind
At all times willingly inclin'd,
To live to my Lord's pleasure;
Why is not the new creature seen
In thought, in action, word and mein,
In it's full stature's measure?
O I—Must sigh.
Until fully—Render'd holy
By his merit,
I with him become one spirit.

6. Yet hark! the Bridegroom's voice I hear,
He whispers in my list'ning ear,
That he my suit approveth;
He, who unto himself, his bride,
The church, betrothed when he died,
Me, needy sinner, loveth:
Thus he—Cheers me;
"I to gladness—Turn thy sadness;
Here is weeping,
Once in joy we shall be reaping.

1071. T. 37.

THEY that are whole need not
The good physician,
But they who know and feel
Their lost condition,
Bewail their wretched state,
To Christ appealing,
Experience of his stripes
The virtue healing.

2. We know, that in our flesh
No good thing dwelleth,
But with ne'er failing skill
Our wounds he healeth;

Thus spirit, body, soul,
Tho' poor and needy,
Can to rejoice in him
Be ever ready.

1072. T. 159.

HOW needful, strictly to enquire
And ask our hearts each day,
"Doth Jesus' love me still inspire,
"My thoughts and actions sway?
"Am I a branch in Christ the vine?
"Am I his own, and is he mine?
"Do I by faith unto him cleave,
"And to his honor live?

2. The Spirit's witness, full and clear,
Will state the real case,
And either draw a contrite tear,
Or thanks unfeigned raise;
Hence will the consequence ensue,
That the full purpose we renew,
To run in faith th' appointed race,
Till we shall see his face.

1073.* T. 167.

FAITHFUL souls, with real blessing,
Celebrate their natal day,
Asking: "are we onward pressing?
"What may Jesus have to say?
"Are the ways of sin unpleasant?
"Do we hold our Saviour fast?
"Are we more like him at present,
"Than we were in seasons past?

2. Great defects are still revealed;
Short we fall of his blest aim;
Then the conscious soul is filled
With a deep, but wholesome shame;
Earnest to improve the morrow,
We our yesterday review,
While the tear of godly sorrow
Saddens, but enlivens too.

3. Jesus, for thy faithful leading
In times past, we humbly raise
Our thanksgiving, thus proceeding
Onward in the path of grace;
While another year we enter,
We renew our vows of love,
All for thee resolv'd to venture,
Our benign conductor prove!

1074. T. 11.

THEY; who know our Lord indeed,
Find in him a friend in need,
And behold in Jesus' face,
Nought but mercy, truth and grace.

2. They can cast by faith their care
On that Lord, who heareth pray'r,
And when they to him draw nigh,
He doth all their wants supply.

3. They who him, their Saviour know,
Lowly at his foot-stool bow;
They, to whom his name is dear,
Greatly to offend him fear.

4. But this very fear is sweet,
While abased at his feet,
He with gentle voice doth chide
Their unfaithfulness and pride.

5. O how wond'rous is his love,
To all, who his goodness prove,
Deep abasement, heav'nly joy,
Their alternate thoughts employ.

6. Wonders without end we see,
Countless mercies, great and free;
Lord, accept our thanks and praise
For thy goodness, truth and grace.

1075. T. 14.

WHO saith he's poor, nor feels within
With deepest shame his need,
Convicted on account of sin,
He is not poor indeed.

2. But he, who knows himself aright,
Is ready to confess,
Instructed by the Spirit's light,
His utter helplessness.

3. How greatly he forgiveness wants
In Jesus' blood, he knows,
With inward spirit's ardor pants,
In him to find repose.

4. Who is so full of tenderness,
And patience, as thou, Lord?
But I must own with shame, alas!
I oft transgress thy word.

6. Oh! from my heart, God Holy Ghost,
This suit I make to thee:
Show me how much my ransom cost,
How great my poverty.

1076.* T. 22.

O LORD, 'fore thee abas'd I fall,
And on thy name for mercy call,
The faults indeed are numberless,
Which humbly I to thee confess.

2. I give myself to thee anew,
My soul and body are thy due,
Form me into thy likeness here,
By means, or gentle, or severe.

3. Grant that I may henceforth to thee
More faithful and obedient be,
O may thy blood and righteousness
My beauty be, my glorious dress.

1077. T. 36.

THY love unchanging is our consolation,
Thy patience and long suff'ring our salvation,
O thou our yesterday, to-day and ever,
Most faithful Saviour,

2. Thy purposes of love remain unshaken,
Tho' we alas! our vows have oft forsaken,
Forgive, bear with us, grant us thy direction,
And kind protection.

3. As a thick cloud let all our sins be blotted
Out of thy book, that nothing past be noted,
As children, chasten us when we are failing,
Heal us, when ailing,

1078.* T. 159.

WHEN in thy spirit's light, O Lord,
Our hearts we strictly search,
Whether we joy to thee afford,
And edify thy church,
Directing every thought and aim
Unto the honor of thy name,
Then our defects so great appear,
We drop a contrite tear.

1079. T. 96.

NO longer to behold the tree,
Where Christ our guilt and curse did bear,
No longer him by faith to see
Nor feel him to our spirit near
This fills the soul with bitter smart,
Yes, God knows this, who knows the heart.

1080.* T. 23.

I AM needy, yet forgiven,
With thy blood my heart enliven,
Give me, Jesus, of thy passion
An abiding, deep impression.

2. With new grace, dear Lord, array me,
Into new degrees convey me,
For thy service make me ready,
Sanctify both soul and body.

1081. T. 22.

ALTHO' my deep depravity
Oft causeth me to mourn and sigh,
My hope to prosper for the Lord
Doth heart-felt joy to me afford.

2. Till to that happy fold I'm led,
Which with celestial joy is fed,
And of life's fountain drinks above,
In endless bliss and perfect love.

IX. Of SANCTIFICATION.

1082.*. T. 200.

TO thee, O Lord, I send my cries,
O let them rise to heaven;
To all my pray'rs, my tears and sighs
A gracious ear be given;
Thy blessed word be my support,
May I, in thee believing,
To thee cleaving,
By faith be purified,
From thee true life receiving.

2. Let neither lust nor fear prevail,
To draw me from my duty,
By aiding grace I shall not fail
To walk in holy beauty;
For who hath ought, but what is giv'n?
Such favor none can merit,
But thy spirit,
Our guide to life and heav'n,
Can graciously confer it.

1083.* T. 151.

GENTLE is the coercion
Of Jesus' pow'r and love,
Without it my exertion
Must unavailing prove;
Humble in heart and broken,
To Christ for strength I flee;
"My grace:" himself hath spoken:
"Sufficient is for thee."

2. If ask'd: "Hast thou already
"In grace such progress made,
"As with steps firm and steady
"Th' appointed path to tread?"
I own: "I'm weak and feeble,
"Alone I cannot stand,
"'Tis Christ, who makes me stable,
"On him I must depend."

3. Is good in contemplation,
I on my Saviour call,
Who gave the intimation,
And worketh all in all;
The wish'd for good effected,
To him I render praise,
Who hath the work directed,
By his enabling grace.

1084. T. 71.

LORD, who did'st sanctify
Thyself, and hast thereby
Procur'd that blessing,
That we before thy face
May walk in holiness,
To thee well pleasing.

2. In true simplicity,
O may we cleave to thee,
Our God and Saviour;
In all things free from blame,
To glorify thy name
Be our endeavour.

3. In heart here purified,
May we in thee abide,
Without cessation;
Thy praise be our employ,
On earth our highest joy,
Thy congregation.

1085.* T. 580.

LORD, take my sinful, worthless heart
As thine, thy grace to me impart,
And deep thy seal impress;
Take me into thy special care,
Secure my soul from every snare,
Thyself find always free access.

2. Make me a bosom friend of thine,
Upon thy breast may I recline,
Preserv'd from needless fears;
And when this earthly house I leave,
Into those mansions me receive,
Where thou wilt wipe away all tears.

1086.* T. 125.

O SHED abroad, Lord Jesus,
Thy love in us, we pray,
And let its influence gracious
Our thoughts and actions sway;
Thus in the path proceeding,
To life eternal leading,
We shall thy word obey.

1087.* T. 9.

WHO thro' Jesus' wounds obtains
Pardon and salvation,
Both for soul and body gains
True sanctification.

1088.* T. 22.

WHENE'ER by sinful lust assail'd,
I thank my God, I need not yield;
But say to av'rice, lust and pride:
"My Lord destroy'd you, when he died!"

2. No parley with the foe I make,
But unto Christ my refuge take,
And when I to my Lord complain,
From sin I quickly freedom gain.

1089. T. 14.

I WANT a principle within,
Of jealous, godly fear,
A sense of each approach of sin,
A dread, lest it come near.

2. Quick as the apple of the eye,
O God. my conscience make,
Arouse my soul, when sin is nigh,
And keep it still awake.

1090.* T. 68.

WHILE we take our seat
At the Master's feet,
Urg'd by love, we in our measure,
His commandments keep with pleasure,
Doth he strength bestow,
We can all things do.

1091.* T. 136.

O HAPPY lot!
To live in blessed union
With Christ, and with his church in close communion,
To look to him,
Prompted by love and need,
To feed by faith, upon his death and merit,
And purified in heart, become with him one spirit,
To love him, tho' we see him not,
O happy lot!

1092. T. 590.

NOW may the very God of peace
Us wholly sanctify,
And grant us such a rich increase
Of unction from on high,
That spirit, soul and body may,
Preserved free from stain,
Be blameless until thy great day,
Lord Jesus Christ; Amen!

X. Of PATIENCE in TRIBULATION.

1093. T. 14.

GOD moves in a mysterious way,
His wonders to perform,
He plants his footsteps in the sea,
And rides upon the storm.

2. Deep in unfathomable mines
Of never-failing skill,
He treasures up his bright designs,
And works his sov'reign will.

3. Ye fearful saints, fresh courage take
The clouds you so much dread,
Are big with mercy, and shall break
In blessings on your head.

4. Judge not the Lord by feeble sense,
But trust him for his grace,
Behind a frowning providence,
He hides a smiling face.

5. His purposes will ripen fast,
Unfolding ev'ry hour,
The bud may have a bitter taste,
But sweet will be the flow'r.

6. Blind unbelief is sure to err,
And scan his work in vain,
God is his own interpreter,
And he will make it plain.

1094. T. 22.

BE still my heart, these anxious cares
To thee are burthens, thorns and snares,
They cast dishonor on thy Lord,
And contradict his gracious word.

2. Brought safely by his hand thus far,
Why wilt thou now give place to care?
How canst thou want, if he provide,
Or lose thy way with such a guide?

3. When first before his mercy-seat
Thou didst thy All to him commit,
He gave thee warrant from that hour,
To trust his wisdom, love and pow'r.

4. Did ever trouble thee befall,
And he refuse to hear thy call,
And hath he not the promise pass'd,
That thou shalt overcome at last?

5. He that hath help'd me hitherto,
Will help me all my journey thro',
And give me daily cause to raise
New Ebenezers to his praise.

6. Tho' rough and thorny be the road,
It leads me home apace to God,
I count my present trials small,
For heav'n will make amends for all.

1095. T. 39.

BEGONE unbelief! for my Saviour is near,
And for my relief he will surely appear,
By pray'r let me wrestle, and he will perform,
With Christ in the vessel, I smile at the storm.

2. Tho' dark be my way, yet since he is my guide,
'Tis mine to obey, and 'tis his to provide,
Tho' cisterns be broken, and creatures all fail,
The word he hath spoken, will surely prevail.

3. His love in times past me forbiddeth to think,
He'll leave me at last unrelieved to sink,
Each sweet Ebenezer I have in review
Confirms his good pleasure to help me quite thro.'

4. Why should I complain then of want or distress,
Temptation or pain? for he told me no less,
The heirs of salvation, I know from his word,
Thro' much tribulation must follow their Lord.

5. How bitter the cup none can ever conceive,
Which Jesus drank up that poor sinners might live!
His way was much rougher, and darker than mine,
Did Jesus thus suffer, and shall I repine?

6. Since all that I meet with shall work for my good,
The bitter is sweet, and the med'cine is food,
Tho' painful at present, 'twill cease before long,
And then, O how pleasant, the conqueror's song.

1096. T. 591.

IF to Jesus for relief
My soul hath fled by pray'r,
Why should I give way to grief,
Or heart-consuming care?
Are not all things in his hand,
Hath he not his promise pass'd?
Will he then regardless stand,
And let me sink at last?

2. While I know, his providence
Disposeth each event,
Shall I judge by feeble sense,
And yield to discontent?

If he worms and sparrows feed,
Clothe the grass in rich array,
Can he see a child in need,
And turn his eye away?

3. When his name was quite unknown,
And sin my life employ'd,
Then he watch'd me as his own,
Or I had been destroy'd;
Now his mercy-seat I know,
Now by grace I'm reconcil'd,
Would he spare me, while a foe,
To leave me, when a child?

4. If he all my wants supplied,
When I disdain'd to pray,
Now his spirit is my guide,
How can he answer nay;
If he would not give me up,
When my soul against him fought,
Will he disappoint the hope,
Which he himself hath wrought?

5. If he shed his precious blood,
To bring me to his fold,
Can I think, that meaner good
He will from me withhold?
Satan, vain is thy device,
Here my hope rests well assur'd;
In that great redemption-price
I see the whole secur'd.

1097. T. 89.

YES, since God himself hath said it,
On his promise I rely,
His good word demands my credit,
What can unbelief reply?
He is strong and can fulfil,
He is truth, and therefore will.

2. In my Saviour's intercession
Humbly still I will confide,
Lord, accept my free confession;
"I have sinn'd, but thou hast died;"
This is all I have to plead,
This is all the plea I need.

1098. T. 585.

O MY soul, what means this sadness,
Wherefore art thou thus cast down?
Let thy griefs be turn'd to gladness,
Bid thy restless fears begone:
Look to Jesus :||: And rejoice in his great name.

2. What tho' Satan's strong temptations
Harrass thee by night and day,
And thy sinful inclinations
Often fill thee with dismay,
Thou shalt conquer :||: Thro' the Lamb's atoning blood.

3. Tho' ten thousand ills beset thee,
From without, and from within,
Jesus saith, he'll ne'er forget thee,
But will save from hell and sin;
He is faithful :||: To perform his gracious word.

4. Tho' distresses now attend thee,
And thou tread'st the thorny road,
His right hand shall still defend thee,
Soon he'll bring thee home to God;
Therefore praise him :||: Praise the dear Redeemer's name!

1099* T. 159.

LOOK up, my soul, to Christ thy joy,
With a believing mind,
With all the ills, which thee annoy,
The way to Jesus find;
Here in this world thou hast no home,
Nor lasting joy: to Jesus come,
He is the Pearl of greatest price;
Who all thy wants supplies.

2. Stedfast in faith to Jesus cleave,
His faithfulness review,
And ev'ry burthen with him leave,
Whose love is daily new:
His ways with thee are just and right,
He puts thy enemies to flight,
However threat'ning they appear,
Take courage, he is near.

3. Thy closet enter, pray and sigh,
To Jesus tell thy grief,
His ear is open to thy cry,
His hand to give relief,

Tho' men thee hate, forsake and grieve,
Thy Saviour thee will never leave,
His word is pass'd: he'll aid afford;
Rely upon the Lord.

4. Lift up thy heart to him on high,
And leave this sordid earth,
Behold with a believing eye
God's excellence and worth;
Devote thy life, thy all to him,
Who did thy soul from death redeem,
In love to thee the cross endur'd,
And life for thee procur'd.

5. Arise and seek the things above,
Let heav'n be all thy aim,
Where Jesus dwells in bliss and love,
And earth and sin disclaim;
The world and all its empty joy
His potent breath will once destroy;
Abiding rest and peace of mind
In Christ alone we find.

1100.* T. 142.

O FOUNTAIN eternal of life and of light,
Where all find refreshment, who seek it aright,
Pure spring of salvation,
And true consolation,
From God's holy temple thy living stream rolls,
Whose waters flow ample for all thirsty souls.

2. Let him that is thirsty, encouraging call!
Now drink of the waters, abounding for all,
The promised blessing
Is sweetly refreshing,
All ye who are ailing and needy draw nigh,
This well-spring ne'er-failing your wants will supply.

3. Thou river of life dost revive soul and mind,
Those whom thou enrichest eternal good find,
Amidst tribulation,
The cup of salvation,
I take, thus with gladness inspired by thee,
All sorrow and sadness affrighted must flee.

4. I plead thy rich promise, O give me to drink,
With fervor of spirit I wholly would sink
Into thy love's ocean,
O let true devotion
My heart be impelling, still onward to move,
To Zion thy dwelling, the city of love.

5. Should bitter be mix'd with the sweet of my cup
O grant me with joy all self-will to give up.
The cup of dire sorows.
Which thou hast drank for us,
To thine thou dost offer in this world of pain,
With thee, they here suffer, with thee they shall reign.

6. O therefore, my Jesus, permit me to rest,
Where saints are no longer by suff'ring oppress'd,
Where joys beyond measure,
And fullness of pleasure
In glory transcendent the conquerors gain,
And where crowns resplendent the faithful obtain.

1101.* T. 82.

FAITHFUL Saviour, we to thee
Will look up incessantly,
Happy in thy peace and blessing,
Filial confidence possessing,
Poor in spirit, rich in grace,
We show forth thy matchless praise.

2. God be prais'd! thy love is known,
Thou expectest this alone,
That disclaiming self-reliance,
We should yield a glad compliance,
With a mind devoutly still,
To thy good and perfectly will.

1102.* T. 157.

WITH undaunted resolution,
Christian heart—where thou art,
Stand without confusion;
Yea should death with its last message,
Call thee hence—Christ's defence,
Leads thro' the dark passage.

2. What are this world's joys and troubles,
But a hand-full of sand,
Vain and empty bubbles:
Yonder are the solid treasures,
Where our Lord—will afford
Endless joys and pleasures.

XI. HYMNS of PRAISE and THANKSGIVING.

1103.* T. 583.

TO thee, the Lord of all, I'll humbly sing,
To thee, my Maker, I'll thank-off'rings bring;
But how can language worthily display
Thy lauds, or to thy name due homage pay?

2. I've nought to give, for what I have is thine,
Thine is my soul and body, and not mine;
My reas'ning pow'rs, my health, my daily food,
Are all thy gifts, and show, that thou art good.

3. That I'm an honourable vessel made,
Is all the work of love unmerited,
And not because I'm worthy: mercy free
Redeem'd my soul from sin and misery.

4. Now while on earth I stay, to thee I'll live,
And to thy name alone all glory give,
Till I with all thy saints, my voice shall raise,
And join in everlasting songs of praise.

1104. T. 585.

WHILE successive years are wasting,
Still our God abides the same;
All his words are everlasting,
All his works his love proclaim;
Men and angels :||: Sing thrice holy to his name.

2. Out of love he man created,
And ordain'd him God's delight,
Nor was this, his love, abated,
When man lost God's image bright;
Then compassion :||: Brought redemption's plan to light

3. Here is love divine pourtrayed.
So that man the lines may trace,
See, O man, God's love displayed,
In thy Saviour's marred face;
Wouldst thou praise him :||: Be thy theme redeeming grace.

4. Bear in mind, how Jesus suffer'd,
He the righteous, for th' unjust,
How his sinless soul he offer'd,
Unto God for sinful dust;
Love thus triumph'd :||: Mighty now to save the lost.

5. Lo, th' incarnate God ascended,
Pleads the merits of his blood,
Now all enmity is ended,
Man is reconcil'd to God;
All the ruin :||: Of his fall is now made good.

6. We shall see him once returning,
Then the sav'd their heads will raise,
He will change their grief and mourning
Into notes of endless praise;
As Jehovah :||: Ev'ry tongue will him confess.

7. Sing with glad anticipation,
Mortals and immortals, sing,

Jesus comes with full salvation,
Jesus doth his glory bring;
Hallelujah! :||: Lord of hosts, of kings, the King!

1105. T. 580.

JESUS, the whole creation's Head,
Lord of the living and the dead,
Endless thy glories shine;
Thy blood-bought church in mercy own;
The church assembled round thy [throne,
Or pilgrims here; we all are thine.

2. Pilgrims on earth, here we may rest,
The sparrow here hath found a nest,
Thine altars, O Lord God!
For all thy blessings and thy care,
Our gratitude in praise and pray'r
Shall still ascend to thine abode.

3. Ye spirits of the just above,
With Christ now perfected in love,
Once our companions here;
In higher strains join us to sing
Blessing and honor to our King,
Till he in glory shall appear.

4. Hail! Lamb once slain, thy precious blood
Hath brought us sinners nigh to God,
Worthy art thou alone!
Accept, O Lord, Ancient of days,
Thy universal church's praise,
Here, and around thy glorious throne.

1006. T. 14.

FOR mercies, countless as the sands,
Which daily I receive,
From God, by my Redeemer's hands,
My soul, what canst thou give?

2. Yet this acknowledgment I'll make,
For all he hath bestow'd,
Salvation's sacred cup I'll take,
And call upon my God.

3. The best return for one, like me,
So wretched and so poor,
Is from his gifts to draw a plea,
And ask him still for more.

1107.* T. 166.

THANKS be to thee, O Lamb of God,
For thy unfathomable grace,
How many benefits bestow'd
Forgotten and unnotic'd pass!
When I thy love astonish'd see,
What lengths, breadths, heights, and depths appear!
Eternity, immensity,
These, these its only limits are.

1108.* T. 114.

THE Lamb of God unspotted, pure and holy,
Who by his death us reconcil'd to God,
And from our sins hath wash'd us in his blood,
Is worthy, that each knee bow 'fore him lowly,
That ev'ry tongue with gladness him confess,
The only Lord, unto the Father's praise.

XII. Of PRAYER and SUPPLICATION.

1109. T. 582.

BEHOLD the throne of grace,
The promise calls me near,
There Jesus shows his cheering face,
And waits to answer pray'r.

2. That rich, atoning blood,
Which sprinkled round I see,
Provides for those, who come to God
An all-prevailing plea.

3. My soul, ask what thou wilt,
Thou canst not be too bold,
Since his own blood for thee was spilt,
What else can he withhold?

4. Beyond thy utmost wants,
His love and pow'r can bless,
To praying souls he always grants
More than they can express.

5. Since 'tis the Lord's command,
My mouth I open wide,
Lord, open thou thy bounteous hand,
That I may be supplied.

6. My soul, believe and pray,
Without a doubt believe;
Whate'er we ask in God's own way,
We surely shall receive.

7. Here stands the promise fair,
For God cannot repent,
To fervent, persevering pray'r
He'll ev'ry blessing grant.

1110. T. 11.

COME, my soul, thy suit prepare,
Jesus loves to answer pray'r,
He himself hath bid thee pray,
And sends none unheard away.

2. Thou art coming to a King,
Large petitions with thee bring,
For his grace and pow'r are such,
None can ever ask too much.

3. Lord, I will not let thee go,
Till the blessing thou bestow,
O do not my suit disdain,
None shall seek thy face in vain.

1111.* T. 10.

THE prayers of the needy,
Thou, Lord, to hear art ready
Thy mercy and forbearance
We ev'ry day experience.

2. When thee in faith addressing,
Thou no good gift nor blessing
Unto thy church deniest,
But all her wants suppliest.

3. In thee we trust for ever,
Since thou to each believer
Afford'st that consolation;
"I've heard thy supplication."

1112.* T. 114.

WHENE'ER with ardent pray'r and supplication,
My mind surveys thy kingdom, gracious Lord,
And recollects the promis'd rich reward,
For thy soul's travail, bitter death and passion,
The hope I cherish, that thy flock of grace,
On earth will still abundantly increase.

2. O Father of thy people, I implore thee,
The church, the fruit of Jesus' suff'rings, bless,
Refresh her oft with copious show'rs of grace,
Her only aim is, to promote thy glory;
May Jesus thousands as a spoil obtain,
And his disciples constant vict'ry gain.

3. Spirit of truth, who Christ's blood-
bought salvation [fice,
Set's forth, and glorifiest his sacri-
May hosts of sinners, list'ning to
thy voice,
Receive with joy the gospel-invita-
tion,
And be enroll'd, as members of his
bride;
His thirst for souls is not yet satisfied.

1113.* T. 159.

ABUNDANTLY our Saviour's hand
Bestoweth gifts and grace,
This we in many a distant land
With inward joy can trace;
When for his work engag'd in pray'r,
We know, he our requests will hear,
And confidently can believe,
A rich increase he'll give.

1114.* T. 208.

CALL to mind that blessed,
And so oft distressed
Cloud of witnesses,
Which thro' the world goeth,
And which no one knoweth,
But the flock of grace:
With them be—as they with thee,
Thou with heav'nly consolation
Favor'd congregation.

1115.* T. 166.

O JESUS, bless thy witnesses,
Spread over them thy arms of love,
Behold them in their destin'd race,
Where bold in faith's bright path
they move;
Support them under ev'ry load,
Console them, when they weep
'fore thee,
And help them, for thy aid bestow'd.
To praise thy name continually.

1116.* T. 590.

MAY God his grace to us dispense,
His blessings on us show'r:
May he lift up his countenance
Upon us evermore:
O may we rightly know his mind,
His saving word proclaim,
That many heathen tribes may find
Salvation in his name.

1117. T. 185.

BLESS, O Lord, we pray, thy con-
gregation,
Bless each choir and family,
Bless the youth, the rising generation,
Bless the children, dear to thee,
Bless thy servants, grant them grace
and unction,
That they may with care discharge
their function,
Lord, on thee we humbly call,
Let thy blessing rest on all.

1118. T. 580.

UPON our King's anointed head,
O Lord, thy choicest blessings shed,
Defend him graciously,
Preserve him in thy fear and love,
Give him true wisdom from above,
To govern so as pleaseth thee.

2. Unto our Father and our King
Thy promis'd aid and succor bring,
Support him, by thy grace;
The branches of his family,
O Lord, crown with prosperity,
And we will give thee all the praise.

1119.* T. 97.

THANKS, adoration, glory, praise,
To thee we render for thy grace,
With ev'ry breath may we proclaim
Thy goodness and extol thy name;
O Lord, thy knowledge spread both
far and near,
May all in thy redemption have a
share.

XIII. Of the CHURCH of CHRIST.

1120. T. 22.

"AS birds their infant brood protect
"And spread their wings to shelter them:"
Thus saith the Lord to his elect,
"So will I guard Jerusalem."

2. And what is then Jerusalem,
The darling object of his care?
What is its worth in God's esteem?
Who built it? who inhabits there?

3. Jehovah founded it in blood,
The blood of his incarnate Son;
There dwell the saints, once foes to God,
The sinners whom he calls his own.

4. Tho' foes on ev'ry side assail,
This city hath a sure defence,
Against her they shall ne'er prevail,
While guarded by Omnipotence.

1121. T. 97.

HOW sweet thy dwellings, Lord, how fair,
What peace, what bliss inhabit there,
With ardent hope, with strong desire,
My heart, my flesh to thee aspire;
How oft I long thy heav'nly courts and thee, [to see!
My Lord and God, the living God

2. One wish, with holy transport warm
My heart hath form'd, and still doth form,
One gift I ask, that to my end
Thine hallow'd house I may attend,
There may I joyful find a safe abode,
There may I view the beauty of my God.

1122. T. 96.

THE consecrated house we love,
Where God vouchsafes to place his name, [move,
Nor will we Lord, from thence re-
But jointly there thy praise proclaim,
And daily to thy courts repair,
To seek thee in the house of pray'r.

2. But oh! the house of living stones
We never can neglect nor leave,
That temple, which the world disowns.
To that in life and death we cleave,
Thro' faith to ev'ry member join'd,
The church, diffus'd thro' all mankind.

1123.* T. 9.

ONE there is to Christ well known,
And by him approved,
Poor and needy, yet his own,
His bride, his beloved.

2. She with a devoted mind
His cross gladly beareth,
In her, to her matchless friend,
Love sincere appeareth.

3. We one Lord and Saviour own,
Even Christ our brother,
Of our flesh and of our bone,
We know of none other.

4. He upon his heart doth bear,
All his souls redeemed,
As his Father's children dear,
Now thro' grace esteemed.

1124.* T. 126.

THE Lord, e're he appeared,
Upon this earth, as man,
Already had prepared
The great and glorious plan,
A church to gather to his praise,
And had decreed beforehand,
How this should come to pass.

2. Tho' man by sin deceived,
God's image forfeited,
Yet Christ this loss retrieved,
By dying in his stead; [slain,
Thou Bridegroom of the church, once
What anguish did it cost thee,
Thy faithless bride to gain!

3. O days of solid blessing,
When Christ, the Son of grace,
All other light surpassing,
His healing beams displays!
Then walking on the narrow way,
Our path we can discover,
Till dawn of endless day.

4. When we shall see our Jesus,
In majesty most bright,
O how will this abase us,
When he his kingdom's might
Shall with his foll'wers deign to share;
Lord Jesus, for thy coming
Thy church on earth prepare!

5. We shall possess for ever
Those joys divine in heav'n,
Of which to the believer
A foretate here is giv'n,
And our redemption by his blood
Shall be our song eternal
Before the throne of God.

1125.* T. 234.

THOU sov'reign Lord of earth and heav'n
And of our hearts, to thee for ever
Be homage paid, and praises giv'n,
For thy eternal love and favor;
The subjects of thy government,
Who from thy death have life obtained,
Their souls and bodies now present
To thee, as trophies dearly gained:
Thou, Lord, this gift entire
Dost of us all require,
As justly due by thee 'tis claimed;
And until all have grace
To live unto thy praise, [ed
The faithful part must stand asham-

2. We worship thee with filial fear,
As part of thy blest congregation,
With all, who with us grounded are
On apostolic truth's foundation,
Where Jesus is the Corner-stone,
And give thee praise for our election,
In thee we put our trust, alone, [tion:
Thou, Lord, wilt lead us to perfec-
O grant us to make known
Thy truth and freely own, [joined;
That faith from works can't be dis-
That piety on grace
Must rest, and faithfulness
With faith must ever be combined.

1126.* T. 221.

THOU monarch of All, thou Lord God of creation!
How wonderful and yet how blest,
Appears in the church thy wise administration, [fess'd;
Of which thou art the Head con-
'Tis here for the needy all help abounds, [wounds,
To keep the eye steady fix'd on thy
The sum is and substance with poor contrite sinners, [are winners.
Of all the wise maxims, whereby they

2. What is it, that makes us stand fast in one spirit,
Lord Jesus, author of our faith?
What is it cements us? 'Tis only thy merit,
Thy wounds and all-atoning death:
Ye heralds of mercy, with courage good [blood,
Redemption proclaim ye in Jesus'
No heart e'er dissolved by Sinai's thunder, [cleave asunder.
But rocks at the message of peace

3. Art thou not refresh'd with divine consolation,
Thou ransom'd, highly favor'd flock,
When drinking with joy of the wells of salvation, [rock?
Which freely flow from Christ the
Who now would be fearful? for us he bled, [finished!"
Who would not be cheerful? "'tis
This doctrine we'll hold and declare without ceasing,
His cross brings us peace, 'tis the source of all blessing.

1127.* T. 155.

JESUS, how do we rejoice,
When contemplating the favor,
Thou hast ever
Shown to those, brought nigh to
By thy blood; [God
Thou hast giv'n to us thy spirit,
Whereby we true life inherit,
And most graciously are led.

2. Yet whence comes it, Lord, that we
Hallelujahs without ceasing
Are not raising?
But the cry is often heard:
"Mercy Lord!"
'Tis because we must abased
Own, thy grace is not so traced
In our walk, as justly due.

3. Is it still thy pleasure, Lord,
That thy Church, tho' poor and needy,
Here stand ready
Thee to serve and to confess?
Grant thro' grace,
That none in thy congregation
Slight thy gracious invitation
Or neglect his heav'nly call.

1128.* T. 26.

CHRIST is the church's Lord and Head;
This makes us hope with confidence,
That he will be our sure defence,
And help in ev'ry time of need.

2. O may our fellowship abide
An honor to his blessed name,
May he in us fulfil his aim,
That we throughout be sanctified.

1129. T. 16.

HIGHLY favor'd congregation,
Lov'd by Jesus and esteem'd,
Ne'er forget thy destination,
Why from this vain world redeem'd.

2. Grounded on thy Saviour's merit,
Bless'd in his communion sweet,
Destin'd heaven to inherit,
And the church above to meet.

3. Witness, here to all around thee
Of thy Saviour's dying love,
Testify: "he sought and found me,
"Else I still should restless rove."

4. Evidence by word and action
That thy faith is not in vain,
That thy highest satisfaction
Centers in the Lamb once slain.

5. By love's closest bonds united,
As the Lord's own family,
Be to serve his name excited,
Be to him a fruitful tree.

6. Grant, Lord, to thy congregation,
What adorns her in thy sight,
Let her walls be call'd salvation,
Be her glory, shield and light.

1130.* T. 14.

THE great salvation of the Lord
Abides his church's joy,
To honor him with sweet accord,
Our fav'rite, bless'd employ.

2. Into the bosom of our Friend
Both joy and grief we pour,
Until our griefs shall have an end,
And sorrows be no more.

3. What comfort, what supreme delight
Do we enjoy, what bliss,
When the Lamb slain appears in sight.
Might the whole world know this!

1131.* T. 69.

LEARN, church of Jesus,
While on earth abiding,
Still at a distance
From thy Lord residing,
To cleave
To him, and in him live.

1132*. T. 14.

HAPPY, O Lord, are they who wait
Thy pleasure to fulfil,
Upon thy statutes meditate,
And learn to do thy will.

2. How blessed is thy family,
Thy kind support they prove,
All may be done by faith in thee,
From strength to strength they move.

1133. T. 168.

O HOW blessed is the station
Of all those, who love the Lord,
Who partake of his salvation,
Trusting in his sacred word:
Bless'd, who in love's bond united,
To his altars are invited,
In his courts on earth they dwell,
There his matchless praise to tell.

XIV. Of the SERVANTS of CHRIST.

1134.* T. 26.

OF Christ our boast we freely make,
Whose grace our stony hearts did melt,
We speak the pow'r divine we felt,
The words, which rocks asunder break.

2. A sinner hears us, and believes,
For when of Christ we witness bear,
The dead his quick'ning voice shall hear,
And whosoever hears it, lives.

3. He hears—and joy o'erspreads his face,
From death to life he passeth o'er,
A stranger to his God no more,
A trophy of redeeming grace.

4. Scarce born again—his watchful eye
Perceives another sinner near,
With guilt oppress'd and sunk in fear,
"Behold the Lamb!" is then his cry.

5. Thus souls with eagerness are sought,
And by the power of the Lord,
Which rests upon the gospel-word,
Are to Christ's saving knowledge brought.

1135*. T. 582.

A MESSENGER of peace
No higher pleasure knows,
Than to direct the human race,
To flee to Jesus' cross,
To Jesus' healing wounds,
And precious, cleansing blood
The source, whence life to us redounds,
And fountain of all good.

2. Servant of God, be fill'd
With Jesus' love alone,
Upon a sure foundation build,
On Christ, the Corner-stone,
By faith in him abide,
Rejoicing with his saints,
To him with confidence, when tried,
Make known all thy complaints.

3. A cheerful life enjoy,
A life of faith in God,
An int'rest, nothing can destroy,
In Christ's atoning blood;
Then tho' the heathen rage,
And devils envious roar,
The Saviour's grace in ev'ry age
Extol for evermore.

1136*. T. 69.

THE witness people,
Who execute God's will,
Are strong, when feeble,
In him confiding still,
While they
Their master's call obey.

1137.* T. 82.

PREACHERS of the gospel-word,
Seek ye first to know the Lord,

And to live in the enjoyment
Of his grace, then your employment
Rays of light will shed abroad
In the family of God.

2. Not for your own worthiness,
(All you are, you are thro' grace)
But because your Lord and Saviour,
Whose bless'd purposes ne'er waver,
Is your sure support and aid,
Counsellor and friend in need.

3. Leaders would ye faithful prove,
Ev'ry other gift above,
Of obedience be possessed,
With this virtue unimpressed,
How could ye at home preside?
How the flock of Jesus guide?

1138.* T. 4.

O JESUS, my Lord,
For ever ador'd,
My portion, my all,
At thy holy feet with abasement, I fall.

2. As sure as I prove
Thy mercy and love
To me, thy poor child, [Shield:
As sure as thou art my Reward and my

3. So sure will I be
Devoted to thee,
And cheerfully stand,
Prepared to follow thy ev'ry com-
mand.

4. Keep me thro' thy grace
So minded always,
That I nought beside [crucified.
May know but thee only, and thee

5. Whene'er I survey
In stillness, and weigh
The proofs of thy grace, [ways.
Experienc'd by me, in so manifold

6. I then at thy throne
Adoring sink down,
With joy and deep shame, [claim.
Thy love to my grateful return hath a

7. For ever be blest,
Thou source of true rest,
Thanks be to thy hand, [the end.
Which led me, and safely will lead to

8. Now am I, tho' dust,
Thy property just,
With thee one in heart,
May nought from thy love me, poor
sinner, e'er part.

9. Soul, spirit and mind
To thee be resign'd,
Thy throne there erect, [canst effect.
Till thou thy whole purpose in me

10. Whatever I do
With thy blood bedew,
May ev'ry thought be [thee.
Intent on enjoying communion with

11. Make me thine abode,
A temple of God,
A vessel of grace, [thy praise.
For thy use prepared, and form'd to

12. The cov'nant is made
With thee, as my Head,
Lord, grant my request, [thee I rest.
To love and to serve thee, till with

1139.* T. 97.

ATTEND, Lord Jesus, to my pray'r,
Unto thyself O draw me near,
Thou know'st the frailty of my heart,
Thy unction unto me impart,
To all my faithfulness and industry,
To give them weight, enabling grace
apply.

2. May I, in thy communion blest,
Enjoy an undisturbed rest,
Make soul and body thine abode,
A temple of the living God,
Thus, Lord, for thy appearing may I
wait,
Then will my joy in thee be quite
complete.

1140.* T. 14.

O GRANT thy servant, thro' thy
grace,
An understanding heart,
Thy dealings with thy church to trace,
And counsel to impart.

2. With heav'nly wisdom me endow,
Thy peace O may I feel;
Presence of mind on me bestow,
To execute thy will.

3. Thus strengthen'd in the inner man,
Supported by thy aid,
I shall thy gracious aim obtain,
And in thy path proceed.

1141.* T. 580.

WITH gladness we will follow thee,
We vow allegiance, bend the knee
To thee, our Lord and Head,
We'll venture freely ev'ry thing,
At thy command, O Christ, our King,
By thee alone we will be led.

1142. T. 590.

O GLORIOUS Master of thy house,
Thy chosen flock's defence,
Upon thee stay'd, my mind is kept
At ease, tho' in suspense!
Most graciously I'm onward led,
Beneath thy tender care,
Thy arm prepares my way, thine eye
Looks out before me far.

1143.* T. 205.

LET thy presence go with me,
Saviour, else I dare not move,
With thy aid and led by thee,
I will go, constrain'd by love;
Serve thy cause with all my might,
Deeming ev'ry burthen light,
And, if favor'd with success,
To thee render all the praise.

1144. T. 146.

O BLESS the ministry,
To which I am appointed,
'Midst weakness may I be
With pow'r divine anointed;
A lowly mind impart,
Obedient, sway'd by grace,
So shall my poor, frail heart
Not easily transgress.

1145.* T. 97.

THOU Master of thy family,
In humble faith we look to thee,
Dispose our hearts, thy blessed will
With resignation to fulfil,
Call forth thy servants: grant them needful grace,
And say to each: "I leave with thee my peace."

1146.* T. 83.

JESUS, grant thy witness-flock
Holy boldness, with submission
To thy mild and easy yoke,
And that lowly disposition,
Gladly poor ourselves to be,
If but souls are gain'd for thee.

2. Long as we continue here,
To thy will be our's resigned,
Tho' a more contracted sphere
Be by thee for us designed;
Ah! we have but little strength!
Give us, Lord, success at length.

1147.* T. 9.

SHEPHERD, help thy chosen few,
Thee in truth to follow,
With thy blood, whate'er we do,
Be thou pleas'd to hallow.

2. Show us daily more and more,
Of thy church's beauty,
Give the impulse and the pow'r
For each sacred duty.

3. Thus shall we with willing feet
On thy service venture,
Thy hard labor makes all sweet,
When on toil we enter.

1148.* T. 232.

JESUS, who died upon the cross,
And shed his precious blood for us;
(To God a pure oblation!)
Is the bless'd object of our faith,
We show the virtue of his death,
Of him we make confession:
O may his love our hearts inspire,
And touch our lips with hallow'd fire;

Led by his spirit and his grace,
May we set forth his matchless praise;
Thus will the Lord, his due reward,
Well-pleas'd regard,
Receiving honor thro' our word.

1149.* T. 14.

THE day will come, when Jesus Christ,
The righteous Judge declar'd,
Will be his servant's crown of joy,
Their endless, great reward.

2. Meanwhile they tread the narrow path,
From worldly fetters freed,
Obedient to their Lord, in hope
They sow the gospel-seed.

XV. Of the SPREADING of CHRISTS'S KINGDOM upon EARTH.

1150.* T. 22.

ALL is the Lord's: the spacious earth
Sets his creative wisdom forth;
What man of all the human race
Is not an object of his grace?

2. Gladly we spend our life and blood,
To serve our Lord, the living God;
High praises we to Jesus give, [live.
Who died, that all mankind might

3. What true disciple e'er would chuse,
At home to cherish selfish views,
If, tho' with hardship and with pain,
One soul for Jesus he might gain?

4. God sends you forth—his will be done,
Your destin'd race with patience run,
Jesus to all the world declare,
His ransom publish ev'ry where.

5. But lay your own foundation sure,
Be clean in heart, in spirit poor,
Devoted wholly to the Lord,
He will the needful strength afford.

6. Fall down in faith beneath his cross,
Cry: "God be merciful to us!"
Lord, let us hear thy cheering voice,
And ever in thy name rejoice.

1151.* T. 228.

WHAT stores of ripe abundant fruit,
Produced from Jesus Christ the root,
Have his disciples gained!
By their laborious agency,
We flocks of Gentile-sheep now see,
To love the Lord constrained;
O yes—Thro' grace,
They on pleasant—Fair and verdant
Fields of pasture
Feed enrich'd by gospel-culture.

2. The hosts of flaming seraphim,
Jehovah—Jesus make the theme
Of their exalted praises;
Ye angels, who obedient fly,
Fulfilling your commission high,
To guard the flocks of Jesus;
Praise him—bless him,
Raise incessant—Songs triumphant
O'er sav'd nations;
Lo! we join your jubilations.

1152.* T. 205.

WOULD the world our passport see,
By which we free entrance gain,
Or ask our authority,
We reply: "the Lamb was slain!"
This is ev'ry where our boast,
He, that higher soars is lost;
For that pow'rful word we raise,
Christ, to thee eternal praise.

2. Ev'ry where, with shoutings loud,
Shouts that shake the gates of hell,
Thy anointed witness-cloud
Of thy great redemption tell;
Are our door-posts, Lamb of God,
Sprinkled with atoning blood,

Thou thy flocks of Gentile-sheep
Wilt from the destroyer keep.

1153.* T. 136.

GOD'S boundless grace
Preserves each faithful servant,
All share his aid, in cold and heat most ardent;
Midst ice and rocks,
Or on the stormy seas,
Are soul and body under his direction;
The shadow of his wings affords complete protection;
The Lord will be about our ways,
O boundless grace!

2. Our life, our death,
Be to thy joy and honor, [the donor,
Who art of life, and each good gift
We say, Amen!
Thou author of our faith, [vior,
Thy name be glorified in our beha-
Whether our pilgrimage be rough or smooth, dear Saviour. [breath,
Be thou our strength, while we have
Our life in death.

1154.* T. 205.

GROUNDED on th' eternal Rock,
Moving in the gospel-way,
Strong and firm 'midst every shock,
Humble, but without dismay;
Such the pilgrim, who in faith
Safely walks the narrow path,
He proceeds from grace to grace,
Till with joy he ends his race.

2. More and more our joys increase,
As we humbly travel on,
Jesus gives abundant grace,
While we lean on him alone;
Thro' the virtue of his blood,
Source of life and ev'ry good,
We preserve a cheerful mind,
His bless'd will to do inclin'd.

3. Then we suit ourselves to those,
Who with us yoke-fellows are,
Glad to soften all their woes,
Glad their ev'ry joy to share;
If to Christ the Vine we cleave,
Daily strength from him receive,
Thro' his pow'r we shall produce
Goodly fruit, matur'd for use.

1155.* T. 79.

MOST gracious Lord and Saviour,
Who dost accept in favor,
Of sinners vile and poor;
May we while here remaining,
Be thy whole aim attaining,
Since thou hast open'd us a door.

2. Lord, should'st thou even gather
Such multitudes together,
As sands upon the coast,
Thou tents for them providest,
Among them thou residest,
As Captain of the ransom'd host.

1156.* T. 582.

AMBASSADORS of Christ,
Know ye the way you go?
A path, not strew'd with blooming flow'rs,
But yielding thorns and woe;
All who Christ crucified,
Their only Saviour own,
Meet oftentimes with treatment base,
Unto their Master shown.

2. Only against offence
With circumspection guard,
By craft or force in ev'ry place
The fiend is striving hard,
God's work's to overthrow,
That in the trying hour,
The servants of the Lord may fall,
Bereft of faith and pow'r.

3. But see, the fields are white,
Go therefore, lab'rers, go,
The Lord leads on to victory,
His pow'r and grace ye know;
Christ, whom ye Saviour call,
Of all is sov'reign Lord, [priest,
Your Captain and your great High-
Ye conquer thro' his word.

4. To Cæsar ever give
The things that Cæsar's are,
And render unto God his right,
Unite in fervent pray'r,
To him let praise ascend;
In undissembled love,
In uprightness and justice walk,
Until ye hence remove.

1157.* T. 68.

LABORERS, go forth
Into all the earth,
Gather souls in distant places,
To reward the death of Jesus,
Throughout all the earth,
Set his suff'rings forth.

2. Open, Lord, a door,
Soon from shore to shore,
Send an host of gospel-preachers,
Shining lights, anointed teachers,
Soon from shore to shore,
Open, Lord, a door.

1158. T. 11.

BRETHREN, what do you desire,
After what do ye aspire?
Whither do your labors tend?
To preach Christ, the sinners' friend.

2. Seems this subject ever new?
Can you give it praises due?
Ne'er be weary to proclaim
Jesus' lovely, saving name.

3. Never, never will we cease
To proclaim the news of peace,
Never, till our latest breath,
Fervent, faithful unto death.

1159.* T. 161.

URG'D by love, on ev'ry station
To the fallen human race,
We will publish Christ's salvation,
And declare his blood-bought grace;
To display him—And pourtray him
In his suff'ring form and beauty,
Be our aim and pleasing duty.

1160.* T. 167.

NOUGHT shall hinder our blest function,
Jesus, since we bear thy name,
And are call'd, taught by thy unction,
Thy atonement to proclaim;
Are we with thy blood besprinkled,
Marked with thy Spirit's seal.
Tho' for death we should be singled,
We in death, would trust thee still.

1161.* T. 205.

WARRIOR, on thy station stand,
Faithful to thy Saviour's call,
With the shield of faith in hand,
Fearless, let what may, befal;
Nothing fill thee with dismay,
Hunger, toil, or length of way,
In the strength of Jesus boast,
Never, never quit thy post.

1162.* T. 185.

WHAT affords the Christian warrior vigor,
Who climbs rocks, or sinks in sands,
Braving now of northern storms the rigor,
Scorched then in southern lands?
Here no case avails, no circumspection,
But depending on his Lord's protection,
In his heav'nly armor clad,
He moves on, serene and glad.

1163.* T. 141.

WHILE the pilgrim travels
On this earthly ground.
Watchful guardian angels
Compass him around;
Like Elisha's servant,
He in faith espies
Hosts with fiery horses,
Flaming chariots rise.

1164.* T. 591.

DOTH our Saviour on us call,
We to his service haste,
For his sake we venture all,
Renounce lethargic rest;
Not despairing to fulfil
The great trust repos'd in us,
We to him submit our will,
And boldly preach the cross.

1165.* T. 583.

THE earth's the Lord's! to cultivate
The land, [stand;
And sow the gospel-seed we ready
In hope, that for his travail he may see
A rich reward, and reap abundantly.

1166.* T. 590.

AH! could we prompt the human race,
To Jesus Christ to turn,
And as the case at Emmaus was,
In love to him to burn,
Who on th' accursed cross was slain,
To rescue the enslav'd,
And doth the scriptures still explain
To such as would be sav'd!

1167.* T. 580.

THOU of all nations the desire,
With ardent zeal our breasts inspire,
And grant that ev'ry field,
With gospel-seed already sown,
In Gentile-lands, or in our own,
May an abundant harvest yield.

1168.* T. 155.

O WHAT songs in highest strain
Will the ransom'd sing in heaven,
With thanksgiving,
To him who brought us to God,
By his blood,
When of ev'ry tongue and nation,
There will be with exultation
But one flock and Shepherd known.

2. Amen, Jesus' words are true,
Surely he his gracious promise
Will accomplish;
Ye, his servants, ready stand,
In each land,
Yea in the most distant places,
Till he comes, to sound his praises,
And make known his saving name.

XVI. HYMNS for SOLEMN OCCASIONS.

1169.* T. 185.

GRACE and peace from God, our blessed Saviour,
Be with all who love his name!
Church of Christ, his service deem a favour,
Joyfully his death proclaim;
Be prepar'd for rest or for employment,
With activity, combine enjoyment,
Serve with zeal and faithfulness,
Love enraptur'd with his grace.

2. Chosen flock thy faithful Shepherd follow,
Who laid down his life for thee;
All thy days unto his service hallow,
Each his true disciple be:
Evermore rejoice to do his pleasure,
Be the fullness of his grace thy treasure,
Should success thy labor crown,
Give the praise to him alone.

1170.* T. 166.

O THOU the church's Lord and Head,
Our only refuge, shield and rock,
The pilgrims' guide support and aid,
Thou faithful Shepherd of thy flock;
Vile as we are, we're surely thine,
Thro' mercy we have life obtain'd,
As monuments of grace divine,
To our astonishment we stand.

2. As part of thy church militant,
An emblem of the church above,
To thy dear Father us present,
(Thou in the bosom of his love,)
That us as children he may own,
Since we're thy dearly earn'd reward,
And send his holy Spirit down,
To train us up for thee, our Lord.

3. We cast ourselves into thy arms,
While we with inward rapture glow;

The flame, which thy pure bosom warms,
Thy never-failing love we know;
Thou, who for us once tasted'st death,
And wast restor'd to life again,
Thy quick'ning Spirit on us breathe,
Come, heav'nly Vine, each branch sustain.

4. We wish, (and what we wish is gain'd,
Since we thy chosen foll'wers are,
And have thy pow'r divine obtain'd,)
To thee well-pleasing fruit to bear;
Thy *servants* we will be thro' grace,
Thy *handmaids*, who look up to thee;
Set us, O Lord, unto thy praise,
Grant we may serve thee faithfully.

1171.* T. 22.

MAY Jesus' blood and righteousness
Fill and adorn this hallow'd place,
Wherein is preach'd his holy word,
And sacramental grace conferr'd.

2. That this redeemed, happy flock
Be firmly built on Christ the Rock,
And of those blessings be posses'd
Which on the Spirit's union rest.

3. May ev'ry place of worship round
With free, electing grace resound,
Inviting men, to Christ to come,
Who calls the weary wand'rers home,

4 The gospel precepts to obey,
And never from the truth to stray,
With an attentive, list'ning ear,
The Spirit's small, still voice to hear.

5. Unto the Father to draw nigh,
Tho' pleading nought but misery,
Yet with full, child-like confidence,
Since Jesus died for our offence.

6. Then doth the Saviour for us plead,
With God the Father intercede,
And say: "These souls thou gavest me,
"They are my blood-bought property.

7. "For them on earth I liv'd and died,
"My thirst for souls is satisfied,
"Since I can claim them as a spoil,
"The dear-earn'd purchase of my toil."

8. The Father's heart thereby is mov'd,
He us accepts in the Belov'd,
With joy confesseth us as his,
And greets us with a pard'ning kiss.

9. We humbly thee adore and praise,
Father of mercy, God of grace,
That souls by thy beloved Son
Redeem'd, by thee to him are drawn.

10. Thou man of sorrows, be ador'd,
Whose death doth life to us afford,
Since thro' thy merits we possess
True joy and solid happiness.

11. God, holy Ghost, bless'd Comforter,
With grateful hearts we thee revere,
Since we by thee convinc'd and taught,
Are to the blood of sprinkling brought.

12. With power from on high endue
Thy flock, O Lord, this day anew,
That many souls with us may feel
Thy pard'ning grace, the Spirit's seal.

13. That thousands by our ministry
May to the truth converted be,
And we may see them flock with us,
Unto the standard of thy cross.

14. We join together heart and hand,
To travel t'wards the promis'd land,
The seed we sow will then be good,
If water'd with the Saviour's blood;

15. As long as we on earth remain,
We will confess the Lamb once slain,
Until we for his victory,
Shall praise him in eternity.

1172. T. 22.

WHERE two or three, with sweet accord,
Obedient to their sov'reign Lord,
Meet to recount his acts of grace,
And offer solemn pray'r and praise:

2. "There:" saith the Saviour: "I will be,
"Amidst this little company;
"to them I will unveil my face,
"And shed my glories round the place."

3. We meet at thy command, O Lord,
Relying on thy faithful word,
Now send thy Spirit from above,
And fill our hearts with heav'nly love.

1173*. T. 101.

DRAW near, O flock of Christ, and bow
With deepest reverence before him,
Yea sink at Jesus' foot-stool low,
And in the dust with awe adore him;
Confess, that in thyself thou nothing art,
But that he is thy All, sole object of thy heart.

1174. T. 230.

JESUS, God of our salvation,
Behold thy blood-bought congregation
Assembled here before thy face,
Pond'ring on thy gracious dealing,
We would express our grateful feeling
And joyful Hallelujahs raise:
But when we in thy light
Discern, how we requite
Thee O Jesus,
We blush for shame—Our's is the blame,
But praise is due unto thy name.

2. Deeply conscious of transgression,
To thee we turn, hear our confession,
Assure us of thy pard'ning love:
O root out whate'er impedeth
Thy Spirit's work or discord breedeth,
Each stumbling-block from us remove;
Those who have gone astray,
Cause to return, we pray,
Faithful Shepherd!
With thee our Guide—May we abide,
Preserve us, lest we turn aside.

1175.* T. 519.

MOST holy Lord and God!
Holy, almighty God!
Holy and most merciful Saviour!
Thou eternal God!
Bless thy congregation,
Thro' thy suff'rings, death and blood;
Have mercy, O Lord!

1176. T. 159.

THIS day is holy to the Lord,
This day the Lord hath made,
We will rejoice with one accord,
And in his name be glad.
Come let us worship and bow down,
With thanks appear before his throne;
He to our songs of praise and pray'r,
Will lend a gracious ear.

1177. T. 71.

'FORE thee, Lord we appear,
Thou list'nest to our pray'r
Wait'st to be gracious;
Thy goodness to display
Unto thy church this day,
To own and bless us,

2. Thy pierced hands, for us
Once nailed to the cross,
Give benediction;
Thy blood from sin us cleanse,
And pard'ning grace dispense,
Without restriction.

1178. T. 594.

ACCEPT, O God of our salvation,
The sacrifice of praise and pray'r;
Upon thy gracious invitation,
Unto thy altars we repair;
Thou bid'st us come: all things are ready,
The treasure of thy boundless grace
Is open to the poor and needy,
They ne'er go empty from thy face.

1179.* T. 185.

JOY divine, and heav'nly peace with unction,
Church of Christ, thy portion be!

Holy Ghost, preserve the deep compunction,
Flowing from Christ's agony:
Father, bless and keep without cessation,
Thy Son's dearly purchas'd congregation;
Slaughter'd Lamb, thy peace divine
Seal our cov'nant, we are thine.

1180. T. 341.

TO Christ we homage pay,
We covenant this day,
Him to serve with all our strength,
Him to love with all the heart,
Him to follow, till at length
We obtain in heav'n our part.

XVII. Of the HOLY COMMUNION.

1181.* T. 599.

LORD Jesus, who before thy passion,
Distress'd and sorrowful to death,
To us the fruits of thy oblation
In thy last supper didst bequeath,
Accept our praise, thou bounteous giver
Of life to ev'ry true believer.

2. As oft as we enjoy this blessing,
Each sacred token doth declare
Thy dying love all thought surpassing,
And while we thee in mem'ry bear,
At each returning celebration,
We show thy death for our salvation.

3. Assurance of our pardon sealed
Is in this sacrament renew'd,
The soul with peace and joy is filled,
With thy atoning blood bedew'd,
This from unrighteousness us cleanseth,
And life abundantly dispenseth.

4. That bond of love, that mystic union,
By which to thee, our Head, we're join'd,
Is closer drawn at each communion,
By love inspir'd, we know thy mind;
And feeding on thy death and merit,
Are render'd one with thee in spirit.

5. Lord, by thy flesh the soul is nourish'd,
When faint, thy blood doth us revive,
And while our faith thereby is cherish'd,
To serve thee, and thy house we strive;
We, by this food invigorated
Are to good works anew created;

6. While thus thou feed'st the poor and needy,
Life from thy death pervades the whole,
And the true members of thy body
In thee, their Head, one heart and soul,
For whom one bread and cup sufficed,
Into one spirit are baptized.

7. Thy flesh to us a pledge is given,
That ev'n our flesh, corrupt and vile,
Shall from the dust be rais'd to heaven,
And with unfading glories smile;
And soul and body be for ever
At home with thee, our Lord and Saviour.

8. O what a striking exhibition
Of love divine is here bestow'd;
Our hungry souls in this fruition,
Find here on earth our highest good:
It proves amidst all tribulation,
Of heav'nly bliss th' anticipation.

1182.* T. 69.

WITH deep devotion,
We in Christ's suff'rings trace
Th' unfathom'd ocean
Of his unbounded grace;
He gave—Himself, our souls to save.

2. His body broken
Upon the shameful cross,
As he hath spoken:
Was giv'n to death for us,
We feed—On everlasting bread.

3. That precious fountain
Of blood, which from him flow'd,
On Calv'ry's mountain,
Is now on us bestow'd:
Here we—Life's well-spring open see.

4. O well-spring flowing
Unto eternal life,
Our souls bedewing,
By thee alone we thrive,
And are—Enabled fruit to bear.

5. The Lord draws near us,
Let us to meet him haste,
He comes to cheer us,
His flesh is our repast, [good.
His blood—Our drink and highest

6. In sweet communion
With Christ our paschal Lamb,
And holy union
With all who love his name,
May we—Abide continually.

1183.* T. 14.

THE nearer we to Jesus draw,
The more he teacheth us. [pain,
What yields him joy, or gives him
What brings us gain or loss.

2. Desirous to display our love,
We gladly would afford,
Touch'd with a sense of gratitude,
Some pleasure to our Lord.

3. He loveth us unspeakably,
Nor lets us pray in vain,
But gives the fearful heart that hope:
"Thy suit thou shalt obtain."

4. Most graciously he doth confess
His dear bought property,
When we upon his flesh and blood
Feed sacramentally.

1184.* T. 14.

NO words can ever fully tell,
What blessings Christ bestows
On me, when I on Calv'ry dwell,
And weep beneath his cross.

2. He who to his own flesh and blood
Can ne'er himself deny,
Saith unto us: "Take courage good,
"Your brother lo! am I."

3. His loving heart I open see,
Replete with tenderness;
He, as his blood-bought property,
Doth even me confess.

4. I am forgiv'n and reconcil'd,
My happiness renew'd,
My heart with deep abasement fill'd,
Is with his blood bedew'd.

5. From all anxiety and dread,
Which else my soul oppress'd,
Thanks be to him, I now am freed,
My cares are sooth'd to rest.

1185.* T. 83.

LORD and God, how are thy sheep
With thee in such close connexion!
Tho' they have thee, still they weep
Tears of longing and affection;
O thou highest good, which we
Cannot prize sufficiently.

1186.* T. 15.

AH! come, thou most beloved guest,
My joy and delectation,
With whose indwelling I am blest,
Source of all consolation.

2. O keep thy banquet, Lord, with
A sinner poor and needy; [me,
Since thou invit'st me graciously.
"Come, all things now are ready!"

3. I open heart ond soul to thee,
Lord Jesus, to receive thee:
For thee I long most ardently,
O may I never leave the.

1187. T. 166.

JESUS, thy feast we celebrate,
Show forth thy death, and praise
Thy name,
Till thou return, and we shall eat
The marriage-supper of the Lamb;
In mem'ry of our dying Lord [end,
The church on earth, till time shall
Meets at his table to record
The love of her departed Friend.

1188. T. 211.

JESUS, Lord of life and glory,
Hear thy people's fervent pray'r,
Us to meet thee now prepare,
We with awe appear before thee;
In this consecrated place,
We approach the throne of grace:
Lord, Lord, God,
Thee we own our only Saviour: :||:
Blessed, truly blessed they,
Who to thee have found the way,
Who of thy body and thy blood, ev'n here partakers are,
And in the supper of the Lamb once in heaven above shall share.

XVIII. Of our DEPARTURE unto the LORD and the LAST JUDGMENT.

1189.* T. 119.

HAD we nought :||:
Nought beyond this life to hope,
Here receiving our full measure,
Did no further prospect ope,
Laid we up no heav'nly treasure,
Wretched were our state in life and death,
Vain our faith. :||:

2. Here we sow, :||:
Here on earth in tears we sow,
He, who here goes forth and weepeth,
Bearing precious seed below,
Brings his sheaves with him and reapeth
There in joy, his sighs and sorrows o'er
Evermore. :||:

1190.* T. 205

WITH thee, Lord, while I remain,
Thou wilt near thy child abide,
Till, thy perfect aim t' attain,
I throughout am sanctified;
All my wants, all my distress,
I to thee, my Lord, confess;
Till I shall from sorrow free,
Live for evermore with thee.

1191* T. 83.

JESUS' suff'rings were for me,
That once my departing spirit
Full of joy and peace might be,
And eternal life inherit;
I'm from judgment freed by faith,
In his meritorious death.

1192.* T. 244.

IN spirit I am waiting,
Lord Jesus, near to thee
Thy suff'rings contemplating:
I know, they were for me!
I thee behold by faith,
Bow down thine head in death;
I hear thee cry: "Tis finish'd."
And watch thy latest breath.

2. Thy sighs, thy groans in anguish,
The tears, which from thee flow'd,
When thou for me didst languish,
Thy wounds and precious blood,
Be present night and day
To me while here I stay,
And at my dissolution,
My soul to heav'n convey.

3 'Midst joy beyond expression,
I shall abased be
With deep humiliation,
When called home to thee;
When I, completely bless'd,
Have leave with thee to rest,
Thy holy feet with rapture
By me shall be embrac'd.

4. O hasten thy appearance!
Yet as it pleaseth thee,
Meanwhile to me thy presence
Vouchsafe continually.
Fix thou my heart and eyes
Upon thy sacrifice,
Until my race here finish'd,
I shall obtain the prize.

1193. T. 14.

O HOW I long with Christ to be,
And in his presence rest;
He draws my soul most pow'rfully,
I to his bosom haste.

2. Meanwhile may I in spirit view
His suff'rings, cross and death,
These to my heart be daily new,
Till I resign my breath.

3. Me for thy coming, Lord, prepare,
Grant I may ready be,
Whene'er thou callest, without fear
To meet and welcome thee.

4. Thou know'st my insufficiency,
All my diseases cure,
O let thy stripes and wounds on me
Exert their healing pow'r.

5. Thus will my wants be well supplied,
Thus will my soul with grace
Abundantly be satisfied,
And kept in heav'nly peace;

6. Until the hour shall strike at last,
When I from sorrow free,
Shall hasten to my arms and breast,
And ever live with thee.

1194.* T. 151.

UNTIL my consummation,
My Saviour's grief and pain,
His wounds and bitter passion,
My comfort shall remain;
To him my Lord, when dying,
I'll look with humble faith,
On him alone relying,
Bless'd then will be my death!

1195. T. 16.

HAPPY soul, thy days are ended,
All thy mourning days below,
Thou by angel-guards attended,
Didst to Jesus' presence go.

2. Trusting in thy Saviour's merit,
Thou beheldst him from above,
Waiting to receive thy spirit,
Reaching out the crown of love.

3. For the joy he set before thee,
Felt'st a momentary pain,
Diedst to live a life of glory,
Suffer'd'st with thy Lord to reign.

1196.* T. 79.

WHEN children, bless'd by Jesus,
To whom their souls are precious,
Depart in early years,
They are not lost, for heaven
To children shall be given,
Eternal happiness is their's.

2. This child is therefore blessed,
Let no one be distressed,
Christ bid it fall asleep:
The body dead, the spirit
Will endless life inherit,
With his redeemed happy sheep.

1197. T. 585.

DAY of judgment! day of wonders!
Hark! the trumpet's awful sound,
Louder than a thousand thunders,
Shakes the vast creation round;
How the summons :||: will the sinner's heart confound!

2. See the Judge, our nature wearing,
Cloth'd in majesty divine;
Ye, who love the Lord's appearing,
Then shall say: "this God is mine!"
Gracious Saviour :||: own me on that day as thine!

3. At his call the dead awaken,
Rise to life from earth and sea,
All the pow'rs of nature shaken,
At his call prepare to flee:
Careless sinner, :||: what will then become of thee?

4. Horrors past imagination
Will surprise thy trembling heart,
When thou hear'st thy condemnation,
"Hence, accursed wretch, depart,
"Thou with Satan :||: and his angels have thy part!"

5. But to those, who have confessed,
Lov'd and serv'd the Lord below,
He will say: "Come near, ye blessed,
"See the kingdom I bestow:
"You for ever :||: shall my love and glory know.

6. Under sorrows and reproaches,
May this thought our courage raise,
Swiftly God's great day approaches,
Sighs will then be turn'd to praise:
We shall triumph :||: while the world is in a blaze.

1198. T. 580.

BEFORE me place, in dread array,
Lord Jesus, that tremendous day,
When thou in clouds shalt come;
To judge the nations at thy bar,
And tell me, Lord, I shall be there;
And meet from thee a joyful doom.

1199. T. 167.

HAIL the happy consummation,
Hail the time when all is done,
Christ appears to full salvation,
Perfects what was here begun:
Hail the Lord to earth returning,
Awful, fearful, joyful day,
Vallies, plains and mountains burning,
Flaming skies are swept away.

2. Hear the awful trumpet sounding,
See the nations all draw near,
"Come to judgment:" still resounding
Till it reacheth ev'ry ear:
Sinners call for rocks to hide them,
Saints repeating: "Come Lord, come!"
Angels charged, now divide them;
Jesus speaks their final doom.

3. Hear the sentence ne'er reversed,
See the mighty gulph between:
"Come ye blessed:"—"Go ye cursed:"
Closeth up the awful scene:
Shout ye saints, behold your Saviour,
Know him by his bleeding wounds:
This will yield you joy for ever,
While the sinner it confounds.

1200.* T. 58.

WHEN Jesus had to his disciples giv'n
His farewell blessing, and went up to heav'n,
While with sorrow filled, they upwards gazed,
Their master's countenance remained impressed
Upon their hearts.

2. When he in like manner
Shall be returning,
His church on earth will change her grief and mourning,
To songs of joy.

3. This reflection fills us
With joy unbounded,
That we the Lord, who for our sins was wounded,
Shall once behold.

4. O might we, poor sinners,
For his salvation,
Hunger and thirst until our consummation,
By day and night.

5. Thus shall we believing,
Ne'er be confounded,
And here already with his peace surrounded,
Taste heav'nly joys.

6. May we cleave to Jesus,
Till we've obtained
The prize, and till our faith and hope have gained
Their highest aim.

7. So as she believed,
Christ's congregation
Shall find it, and behold the Lord's salvation,
In endless bliss.

8. At his blest appearing,
Freed from all weakness,
Our bodies shall be chang'd into his likeness,
By his great pow'r.

9. Amen, Lord, afford us
Thy kind direction,
Keep us from evil, under thy protection,
Always secure;

10. Till we shall in heaven
Behold thy glory,
And free from sin and sorrow there adore thee,
World without end!

INDEX.

N. B. The verses marked with an asterisk (*) begin a hymn.

D

E

F

G

H

L

M

N

O

TABLE OF TUNES.

Note. The numbers of the Tunes correspond with those in the Tune Book, in use in the Congregations of the Brethren.

BOOKS PUBLISHED,

Relating to, or in use among the

UNITED BRETHREN.

1. AN EXPOSITION of CHRISTIAN DOCTRINE, as taught in the PROTESTANT CHURCH of the UNITED BRETHREN or UNITAS FRATRUM. Written in German, by AUGUST GOTTLIEB SPANGENBERG, with a Preface by BENJAMIN LATROBE. Second editon, revised. Price 8s. in boards.

2. HARMONY of the FOUR GOSPELS; or, The History of our Lord and Saviour JESUS CHRIST; in which every thing and circumstance, mentioned by the four Evangelists, is brought into one narrative; so that the reader hath here collected together, in one series, all that is recorded of the Acts of the Days of the SON OF MAN, in the very words of our English Version. Price, bound, 4s.

3. A SUMMARY of the DOCTRINE of JESUS CHRIST; to be used for the Instruction of Youth in the Congregations of the UNITED BRETHREN. New Edition, 8vo.

4. SOUND DOCTRINE extracted from the Writings of *The most eminent Reformed Divines*, chiefly OF THE FRENCH PROTESTANT CHURCH. *Translated from the French*, 8vo.

5. A SUCCINCT VIEW of the MISSIONS established among the HEATHEN by the CHURCH of the BRETHREN, or UNITAS FRATRUM. By BENJAMIN LATROBE. Price 6d.

6. A BRIEF ACCOUNT of the MISSION established among the Esquimaux Indians on the Coast of Labrador, by the Church of the Brethren. Price 6d.

7. AN ACCOUNT of the MANNER in which the PROTESTANT CHURCH of the UNITAS FRATRUM, or UNITED BRETHREN, preach the gospel, and carry on their Missions among the Heathen. Translated from the German of the Rev. AUGUST GOTTLIEB SPANGENBERG. Price sewed 1s. 8d.

8. A COLLECTION of HYMNS, for the Use of the UNITED BRETHREN. New Edition, revised and enlarged 1809.

9. A COLLECTION of HYMNS for the USE of CHILDREN. New Edition, revised and enlarged. Price 1s. bound.

10. HYMN-TUNES, sung in the CHURCH of the UNITED BRETHREN Collected by CHRISTIAN IGNATIUS LATROBE. Price half-bound, 8s.

11. The WORKS of the late Rev. JOHN GAMBOLD, A. M. formerly Minister of Staunton-Harcourt, Oxfordshire, and late one of the Bishops of the UNITAS FRATRUM, or UNITED BRETHREN. To which is annexed, the Life of the Author, with a Head, Crown Octavo.

12. SELECT NARRATIVES extracted from the HISTORY of the CHURCH, known by the name of UNITAS FRATUM; or the UNITED BRETHREN. Chronologically arranged. PART 1st. containing the ANCIENT HISTORY. Translated from the German. Price in boards, 3s.

13. A CONCISE HISTORICAL ACCOUNT OF THE PRESENT CONSTITUTION OF THE PROTESTANT CHURCH OF THE UNITED BRETHREN, &c. translated from the Fourth improved German edition.

All the above Books are sold by JOHN LEFEBVRE, No. 2, Chapel-Place, Nevil's-Court, Fetter-lane, LONDON; BINNS, BATH; and at all the *Settlements* and *Chapels* of the UNITED BRETHREN, in the UNITED KINGDOM.

Printed by T. Cunningham, Scotland-street, Ashton-under-line.

Milton Keynes UK
Ingram Content Group UK Ltd.
UKHW051058060224
437337UK00005BA/237